THE
I·N·D·O·O·R
GARDEN
BOOK

THE
I·N·D·O·O·R
GARDEN
BOOK

JOHN·BROOKES

Crown Publishers, Inc.
NEW YORK

Consultant editor
Richard Gilbert

Project editor
Elizabeth Eyres

Art editor
Jane Owen

Editors
Sophie Mitchell/Tim Hammond

Designers
Cheryl Picthall/Ann Cannings

Art director
Anne-Marie Bulat

Editorial director
Alan Buckingham

American editor Marjorie J. Dietz
First published in Great Britain in 1986
by Dorling Kindersley Publishers Limited, London

Published in 1986 in the United States of America
by Crown Publishers, Inc.,
225 Park Avenue South, New York, New York 10003
and represented in Canada by
the Canadian MANDA Group.

Library of Congress Cataloging-in-Publication Data
Brookes, John 1933—
   The indoor garden book.

   1. Interior landscaping. 2. House plants in interior
decoration. 3. Flower arrangement. I. Title.
SB419.25.B76 1986   747'.98   86-11613
ISBN 0-517-56313-4

10   9   8   7   6   5   4   3   2

First American edition

Typesetting
Modern Text

Reproduction
Reprocolor International

Printed and bound in Italy
by Arnoldo Mondadori, Verona

Contents

Introduction **6**

·1·
THE DECORATIVE QUALITIES OF PLANTS

Plant form **12** Leaf size **14** Leaf shape **16**
Leaf color **18** Leaf texture **20** Flower size **22**
Flower shape **24**

·2·
PLANT DISPLAY

Matching plants to containers **28**
The principles of arrangement **32**
Lighting plants **36** Styling with plants **40**
Grouping plants in a single container **46**
Training climbing plants **50**
Planting hanging baskets **54**
Growing bulbs indoors **59**
Planting window-boxes **62**
Planting bottle gardens **66** Planting terraria **68**
Cacti and succulent gardens **70**
Making water gardens **72**
Caring for bonsai **74**

·3·
CUT-FLOWER ARRANGING

Using the color wheel **78**
Cutting and preparing flowers **80**
Supports for flower arrangements **82**
The principles of arrangement **83**
A spring flower arrangement **86**
A summer flower arrangement **88**
An autumn flower arrangement **90**
A winter flower arrangement **92**

·4·
DRIED-FLOWER ARRANGING

How to dry flowers **96** Arranging flowers
in a basket **100** Further ideas for
arrangements **103** Making dried-flower trees **104**
Decorating a basket of pot-pourri **106**
Making wreaths **108** Making decorations **110**

·5·
THE ROOM-BY-ROOM GUIDE

Mini-climates in the home **114** Living rooms **116**
Dining rooms **130** Kitchens **136** Bedrooms **140**
Bathrooms **144** Halls and entrances **148**
Stairs and stairwells **152**
Sunrooms and conservatories **154**

·6·
THE PLANT FINDER'S GUIDE

How to use the plant finder's guide **160** Upright plants **162**
Arching plants **168** Rosette-shaped plants **172**
Bushy plants **176** Climbing plants **184** Trailing
plants **188** Creeping plants **192** Bulbs **194**
Cacti and succulents **196** The color guide to
flowering house plants **202** The seasonal guide to
flowering house plants **208** The cut-flower
guide **209** Spring flowers **210**
Summer flowers **214** Autumn flowers and
berries **218** Winter flowers and berries **222**
Foliage **224** The dried-flower guide **229**
Dried flowers **230** Dried foliage, cereals
and grasses **236** Dried seed heads and fruits **238**

·7·
PLANT CARE

Requirements for healthy plants **242** Light **244**
Temperature and humidity **246** Watering **248**
Feeding **252** Pots and potting mixtures **254**
Repotting and potting on **256** Growing plants
in artificial light **258** Hydroculture **260**
Pruning and training **262** Propagation **264**
Problems, pests and diseases **270**

Glossary **278** Index **282** Acknowledgments **288**

Introduction

For those of us living in the colder parts of the northern hemisphere, the long months of winter sometimes stretch from October to April—nearly half the year. While green thoughts and nursery catalogues may sustain some plantsmen through this long period, others may seek a more practical outlet for their horticultural interests, or just the sight of greenery and flower color in their home. And for those residing in towns, this yearning for a contact with nature lasts throughout the year. It is to all these that *The Indoor Garden Book* is directed.

Indoor plants provide contact with nature for they are living growing things, and interesting because of it; at the same time they will enhance almost any interior by adding natural forms, colors and fragrances. However, used at random they look messy and may be at odds with the decoration of a room. Professional designers are well aware of the decorative qualities of plants and how they can be used to complement a decorating scheme. But this skill in matching plants to interior decoration, and in placing them effectively in a room, can be easily learned through practice and through an appreciation of the different decorative qualities of plants and flowers. This book sets out to show you how to get to know your plants and flowers and appreciate their shapes, colors, sizes, textures and seasons within an interior setting.

How to use your indoor plants

Begin your decorating by thinking about the sort of space you want to fill with plants. Do you want one large dramatic plant to act as a single focal point or a smaller group of

A Victorian flavour
The classic late nineteenth-century interior is dark and cluttered with heavy draperies and over-stuffed furniture. Several large Kentia palms (*Howea belmoreana*) might be placed in the room, with gloxinias (*Sinningia* sp.) clustered on side tables. Here, a series of hanging baskets helps to break up the large expanse of window and lightens the gloom of the dark wooden panelling.

Period romanticism
A more romantic approach to the interior appeared around the turn of the century, combined with a re-appraisal of simple garden flowers. This torso is surrounded by a group of poinsettias (*Euphorbia pulcherrima*) whose lush flowers echo the color of the sculpture; the effect is rich and voluptuous.

Traditional country-house style
Though modern, this room is a scaled-down version of a traditional, grand, country-house interior with bright colors, a fireplace, deep upholstery and an arrangement of garden flowers. Strongly colored exotic house plants would appear alien in this setting, and although some orchids (*Cymbidium* sp.) have crept in here, their color is sufficiently delicate to blend in with the decoration.

plants to contrast shapes, colors or textures? Perhaps you only have space to use plants in a hanging basket, or trained round a piece of furniture, or round part of the structure of the room. Step-by-step projects in the chapter on *Plant Display* show you how to put these ideas and many more into practice. A simple arrangement of fresh flowers will immediately lighten the mood of a room and, in the *Cut-Flower Arranging* chapter, a selection of cut flowers and foliage, including commercially available material and garden varieties, have been used to create a series of seasonal displays. In winter, cut flowers are expensive, so it is worth considering the use of dried material in the home to sustain the colors and mood of summer and autumn. The chapter on *Dried-Flower Arranging* shows you how to make trees, wreaths and decorations as well as flower arrangements. In *The Plant Finder's Guide*, decorating tips are given on how to use each of the featured plants to best effect, while *The Room-by-Room Guide* shows how plants and flowers can be used in a variety of novel and exciting ways in different parts of the house.

Styling with plants

Never has there been such a range of styles for living as there is today. Yet all—even the most modern—are subtly influenced by the past. Recognizing the component parts of a style of décor helps to define the qualities you need in a plant to enhance that style. To illustrate this, and show how to approach your decorative schemes, I have chosen a selection of contemporary styles of decoration and analyzed them, to show how plants contribute to the overall styling.

American colonial style
Another trend in interior decoration is one which is strongly influenced by the houses and artefacts of colonial North America. The early homesteaders were gardeners, and this is reflected in the way that herbs and vegetables, along with country flowers, are used for decoration in this style. The daisy bushes (*Chrysanthemum frutescens*) in rough wicker baskets used in this bedroom are typical.

Simple rustic style
In Britain, nostalgia for a rural past took another turn when stripped-pine furniture and small-print fabrics appeared in the 1960s. The style is comfortable and unpretentious, with much allusion to country pursuits. Country flowers, such as these daffodils (*Narcissus* sp.), and dried flowers find a place here.

The influence of the exotic
The hippy movement of the 1960s brought the east closer to the west, and fabrics, carpets and ornaments from the east have now found their way into many homes. The rich patterns and colors of many ethnic textiles suit the strong forms and bold colors of tropical and semi-tropical plants.

The history of indoor plants

Plants have been used indoors for many centuries. The Dutch interest in painting interiors and flower-pieces went hand-in-hand with an increasing interest, throughout the western world, in the cultivated plant. Again, the Dutch tulip craze of the 1630s must have influenced other countries, but travellers, since the returning Crusaders, would also have brought plants home and fostered them indoors prior to the advent of glass. We know, too, that herbs were used extensively indoors: for strewing, medicinal and culinary purposes. In the seventeenth century, orangeries, structures made of brick or stone with large south-facing windows, were built to shelter orange trees in winter. But it was not until the introduction of glass structures, which could be heated, that plants could be grown inside to any degree.

Tropical fruit was initially cultivated in primitively heated houses; pineapples, guavas and limes were grown—and also the first camellias. Later, there followed the date palm and banana. Succulents, such as the aloe and agave, were also raised for medicinal purposes and to decorate terraces in summer. During the nineteenth century, the conservatory became a standard addition to larger houses; house plant cultivation moved into the realms of fashion, with fern houses, palm houses, and houses for exotic plants being all the rage. Simple potted plants too began to escape from the conservatory to become the necessary accompaniment to the heavy, draped look of the late nineteenth-century interior—although the smoke from open fires did the plants little good. Floristry became a fashionable lady's accomplishment.

One reaction to this style was to seek inspiration from what

The influence of the 1930s
This contemporary bathroom looks back to the 1930s in its monochromatic color scheme and the geometric form of the metal-framed mirror. The simplicity calls for plants with a strong form, and these dragon trees (*Dracaena marginata*) add softness and interest to a setting which might otherwise look clinical.

The oriental look
This modern interior is heavily influenced by the austerity of a traditional Japanese home. Colors are largely neutral and are offset by carefully positioned areas of bright color—the pink leaf margins of the ti plant (*Cordyline terminalis*) in the foreground pick up the color of the cushions. The bare branches are chosen for their linear forms.

Linear austerity
The evolution of the Modern movement in architecture and interior design was complex, with influences from Japan, Scandinavia, Italy and America. But it was typified by more severe linear forms, a lack of pattern, and "designer" furniture in laminated wood or metal and leather. This type of hard-edged interior is softened and enriched by the use of large plants, such as these Kentia palms (*Howea belmoreana*)— which here also help to link indoors with outdoors.

must have been a continuing, unsophisticated, cottage tradition of keeping temperate plants indoors to root or over-winter, and of hanging herbs from the rafters to dry. An alternative Modernist movement at the beginning of this century used specific plants in its interiors—the lily being a great favorite. But the real origins of the use of house plants lie in Scandinavia where, traditionally, plants were brought indoors to relieve the bleakness of a long winter; and it was not until after the Second World War that they really became part of the modish interior. It was then that house plants as we know them started to make their appearance, with species from Asia, Africa and tropical America becoming available. Since then, new varieties have been bred that need less maintenance and, with the right environment and management, they can be kept very successfully indoors.

Choosing plants

The plants, which are or are not suitable for you, will depend on the particular type of decoration you have, for currently there are a number of interior styles. Your selection will depend on personal taste and on what it is practical to maintain—given the specific limitations of day- and night-time temperatures, light availability, the presence of drafts, children and pets, and, of course, available space.

The industrial style
During the 1970s, a new style of design appeared, which made use of industrial artefacts. The hard lines and strong colors of this style called for the use of large plants with distinctive shapes, and flowers with strong forms and colors.

A softer approach
In the 1980s, a softening of the high-tech style has occurred with the introduction of subtle pastel colors. In this interior, the rooms blend into each other to create a feeling of space and light, and large plants, such as these weeping figs (*Ficus benjamina*), can be used in an architectural way to link the spaces.

Classical eclecticism
Another current mood is a classic look characterized by discreet colors and patterning, and bold pieces of furniture which may be modern or traditional. Plant groupings are strong and simple; they are part of the overall conception of the room, but punctuate rather than dominate the setting.

·1·

THE DECORATIVE QUALITIES OF PLANTS

The photographs in this opening chapter demonstrate the astounding diversity of plant form—from striking architectural plants with bold foliage to relatively inconspicuous ground creepers. There is a tremendous range of growing habit, as well as leaf and flower size, shape, color and texture. Cut flowers, too, provide a kaleidoscopic array of colors—rich and vibrant or subtle and subdued. The flower heads may be large or small, flat, spiky, spherical or more complex, and these shapes themselves may suggest an appropriate way to display the material.

Bear these decorative qualities in mind when choosing plants and flowers, so that their characteristics will enhance the mood of your home. Think about the form and size of a plant if you want it to be part of the landscape of your room, or link parts of the room that have different functions. When planning smaller groups of plants, or arrangements of flowers, consider their colors and textures in conjunction with wall colors and fabric textures, so that the display and its setting show a sense of overall harmony.

Infinite variety
One of the principal joys of using plants in the home is the diversity of decorative qualities they provide. Here, a random selection of freshly cut flowers, leaves and berries gives some indication of the range of color, texture, size and shape available.

Plant form

Of all plant characteristics it is shape that probably creates the strongest initial impression. Shape is primarily to do with the general outline of the plant, but it also embraces other characteristics that contribute to the plant's overall form: the density of the growth, the size and number of individual stems and branches, the way the leaves or leaflets are arranged and the "weight" of the foliage. Of course, shape is always changing as a plant grows, but certain generalizations can be made and throughout this book I have used a system of classification that divides plants into eight different shape categories: upright, arching, weeping, rosette-shaped, bushy, climbing, trailing and creeping. These are the categories used in *The Plant Finder's Guide* and here you will find a plant to illustrate each one of them.

Coconut palm
Cocos nucifera (see p.169)
This plant has an *arching* shape, as do most of the palms and ferns; its sword-shaped fronds have a hard outline.

Japanese fatsia
Fatsia japonica (see p.181)
The overall shape of this plant is *bushy* but the large fingered leaves have a strong individual outline.

Creeping fig *Ficus pumila* (see p.193) With its spreading shape, this *creeping* plant resembles a green carpet when allowed to ramble; it can also trail or climb.

Heartleaf philodendron
Philodendron scandens (see p.188)
Plants usually combine different elements of
shape; this *trailing* philodendron has beautifully
shaped leaves as well as stems that trail
in an attractive way.

Algerian ivy
Hedera canariensis (see p.184)
The shape of its support will
dictate the overall shape of a
climbing plant, but individual
foliage will give an outline that
may be delicate or bold.

Stick yucca
Yucca elephantipes (see p.167)
Plants with *upright* growth and
spiky leaves have a simple
bold shape.

Ponytail
Beaucarnea recurvata (see p.171)
The soft shape of this *weeping* plant is created by
the mass of drooping, grasslike leaves.

Bird's nest bromeliad *Nidularium innocentii*
(see p.175) Most *rosette-shaped* plants
have a strong outline that demands attention.

Leaf size

In many fields successful design often relies on the simple repetition of elements of similar sizes. This principle holds good for the arrangement of plants but impressive effects can also be achieved by emphasizing differences in scale.

For example, the delicate tracery of small climbing plants can be highlighted by juxtaposing them with broad expanses of leaf of an uncomplicated shape.

Dwarf coconut palm
Microcoelum weddellianum
(see p.170) Juxtapose these small slender fronds with other larger palms.

Kentia palm
Howea belmoreana (see p.170)
Display large plants on their own, or in groups with spiky-leaved plants.

Rosary vine
Ceropegia woodii (see p.201)
A plant which looks best on its own; allow the stems
to trail from a hanging basket or shelf.

Elephant's ear philodendron
Philodendron hastatum
(see p.187)
A large-leaved climber best
used as a feature plant or as a
foil for low-growing plants.

Heartleaf philodendron
Philodendron scandens
(see p. 188)
Use in a hanging basket or
arrange around a large-leaved
philodendron.

Leaf shape

Leaf shape is a very strong visual characteristic of a plant and a striking display can be achieved by concentrating solely on either contrasting or harmonizing leaf shapes. There is a great variety of leaf shapes to choose from—lance-shaped leaves, oval leaves, heart-shaped leaves, wavy-edged leaves and even leaves shaped like a violin. The shape of its leaves can be the most important feature of a plant or it can be a secondary charm.

Pothos vine
Scindapsus pictus "Argyraeus" (see p.188) Heart-shaped leaves with acutely pointed tips.

Swiss cheese plant
Monstera deliciosa (see p.187) The large oval leaves become perforated as the plant gets older.

Passion flower
Passiflora caerulea (see p.185) Fan-shaped leaves with many deeply cut lobes.

Grape ivy
Cissus rhombifolia (see p.186) The leaves have pointed tips and scalloped edges.

Fiddle-leaf philodendron
Philodendron bipennifolium (see p. 169) The young irregularly shaped leaves become violin-shaped when mature.

Asparagus fern
Asparagus setaceus (see p.183) Wiry stems carry triangular sprays made up of feathery branchlets.

Dumb cane
Dieffenbachia exotica
(see p.163)
The long oval leaves have wavy
margins and a distinct point at
their tip.

Weeping fig
Ficus benjamina (see p.171)
Small, slender, oval leaves with
curved edges and pointed tips.

Stick yucca
Yucca elephantipes
(see p. 167)
Long, narrow, spiky leaves with
finely toothed edges.

Silk oak
Grevillea robusta (see p.166)
The leaves are highly divided
giving a delicate fernlike
appearance.

Boston fern
Nephrolepis exaltata
"Bostoniensis".
(see p. 170)
The fronds are divided into
narrow leaflets giving a graceful
feathery appearance.

False aralia
Dizygotheca elegantissima
(see p.165)
Narrow leaflets with saw-
toothed edges radiate like
spokes from the top of
each stem.

Leaf color

The range of color found in leaves is startling: from the variety of different greens to leaves with all-over colors from silver-white to deep purple, as well as those which are patterned or mottled with contrasting colors. Dramatic displays can be made with foliage plants by concentrating on the interplay between two, or at most three, colors.

Wandering Jew
Zebrina pendula (see p. 189)
The leaves are finely marked with two translucent green stripes.

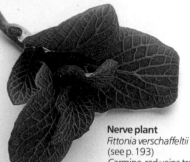

Nerve plant
Fittonia verschaffeltii
(see p. 193)
Carmine-red veins traversing olive-green leaves create a dramatic color contrast.

Angel wings
Caladium hortulanum hybrids (see p.182)
Paper-thin leaves with very delicate markings in combinations of red, pink, white and green.

Painted nettle
Coleus blumei
(see p.177)
Leaf color and pattern varies, with rich mixtures of yellow, red, orange, green and brown.

Croton
Codiaeum variegatum pictum
(see p.164) Leaves in a range of warm exotic colors mottled with spots, blotches and veins.

Blushing bromeliad
Neoregelia carolinae "Tricolor" (see p. 174)
Green- and cream-striped leaves which become suffused with red at flowering time.

Peacock plant
Calathea makoyana (see p. 165)
Leaves which look as if they
have been hand-painted with a
spectacular pattern of dark
blotches.

English ivy
Hedera helix hybrids
(see p.190)
The mid-green leaves have
darker green blotches and
cream margins.

Ti plant
Cordyline terminalis (see p.163)
The striped leaves are outlined
in a vivid pink.

Angel wings
Caladium hortulanum hybrids.
This young leaf, from the same
plant as the leaf to its left, shows
the color variation that can
occur on the same plant.

Silvered spear
Aglaonema crispum
"Silver Queen" (see p.164)
Beautiful dark-green leaves
heavily marked with silvery-
green blotches.

Eyelash begonia
Begonia "Tiger Paws"
(see p. 193)
The bright-red markings on the
undersides of the emerald-green
leaves show through as brown
on the upper surface.

Strawberry geranium
Saxifraga stolonifera "Tricolor"
(see p.190)
Olive-green leaves with a pink
margin and fine pink hairs.

Polka-dot plant
Hypoestes phyllostachya
(see p.179)
Dark olive-green leaves which
are heavily spotted with pink.

Leaf texture

There are as many variations in leaf texture as in shape, size or color. Very few leaves have no textural quality and textures can vary from glossy to matt, from hairy to wrinkled, from ribbed to quilted, each variation giving added interest to the plant. Subtle displays can be made by juxtaposing plants with contrasting leaf textures.

Norfolk Island pine
Araucaria heterophylla (see p.166)
Tiers of needle-covered branches give an overall filigree lightness.

Cast-iron plant
Aspidistra elatior (see p.165)
Distinctive ribbing marks run along the length of these leathery leaves.

Bird's nest fern
Asplenium nidus
(see p.173)
The lance-shaped leaves are extremely smooth and shiny with a central rib.

Emerald ripple peperomia
Peperomia caperata
(see p.180)
The heart-shaped, dark-green leaves have a corrugated surface with a waxy feel to them.

Painted-leaf begonia
Begonia rex-cultorum (see p.183)
The highly decorative foliage is covered in pimples giving it a curious rough texture.

Delta maidenhair fern
Adiantum raddianum
(see p.183)
Leaves have a soft filmy texture
and are arranged on gracefully
drooping fronds.

Purple velvet plant
Gynura aurantiaca (see p.191).
The toothed leaves are covered
in soft purple hair, giving them a
furry texture.

Staghorn fern
Platycerium bifurcatum (see p.191)
The antler-shaped fronds are
covered with fine, white,
feltlike scurf.

Prayer plant
*Maranta leuconeura
erythroneura* (see p.178)
Bright-red veins stand out from
the surface of the satiny leaves.

Columnea
Columnea "Banksii" (see p.189)
The dark-green paired leaves are
fleshy with a waxy texture.

Flower size

The beauty of flowers does not depend solely on their color, although it is an important factor. Size contributes to the unique appeal of a particular bloom and is a major consideration when planning an arrangement. Use flowers which are in scale with one another and, when choosing a container, make sure that its size is suitable for your flowers.

Mimosa
Acacia longifolia (see p.212)
This evergreen shrub produces short-stemmed clusters of fragrant, golden-yellow flowers the size of peas.

Delphinium
Delphinium elatum (see p.217)
The tall spikes of these cut flowers are suitable for any kind of large arrangement.

Chrysanthemum
Chrysanthemum hybrids (see p.222)
These flowers, the largest
of the numerous cut varieties of
chrysanthemum, are the size of
grapefruits.

Poinsettia
Euphorbia pulcherrima (see p.178)
These striking house plants have large,
bright red bracts which form a circle
around the insignificant flowers.

Cornflower
Centaurea cyanus (see p.217)
The single, small, round heads of
these cut flowers are the size
of golfballs.

Anemone
Anemone coronaria (see p.222)
These brightly colored, poppy-
like flowers have heads as large
as tennis balls

Flower shape

Flowers come in an immense variety of shapes from the simple petalled blooms of the primrose to the exotic, petalless, globular flowers of the nodding pincushion. Successful flower arrangements depend upon an appreciation of shape, and the natural outline of the flower can be used as a key to the overall design. Use long, thin flower spikes for outline and rounded shapes for focal point in large displays.

Bells-of-Ireland
Moluccella laevis (see p.217)
These are long spikes of small white flowers surrounded by green cuplike bracts.

Kalanchoe
Kalanchoe blossfeldiana (see p.196)
The small flowers of this house plant grow in dense clusters and may be cut and used in a vase.

Painter's palette
Anthurium andraeanum (see p.182)
These strange-looking blooms consist of a waxy, shield-shaped bract and a protruding cylindrical flower spike.

Baby's breath
Gypsophila paniculata (see p.213)
The loose clusters of tiny single or double flowers create a hazy effect which is emphasized by displaying them alone in a glass container.

Transvaal daisy
Gerbera jamesonii (see p.217)
These large single or double flowers come in vivid colors and provide focal interest in mixed arrangements.

Pansy
Viola wittrockiana (see p.213)
These attractive heart-shaped flowers have layers of soft, lobed petals.

Bird-of-paradise
Strelitzia reginae (see p.164)
These unusual flowers consist of a green bract supporting orange-and-blue flowers which stand erect like the crest of a tropical bird.

Zonal geranium
Pelargonium hortorum hybrids (see p.178)
These rounded clusters of small flowers are available in a wide range of colors.

Orchid
Dendrobium sp. (see p.223)
These long-lasting flowers grow
in arching sprays that bloom
right down the stems.

Peruvian lily
Alstroemeria pelegrina (see p.213)
The trumpet-shaped flowers are
borne at the ends of the
long stems.

African violet
Saintpaulia hybrids (see p.175)
The single or double flowers of
these house plants grow in
clusters on a
short stem.

Gentian
Gentiana sp. (see p.217)
These small flowers are
shaped like a funnel.

Sword lily
Gladiolus sp. (see p.215)
These elegant cut flowers
have tall, one-sided spikes
of single florets.

German violet
Exacum affine (see p.178)
The flowers of this house plant
are small and saucer-shaped
with a single layer of petals.

Tuberous begonia
Begonia tuberhybrida
(see p.176) These house plants
carry both single and double flowers
which are large and roselike.

Nodding pincushion
Leucospermum nutans (see p.221)
These unusual globular blooms
are covered with protruding spikes.

Carnation
Dianthus caryophyllus
(see p.215) These double flowers,
which grow on clustered stems, have a
"ruffled" appearance.

Poison primrose
Primula obconica (see p.181)
This house plant has clusters of
brightly colored blooms on a
single stalk.

·2·
PLANT DISPLAY

The arranging, grouping and positioning of plants and flowers is an art, not a science. It is a matter of taste, and therefore not an area in which there are hard-and-fast rules. However, there are guidelines, and it is possible to give advice on what is likely to look good and what is not. Perhaps the most important thing to remember is that every plant arrangement must be designed in context. This means taking into account not only the appearance of the plant itself, but also the container you intend to put it in, the background against which it will be seen, and the room features or items of furniture by which it will be surrounded. Arrangements may consist of a single plant in a simple pot, a formal grouping of associated plants, a jungle-like garden room or conservatory overflowing with greenery, a single vase of bright, colorful, cut flowers, or a mixed display that incorporates any or all of these elements. In each case, the first thing to do is to look at the plants and flowers themselves and see them in terms of the qualities described in the previous chapter. Only then turn to the choice of container and make your selection not just on the basis of choosing the right size for your plant's health, but also in terms of how the container can add to your display, and how it can enhance the mood you want to create.

Co-ordinating plants and containers
The color of flowering house plants can be picked up, and reinforced, by the color of their containers. Here, the color of the containers holds the group together and, at the same time, because they are a less assertive pink than the flowers, attention is focused on the plants.

Matching plants to containers 1

The criteria to be borne in mind when selecting a container for your plant are many and complex, and for every rule formulated it is possible to show an example that breaks it successfully. In every case the decision will be tempered by personal taste and preference but it is worth setting down some basic guidelines.

The most important consideration is the proportion of the container to the plant. In general, the smaller the plant the more it should equal the height of its container. To find out what combinations will work together it is best to try various permutations of container with your plant, standing back to appreciate the result in each case. Having selected a container whose proportions suit the plant, make sure that both together will suit the particular place in which you want to put them. This is fundamental to the success of the arrangement for not only the container, but also the plant inside it, must be suitable for the setting both practically and aesthetically.

It is essential to choose a style of container and a type of plant that will reflect and enhance the ambience of the room for which they are intended. The style of the container depends on the material of which it is made and on its shape, color and texture. The style of a plant can be analyzed in a similar way: for instance, the spiky-leaved yucca has a hard-edged modern look to it, while a begonia with lush flowers and a soft outline will suit a more traditional setting. So do not be tempted to buy a yucca in an aluminium pot if you have a period house decorated with chintzes.

Containers for different-shaped plants

Scarlet star
Guzmania lingulata

Pothos vine
Scindapsus pictus
"Argyraeus"

English ivy
Hedera helix hybrids

Conical glass bowl
The crisp linear form of this bowl comple-ments the red flowers and strong outline of these rosette-shaped plants.

Spherical ceramic pot
The trailing pothos vine hangs attractively over the edge of this rounded pot. The simplicity of the pot, both in shape and color, shows off the silver variegation in the leaves.

Tall terracotta pot
An English ivy displayed in this way needs a tall pot to show off its trailing stems. A tall upright plant would look out of proportion in such a container.

Boston fern
Nephrolepis exaltata
"Bostoniensis"

Button fern
Pellaea rotundifolia

Ponytail
*Beaucarnea
recurvata*

Classical lead urn
The height of this imitation lead urn sets off the Boston fern's arching fronds. The combination has a formal look reinforced by the urn's classical design.

Round ceramic pot
The simple shape of this container sets off the delicate outline of the button fern's arching fronds. The dark matt-green leaf color goes well with the blue of the pot.

Low terracotta dish
The bizarre shape of the weeping ponytail plant calls for a plain container such as this terracotta dish. As the roots like to be pot bound, the container is very small for a plant of this size.

Angel wings
Caladium hortulanum
hybrids

Japanese fatsia
Fatsia japonica

Cape leadwort
Plumbago auriculata

Glazed ceramic planter
The bare stems of the bushy angel wings are set off by the attractive shape of the green planter. This unassertive color allows the patterns in the leaves to stand out well.

Handled rush basket
This vigorous Japanese fatsia with its broad fingered leaves and bushy shape demands a simple but sturdy-looking container.

Hooped rush basket
The hooped handle of this basket forms a support for this small, climbing Cape leadwort. The rough texture of the basket goes well with the rather untidy stems.

Baby's tears
Soleirolia soleirolii

Flat terracotta dish
The flat open shape of this dish suits the creeping habit of dainty baby's tears. The rustic terracotta goes well with the fresh green of the plant's tiny leaves.

Rabbit's ears cactus
Opuntia microdasys

Tip yucca
Yucca elephantipes

False aralia
Dizygotheca elegantissima

Square fiberglass planter
The austere form of the upright spiky-leaved yucca is shown off by the extreme simplicity of its white fiberglass container.

Rustic wooden barrel
The arresting shape of this upright cactus requires a container with a simple form. The rough wooden barrel goes well with its vigorous spiny texture.

Large terracotta planter
The success of this combination relies on the contrast between the solidity of the terracotta pot and the filigree effect of this upright plant's bronze-colored foliage.

Matching plants to containers 2
Groups of containers

One of the ways of adding interest to the layout of a room is by grouping pots and other containers with plants, as incidental points of interest. You can use containers of the same color to hold a group of plants together and to stabilize the mood of an area within a room. Few groupings of this sort are important enough to become the focal point in a very large room, but can work well in a smaller area.

When choosing your containers, think carefully about how they will match your plants, and about how plants and containers will work together as a group, both in terms of themselves and in terms of their setting.

Counterpoint with color *right*
These containers were chosen to set up a pleasing interplay of color between themselves and the plants. The black and red containers pick up and complement the leaf colors of both plants.

Painted-leaf begonia
Begonia rex-cultorum

Black aluminium planter

Croton
Codiaeum variegatum pictum

Red plastic container

Baby's tears
Soleirolia soleirolii

Terracotta pots

Terracotta pots *above*
A simple classical grouping of containers that share the same style and color helps control the random, profligate growth of the plants, and contributes to the effect of a balanced arrangement.

Playing with scale *above*
This group works through the repetition of container shape and texture set off by a dramatic contrast in scale of the containers. The use of the same plant in each pot contributes to the satisfying unity of the group.

Tall and small *right*
Here, the contrast in shape and scale between the two containers is enhanced by the use of the same plant in each. The monochromatic color scheme of the pots helps to hold the group together and picks up the silvery-gray leaf variegation in the pothos vine.

Grey ceramic container

Polka-dot plant
Hypoestes phyllostachya

Repetition *below*
A small plant in a small pot may need reinforcement: this can be achieved by using a larger specimen of the same plant in a larger pot. These pots pick up the very dark-green color of the polka-dot plants' leaves and contrast well with their pink variegation.

Pothos vine
Scindapsus pictus "Argyraeus"

White ceramic pot

Black ceramic containers

Unusual containers

Many containers are expensive to buy, particularly if you are thinking of using several of them. It is worth having a look at everyday household objects—wastepaper baskets, preserving pans, galvanized buckets, coal scuttles, kettles, watering cans, china and enamel bowls—which can take on a new look and a new lease of life if used imaginatively. There are no rules for improvisation, it is just a question of what looks right for the plants and for the style of setting they are to inhabit. Experiment with putting potted bulbs in wicker shopping baskets, ivies and other trailing plants in shiny ice coolers, small cacti in colorful pencil holders and any other combinations that suggest themselves. Even an old chimney pot can make an attractive container for a rustic setting (either stand the plant on top of it, in its own planter, or rest the planter on a pile of bricks inside the chimney pot). If you use a container without drainage holes, line it with a layer of gravel, vermiculite or clay pot fragments before planting.

A bird-cage *right*
The delicate bars of the cage provide an elegant framework for the creeping fig (*Ficus pumila*) to ramble over. This plant will climb and trail, as well as creep, and all three habits of growth can be seen here.

An animal container *below*
An out-of-the-ordinary container can attract attention, add an element of humor, and greatly increase the impact of a single plant display—as this rhinoceros pot clearly demonstrates.

A china bust *right*
You can use an object as a container to set up an association and convey a particular mood. Here the combination of fronds of ivy trailing over a classical head recalls overgrown antique statuary.

The principles of arrangement 1
Balancing groups

Making an arrangement of growing plants means both grouping plants together with their containers, as you might on a shelf or table-top for example, as well as placing plants in a room. Special advice for arranging plants in room settings appears in *The Room-By-Room Guide*; but it is easiest to start looking at good groupings of plants together with their planters.

The key to a good arrangement is that it should have visual balance. As a simple rule of thumb, a larger plant has more visual weight than a smaller one. However, certain plants have striking leaf color, shape or texture which attracts the eye instantly; so a small example of such a plant will have as much visual weight as a large example of a less dramatic plant.

Symmetrical arrangements

Asymmetrical arrangements

Symmetry
Two identical creeping figs (*Ficus pumila*) either side of a Norfolk Island pine (*Araucaria heterophylla*) create a perfectly symmetrical arrangement. If a vertical line ran through the middle of the group each side of the line would exactly mirror the other.

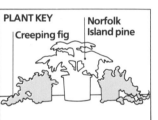

PLANT KEY | Creeping fig | Norfolk Island pine

Asymmetry
The pine has more visual weight than a single creeping fig and needs to be balanced by two of the latter. Space can be used to adjust balance: here, merging the two trailing plants together a little gives them more visual weight than when they are separated.

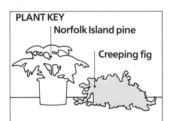

PLANT KEY | Norfolk Island pine | Creeping fig

Balancing plants and objects *left*
Two striking bromeliads stand on a console table, either side of a
centrally placed urn. To hold this group together, and to highlight
the sense of symmetry, ashtrays have been positioned either side
of the urn. The success of the arrangement is reinforced by the way
the red of the flowers and the green of the urn echo colors in the
painting behind them.

Formal balance through symmetry *above*
In general, perfectly symmetrical arrangements suit plants with a very
regular shape and rather formal look, such as the common myrtles
(*Myrtus communis*) placed either side of this mirror. Bay trees or
orange trees would also be appropriate in this context. The simple
table arrangement is made of a single flamingo flower (*Anthurium* sp.)
and palm frond (*Howea* sp.).

The principles of arrangement 2
Using contrast

If a successful arrangement is one that balances visually, what makes it not merely successful but outstanding? The answer: contrast—the setting off of opposites against one another. You can use bold contrasts of shapes and scale or more subtle contrasts of textures and colors. Compose your groups by experimenting with several different plants—choosing ones which like similar conditions—relying upon your eye to tell you what works and what does not. When planning a group, the best way to use contrast is to restrict it to just one, or at most two, elements. The effect of contrast will always be stronger if it is part of an arrangement that displays some sense of overall order and harmony.

Shape
The upright, spiky-leaved yucca (*Yucca elephantipes*) contrasts with the low, rounded forms of the cacti. The strong form of the yucca gives it a visual weight that needs to be balanced by a number of small cacti. The introduction of the spiky-leaved but low-growing queen agave (*Agave victoriae-reginae*) on the left creates a pleasing link between the two dominant elements in the composition.

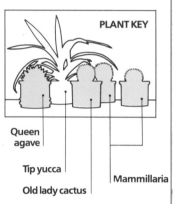

PLANT KEY

Queen agave

Tip yucca

Old lady cactus

Mammillaria

Texture *left*
The filigree lightness of the large delta maidenhair fern (*Adiantum raddianum*) has a similar visual weight to the dense mass of the emerald ripple peperomia leaves (*Peperomia caperata*) because of the different sizes of the plants. The plants balance visually simply by being placed side-by-side.

Maidenhair fern

Emerald ripple peperomia

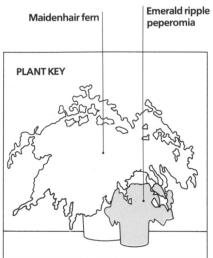

PLANT KEY

Scale

The three plants in this group share the same sort of shape and the same sort of texture—they are all spiky-leaved. Yet they vary enormously in scale. The small queen agave (*Agave victoriae-reginae*) is only a few inches high, whereas the large stick yucca (*Yucca elephantipes*) rises to a height of about 5 ft. Their similarity in shape and texture, and the fact that they are displayed in all-white containers, serve to emphasize the contrasts in scale. Another way of using contrasts of scale effectively is to group plants in a row—along a mantelpiece or shelf for example—using plants of the same kind but of different heights.

PLANT KEY

Stick yucca

Tip yucca

Queen agave

Color *right*

Three pink elatior begonias (*Begonia* "Elatior" hybrids) are offset by a single white-flowered variety. By slightly overlapping the three pink plants and setting the white one a small distance away, neither color predominates but each is strengthened by the element of contrast. Another way of using color is to juxtapose a plant with variegated leaves with a flowering plant that picks up one of the colors in the leaves.

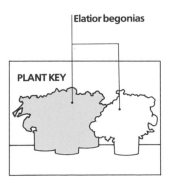

Elatior begonias

PLANT KEY

Lighting plants

The chances are that your plants are seen as often in the evening, when they are lit by artificial light, as they are during the day. In addition to background lighting, you can use directional lighting to highlight plants and flowers. This type of lighting, where the beam of light is narrow enough to pick out a single object, throws plants into relief, accentuating shape, defining color and emphasizing texture. Dramatic effects can be achieved through the interplay of light and shade created by directional lights, and the most ordinary of plants can be made into something outstanding.

Another consideration is the quality of light that you want. Incandescent tungsten bulbs, which are the most popular, give out a warm light which emphasizes yellows and reds; while tungsten halogen bulbs give out a more concentrated beam of colder light. To increase the warmth of a light, buy color-coated bulbs or translucent shades in warm colors. Plants should not be placed right next to the light source, as the heat transmitted by the bulb will damage the leaves. A safe distance is about 2 ft away from a 100 watt incandescent bulb.

Natural light

Light acts on the green pigment chlorophyll, which is present in all plants, to start the process called photosynthesis. The violet/blue and red wavelengths are most important for plant growth: the blue stimulates foliage and the red flowering. Incandescent bulbs are low in blue wavelengths and have only a limited effect on plant growth; but there are special lights which can be used as a substitute for daylight (see pp.258-9).

The amount and quality of daylight that a plant needs depends upon its original habitat in the wild. Some plants need full sunlight, some prefer filtered light, which can be given by diffusing daylight with Venetian blinds, lace or muslin, and others good indirect light. The quality of the natural light in your room will dictate the areas in which you can display your plants. At the same time, think about how they will be lit at night, so that their position allows enough natural light for healthy growth and for a directional light to show them off in the evening.

Using a window as a frame *left*
The filtered light received from this tiny window suits the Japanese fatsia (*Fatsia japonica*) and silhouettes its brilliant-green foliage. The scale of the plant and the window are perfectly matched.

Sun on a windowsill *below*
A symmetrical group of a white Cape primrose (*Streptocarpus* sp.) set between two carved birds is arranged on a wide windowsill. The light emphasizes the brilliant white of the flowers, and gives a translucent quality to the leaves which fall directly in its path.

Lighting effects 1

Downlighting

Use a downlight or pendant light over a table to direct light on to a central decoration, such as a flower arrangement, or to hold together a group of small plants.

Using a pendant light *left*
A pendant light suspended a little way above a terracotta bowl of baby's tears (*Soleirolia soleirolii*) picks up the detail of the foliage.

LIGHTING SET-UP   Down light

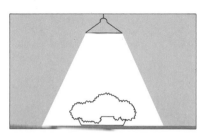

Using a downlight *right*
A downlight recessed into the ceiling casts an intense beam of light over the plants and objects arranged on this table. It illuminates a bowl of pinks (*Dianthus* sp.), a large bromeliad (*Portea petropolitana extensa*) and a maple tree (*Acer* sp.), which has been brought inside for a temporary display.

Uplighting

Lighting a single plant or a group of plants from below, with an uplighter or floor-mounted spotlight, throws strong shadows on to the wall and ceiling above. The quality of the shadows can be controlled by the position of the lights.

LIGHTING SET-UP   Side view

Back light   **Front light**

Uplighting from behind
An uplight placed behind the plant creates an abstract pattern of dramatic but distorted shadows, and reduces the plant itself to an attractive silhouette.

Uplighting from in front
Placing the lamp in front of the plant reveals detail and color in the plant itself, and creates a shadow which echoes the plant's natural shape and form.

Lighting effects 2

Frontlighting and backlighting

By using a spotlight on a table or shelf, you can create a dramatic lighting effect in a small area. Frontlighting will give strong shadows which will enhance the natural shape of plants or flowers, while backlighting produces a softer effect.

LIGHTING SET-UP   **Side view**

Back light

Front light

Backlighting *above*
This light creates an overall warm, translucent quality.

Frontlighting *below*
The shadows enhance the tulips' (*Tulipa* hybrids) distinctive shapes.

Sidelighting
Use a wall- or ceiling-mounted spotlight to beam light on to a plant or flower arrangement. With this flexible type of lighting, the angle of beam can easily be adjusted.

Sidelighting from above *below*
This angled light illuminates the soft texture and filigree pattern of the delta maidenhair fern's (*Adiantum raddianum*) foliage.

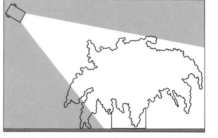

LIGHTING SET-UP

Side light

Sidelighting dried flowers
Kitchens are rooms where different types of lighting are needed: bright lights to illuminate working areas and softer, moodier lights for eating areas. Here, two angled spotlights focus beams of light on to dried flowers, revealing their colors and textures. The candles on the table add another warm light.

Styling with plants 1

Few of us have the opportunity of designing a room from scratch—in one go selecting all the materials, furniture, decorative objects and plants needed to create a recognizable style of interior decoration. In spite of practical limitations on the scope of your ideas, it is well worth looking at how plants can be used to evoke and enhance particular decorative styles. Plants and flowers are an integral part of many styles, often being the inspiration for decorative motifs of all kinds. On the following pages you will find an analysis of some of the most popular contemporary styles of interior decoration, combined with advice on what types of plants and flowers to display with them.

Country style

Country style seeks to bring the garden into the house. Flower patterns are everywhere—on wallpaper, curtains, cushions and china—and can be given added freshness by the presence of fresh flowers. Country style can be formal or relaxed, suitable for the town as well as the country. Objects do not have a particular place but rely on number to create a comfortable, lived-in atmosphere. Nostalgia for rural values is an important ingredient of this style which prizes well-crafted wooden furniture, homely designs, natural fabrics and warm colors.

Plants for a country kitchen *right*
Simple glazed pots are filled with an informal array of variegated English ivy (*Hedera helix* hybrids), thyme (*Thymus vulgaris*) and a sickle-thorn asparagus fern (*Asparagus falcatus*).

Elements of formal country style *left*
Color is more important than shape in country style. Here, foliage and flowering plants with a soft shape complement the patterns found on wallpaper, china and fabric, as do the fresh flowers which are those commonly found in an old-fashioned garden. This type of country style is more formal in feel than that featured opposite. The textures—of bone china and chintz—have more luster than those of terracotta and unvarnished wood.

PLANT KEY

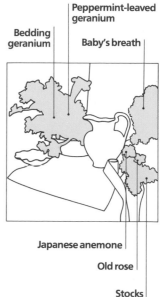

Bedding geranium

Peppermint-leaved geranium

Baby's breath

Japanese anemone

Old rose

Stocks

Floating flower-head table display *above*
Many types of geranium heads (*Pelargonium* sp.) have been floated in water on two plates to make a colorful display suitable for a center-piece on a country dining table.

Echoing floral patterns *left*
Flowers are everywhere— on fabric, on china and massed together in dried bunches to create a crowded effect reminis-cent of a well-stocked country garden.

Elements of informal country style *right*
Again, the shape of plants or flowers is less important than their color. Flowers such as these Michaelmas daisies (*Aster novi-belgii*) are fresh and warm in color, without being vibrant. Dried seed heads have rough textures and monochromatic colors that mix well with the colors and textures of wood, terracotta and basketry. Dried flowers have an immediate asso-ciation with the countryside, and their soft yellows and blues pick up the colors on the hand-painted ceramics.

PLANT KEY

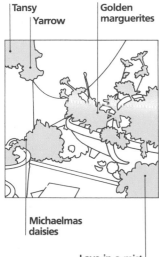

Tansy
Yarrow
Golden marguerites
Michaelmas daisies
Love-in-a-mist seed heads

Styling with plants 2
Ethnic style

The many manifestations of what can be termed "ethnic" style reflect the traditional cultures of various groups throughout the world. It is based on artefacts made by traditional methods and characterized by the use of lively patterns, which can be abstract or figurative.

Using ethnic textiles *above*
A beautiful kilim is the inspiration for this arrangement; its colors are echoed in the ceramic dish and the ochre-colored centers of the marguerites (*Chrysanthemum frutescens*).

South-American style *left*
The brilliant flowers and strong form of this Easter cactus (*Rhipsalidopsis gaertneri*) show up well against the rough texture of the stone shelf and stone carving.

Elements of ethnic style *left*
Plants with a strong outline and solid shape are needed to stand up against the abundance of patterns. Cacti are an obvious choice, particularly with objects of South-American origin as shown here. Colors should be warm to harmonize with the colors of natural dyes. Dried flowers, pebbles and bleached driftwood would all fit in to this decorative scheme.

PLANT KEY

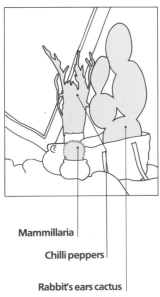

Mammillaria

Chilli peppers

Rabbit's ears cactus

Oriental style

The Far East has been a source of inspiration for decoration over several hundred years. As a decorative style it can be interpreted in a number of different ways, since each area—China, Malaya and Japan—has its own recognizable national style influenced in part by the indigenous flora.

Contrasting textures in the Japanese style *left*
The spiky leaves of the bonsai are echoed by the floating chrysanthemum heads and the harsh texture of the rock is offset against the smooth ceramic plate.

Oriental simplicity *above*
Another simple group which relies on strong forms and contrasting textures for its effect. The spiky-leaved iris (*Iris pallida*) and simple fans have an abstract quality very much in an oriental style.

Elements of oriental style *right*
A key element in oriental style is the concentration on a few simple shapes and large areas of neutral color, offset by focal points of bright color. Here, the contrast in texture between the coarse-weave bamboo mat and the glistening lacquer table is typically oriental. The feathery umbrella plant (*Cyperus* sp.) suggests bamboo while the vivid basket plant (*Aeschynanthus lobbianus*) adds a more tropical Malaysian feel to the group.

PLANT KEY

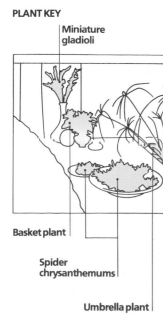

Miniature gladioli

Basket plant

Spider chrysanthemums

Umbrella plant

Styling with plants 3
High tech

This is a style based on the utilitarian shapes and materials of industrial products. Decoration is minimal and the overall effect is hard and clinical looking; it is the antithesis of anything organic. Plants need to have a vigorous outline, and flowers must be strong in color so that they are not swamped by gleaming metallic surfaces and vibrant primary colors.

Using vivid colors *above*
Use flowers with clearly defined shapes and strong colors such as this flamingo flower (*Anthurium andreanum* hybrids). The flowers look almost "unreal" as the texture of the deep-red bracts resembles shiny plastic.

Using strong forms *left*
The aggressive form of a Peruvian apple cactus (*Cereus peruvianus*) emerges in the foreground of this picture. Bright lighting and the reflective white tiling call for large, dominant plants such as the umbrella plant (*Cyperus* sp.) in the background.

Elements of high tech *right*
Suitable plants are those with a great deal of visual weight, such as large agaves, yuccas and cacti. Here, the plants have a well defined shape and foliage whose plain-green color goes well with the red plastic container and red rubber flooring.

PLANT KEY

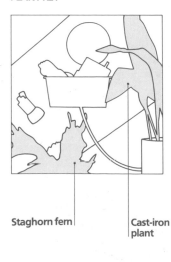

Staghorn fern

Cast-iron plant

Art deco

The art deco style of the 1920s and 1930s is still a source of inspiration for interior decoration. It is characterized by the use of strong geometric forms, monochromatic colors and reflective surfaces, such as chrome and lacquered wood.

Informal art deco *above*
Tulips (*Tulipa* hybrids) have a strong shape which suits this style—particularly when they are massed together in a vase of the period.

Formal art deco *right*
This picture shows the geometric shapes, shiny textures and monochromatic colors which are all hallmarks of the style. The regal lilies (*Lilium regale*) in the circular vase, and the ponytail, with its bold shape, hold their own against the strong outlines of the chairs.

Elements of art deco *left*
Plants with a strong outline are needed to complement the hard lines and solid forms of this style. Here, the hard-edged shape of the sculpture is repeated in the form of the lily flowers. The white of the flowers is in keeping with the monochromatic color scheme. The linear form of the silvery-mauve rosary vine (*Ceropegia woodii*) in the ceramic light fitting is silhouetted against the wall.

PLANT KEY

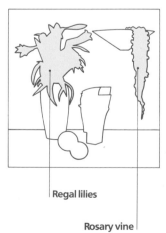

Regal lilies

Rosary vine

Grouping plants in a single container 1

For a large arrangement, quite dramatic effects can be achieved by grouping several plants together in a single container. Plants grow better when they are grouped together; a micro-climate is established with the moisture given off by one plant becoming available to its neighbor. The individual plants tend to grow into each other and show each other off.

The plants may either be all of the same kind, or they may form a mixed group of several different types with similar growing needs. They can either be knocked out of their pots and planted in a common potting mixture, as shown here, or, if they are for a temporary display, they can be left in their individual pots and stood in moist peat. If you are potting the plants, select a fairly deep container, so that the potting mixture does not dry out too quickly, and always include a layer of porous material at the base of the container if it is without drainage holes. This method has the advantage that it usually gives the plants a bigger root run, but it does make it more difficult to remove an ailing plant, or to group plants with different watering needs. Sometimes a combination of the two methods is best, allowing you to give a single plant special treatment.

An alternative planting with begonias
A striking and colorful foliage group can be made by planting together a number of painted-leaf begonias (*Begonia rex-cultorum*). These plants have extremely decorative leaves with striking patterns in red, silver, green and black. Choose specimens with different sorts of leaf patterns and textures to create a subtle interplay of colors. Plant them in peat-based potting mixture and put them in a warm part of the house in indirect light.

Equipment and materials

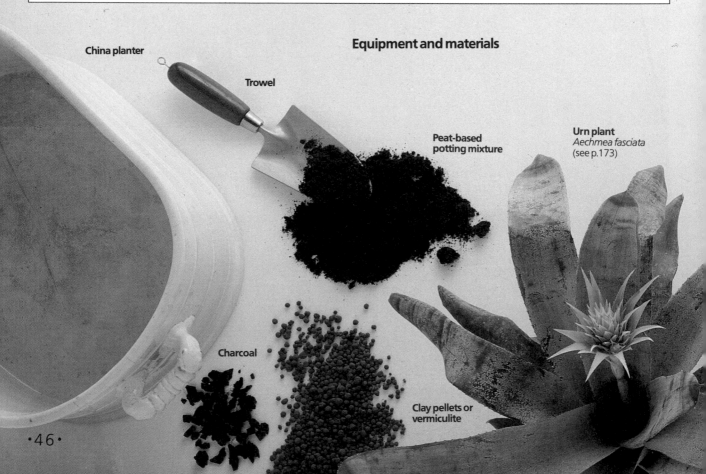

China planter

Trowel

Peat-based potting mixture

Urn plant
Aechmea fasciata
(see p.173)

Charcoal

Clay pellets or vermiculite

Planting a large container

In general, the strongest arrangements of this type are the simplest ones. Often, mixed plantings do not work because they show too much variation in shape and texture; the overall effect is untidy and difficult to place in a room. Here, I have chosen to group together several exotic-looking urn plants. Their vigorous shape called for a simple container and I chose a white china planter whose color picked up the white sheen on the leaves of the plants.

The finished arrangement
To keep the urn plants in good condition, put them in a warm, sunny place and keep their natural "vase"— formed by the rosette of leaves—filled with water. Small pale-blue flowers will emerge from the pink bracts; these do not last for long but the bracts will remain attractive for up to six months.

Building up the arrangement

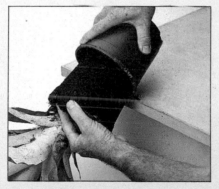

1 Line the bottom of the planter with ¾in of porous clay pellets or vermiculite and scatter pieces of charcoal over them. Fill the planter half-full with potting mixture and place one of the plants on the mixture to check that the top of its pot is level with the top of the planter.

2 To remove the urn plant from its pot, first water it well and then, holding the plant between your first and second finger, hit the pot hard against the edge of a table, or strike the base hard with your fist.

3 Build up the potting mixture at the back of the planter, and as you position each plant in the potting mixture tilt it out slightly so that the rosette of leaves and flower heads can be appreciated.

PLANTS
Mini-climate 1
Warm, sunny

An alternative planting with saffron spikes
Grouping saffron spikes (*Aphelandra squarrosa* "Louisae") in the same china planter makes another simple and effective group. Their strong shape and exciting leaf and flower color are intensified when the plants are massed together.

Grouping plants in a single container 2
Arranging plants in a basket

The choice of a basket as a container will dictate the types of plants which are suitable to be displayed in it. A rush basket calls for unsophisticated plants such as cinerarias (*Senecio cruentus*) and German violets (*Exacum affine*), as well as the examples illustrated here. Potted bulbs can be used in spring and should be massed together in the basket just before they begin to flower.

The plants which you select are for a temporary arrangement as you display them for their flowering period, or when their foliage is at its best. Given that their moment of glory is short there is no need to unpot the plants into a potting medium; and, since they are in separate pots, you can choose to group together plants with different watering needs so long as they like similar amounts of light and heat.

An alternative display with kale
These ornamental kale (*Brassica oleracea acephala*) look like giant flowers when grouped together. Their leaves of rich purple or ivory, both edged with green, can be frilled or plain and are shown off to great effect when several plants are packed together as shown here. Ornamental kale are available in late summer and autumn and, provided that they are given plenty of light and kept in a cool place, they will remain fresh for several weeks.

PLANTS
Mini-climate 5
Cool, filtered sun

Equipment and materials

Rush basket

Plastic lining

Clay pellets or vermiculite

Peat

Scissors

English ivy
Hedera helix hybrids
(see p.190)

Building up an arrangement with primroses and ivy

1 Place a piece of plastic (a trash can liner is suitable) in the basket to form a watertight skin. Cut it to shape allowing a small overhang which will eventually be tucked in. Cover the bottom of the basket with a layer of porous clay pellets or vermiculite about 1in deep.

2 Fill the basket with 2in of damp peat. Stand the pots inside and start to build up the composition. Put the three taller, salmon-pink poison primroses at the back, packing peat around the pots as you go, then let the variegated ivy trail down one side to soften the overall shape.

3 Finally, put the remaining primroses at the front of the basket. Make sure that all the pots are standing upright because you will still need to water them—the primroses in particular like plenty of water. To keep the display looking fresh, take off individual flowers as they fade and remove any yellowing leaves. These primroses should last from 6-8 weeks provided they are kept in a cool place.

Poison primrose
Primula obconica
(see p.181)

An alternative display with begonias
Another filling, suitable for a warmer place in the house, would be a collection of small-leaved eyelash begonias (*Begonia* "Tiger Paws"). Their striking green-and-bronze foliage creates a strong enough pattern for them to stand on their own.

Training climbing plants 1

Climbing plants need to be provided with some kind of support in order for them to grow upright. Plants that use aerial roots to climb, such as the philodendrons, Swiss cheese plants (*Monstera deliciosa*) and pothos vines (*Scindapsus pictus* "Argyraeus"), like to grow over a constantly moist medium. A pole made out of wire netting stuffed with sphagnum moss is an excellent, sturdy support, and particularly suitable for climbing plants with thick stems and large leaves. Plants which climb by means of curly leaf tendrils, such as passion flowers (*Passiflora caerulea*) and ivies (*Hedera* sp.), can be trained on canes, wire hoops and trellis work.

Making a moss-pole

Equipment and materials

Moss-poles can be bought ready-made, but if you make your own with wire netting you can provide far moister moss for the roots of climbing plants. You will need about three or four small plants to grow up a moss pole about 3ft high. Once it is made, remember to keep the moss constantly moist, otherwise the aerial roots will not grow into it.

Sphagnum moss

Bamboo sticks

Terracotta half-pot

Tamping stick

Wire cutters

Drainage dish

Chicken wire

Roll of corrugated paper

Peat-based potting mixture

Trowel

Heartleaf philodendron
Philodendron scandens
(see p.188)

PLANTS
Mini-climate 3
Warm, shady

Wires

Building up the arrangement

1 To form the shape of the moss-pole, take a roll of corrugated paper and wrap chicken wire round it. Cut the wire so that it is 2in wider than the paper. Join the two cut edges together to form a column shape.

2 Cut two lengths of bamboo, thread them through the netting about 1½in from the bottom. Lash them together where they cross each other, and to the wire column, then wedge them into the pot.

Training plants in the house

Climbing plants can be trained up a blank wall, to make it an attractive feature, and trained round mirrors, doors and windows, to frame them with fresh greenery. To provide support for the plant, string runs of wire or strong nylon cord between nails or screw eyes, and then attach the plant to the support with plant ties, to help maintain the shape that you want.

Training a plant up a wall *right*
The emerald fern (*Asparagus densiflorus* "Sprengeri") is often displayed as a trailing plant, but here its soft, feathery stems have been trained round a picture.

Training a plant round a mirror *above*
A grape ivy (*Cissus rhombifolia*) makes an unusual frame for this large mirror. This attractive vine clings to any support with its wiry tendrils and grows very rapidly—about 2-3ft a year. It is an extremely tolerant plant which thrives in a wide range of conditions.

3 Fill the pot two-thirds full with potting mixture. Start to fill the empty column of chicken wire with sphagnum moss, using a wooden stick to pack it together tightly, and continue until it is full.

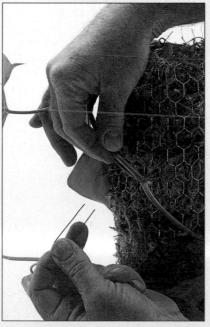

4 Pot the heartleaf philodendrons and attach their stems to the pole with wire, bent to form a hairpin shape.

5 Water the sphagnum moss and the potting mixture well before putting the moss-pole in a warm, shady position. Spray the pole every day to keep the moss thoroughly moist.

Training climbing plants 2
Making a wire support

Many plants suitable for indoor use are rampant climbers in the wild. They are often bought trained round a wire support which is soon outgrown. It is then a good idea to open the plant out and train it round a larger support which will show off foliage and flowers more effectively. Try to match the scale of the plant to the scale of the support: here I trained passion flowers round hoops of wire which suited the delicate tracery of the plants' foliage.

Equipment and materials

Soil-based potting mixture

Pliers

Wire

Plant ties

Glazed ceramic container

Clay pellets or vermiculite

Passion flower
Passiflora caerulea
(see p.185)

**PLANTS
Mini-climate 1**
Warm, sunny

The finished arrangement
Covering one hoop less thickly than the others made the arrangement a more interesting shape. It also gave it a lightness of effect which will make the transitory opening of the curious flowers more visible. You will need to tie in the shoots very regularly in order to maintain the overall shape of the display. If you cut the plants back, as far as the main stems, at the beginning of winter and put them in a cool, frost-free place they should grow back again in the spring.

Building up the arrangement

1 Cut two lengths of wire of the same size to form two hoops. Place them in the container to check that they are in scale with it. Put the hoops to one side; they will be held in place by the potting mixture once you have started planting.

2 If your container has a drainage hole, place a piece of broken shard over it; then line the pot with 1in of vermiculite or clay pellets and fill three-quarters full with potting mixture. Unwind a passion flower from its previous support and repot it, firming potting mixture around its roots. Place one hoop in the pot and wind the plant's stems around it.

3 Place the other wire hoop in the container at a 90 degree angle to the other and fix the pair together with plant ties. Remove any dead leaves or unwanted shoots as you go. Plant the last passion flower, training one stem up the remaining bare hoop, and arranging the other stems on the opposite side.

Other ornamental supports

Using bamboo, rattan or wire you can make many different shapes of support. Bamboo stakes can be made into trellis or, for a more unusual effect, into obelisks. Rattan is flexible and can be used to make any sort of rounded form.

Trellis work *below*
Woodland strawberries (*Fragaria vesca* "Alpine") bear small fruit and make an attractive display.

Rattan canes

Bamboo trellis

Bamboo stakes

Creeping fig
Ficus pumila

Rattan hoop

Plastic trellis

Planting hanging baskets 1

Most of us are familiar with hanging baskets displayed on terraces, balconies or porches, but seldom see them used indoors to advantage. When selecting a basket for an indoor display think carefully about its setting: a wire basket is only suitable for a room with a water-resistant floor, such as a conservatory. A practical, but less attractive, alternative is a solid plastic basket with a raised platform inside, a filling tube and water-level indicator, or another type which incorporates a drip-tray. But there is nothing to stop you using a terracotta container or rush basket, if you make your own rope hangings, or using a wall basket in an appropriate material.

It is important to secure the basket properly because it will be very heavy when wet. The chain or rope support should hang from a hook firmly anchored in a ceiling joist, not set into the plaster.

When deciding upon a planting scheme for a basket, remember that you are trying to blend the arrangement with your décor. Limit yourself to one type of plant unless your setting is very plain. For an outdoor planting you can afford to be less restrained with your color, but it is sensible to choose species which are used to heat and the drying effect of wind.

Planting a wire basket

The attraction of a wire basket is that, once the plants are established, it becomes a spherical mass of flowers or foliage. Here, I set out to create the effect of a large ball of flowers by planting white and blue Italian bellflowers. These should flower continuously from August to November provided they are watered well in warm weather—a good reason for putting this display in a conservatory.

Cross-section of the planted basket

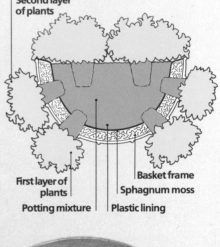

Second layer of plants

First layer of plants

Potting mixture

Basket frame

Sphagnum moss

Plastic lining

Bucket

Plastic lining

Wire basket

A garden room filled with hanging baskets

This light garden room provides an excellent setting for an array of hanging baskets. A dramatic staghorn fern (*Platycerium bifurcatum*) is the focal point of the display. This is flanked on the left by a grape ivy (*Cissus rhombifolia*) in a wicker basket and an impatiens (*Impatiens* sp.), and on the right by several spider plants (*Chlorophytum comosum* "Vittatum"). Notice the wicker wall baskets—one containing dried flowers, the other another grape ivy.

Building up the arrangement

1 Rest the basket on the rim of a flat-bottomed bowl or bucket. Line it with a 2in layer of damp sphagnum moss. Then, cut a circle of plastic sheeting to fit inside, leaving an overlap of 4in. Make a circle of holes in the plastic 2in up from the bottom.

2 You will need to divide some of the larger plants into two to fit them through the holes. First, water the plants before taking them out of their pots; then, holding the plant in both hands, plunge your thumbs into the middle of the potting mixture and pull apart. Insert the divided plants from the outside, pushing the roots through the sphagnum moss and the holes in the plastic.

4 Fill the gaps in the top with blue-flowered plants and, when the basket is filled, tuck in the overhanging plastic. Water the basket well before replacing the chains and hanging it in a sunny place.

3 Push one row of plants around the bottom of the basket, cover with a layer of potting mixture, firming it down around them, and then place more plants higher up the sides of the basket to fill the gaps. Plant several large white specimens in the top.

PLANTS
Mini-climate 4
Cool, sunny

Italian bellflower
Campanula isophylla
(see p.191)

Equipment and materials

Scissors

Peat-based potting mixture

Trowel

Sphagnum moss

Planting hanging baskets 2
Planting a wicker basket

Hanging baskets can add freshness and color to a room, particularly where space at floor level is limited. Think about the place where your basket is to hang and select your plants with an eye to the decorative effect you want, bearing in mind that the plants should like the place you have chosen and be broadly compatible in their requirements. The container you use should not detract from the natural colors of the plants. I felt a wicker basket suited this display where I have chosen to group ferns together, accentuating contrasts of plant form and leaf shape.

Equipment and materials

Wicker basket

Floral foam matting

Foil

PLANTS
Mini-climate 2 Warm, filtered sun
Mini-climate 3 Warm, shady

Clay pellets or vermiculite

Trowel

Peat-based potting mixture

Charcoal

Asparagus fern
Asparagus setaceus
(see p.183)

Emerald fern
Asparagus densiflorus "Sprengeri"
(see p.191)

Scarlet star
Guzmania lingulata
(see p.174)

Bird's nest fern
Asplenium nidus
(see p.173)

Boston fern
Nephrolepis exaltata
"Bostoniensis"
(see p.170)

Cretan brake
Pteris cretica
(see p.183)

Delta maidenhair fern
Adiantum raddianum (see p.183)

Sphagnum moss

The finished arrangement
The final addition of the scarlet stars creates a splash of color and links the display to its setting by echoing the red of the poppies in the painting. After completing the planting I placed the rope hangings round the basket and hung it from the ceiling by a north-facing window. It is a good idea to use a hook with a universal joint so that the basket can be rotated to ensure plants get an even supply of light.

Building up the arrangement

1 Line the basket with foil to prevent rotting, then place foam matting on top and trim to fit. Put some pieces of gravel at the back of the basket to form a higher area for planting. Line the basket with porous clay pellets or vermiculite.

2 Fill the basket with peat-based potting mixture, adding about a handful of charcoal to prevent the mixture turning sour. Allow enough room at the top for watering. Position the first plant where the compost has been built up over the gravel. Use a bushy asparagus fern with delicate feathery fronds to give height to the arrangement.

3 At this stage, it is a good idea to plan the rest of the arrangement by positioning your plants, still in their pots, until you are satisfied with the design. Here I put two trailing emerald ferns either side of the asparagus fern.

continued over

4 To give more substance to the back of the design put two more Boston ferns either side of the asparagus fern. When planting, tilt the ferns out to the side so that their fronds overhang the sides of the basket.

5 To fill the foreground add a delta maidenhair fern and a Cretan brake. The delicate fronds of the delta maidenhair fern and the unusual branching of the Cretan brake provide further variation in leaf shape and color.

6 Placing a bird's nest fern on the left sets up a pleasing contrast between its broad straplike leaves and the surrounding feathery fronds. Finally, add the two scarlet stars, cover any visible potting mixture with damp moss and water well before hanging.

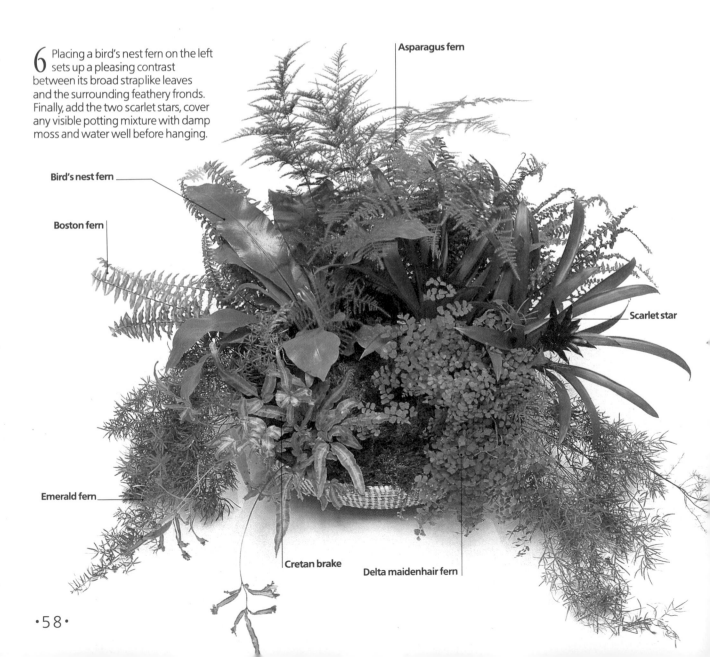

Asparagus fern

Bird's nest fern

Boston fern

Scarlet star

Emerald fern

Cretan brake

Delta maidenhair fern

Growing bulbs indoors 1

A mass of temporary flowering bulbs can make a beautiful grouping, particularly when there is little other color around. Most bulbs can be grown in containers without drainage holes, as well as conventional pots. Plant them in soup tureens, vegetable dishes, china pots or glass vases using potting mixture, or grow them hydroponically in pebbles and water.

When garden bulbs are grown in the house they have to experience an artificial "winter" before they will bloom. They will not flower properly unless they are kept cool (30-45°F) and dark for eight to ten weeks. You can buy "prepared" bulbs which do not need to be kept in the dark (although they must be kept cool) but these are more expensive. Buy bulbs as soon as you see them on sale—usually in early autumn—and plant them right away. It is a good idea to buy several types so that you can keep replacing fading specimens with fresh ones. Plant bowls of early-flowering crocuses which can be white, yellow, bronze, mauve or purple. Plant hyacinths for their scent as well as their large flowers. Choose daffodils for their fresh and cheerful colors, and lily-flowered and kaufmannia tulips for their strong shapes and colors.

A windowsill of bulbs *above*
Amaryllis (*Hippeastrum* hybrids), daffodils (*Narcissus* hybrids) and hyacinths (*Hyacinthus orientalis* hybrids) line a windowsill. This is a good place to display your bulbs since the cooler the plants are kept, the longer they will last.

Crocuses in a basket *below*
A mass of bulbs and foliage spilling over the edges of a basket can look stunning. Here, brilliant white crocuses (*Crocus* hybrids) have been mingled with the graceful grasslike foliage of the bulrush plant (*Scirpus cernuus*).

Growing bulbs indoors 2

Although bulbs can be bought from retailers, there is such an enormous range of hybrids available that it is worth looking through a specialist catalogue to select bulbs whose colors and shapes particularly appeal to you. For fresh color and delicate fragrance, daffodils are a good choice. Certain species of daffodils, including *Narcissus* "Cragford" which I have used here, can be grown in gravel or stones instead of potting mixture or bulb fiber. Plant them in glass containers which allow the texture of the gravel to be seen. If you plant the daffodil bulbs in October, and "winter" them as shown below, they should be in flower by Christmas.

Indoor bulbs which flower later in the spring or in the summer include the amaryllis (*Hippeastrum* hybrids), which has huge, trumpet-shaped flowers, and several lilies including the fragrant, white Easter lily (*Lilium longiflorum*).

Equipment and materials

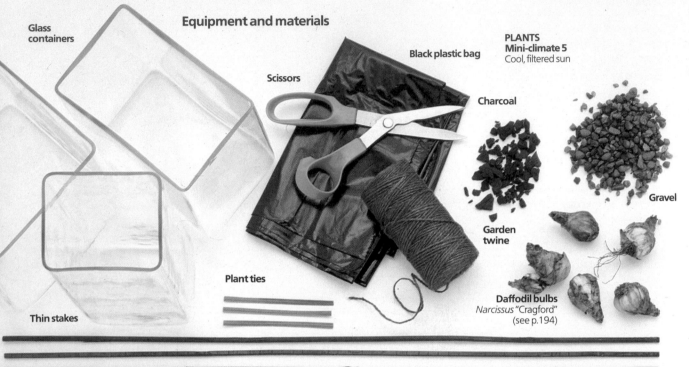

Glass containers

Scissors

Black plastic bag

PLANTS
Mini-climate 5
Cool, filtered sun

Charcoal

Garden twine

Gravel

Plant ties

Thin stakes

Daffodil bulbs
Narcissus "Cragford"
(see p.194)

Building up the arrangement

1 Mix some gravel with about 20 small pieces of charcoal, having first washed the gravel to remove any dirt which would cloud the water. Fill the container so that it is about three-quarters full of gravel and start planting the first bulbs, making a depression with your finger for each bulb to sit in.

2 Place the bulbs in position with their "noses" coming out of the medium. You should be able to fit about nine bulbs in a container of this size, but make sure that the bulbs do not touch each other. Fill the spaces between the bulbs with more gravel and add water until it is close to, but not touching, the bottom of the bulbs.

3 If you use prepared bulbs or those of the paper white narcissus, they can grow in the light, but other bulbs must be kept in the dark. Cut a black plastic bag in half, secure it round the container with garden twine or string and stand in a cool, dark place. Look at the bulbs after about four weeks to see if they need more water.

4 After eight to ten weeks, about ½in of growth should be visible and the bulbs can be brought out into the light. Once the daffodils have reached their maximum height, some of their stems and leaves will need support. Attach any untidy leaves or bending stems to thin green stakes with plant ties. Alternatively, use the stakes at an early stage—when about 4in of top growth has appeared—to support the stems and leaves as they grow.

5 Most spring bulbs do not like very warm rooms. If temperatures are high, their stems become elongated and the leaves soft and sappy. When the flowers have died, remove the dead heads and plant the daffodil bulbs outdoors.

Other indoor bulb displays

It is best to plant one color of a flower per pot because different colors may flower at different times. Hyacinth (*Hyacinthus orientalis* hybrids) bulbs vary so much that it is safest to plant single bulbs in 3in pots. Once the flower buds are well developed, group bulbs together at the same stages of development.

Hyacinths in full bloom *left*
Hyacinths have large flower heads and, when planted en masse, make an eye-catching and fragrant display.

Pots of daffodils *above*
A cheerful display of daffodils (*Narcissus* sp.) in clay pots. Grass seeds have been sown on the surface of the potting mixture for decoration.

Planting window-boxes 1

Window-boxes are usually thought of as outdoor containers but there is no reason why they cannot be used indoors, provided you have a window which opens outwards or upwards with a suitable sill. There are many types of boxes: plastic is a light, cheap material suitable for use indoors or out and, if planted with trailers, will hardly be visible through the greenery; fiberglass comes in authentic-looking imitations of lead and stone, and is extremely light but correspondingly expensive; stone is always attractive but is too heavy for most sills and better used on the ground; terracotta suits period houses and formal interior settings; wood is a very useful material for an outdoor box as it can be made to measure and, if fitted with a waterproof zinc liner which can be lifted out, is easy to replant with the new season's flowers.

Your window-box should have holes at the bottom to prevent the lower layers collecting sour water and causing roots to rot. Wooden, stone and terracotta boxes have holes drilled and plastic ones have indentations which you can tap out with a screwdriver. Always fit a drip-tray underneath the box to prevent any surplus water overflowing. Whether your box is to go indoors or out, select one that is as deep as is practical; this will prevent the potting mixture from drying out too quickly, although you will find that any box will need very frequent watering in warm weather. If your box is placed high-up where it could fall and cause damage below, secure it in place with a brace on either side attached to the window surround, or within an angled bracket fixed to the wall or window. Never use window-boxes on weak or rotten sills.

Types of window-box

The material of your window-box should be in keeping with the style of your house—if it is to go outside—and the style of your room—if it is to go inside. In either case, it is best to choose a box which is as low-key as possible to show off the plants. If you use a purpose-made wooden box it can be painted to match the color of your walls. Your choice of plants will depend on the season in which you are planting, and on the orientation of your window.

A cedarwood box *left*
This deep, wooden window-box sits snugly on its sill. Its simple planting of scarlet geraniums (*Pelargonium hortorum* hybrids) will flower for almost all the year and makes an eye-catching display set against the deep-yellow wall.

A painted wooden box *below*
This box of painted wood is almost completely obscured by the purple lobelia (*Lobelia erinus pendula*) trailing over it. Deep-pink primroses (*Primula obconica*) and marguerite daisies (*Chrysanthemum frutescens*) complete a colorful summer planting attractively framed by the wrought-iron sill-surround.

A brass box *above*
The glistening brass of this indoor window-box is set off by the austere, white-leaded window. It is planted with blue German violets (*Exacum affine*) whose golden stamens pick up the color of the brass. Other alternatives suitable for a brass box would be a bronze-leaved wax begonia (*Begonia semperflorens-cultorum*) or impatiens (*Impatiens wallerana* hybrids), rust-colored florist's chrysanthemums (*Chrysanthemum morifolium* hybrids) or a collection of richly colored painted nettles (*Coleus blumei*).

Planting an indoor window-box

Begin by thinking about what types of plants will like the quality of light offered by your window and make sure that those you choose have similar growing needs. For this summer group I used a plain white plastic window-box and chose pink and purple Cupid's bowers and a tradescantia with pink stripes to pick up the color of the flowers. Alternative plantings for a spring box would be bulbs or herbs and for a winter box you could use daffodils.

Building up the arrangement

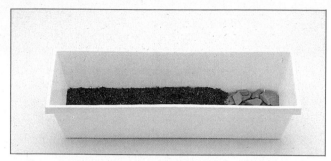

1 Line the box with a layer of shards making sure that the pieces face downwards so that water will drain off them (If you do not have any broken terracotta pots, most garden centers will supply shards free of charge). Add a 2in layer of potting mixture, putting more at the back to give height to the back of the arrangement.

2 Set the plants out in the box and experiment with the design until you are satisfied that it looks balanced. Begin by planting six purple Cupid's bowers along the length of the box, leaving room between them for the pink-flowered kinds and the trailing foliage of the tradescantia.

3 Place a tradescantia in the center of the box, letting some stems trail down in front and threading the others through the Cupid's bowers. Finally, fill the remaining spaces with pink Cupid's bowers and another tradescantia.

The finished arrangement
Both plants like a sunny position and will be happy on a south-facing windowsill. The Cupid's bowers will flower from June until October and, as they grow, will trail attractively over the edge of the box.

Equipment and materials

PLANTS
Mini-climate 1
Warm, sunny

Shards

Tradescantia
Tradescantia fluminensis
"Variegata"
(see p.189)

Soil-based potting mixture

Cupid's bower
Achimenes grandiflora
(see p.181)

Window-box and drip-tray

Trowel

Pruners

Planting window-boxes 2
Planting an outdoor window-box

Winter is the season when you long to see greenery and colorful flowers. One way of improving the view from your windows, particularly if you live in the city, is to plant a window-box using plants with colorful berries and ever-greens with attractive foliage. The window-box I have planted below will need protection from the frost, since the Christmas cherries and florist's chrysanthemums are not hardy; put it at a window where it can easily be brought inside in cold weather or, alternatively, use it as an indoor window-box for a cool place.

Building up the arrangement

1 Line the window-box with 1in of clay pellets (you can also use shards or gravel) to provide drainage. Place a layer of potting mixture over the pellets to a depth of about 2in.

2 With the plants still in their pots, experiment with the design, putting the Christmas cherries in the middle and the chrysan-themums at the edge. Place the ivies in the box to see where their trailing stems will look best.

3 Take the plants out of their pots and shake off excess potting mixture. Put two Christmas cherries in the center of the box and plant the florist's chrysanthemums on either side. Let the four small ivies trail down at the sides and in the front of the box. Firm potting mixture around the plants and water well before putting in position.

Florist's chrysanthemum
Chrysanthemum morifolium
hybrids (see p.181)

Equipment and materials

Clay pellets
or vermiculite

Trowel

Peat-based
potting mixture

English ivy
Hedera helix hybrids
(see p.190)

Terracotta
window-box

PLANTS
Mini-climate 4
Cool, sunny
Mini-climate 5
Cool, filtered sun

Christmas cherry
Solanum capsicastrum
(see p.180)

Other ideas for window gardens

There are other ways to decorate windows besides using window-boxes. You can set potted plants on tiers of glass or plastic shelves across a window, or use wooden shelves lined with metal to protect them from water. Your choice of plants will depend upon the orientation of your window. Place sun-loving desert cacti and succulents and tropical species at a south-facing window, flowering plants at west- and east-facing windows, and plants which like indirect light at north-facing windows. Alternatively, it is possible to build a special window for plants, similar to a miniature conservatory.

Tiers of plants *right*
Rows of plants ranged on glass shelves obscure the view but make an attractive display in themselves. Placing all the plants in the same type of container introduces a sense of order into a crowded arrangement. Most of the plants shown here are desert cacti and succulents which are used to bright sunlight in the wild. Plants with variegated leaves, such as the polka-dot plant (*Hypoestes phyllostachya*) on the bottom shelf, will also thrive in good light, which will intensify the color of their foliage.

A miniature conservatory *below*
Plants benefit from being grouped together and, if they are also given good light, they will grow fast. In a glass box, such as the one shown here, it is necessary to provide some form of shade from the summer sun, to ensure good ventilation, and to increase the humidity, particularly when it is hot. To do this, stand plants on trays filled with moist pebbles.

Planting bottle gardens

Bottle gardens provide optimum growing conditions for plants which like a humid atmosphere, so it makes sense to plant particularly slow-growing specimens if you want your garden to look attractive for a year or more. Tempting as it may be to plant African violets (*Saintpaulia* hybrids), it is not a good idea since, once the flowers fade, they can look very dull. It is best to create a colorful effect by using plants with variegated leaves and to build an interesting group with contrasts of shape and texture. Any sort of bottle is suitable, provided plants can be passed through the neck. If the bottle is made of colored glass it will block out some light and, to compensate for this, you should move the garden into brighter light than would be normal for the plants inside.

Circle of paper

Funnel

Glass bottle

Maidenhair fern
Adiantum raddianum microphyllum
(see p.183)

Sphagnum moss

Clay pellets or vermiculite

Peat-based potting mixture

Charcoal

Equipment and materials

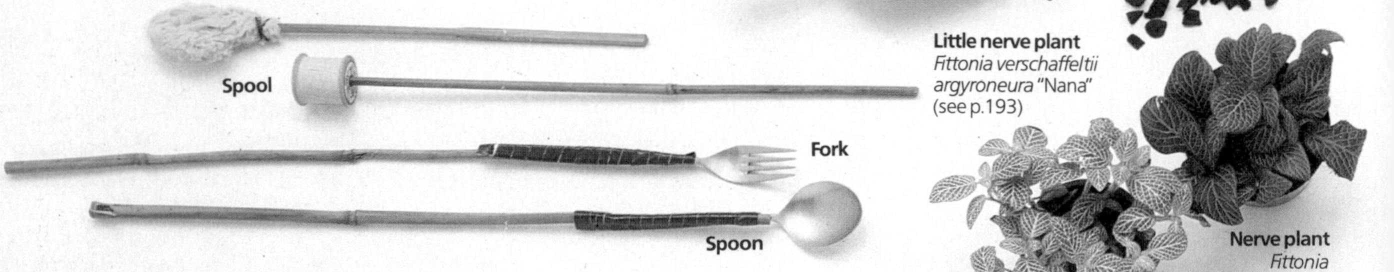

Sponge

Spool

Miniature trowel

Little nerve plant
Fittonia verschaffeltii argyroneura "Nana"
(see p.193)

Fork

Spoon

Nerve plant
Fittonia verschaffeltii
(see p.193)

Building up the arrangement

Australian maidenhair fern
Adiantum hispidulum
(see p.183)

PLANTS
Mini-climate 3
Warm, shady

1 Cut a circle of paper the same size as the planting area of the bottle and experiment with the design—placing the taller plants at the back and the low-growing ones in the foreground.

2 Pour a 1in layer of clay pellets or vermiculite into the bottle through a funnel made of stiff paper. Add a handful of charcoal, and fill the bottle with 2-3in of damp peat-based potting mixture.

3 Build up the potting mixture at the back of the bottle to give more height to the group. Use the spoon to smooth out the surface of the mixture and make a hole at the back for the roots of the first plant.

4 Remove a maidenhair fern from its pot and shake off excess potting mixture. Stick the fork into the root ball and lower the plant into the hole made for it. Release the plant, cover the roots and gently firm down the potting mixture around it.

5 Put another maidenhair fern at the back of the group and then add an Australian maidenhair to vary the outline. Make sure that the plants are not too close together—leave about 2in between them to allow room for growth.

PLANT KEY

Maidenhair fern

Australian maidenhair fern

Little nerve plant

Nerve plant

Peat-based potting mixture

Charcoal

Clay pellets

6 Place the little nerve plants in the foreground. Their solid silver-veined leaves provide a pleasing contrast to the mass of delicate fronds above them. Then, to give the arrangement a focal point and to add color, plant a nerve plant with red leaf veins in the centre. Finally, decorate any bare area of potting mixture with sphagnum moss, and pour a cup of water into the bottle by directing it against the glass. You can put a cork in the top to make the atmosphere more humid, but it will make the glass mist up more quickly.

Planting terraria

Terraria are glass cases that offer the same humid environment as bottle gardens, since the moisture given off by the leaves of the plants inside condenses and runs back into the soil. As it is easier to prune and remove plants from a terrarium than from a bottle garden, you can use suitable fast-growing kinds such as the mosses and polka-dot plants planted in the terrarium opposite. For the same reason, small flowering plants such as miniature gloxinias (*Sinningia pusilla*) can be planted, and replaced when they have faded. Here, I used a leaded-glass terrarium resembling a tiny conservatory which suggested the choice of palms to form the background of the group.

Equipment and materials

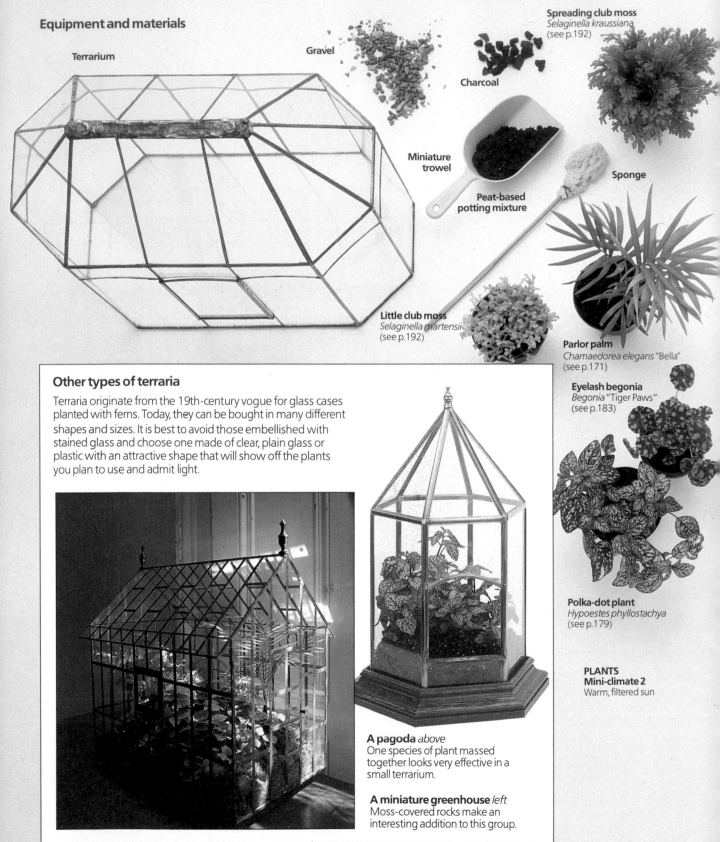

Terrarium

Gravel

Charcoal

Spreading club moss
Selaginella kraussiana
(see p.192)

Miniature trowel

Peat-based potting mixture

Sponge

Little club moss
Selaginella martensii
(see p.192)

Parlor palm
Chamaedorea elegans "Bella"
(see p.171)

Eyelash begonia
Begonia "Tiger Paws"
(see p.183)

Polka-dot plant
Hypoestes phyllostachya
(see p.179)

**PLANTS
Mini-climate 2**
Warm, filtered sun

Other types of terraria

Terraria originate from the 19th-century vogue for glass cases planted with ferns. Today, they can be bought in many different shapes and sizes. It is best to avoid those embellished with stained glass and choose one made of clear, plain glass or plastic with an attractive shape that will show off the plants you plan to use and admit light.

A pagoda *above*
One species of plant massed together looks very effective in a small terrarium.

A miniature greenhouse *left*
Moss-covered rocks make an interesting addition to this group.

Building up the arrangement

1 Line the terrarium with ½in of gravel, spread lumps of charcoal over it and then fill with 2in of damp potting mixture Place some of the plants you have chosen inside the terrarium and plan your group.

2 Make a depression and plant the tallest parlor palm, spreading the roots out horizontally and gently packing potting mixture around them. This will not harm the plant and will slow down its growth.

3 Plant another parlor palm at the back of the terrarium on the left. Then, beneath it place an eyelash begonia next to a little club moss which matches the brilliant green in the begonia's leaves.

PLANT KEY

Parlor palm

Spreading club moss

Polka-dot plant

Little club moss

Eyelash begonia

4 Put another little club moss in the front of the terrarium and a spreading-club moss behind the larger parlor palm to give it more bulk. Then, fill the remaining spaces around the palm with polka-dot plants, and decorate any bare potting mixture with gravel. Mist-spray plants and potting mixture and close any aperture.

Cleaning the terrarium
Use a small sponge attached to a bamboo stake to remove condensation or algae from the inside surface of the glass.

Cacti and succulent gardens

Cacti and succulents with similar growing needs can be planted together to make a miniature desert landscape. As they do not have deep root systems, they can be planted in shallow containers. If your container does not have drainage holes, line it with porous material to prevent the roots from rotting, and water the plants more sparingly than is recommended in *The Plant Finder's Guide*.

Queen agave
Agave victoriae-reginae
(see p.200)

Bishop's cap
Astrophytum myriostigma
(see p.198)

Equipment and materials

Coarse sand

Trowel

Gravel

Soil-based potting mixture

**PLANTS
Mini-climate 4**
Cool, sunny

Powder-puff cactus
Mammillaria bocasana
(see p.199)

Terracotta dish

Mammillaria
Mammillaria sp.
(see p.199)

Building up the arrangement

1 Line the container with 1in of gravel. Mix coarse sand and soil-based potting mixture together in measures of one part of sand to two of soil. Spread a 1in layer of this mixture over the gravel.

2 With the plants still in their pots, experiment with the design. Consider any decorative pebbles which can be used on the surface of the potting mixture.

Brown paper

3 Fold up a piece of brown paper, wrap it round the spines of the cactus and lift the plant out with one hand, pulling the pot away with the other.

4 Lift the queen agave out of its pot and place it at the back of the dish. Plant the two bishop's caps and mammillarias, trickling the potting mixture gently around their roots.

Decorative finishes

Most nurseries and garden centers stock a wide variety of stone chippings, pebbles and gravel that can be used to decorate the surface of the potting mixture. Marble chips can be obtained from stone masons, and aquarium dealers often have a good selection of colored pebbles. Coverings of pebbles and gravel tend to look best with cacti and succulents, since they are in keeping with the plants' arid or semi-arid natural habitat, but try out other finishes as well.

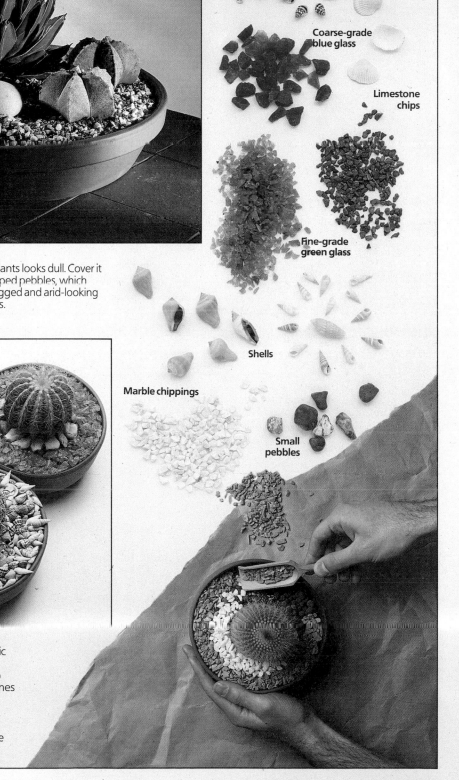

Pebbles

Shells

Coarse-grade blue glass

Limestone chips

Fine-grade green glass

Shells

Marble chippings

Small pebbles

Decorating a cactus garden
A large area of potting mixture between plants looks dull. Cover it with stone chippings and interestingly shaped pebbles, which resemble rocks, and you have a suitably rugged and arid-looking miniature landscape for these desert plants.

Patterns and textures *above*
Building up a series of decorative concentric rings made out of contrasting colors or materials is simple and effective. The sharp conical shells are arranged to mimic the spines of the cactus.

Adding a decorative finish *right*
Using a small scoop or spoon, add a thin layer of decorative material to the top of the potting mixture.

Making water gardens

Hydroculture is a relatively new name for an old practice of growing plants in containers filled with water and aggregate to which soluble plant foods are added. In place of soil, plants are held in position by the aggregate. Special containers are available (see pp.260-1) but you can make a simple and attractive planting in a glass vase.

It is best to use plants that have already made roots in water before putting them into the new medium, since the roots made in water are quite different from those made in soil. "Prepared" plants can be bought, or you can use cuttings of soft-stemmed plants that have been rooted in water. If you do transfer a plant from soil to water you must wait for the old roots to be replaced by new succulent ones. This process takes between 8-12 weeks and, during this time, the plant will need to be encased in a plastic bag to keep it in a warm and humid atmosphere.

Equipment and materials

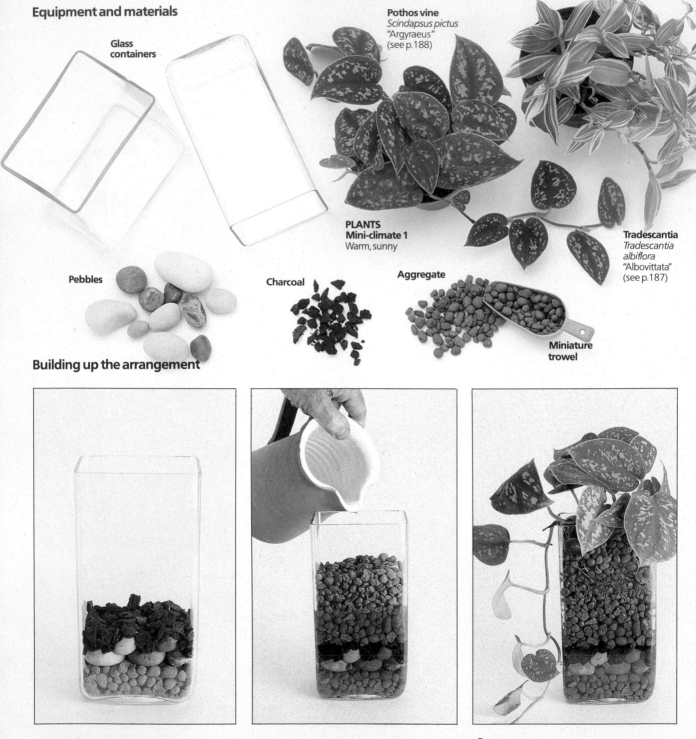

Glass containers

Pothos vine
Scindapsus pictus
"Argyraeus"
(see p.188)

**PLANTS
Mini-climate 1**
Warm, sunny

Tradescantia
Tradescantia albiflora "Albovittata"
(see p.187)

Pebbles

Charcoal

Aggregate

Miniature trowel

Building up the arrangement

1 Line the container with ¾-1 in of aggregate which has previously been soaked to wash away impurities. Place a layer of pebbles over it and add some charcoal to keep the water sweet.

2 Fill the container two-thirds full with aggregate. Pour in enough water to fill the container one-third full and let the aggregate absorb the water.

3 Place the plant inside the container and trickle aggregate around its roots. If you are moving a plant grown in potting mixture carefully wash all traces of it away before planting.

The finished arrangement
A pothos vine and a tradescantia have been planted in aggregate decorated with pebbles to create layers of different textures in the transparent containers. Plants are fed by adding food in the form of a powder or a sachet which releases nutrients into the water when they are needed (see p.260).

Alternative arrangements

Almost any plant can be successfully grown by hydroculture. It is a technique that has several advantages over conventional methods: it is convenient for apartment dwellers since potting mixture does not have to be stored; it is less messy; watering and feeding are simpler; growth is more vigorous; and plants are not subject to soil-borne pests and diseases.

A vegetable garden *above*
The sweet potato (*Ipomoea batatas*) is usually grown for its tuberous edible roots; here the root is growing in water and decorative heart-shaped leaves rise from it.

An oriental garden *left*
This umbrella plant (*Cyperus* sp.) likes boggy conditions in the wild and is therefore a natural candidate for hydroculture. Here, I built up a layer of white pebbles at the front of the container and filled the rest of it with the aggregate.

Caring for bonsai

The word bonsai means literally "plant in a tray". It is a technique by which any tree or shrub can be turned into a dwarf specimen by restricting its growth, and by pruning its roots and branches. As developed by the Japanese and Chinese, the technique was applied mainly to hardy trees of all kinds, such as maple, silver birch, beech, larch and pine. Today, these are referred to as "outdoor" bonsai since they need to spend most of the year outdoors. They should not be brought into a heated room for more than a few days in winter, but in summer, when the temperatures inside are similar to those outside, they can be brought in more frequently. A new development is the "indoor" bonsai: these are tropical or semi-tropical species which are happy to be kept indoors all the year round.

All bonsai need a great deal of light and, as their roots are restricted in a very small container, they must be watered frequently, particularly in warm weather.

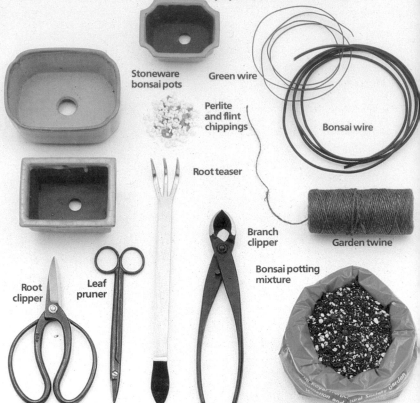

Equipment and materials

Stoneware bonsai pots

Green wire

Perlite and flint chippings

Bonsai wire

Root teaser

Root clipper

Leaf pruner

Branch clipper

Garden twine

Bonsai potting mixture

Indoor and outdoor trees

Bonsai can be grown from seed or cuttings, or bought as young and mature plants. If properly cared for, these trees can live for many years; their price depends on age and the complexity of the shape of the tree.

Bonsai should be grown in shallow frost-proof pots with large drainage holes. Imported from Japan, these pots come in a variety of shapes and in plain, subtle colors which do not detract attention from the trees.

An outdoor bonsai
This Japanese maple (*Acer palmatum* "Dissectum") has a double twisted trunk and graceful upright shape. The leaves turn this beautiful, coppery-pink color in autumn.

An indoor bonsai
This fig (*Ficus retusa*) is 15 years old and its trunk has splayed roots with an interesting shape. Display at an east- or west-facing window, but provide shade for it from the late afternoon sun.

Training and pruning

The Japanese have many different styles of bonsai, named according to their shape and the angle of the trunk in the pot. You can train your tree to grow in unusual shapes with wires, and by pruning the branches and leaves. To wire branches, it is best to use specially imported bonsai wire, which is very stiff, to hold branches rigid in the position you want to train them to follow. Training and pruning should be done in the very early spring, just before the new growth appears. Leaf pruning can be done all through the growing season and will encourage the growth of smaller leaves, which are in scale with the tree.

Complementary shapes *left*
Before you start to train and prune your tree, decide what shape you want it to have. If you want to display it with another tree, put the two together. Here, the smaller tree is to be trained to a fan shape with a flat top to complement the taller specimen behind it.

1 Loop the bonsai wire round the trunk of the tree and push it into the shape you want the branch to follow. Secure the branch to it with thinner garden wire.

2 Prune the stem back almost to the point at which it is wired. Cut just above the leaf axil as this is where new growth will develop.

3 Continue to prune the tree, cutting out all unwanted branches and shortening any long branches by half. Shorten all stems, and where there are multiple shoots crowded together leave just one.

Root pruning and repotting

Established bonsai need repotting every two or three years in spring in order to replenish the potting mixture, and to restrict their roots. They should not be moved into a larger pot because this will encourage them to grow bigger. Use a special soil-based potting mixture which is well-aerated and rich enough to sustain active growth. If you plan to prune your tree as well as repot it, leave three weeks between each operation so that the plant can recover its strength.

1 Take the plant out of its pot. Remove excess potting mixture by gently teasing it from the roots with a special tool or kitchen fork.

2 Prune the roots with a pair of root clippers, cutting away about half the growth and any damaged roots.

3 Line the pot with perlite and flint chippings. Tie the roots up with garden twine and thread the ends through the drainage holes to hold the plant rigid until new roots appear.

·3·
CUT-FLOWER ARRANGING

There is a special joy in using cut flowers in the house; they have an immediate freshness which house plants seldom achieve. Many books have been written about the techniques of flower arranging but, apart from the Japanese *ikebana* arrangements, where different combinations of flowers have symbolic meanings, it cannot be learned by following a set of rules.

The beauty of an arrangement is in the flowers themselves, and the way they are arranged should enhance their inherent qualities rather than impose a formal structure at odds with their natural habit of growth. My personal preference is for simple, informal arrangements which allow the natural shapes, colors and textures of the flowers to be appreciated.

While flower arranging cannot be learned systematically, you will find that, through practice and experiment, you will discover the qualities of different flowers and foliage and acquire an instinctive feeling for how to arrange them. The design of a flower arrangement depends on an appreciation of shape, color and texture and an ability to orchestrate these qualities to produce a harmonious group.

Always think about the setting for your arrangement before you choose the flowers and, at the same time, decide whether it is to be a dramatic display for a special occasion or an informal day-to-day display. These considerations will dictate the size, shape and overall color scheme and help you to create a display which complements its surroundings.

A simple arrangement of orchids
The vibrant color of these orchids
(*Phalaenopsis* hybrids) is set off by the black
vase. The simple lines of the container
allow the intricate shape of the
flowers to stand out.

Using the color wheel

Successful flower arranging depends upon an appreciation of color. The ability to mix colors together comes with experience, and, by experimenting with colors yourself, you will soon develop an instinctive feeling for how to use them. It is also useful to know a little about color theory. Here, a selection of cut flowers and foliage has been arranged in a circle with the colors following the same order as the spectrum—this is known as the color wheel.

Triadic color schemes
Orange, violet and green are secondary colors produced from an equal mixture of the two primary colors either side of them on the wheel. Used together they form a triadic color scheme, as they are equidistant from each other on the color wheel. You can put red, blue and yellow together for a strong triadic combination or, for a more subtle effect, use shades of orange, violet and green.

BLUE
Primary

GREEN
Secondary

YELLOW
Primary

The color wheel
The wheel is composed of primary and secondary colors and each segment of color represents a whole family of tints (the color plus white), shades (the color plus black) and tones (the color plus gray).

Complementary color schemes
Each secondary color is the complementary color of the one primary not used in its make up. For instance, violet, which is formed from red and blue, is the complementary of yellow. Use two complementary colors, in a variety of shades and tones, as the theme of an arrangement.

Analagous color schemes
Analagous, or related, colors are harmonizing colors from adjacent sections of the wheel. Strong reds, oranges and yellows may look harsh together, so use shades of each color for a more subtle scheme. Monochromatic color schemes use various shades of the same color, and very beautiful and sophisticated displays can be made by using a variety of plant material in just green or gray.

VIOLET
Secondary

RED
Primary

ORANGE
Secondary

PLANT KEY

Carnation Rose Transvaal daisy Lily Chrysanthemum Chrysanthemum Rose Daffodil Cypress Fern Iris Brodiaea Hyacinth Statice Anemone

Cutting and preparing flowers

It is important to realize when you cut a flower that it is still alive and growing. The best time to cut flowers is in the morning, when they contain most fluid. Failing this, cut your flowers in the evening, when the plant will have been producing food all day, giving it a reservoir of nutrients to help it survive in the container. Once picked, slit the stems and put them straight into deep water, then leave them in a cool place for several hours.

When choosing flowers at the florist, make sure that petals are firm and colors are strong, and that foliage is green and not beginning to wilt. A good way of telling how fresh flowers are is to look at their stamens. If they are hard, this indicates that the flower has only recently opened. Never buy flowers that have been left outside in hot sun.

Cutting soft stems

When a freshly cut flower is left out of water, the water-transporting tubes start to close up. To help a soft stem take up water, cut the stem as cleanly as possible by using a sharp knife or florist's scissors. If you have only a few flowers to arrange, cut the stems in water so that water, not air, is drawn up immediately.

1 Cut the stem at a 45 degree angle to increase the surface area for water intake. It will also stop the stem resting flush against the bottom of the vase, thus cutting off its water supply.

2 Make a vertical slit about 2in long to further increase the area capable of taking up water. Put the cut stems in deep water for a long drink before arranging. This ensures that they become full of water (turgid), and will therefore last longer.

Cutting woody stems

Cut woody stemmed flowers and foliage at a 45 degree angle using pruners. If the stem is very hard, remove the bark from the base of the stem as well. Do not hammer the stems, since this reduces their capacity to take up water. Strip off all the leaves that will be underwater in your vase, as they will rot and foul the water.

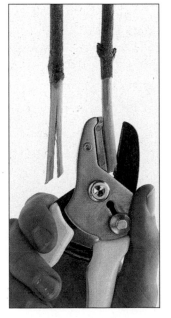

1 With stems which are particularly woody, such as roses (*Rosa* sp.), lilac (*Syringa* sp.) and foliage sprays, scrape off 2in of bark with a sharp knife.

2 Make a 2in slit with pruners or a sharp knife to increase the surface area for water intake.

Sealing bleeding stems

Daffodils, euphorbias, poppies (*Papaver* sp.) and many other plants bleed when cut, exuding either a sticky or milky juice. (The milky juice of euphorbias can cause skin irritation.) This sap flow results in a loss of nutrients to the flower head and, if lost into the flower water, will block up the water-conducting tubes of the stem and encourage bacteria; so spend a little extra time conditioning flowers which bleed, before using them in an arrangement.

1 Seal bleeding stems by first cutting them at an angle and then either dipping them in boiling water or placing them in a flame for 30 seconds. This will not prevent them from taking up water.

2 Place the treated stems, by themselves, in warm water until they have finished bleeding. They can then be arranged with other flowers.

Useful tips

● To prolong the life of flowers with hollow stems, such as delphiniums (*Delphinium* sp.) and Cape lilies (*Crinum* sp.), fill each stem with water and plug the end with cotton wool.

● Harden weak stems by putting them in water containing a special florist's conditioning solution. Leave in a dark place where water loss by transpiration will be reduced.

● Condition young foliage by immersing it completely in water for two hours before arranging.

● To remove thorns from roses, rub the stems very hard with the back of a pair of scissors. Roses are much easier to arrange once the thorns have been removed.

● Add one or two drops of household bleach to your arrangement water, as this will help prevent the growth of bacteria. Dissolve a teaspoonful of sugar in warm water to provide flowers with valuable glucose.

● Add water to your arrangement daily. You will find that certain flowers, such as dahlias (*Dahlia* hybrids), asters (*Aster novi-belqii*) and stocks (*Matthiola incana*), foul their water very quickly, so it is worth changing their water completely once a day.

● Remove any dying heads immediately, as they emit an ethylene gas which will cause wilting in other flowers.

● Position your arrangements away from bright sunlight, heat and drafts. These will all shorten the life of your flowers, since they increase transpiration.

● Mist-spray your flowers daily with a fine spray of luke-warm water. This will make them last longer.

Removing an airlock

If your flowers have been out of water for some time, it is possible that air may be trapped in the stems. Air-bubbles prevent water from being taken up into the stem and lack of water will cause the flowers to wilt prematurely.

Preparing tulips

Forced tulips (*Tulipa* hybrids) have weak stems which droop in an awkward way, making them difficult to arrange. They can be straightened by wrapping them in paper and putting them in warm water containing a conditioning solution.

Pricking a tulip to remove an airlock
To release trapped air, sterilize a needle in a flame, then prick the stem just below the flower head.

1 Having cut and slit the stems, and removed some of the leaves, wrap the flowers in brown paper, newspaper or waxed florist's tissue which will retain its rigidity in water.

2 Stand the tulips in warm water for several hours. To assist the process and strengthen the stems, add special florist's conditioning solution to the water; this contains sugar for food and a bactericide.

Supports for flower arrangements

Using wire netting

Crumpled chicken wire is an effective stem holder, particularly for woody stems or heavy flowers. It can be used on its own—and is the best anchor for flowers which will only last if arranged in deep water—or it can be used with floral foam for extra support. You can buy chicken wire by the foot in various gauges: use the fine gauge for slender stems and the wider gauges for more robust flowers and foliage. If you need to support one, or several, very heavy stems, secure them on a pinholder attached to the bottom of the container with adhesive clay, using wire netting as well if necessary.

1 Cut a piece of wire netting with wire cutters to make a square several times larger than the aperture of the container. You can use ordinary household objects, such as this mixing bowl, as a water-tight container inside a more decorative outer container, such as a wicker basket.

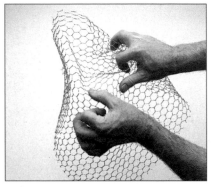

2 Crumple the wire in your hands molding it so that it will fit into the bowl and have an uneven surface. Be careful to avoid scratching yourself against the raw edges of the metal.

3 Place the crumpled wire in your container. For larger arrangements it may be necessary to secure the netting in place by passing wires, or pieces of colorless adhesive tape, over it, and securing them beneath the container.

4 Place the mixing bowl filled with crumpled wire inside the basket, and insert the first stems through the layers of netting which will secure them.

Using floral foam

Water absorbent floral foam is another useful stem holder which will support flowers in place at any angle. It is available in several shapes and sizes: in large bricks for large arrangements and in cylinders and squares for smaller displays. The foam can be used whole, or cut to fit any shape of container. Floral foam should be soaked in water for half an hour before use, since it will otherwise suck water out of the flowers as they are being arranged. If you are arranging long- or heavy-stemmed flowers, you may need to secure the foam in position with clear adhesive tape. A block of floral foam can be re-used several times.

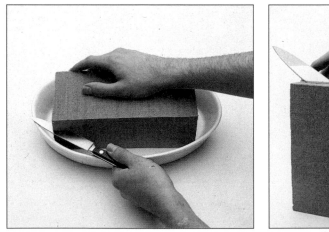

1 Place the floral foam in the container. For a low arrangement (shown made up on p.85), trim down the floral foam so that it is flush with the side of the container. If you want to insert stems at an angle, so that they will point downwards, allow several inches of floral foam to extend above the rim of the container.

2 Having soaked the floral foam in water, insert the stems by pushing them carefully into the foam. Top up the container with water once all the flowers are in position.

The principles of arrangement 1

Where do you begin with a flower arrangement if you are starting from scratch? First of all, think about where the arrangement is to go, and plan it with the setting in mind. Consider how it will be lit and the angle from which it will be seen. Then think about a suitable container for the place you have chosen. Containers range from kitchen bowls, jugs and baskets to purpose-made vases in all sorts of shapes and materials. Before you start to arrange your flowers, look at their shapes, textures and colors and work out a design based on a simple shape. Prepare and condition the flowers as described on pp.80-1, and select the first stems to establish the basic outline for the arrangement. Then fill out the shape, placing the largest foliage and flowers at the bottom and the most slender at the top. Position the most striking material in the center of the arrangement.

Making a large informal arrangement *right*
For a large arrangement, avoid following a shape too rigidly; allow the natural outlines of the flowers to show. Here, I have established the outline with foliage, white lilac (*Syringa* sp.) and baby's breath (*Gypsophila paniculata*), and added red flowers for focal interest.

A triangular arrangement

Fill the vase with floral foam or wire netting. First, establish the apex of the triangle and the outline of the two sides with chrysanthemum (*Chrysanthemum* hybrids) sprays. Then strengthen the shape with holly (*Ilex aquifolium*), choosing branches with a suitable outline and good berries. Add the corn-shaped heads of chincherinchee (*Ornithogalum thyrsoides*) for outline, and use some large chrysanthemum heads for focal point.

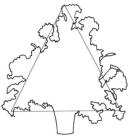

FLOWER KEY

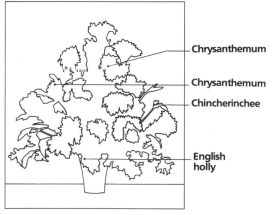

- Chrysanthemum
- Chrysanthemum
- Chincherinchee
- English holly

The principles of arrangement 2

A circular arrangement

This shape of arrangement suits all types of cottage flowers. Put floral foam inside the vase so that it is flush with the top. Establish the shape with baby's breath (*Gypsophila paniculata*) and then strengthen it with white lilac (*Syringa* sp.). Then add sprays of white daisy-shaped chrysanthemums (*Chrysanthemum* hybrids), orange lilies and pink-and-green Peruvian lilies (*Alstroemeria* sp.).

FLOWER KEY

White lilac
Lily
Chrysanthemum
Peruvian lily
Baby's breath

A semi-circular arrangement

This thin, lozenge-shaped container and the bare twigs suggested a stark, modern arrangement. Insert wire netting into the top of the container and let it extend a little way over the edge, so that stems can be inserted at an angle. Establish a semi-circular shape with the twigs, letting one trail down in front. Insert the orchid stems so that they follow the lines of the twigs.

FLOWER KEY

Dogwood | Orchid

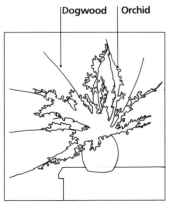

A vertical arrangement

FLOWER KEY

White iris
Iris leaves

The stiff, linear form of the iris (*Iris* sp.) and vertical container suggested this oriental-style arrangement; sword lilies (*Gladiolus* hybrids) would also be suitable. Fill the vase with floral foam so that it extends about 1 in above the edge. Insert one stem to establish the height and arrange the others at different heights.

A low triangular arrangement

I have used irises again to make this low horizontal arrangement. Establish the outline on both sides with blue flowers, then add iris leaves for outline. Cut the stems of the white irises short and insert them in the middle at varying heights for focal interest.

FLOWER KEY

Blue iris
Iris leaves
White iris

A spring flower arrangement

Daffodils (*Narcissus* hybrids) are simple flowers that look best arranged informally; they do not mix well with other flowers in a more formal display. I like to arrange them so that their stems curve outwards, mimicking the way they grow in clumps in the wild. Mass the flowers together in a simple wicker basket and include some of their own foliage to increase the natural look of the display. Put the arrangement on a side table, or use it as a centerpiece for a country kitchen table. If you place the arrangement in a cool spot, the flowers will last much longer.

Building up the arrangement

1 Place a glass mixing bowl inside a circular reed basket and cut a block of floral foam to fit inside so that it is flush with the top. Cut a large piece of wire netting, mold it into peaks, and secure it around the edge of the basket.

Equipment and materials

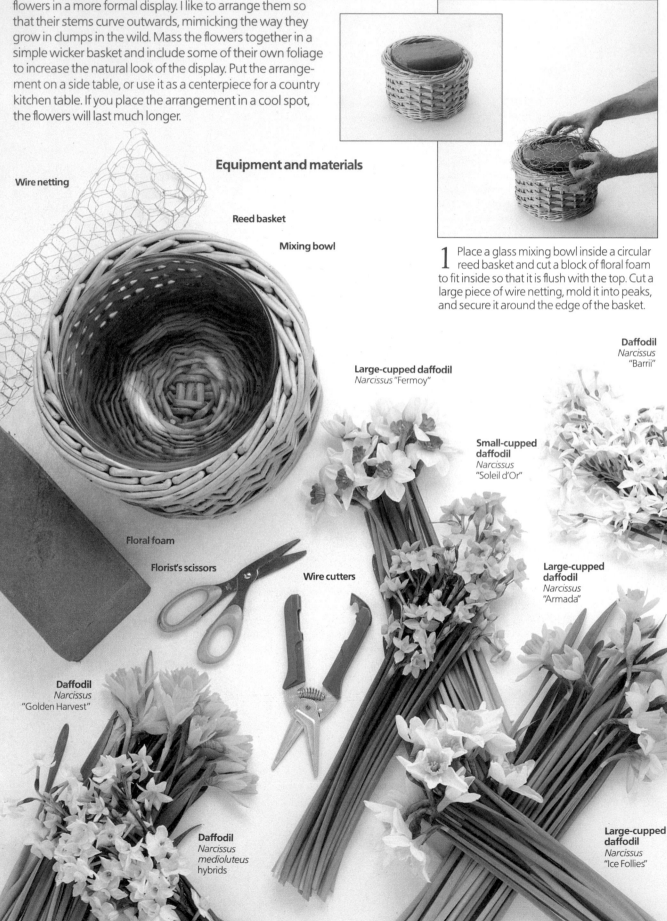

Wire netting

Reed basket

Mixing bowl

Floral foam

Florist's scissors

Wire cutters

Large-cupped daffodil
Narcissus "Fermoy"

Daffodil
Narcissus "Barrii"

Small-cupped daffodil
Narcissus "Soleil d'Or"

Large-cupped daffodil
Narcissus "Armada"

Daffodil
Narcissus "Golden Harvest"

Daffodil
Narcissus medioluteus hybrids

Large-cupped daffodil
Narcissus "Ice Follies"

2 Daffodils have stems which exude a sticky juice, so seal them before arranging (see p.80). Begin by outlining a semi-circular shape, arranging the flowers with their leaves.

3 Continue to fill in the basic shape, using the larger daffodils and leaves, cutting the stems to the height you want. Rotate the arrangement as you work, for, if used as a centerpiece, the display will be seen from all angles.

4 Use small daffodils, also known as jonquils, to fill in any obvious spaces. Add more large flowers and leaves to emphasize the outline and give body to the arrangement; bend down some of the lower stems below the line of the basket to give a slightly more rounded shape. Other flowers can be cut down and positioned to give body to the middle of the arrangement. Cut a few of the smaller ones very short and insert them around the edges of the basket so that they disguise the wire netting.

A summer flower arrangement

There is such a profusion of flowers in the summer that you should think carefully about the setting for your arrangement, and the effect you wish to create, before picking or buying the flowers. Here I wanted to create a display with a light and airy feel suitable for a side table or an alcove.

I chose to contrast strong shades of blue and golden yellow against a subtle background of gray and white flowers and green foliage. Taking an asymmetrical triangle as my basic shape, I selected a white oval casserole dish as a container since it will be obscured by the flowers.

Building up the arrangement

1 Cut a block of foam to extend above the rim of the container and secure in position with adhesive clay. Form the outline with the strongest shapes—the cylindrical globe thistles and the dried sea holly.

2 Fill the shape out laterally with eucalyptus and, at the front of the arrangement, push sprigs of foliage into the foam so that they hang down over the edge of the container. Add the deep yellow flowers of St John's wort to create focal points of color.

Equipment and materials

Florist's scissors

Pruners

Golden marguerite
Anthemis tinctoria "E.C. Buxton"

Stub wires

Eucalyptus
Eucalyptus gunnii

Casserole dish

Sea holly
Eryngium giganteum

Marguerite daisy
Anthemis cupaniana

Tutsan St John's wort
Hypericum androsaemum

Yellow yarrow
Achillea filipendulina "Coronation Gold"

African lily
Agapanthus "Headbourne Hybrids"

White yarrow
Achillea sp.

Floral foam

Globe thistle
Echinops ritro

Butterfly bush
Buddleia davidii "White Cloud"

3 Now strengthen the yellow areas by adding several golden yarrow heads to create yellow focal points in the middle of the design. As you position each flower, you will need to cut the stem to an appropriate length to maintain the overall shape. Place the most dominant yarrow head right into the center of the group, cutting its stem short so that your eye is led into the design. Add a couple of sprigs of white yarrow to fill out the base of the arrangement.

4 The largest flowers should be positioned at the base of the arrangement. Use the long and heavy heads of the sweetly scented butterfly bush at the front, and at the sides, to give them more bulk. As the arrangement fills out in all directions, the foam and the casserole dish become obscured by the delicate mass of flowers and foliage.

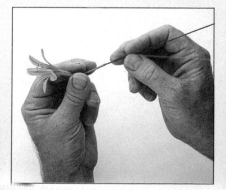

5 Since a full African lily head would be out of scale with the other flowers, pull off the individual florets and wire them by pushing a fine-gauge stub wire up the length of each stem.

6 Lighten the design with touches of golden and white marguerite daisies. Finally add the wired African lily florets, concentrating them on the right-hand side of the design to balance the daisies on the left.

An autumn flower arrangement

The colors of autumn are much darker than those of spring and summer. Here I chose to contrast russet- and gold-colored flowers and berries with deep-purple foliage, highlighted with scarlet dahlias and rose hips. I decided to make a horizontal arrangement designed to be seen from above—either on a low table or as a table centerpiece— where the addition of fruit would enhance the autumnal feel of the display. Since the arrangement may be put on a table where people eat, it should be low enough to allow conversation across it. I chose a wooden basket, whose natural color harmonized with the flowers, and fitted a glass pie dish inside the basket to act as a watertight container.

Equipment and materials

Wooden basket

Glass dish

Floral foam

Stub wires

Pruners

Florist's scissors

Cotoneaster
Cotoneaster sp.

Elder
Sambucus nigra
"Aurea"

Stonecrop
Sedum spectabile
"Atropurpureum"

Crab apples
Malus
"Golden Hornet"

European cranberry bush berries
Viburnum opulus
"Fructo-Luteo"

Dahlia
Dahlia hybrids

Barberry
Berberis thunbergii
"Rose Glow"

Rose hips
Rosa sp.

Rose hips
Rosa moyesii

Coneflower
Rudbeckia fulgida deami

Ragwort
Ligularia dentatum
"Desdemona"

Building up the arrangement

1 Cut a piece of foam to fit the glass container, allowing it to extend above the rim so that stems can be pushed in horizontally. Lay two purple elder branches and two circular ragwort leaves over the foam to establish the overall shape which will relate, of course, to where you plan to put the arrangement.

2 Once you are satisfied with the outline, decide whether you are going to look down on your arrangement or whether it will be seen from the side, and plan the design accordingly. Slide the foliage into the foam, then, to give bulk to the arrangement, add the purple stonecrop flowers.

3 Add the golden coneflowers for focal interest and open out the arrangement by adding a couple of stems of barberry, following the lines established by the elder. Put a sprig of cotoneaster berries at the front to fill an empty space. The flowers and branchlets which you are using should have been cut at an angle, and the stems split, to provide a greater area for water intake. Be careful not to push the cut stems flush with the side or bottom of the container as this will reduce the amount of water available to them.

4 Wire several stems of crab apples together and add the bunch to the arrangement. Add dahlias to create bold points of color and echo their scarlet tones with stems of rose hips placed at one end of the display. At this stage, fill the bowl with cool water and move it to its setting. You will need to top up the water after a day or so as the floral foam absorbs a considerable amount.

5 European cranberry bush berries are sparsely distributed on their stems, so wire two sprigs together. Hold the stems tightly and wrap a fine-gauge stub wire around them. The wired bunch can easily be pushed into the foam.

6 Add several bunches of the wired berries to fill the hole at the front of the display and reinforce the red area on the right by adding another stem of rose hips. Place a bunch of grapes and a few crab apples beside the arrangement.

A winter flower arrangement

Flowers are at a premium in winter, but in the garden you will find a surprising amount of material suitable for arrangements. Some of the autumn berries remain, much of the variegated foliage is in good condition, small buds are beginning to open on shrubs and trees, and the early flowering hellebores appear after Christmas. Here, I have made a predominantly green arrangement, exploiting the different shapes of the foliage and adding white and yellow flowers and orange berries for color. An old pottery jug makes a suitable container for this unsophisticated display.

Building up the arrangement

1 Shave the sides off a block of floral foam so that it will fit inside the jug, and push it in so that it is flush with the top. Begin the arrangement by inserting branches of witch hazel and cypress.

Equipment and materials

Floral foam

Pruners

Pottery jug

Winter-flowering cherry
Prunus subhirtella
"Autumnalis"

Hellebore
Helleborus corsicus lividus

Laurustinus
Viburnum tinus

Stinking iris
Iris foetidissima

Persian ivy
Hedera colchica
"Paddy's Pride"

Mahonia
Mahonia sp.

Black calla
Arum italicum
"Pictum"

Silk tassel bush
Garrya elliptica

True cypress
Cupressus glabra

Witch hazel
Hamamelis mollis

2 Position a large branch of mahonia in the center of the arrangement and a tall spray of the silk-tassel bush, covered with some early catkins, behind; this establishes the height and basic triangular shape of the display.

3 Insert a large flower head of hellebore in the center as a focal point, after trimming off all the lower leaves and some of the upper ones. Place a spray of laurustinus to fill out the space at the back of the arrangement.

4 Now position the yellow-and-green ivy leaves and place the bright-orange iris berries at the top of the arrangement. Add the narrow, spiky iris leaves to contrast with the heavier forms of the other foliage, and place a branch of winter-flowering cherry behind the cypress on the left. Finally, include the highly patterned black calla leaves to provide interest at the base of the container. This arrangement should remain attractive for about a fortnight, providing you put it in a cool place and top up the water level every day.

·4·
DRIED-FLOWER ARRANGING

Living plants require regular care and a particular environment in order to thrive, and the beauty and freshness of cut flowers lasts for a few weeks at most. But dried flowers need neither water nor light and, once arranged, they do not flop or drop their petals. Dried arrangements can be put anywhere and, through the winter, when fresh material is hard to come by, will evoke the abundance of the summer season. As with fresh flowers, the principles of proportion and use of color, texture and shape apply to each display. Containers are important: baskets—plain or painted— terracotta pots and glass vases all help show dried flowers to their best advantage. Do not restrict yourself to flower arrangements—garlands and wreaths are simple to build up with dried material. Make a dried-flower tree, or mix up a fragrant pot-pourri whose heady scent may be reminiscent of a late spring meadow or warm summer night. Drying herbs and bunches of flowers in your kitchen will also bring back the smells of summer.
If dried displays catch your imagination, enjoy discovering all the different forms they can take. As well as flowers, you can include leaves, grasses, berries, cereals, fruits and seed heads, to give countless variations of color and texture. You will soon develop a "collector's eye"—scanning every garden, bank and hedgerow for suitable materials to be dried and incorporated in your arrangements.

An informal arrangement of dried flowers
A collection of dried flowers, grasses and
seed heads have been massed together in a
simple terracotta container. The arrangement
is held together by its autumnal color
scheme and complemented by the orange
pumpkin placed beside it.

How to dry flowers 1

Drying flowers requires neither time-consuming techniques nor expensive equipment. Many plants need only to be collected at the right time, tied in bunches and hung up to dry. Others, depending on their shape, can be dried upright or laid flat. The more delicate garden flowers, or those likely to lose their color if air-dried, may be put in an airtight box and covered with a suitable desiccant.

Although the techniques by which plants are dried are not difficult to follow, you will find that, however careful you are, your results will vary from year to year as the process is affected by the weather conditions. Pick flowers only when the weather is dry, and begin the drying process as soon as possible after you have picked them. Avoid putting them in direct sunlight, as this causes colors to fade.

Air-drying

This technique is suitable for most flowers, grasses and seed heads. Arrange them in small bunches, hanging large flowers, such as hydrangeas (*Hydrangea* sp.), separately

so that they do not touch each other. Check after a day or two and if those with fleshy stems, such as delphiniums (*Delphinium* hybrids), are not drying, apply moderate heat.

Drying in bunches

1 Strip the leaves off the stem as far as the flower head, unless they form a natural rosette around the flower, as those of straw flowers (*Helichrysum bracteatum*) do, in which case leave them so the stems do not look so naked.

2 Tie up the flowers with an elastic band so that the bunch stays together as the stems contract. Do not make your bunches too large, otherwise the flowers in the middle will fail to dry and will become moldy.

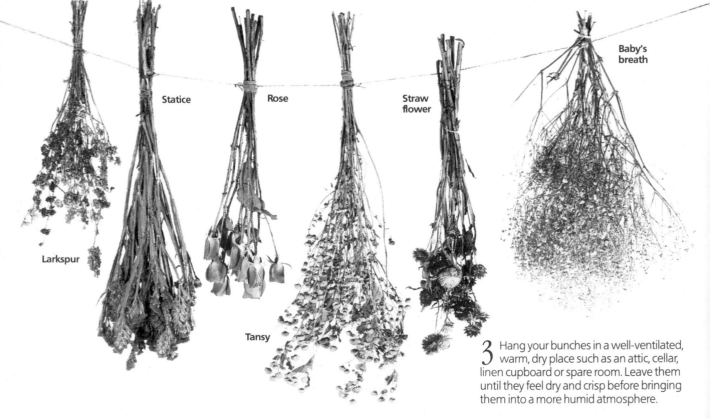

Larkspur

Statice

Rose

Tansy

Straw flower

Baby's breath

3 Hang your bunches in a well-ventilated, warm, dry place such as an attic, cellar, linen cupboard or spare room. Leave them until they feel dry and crisp before bringing them into a more humid atmosphere.

Drying upright

Most flowers which can be air-dried can also be dried upright. Use this method for flowers or grasses with particularly delicate heads, as it will preserve them better. Leave the flowers standing in a little water until they have absorbed it all and become crisp to the touch.

Drying flat

Most seed heads, grasses and seed pods can be dried in open boxes or laid flat on newspaper or brown paper.

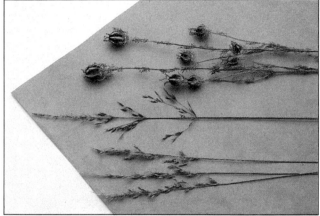

Preserving in desiccants

This is a slightly more complicated process, but it is worth using on more delicate flowers and on roses, which lose some of their color when air-dried. You need an airtight container, such as a biscuit tin or plastic food box. It need only be large enough to dry the flower heads; as wire stems are attached once they are dry.

1 Line your container with 1 in layer of equal parts of borax and alum. Alternatively, use silver sand and silica gel crystals, and heat the mixture to eradicate moisture.

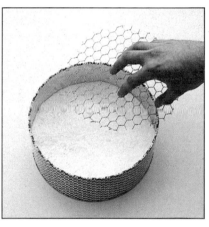

2 Cut a piece of wire netting to fit the container and lay it on top of the desiccant mixture. This will keep the flower heads upright.

3 Take a flower, such as a Transvaal daisy (*Gerbera* sp.) and cut about 1 in below the head, leaving enough stem to insert the wire into, when the flower has dried.

4 Place the flower heads in the netting, making sure that they do not touch. Dry flowers of one type together so that they will be ready at the same time.

5 Add more of the desiccant powder, sieving it over the flower heads to avoid damaging them. Continue until they are covered by about 1 in of powder.

6 Seal the container and leave undisturbed in a warm, dry place for four to fourteen days, depending on the density of the flowers.

How to dry flowers 2

Preserving in glycerine

This is a preserving, rather than a drying, method which can be used for whole branches of foliage, berries and large leaves. It is also suitable for preserving long flower spikes, such as foxgloves (*Digitalis* sp.). The stems are placed in a mixture of glycerine and near-boiling water and left until they have absorbed enough of the solution. This takes about a week for light foliage, and from six to eight weeks for heavy foliage. The leaves gradually become deeper and richer in color, and when

drops of glycerine appear on them they will have absorbed enough of the solution. Remove them, as excessive absorption will cause wilting, and wipe them clean. Immerse single leaves and very tall branches, when the top stems might not take up the mixture, in a bath of glycerine and water solution.

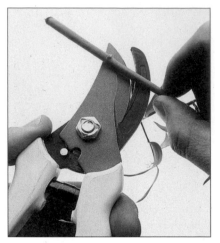

1 Remove the lower leaves from the stems with pruners. Cut them at a 45 degree angle, pare away any bark from woody stems, and make a 2in slit to increase the area for glycerine intake.

2 Mix one part of glycerine with two parts of near-boiling water in a narrow container and stir the solution vigorously.

3 Pour the glycerine and water solution into a heatproof container. Fill to a depth of 4in, so that it will cover the prepared part of the stems.

4 Stand the stems in the solution and place the container with the foliage in a cool, dark room until the leaves have absorbed sufficient glycerine.

Pressing

Most leaves—including ferns, gray-tinted shrubs and maples (*Acer* sp.)—can be dried by pressing. Only a little pressure is needed for large leaves and ferns, otherwise they become too brittle to arrange. Once covered in blotting paper or newspaper, they can be put under a carpet or mattress and left to dry for about a week. Smaller leaves, bracts and the delicate heads of wild flowers can be put in a bought press and left for a fortnight.

Two methods of pressing leaves
Place large leaves between pages of blotting paper, and small leaves and flowers between the absorbent sheets of a bought flower press.

Making pot-pourri

Pot-pourri means "rotten pot"—the original method was to mix dried petals with salt so that they fermented, giving off a strong scent. Although its smell is more fugitive, the dry pot-pourri is much easier to make.

Rose petals

Larkspur
Delphinium consolida

Hop-clover
Trifolium agrarium

Juniper berries

Pot-pourri essence

Rose petals for decoration

Bay leaves
Laurus nobilis

Dried lemon peel

Orris root powder

Sea holly
Eryngium maritimum

Lemon-scented geranium leaves
Pelargonium crispum

Larkspur
Delphinium consolida

Lavender
Lavandula sp.

1 Dry petals, leaves and the lemon peel on a surface that allows plenty of air to circulate round them. It will take up to ten days for them to become crisp.

2 Mix all the petals and leaves together. Crush the lemon peel into small pieces and add it to the mixture with the spices and a few drops of essence.

3 Add dried flower heads and rose petals dried in borax for decoration. Seal the container and leave it for six weeks to mature, shaking it occasionally.

Ingredients for pot-pourri
Sachets have been filled with dried flowers and leaves from the terracotta bowls. These bowls contain some of the most popular ingredients for making pot-pourri. Lavender has a strong scent and is an ingredient of many pot-pourris. Sweet-scented roses are often used as the base of a pot-pourri and the whole heads, as seen here, can be added for decoration. The small grape hyacinth florets (*Muscari* sp.) are intensely blue and help to give color to a pot-pourri.

Arranging flowers in a basket

The place where you decide to put an arrangement will help to suggest an appropriate size and shape. I selected a windowsill where the flowers would be attractively framed by the window. For a display such as this, which will not be seen in the round, I chose a flat-backed asymmetrical triangle as my basic shape.

I decided to use blues, whites, creams and yellows, adding cereals and seed heads to give substance and texture to the design. Let an arrangement reflect the natural growth of the flowers themselves. Here, the graceful curve of the barley lent itself to trailing over the sill, contrasting with the stiffer wheat used to outline the shape.

Equipment and materials

Basket

Floral foam

Knife

Florist's scissors

Stub wires

Dried moss

Wheat
Triticum vulgare

Larkspur
Delphinium consolida

White statice
Limonium sinuatum

Barley
Hordeum vulgare

Everlasting
Helipterum roseum

Sea lavender
Limonium latifolium

Blue statice
Limonium sinuatum

Baby's breath
Gypsophila paniculata

Poppy seed heads
Papaver sp.

Lady's mantle
Alchemilla vulgaris

Oregon grape
Mahonia aquifolium

Sea holly
Eryngium maritimum

Oats
Avena sp.

Heath
Erica sp.

Rose
Rosa sp.

Love-in-a-mist seed heads
Nigella damascena

Dyed baby's breath
Gypsophila paniculata

Straw flower
Helichrysum bracteatum

The finished arrangement
This light and delicate arrangement suits the small window with its pretty lace pelmet and neutral-colored curtains. Think carefully about the décor of your room before selecting flowers and a container so that the colors and style of your display will be in keeping with its surroundings.

Building up the arrangement

1 Cut one block of foam—using the stiffer variety made for dried flowers—for the center of the basket and two smaller ones to fit either side. Press the foam down firmly and shear off all edges with a knife. Cut some wires into thirds and bend to form a hairpin shape. Cover the foam with dried moss secured with the wire pins. Position the wheat to establish the shape of the design.

2 Having established the height using the basket as a guide—it should be a third of the overall height—start to establish the shape of the arrangement with the sea lavender. When you cut the foam, make sure that it extends above the rim of the basket so that flowers can be inserted downwards.

continued over

3 Introduce color and tone with larkspur and blue statice to the left and white statice to the right. Take a few blue flowers over to the right to help link the two sides of the design.

4 Elongate the design with barley and everlastings wired into small bunches (see p.110). Add lady's mantle and baby's breath and position the poppy seed heads and the sea holly in the center for focal interest.

5 Cross the design with love-in-a-mist seed heads and infill with oats to give bulk to the paler side of the group. Fill the spaces with the darkest elements in the design—Oregon grape, dyed gypsophila and heath. Add the roses and the straw flowers which should be wired to give them extra length. Then, having put the display in its setting, stand back and adjust the outline as necessary.

Wheat

Love-in-a-mist seed head

Blue statice

Larkspur

Lady's mantle

White statice

Poppy seed head

Sea holly

Heath

Rose

Oats

Everlasting

Barley

Dyed baby's breath

Oregon grape

Straw flower

Sea lavender

Further ideas for arrangements

There are an enormous number of ways in which dried flowers can be arranged. For informal displays use baskets of any kind, or earthenware pots, as containers. Try filling a large basket with grasses, seed heads and cereals in creams, beiges and very pale greens, inserting stems at an angle so that the flowers appear to radiate from the center. Alternatively, fill an earthenware pot with bunches of flowers.

Neutral tones *below*
A tall container can set off a rounded mass of flowers, and frosted glass will disguise stems and wires. Here the neutral colors of the vases do not overshadow the delicate flowers of sea lavender (*Limonium latifolium*) on the right and flowering onion (*Allium* sp.) on the left.

Still life *above*
Arrange dried hydrangeas (*Hydrangea macrophylla*) in a simple vase and the subtlety of their color and texture is enough to make an attractive display. The figs, grapes and pomegranates complete a still life group which looks good enough to paint.

Informal groups *left*
Bunches of flowers placed in baskets can look very effective in the right kind of setting. Here, the neutral tones and rough textures of the love-in-a-mist (*Nigella damascena*) and poppy (*Papaver* sp.) seed heads suit the coarse-weaved basket. A sheaf of ribbed seed pods in the foreground picks up the textures of the baskets.

Making dried-flower trees

Dried-flower trees are much easier to make than you might imagine and, once you have mastered the basic techniques, you can experiment with different types of flowers and different shapes of tree. Here, I have used pink, blue and white flowers and parchment-colored seed heads to make a light and delicate tree.

Blue larkspur
Delphinium consolida

Bells-of-Ireland
Moluccella laevis

Blue statice
Limonium sinuatum

Equipment and materials

Sea lavender
Limonium latifolium

Poppy seed heads
Papaver sp.

Winged everlasting
Ammobium alatum

Everlasting
Helipterum roseum

Straw flower
Helichrysum bracteatum

Pink larkspur
Delphinium consolida

Wire cutters

Ribbon

Baby's breath
Gypsophila paniculata

Plastic pot

Stub wires

Pink statice
Limonium sinuatum

Ball of floral foam

Sea holly
Eryngium maritimum

Stones

Fresh moss

Interior wall filler

Bamboo stick

Building up the arrangement

1 Take a plastic plant pot 4½-5in in diameter, line it with foil and fill with stones in order to secure a bamboo stick about 14in high. Spoon a mix of wall filler into the pot until it reaches the surface.

2 Push the ball of floral foam on to the bamboo stick. Make sure that the stick only goes half-way through the foam. Pack moss around the outside of the ball.

3 Attach the moss to the foam with pins, made by cutting stub wires into thirds and bending the pieces over. As you work, be careful not to push down too hard on the foam ball.

4 Start to outline the shape with the blue larkspur and blue statice. You will find that you need to break small branches of flowers off the main stems to achieve the right scale for this size of tree.

5 Break off some small segments of sea lavender, and place them where they will be seen. Wire together some winged everlastings to form small bunches, and add to cover the surface of the tree. Infill with pink statice and pink larkspur.

6 Add the round heads of straw flowers and pink everlastings to fill some of the gaps. Place poppy seed heads, sea holly and small pieces of bells-of-Ireland to give texture, and finally add small sprigs of baby's breath to soften the outline.

Other types of dried-flower tree

For a strong and simple country-style tree, use the flat heads of golden yarrow (*Achillea filipendulina*) to form the tree itself and use a plain terracotta pot for the base. To create a different type of tree, take a branch with an interesting outline and decorate it with rough-textured flowers, cereals and seed heads in creams, browns and greens.

7 Place the completed tree in a white pot and put some moss and a few flower heads over the stone base. You can leave the bamboo stick plain, or decorate it with ribbon to create a maypole effect. Take two strips of ribbon, glue them to the top of the stick and twine them round it, securing at the bottom with sticky tape.

A tree for Christmas
The basic form of this tree is the same as the one featured above. Instead of flowers, I have covered the foam base with wired pine cones, and added a few artificial fruits to add color and give it a more festive look.

Decorating a basket of pot-pourri

The art of making pot-pourri is experiencing something of a revival. Consequently, there are many bought varieties to choose from or it is possible to make your own by following the recipe on p.99. Pot-pourri is valued not only for its subtle smell but also for the attractive colors and textures of the dried petals from which it is made. Put it in a pretty basket decorated with dried flowers and you will have a delicate and sweet-smelling display with many decorative uses. If you wish to add a spicy quality to the fragrance of the pot-pourri, place a pomander in the middle of the basket. Alternatively, these can be decorated with ribbon and hung around the house or put in drawers.

Equipment and materials

Wicker basket

Dried flower heads

Pomander

Pot-pourri

Larkspur
Delphinium consolida

Chicken wire

Binding wire

Cotton wool

Wire cutters

Pot-pourri essence

Rose
Rosa sp.

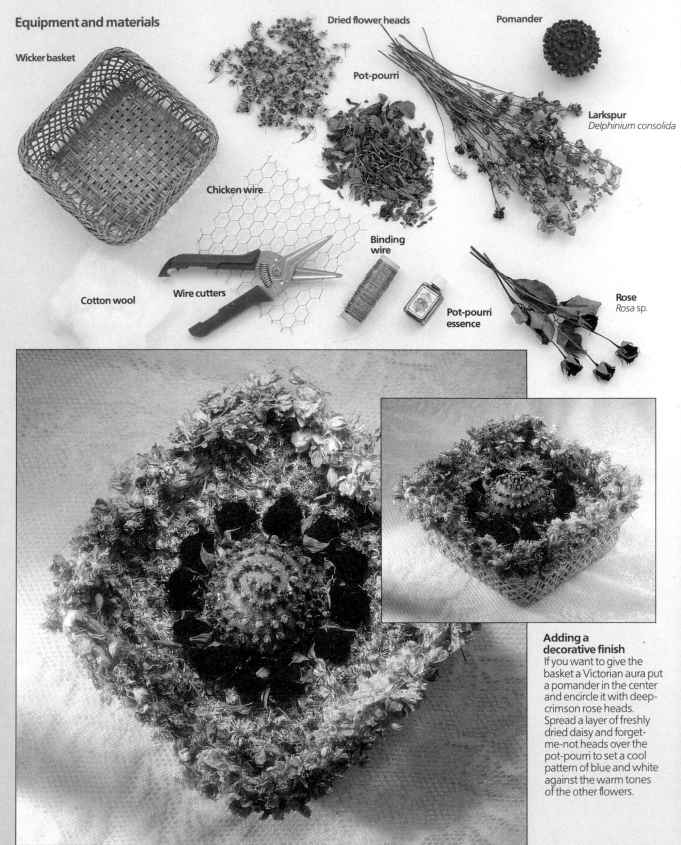

Adding a decorative finish
If you want to give the basket a Victorian aura put a pomander in the center and encircle it with deep-crimson rose heads. Spread a layer of freshly dried daisy and forget-me-not heads over the pot-pourri to set a cool pattern of blue and white against the warm tones of the other flowers.

Building up the arrangement

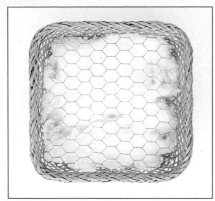

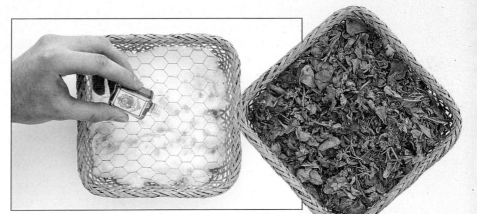

1 Line the basket with a thin layer of cotton wool. Cut a piece of fine chicken wire to fit inside the basket resting on the cotton wool. This will keep the pot-pourri dry and stop it becoming "fusty" by allowing air to circulate underneath it.

2 Sprinkle a few drops of bought pot-pourri essence (or use your own essential oils distilled from fresh flowers) to enhance the existing natural fragrances. Fill the basket two-thirds full with pot-pourri made from rose petals, lavender, scented-leaved geraniums, dried lemon peel and orris root (see p.99).

3 To make the garland, take three stems of larkspur and bind them together using fine binding wire. Arrange the stems so that the flowers are equally distributed along the garland and wrap the wire around the stems being careful not to damage the flowers.

4 Continue to make the garland until it is long enough to fit right round the basket. As an alternative to the pink larkspur you could use blue larkspur mixed with deep red straw flowers or immortelles.

5 As the garland is flexible, adjust it to the shape of your basket and secure it in position with wire. The illustration opposite shows how to add a decorative finish using blue and white dried flower heads and a pomander centerpiece.

Making a pomander

Take an orange—preferably a Seville orange—and, if you are planning to hang up your pomander, place masking tape on the orange where the ribbons will go. Stick the cloves into the orange and then roll it in the orris root and cinnamon. Put it in a dark, well-ventilated place for several weeks.

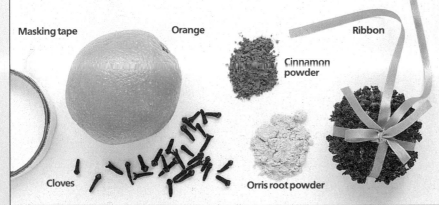

Masking tape **Orange** **Ribbon** **Cinnamon powder** **Orris root powder** **Cloves**

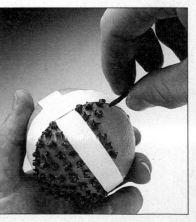

Inserting the cloves *above*
Stick the cloves into the orange leaving the width of one head between them.

Making wreaths

Wreaths made out of dried materials can be used in a
number of ways. They can be hung on a door, on a wall, or
from the ceiling, or used flat to make a table decoration.
Here, I have made a rough-textured wreath with brown
nuts and neutral-colored grasses, highlighted with the
warm tones of yellow, orange and red flowers.

Equipment and materials

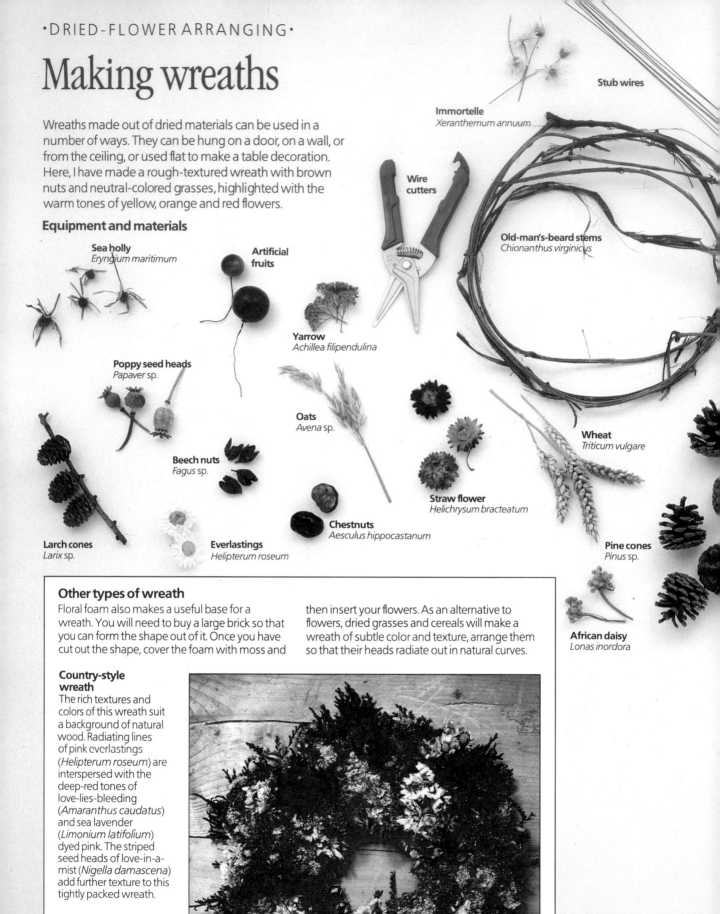

Stub wires

Immortelle
Xeranthemum annuum

**Wire
cutters**

Old-man's-beard stems
Chionanthus virginicus

Sea holly
Eryngium maritimum

**Artificial
fruits**

Yarrow
Achillea filipendulina

Poppy seed heads
Papaver sp.

Oats
Avena sp.

Wheat
Triticum vulgare

Beech nuts
Fagus sp.

Straw flower
Helichrysum bracteatum

Larch cones
Larix sp.

Everlastings
Helipterum roseum

Chestnuts
Aesculus hippocastanum

Pine cones
Pinus sp.

African daisy
Lonas inordora

Other types of wreath

Floral foam also makes a useful base for a
wreath. You will need to buy a large brick so that
you can form the shape out of it. Once you have
cut out the shape, cover the foam with moss and
then insert your flowers. As an alternative to
flowers, dried grasses and cereals will make a
wreath of subtle color and texture, arrange them
so that their heads radiate out in natural curves.

Country-style
wreath
The rich textures and
colors of this wreath suit
a background of natural
wood. Radiating lines
of pink everlastings
(*Helipterum roseum*) are
interspersed with the
deep-red tones of
love-lies-bleeding
(*Amaranthus caudatus*)
and sea lavender
(*Limonium latifolium*)
dyed pink. The striped
seed heads of love-in-a-
mist (*Nigella damascena*)
add further texture to this
tightly packed wreath.

Building up the arrangement

1 Make the circular base of the wreath with old-man's-beard stems. Wrap the thickest stems around each other about four times, forming a circle, then wrap the thinner parts of the stems over this. Vine prunings can also be used as the base.

2 Beech nuts, chestnuts, pine cones, and straw flowers need to be wired. To wire a pine cone, insert a wire between the scales of the cone and twine the shorter side of the wire around the longer.

3 Encircle the wreath with wired pine cones. Wire the chestnuts by pushing a stout needle through the center to make a hole (see step 2). Wire the beech nuts in the same way as the pine cones.

4 Add groups of wired chestnuts to the wreath. Insert larch cones on their short stems, wired beech nuts, poppy seed heads, sea holly, wheat and oats to create the main body of the wreath.

5 Add everlastings, yellow, orange and red straw flowers, immortelles, yarrow and African daisies wherever there are holes which need filling.

6 You can leave the wreath as it is or, if you want to decorate it for Christmas, add some red artificial fruits and a large red ribbon to attach it to a door knocker.

Pine cone

Larch cone

Chestnut

Wheat

Immortelle

Beech nut

Poppy seed head

Yarrow

Sea holly

Straw flower

African daisy

Oats

Everlasting

Making decorations

Dried flowers can be used to make decorations for festive occasions. Floral balls, corn stars and "snowy" pine cones make unusual tree decorations and a brightly colored chain of straw flowers can be hung on a tree or chimneypiece.

Floral balls

Straw flowers
Helichrysum bracteatum

Wire cutters

Stub wires

1 Push a wire through the center of each flower, bending it over at the top and pulling it back through the flower head.

2 Wire five flowers, then arrange them so that they form a ball. Twist one of the wires around the others to secure them.

Corn stars

Wire cutters

Everlasting
Helipterum roseum

Wheat
Triticum vulgare

Ribbon

1 Cut the corn stalk between the nodes to make 4in lengths, and strip off the outer sheath. Make a slit in one stalk and slip another through it at 90 degrees.

2 Continue until you have a star with as many points as you require. Take the ribbon and twist it under and over each prong of the corn to make a central disc.

Snow-covered pine cones

Pine cones
Pinus sp.

Washing powder

Stub wires

Wallpaper paste

1 Wire the pine cones as shown on p.109; dip each one into a solution of wallpaper paste until half of the cone is covered in paste. Take it out and shake well to remove the excess paste.

2 When the paste feels tacky, dip the cones in the washing powder, making sure that they receive an even covering of white. Shake off any excess and leave them to dry before hanging on the tree.

A chain of dried flowers

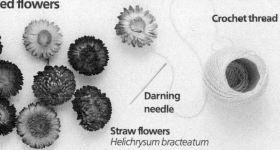

Crochet thread

Darning needle

Straw flowers
Helichrysum bracteatum

Cut a piece of thread to the length that you require. Thread the darning needle and push it through the center of each straw flower. As you thread each flower, make sure that its front faces the back of the one it is next to on the chain; this will ensure a more even effect.

·5·

THE ROOM-BY-ROOM GUIDE

Pot plants and flowers have been used to decorate rooms since as early as the seventeenth century, but it was the start of the nineteenth century that saw a vast influx of exciting new plants into Europe. This was when the first painted-leaved begonias, paper flowers and a large array of tropical foliage plants arrived, and those who could afford them began to display them in their homes and conservatories. However, it is only recently that an enormous range of plants have become available to everyone.

The following pages display the different rooms in the house and show how plants can be actively incorporated into the decorative scheme of a room, rather than being merely random extras. Each room in the home has a different function and its practical use will determine the sort of environment, or *mini-climate*, it can offer to plants. Each room also has a specific mood and plants can be used to enhance this particular atmosphere.

The period of your house and the style of your room will determine the way in which you display your plants. A traditional interior calls for plants to complement an existing setting and, for instance, co-ordinate with fabrics or a collection of objects. A modern interior may call for plants to be used in an architectural way, as an integral part of the landscaping of the room.

Using plants and flowers in a room
These two milkbush plants (*Euphorbia tirucalli*) are used as a counterbalance to the large bookcase, and are of a scale to match it. They like the warm conditions of a living room and are easy to keep provided they are not overwatered. The vase of flowers on the table is part of an incidental coffee table grouping.

Mini-climates in the home

Throughout this book I have used a system of mini-climates to identify the different environments offered by the average home. Each plant featured in *The Plant Finder's Guide* has a mini-climate reference indicating its optimum levels of heat and light. This need not be interpreted too rigidly; a great attribute of many of our most popular house plants is their tolerance of a wide range of growing conditions. In much of the USA and Canada where summer temperatures run very warm indoors and outdoors it is impossible to provide consistent summer indoor temperatures of 50°-60°F. One solution is to summer the plants outdoors in light shade. Also, plants grown in city apartments may not receive the suggested amount of light. A solution is to provide artificial light, usually from fluorescent tubes (see p.244 and p.258).

Winter sunshine will not harm any plant grown in northern latitudes, and one that ideally needs filtered sun when the sun is high may need direct sunlight in winter, when the sun is weaker and days shorter.

Very few plants will suffer if placed in a higher temperature than that recommended—as long as higher levels of humidity, and probably a little more water, are provided for them. Water plants less if you grow them cooler than the given mini-climate, and remember that it is much better to underwater than to overwater.

Very high summer temperatures often cannot be brought down without the aid of air conditioning units, which dry the air. A high level of humidity, adequate watering and frequent mist-spraying will all help to counteract this but, in any case, do not keep plants near an air conditioning unit.

When choosing plants to group together indoors, it is not enough merely to consider their decorative qualities; if the display is to remain attractive, you must also ensure that the mini-climate requirements of the plants are compatible. A plant which likes direct sunlight can be put quite happily with a plant that likes filtered light, but it is not sensible to group a tropical shade-lover with a temperate flowering plant.

Mini-climate 1
Warm, sunny

A *warm* room is one kept at a temperature of 60°-70°F—a range preferred by many house plants. Ideally, for the comfort of people, the day temperatures are 65°-70°F and the night range between 60°-65°F or even lower, which the plants can tolerate.

A *sunny* position is one that gets direct, unobstructed sunlight for part of the day. A plant standing in or very near to a south-facing window is in a sunny position; those in east- or west-facing windows receive less sun each day.

White walls contribute to brightness of the room by reflecting light.

Hanging basket receiving direct light, but away from heat rising from stove.

Two large windows provide plenty of direct sunlight for plants and flowers.

Steam rising from kettle increases humidity in the kitchen.

Timber ceiling absorbs heat, preventing sudden temperature changes.

Hot air rises, creating warm conditions for these tropical plants.

Bare brick wall catches light and has heat-retaining qualities.

Full-length windows provide the amount of light needed for this large, plant-filled room.

Mini-climate 2
Warm, filtered sun

A *warm* room is one kept at a temperature of 60°-70°F—a range preferred by many house plants. Ideally, for the comfort of people, the day temperatures are 65°-70°F and the night range between 60°-65°F or even lower, which the plants can tolerate.

A room receiving *filtered sun* may face south, east or west (or south-east or south-west) but direct sunlight is baffled by translucent blinds or curtains, a tall building or leafy tree outside a window.

Sub-tropical plants thrive in these conditions.

Fine net curtain serves as filter for sunlight.

White fittings and large mirror over bath reflect light, greatly increasing room brightness.

Steam rising from bath provides high levels of relative humidity.

Leafy tree outside window serves to baffle sunlight.

Venetian blind needed to filter direct light by the coast or in lower latitudes.

Wall-mounted mirror reflects sunlight and increases brightness of the room.

Umbrella plant benefits from filtered sun and humidity of the bathroom.

Mini-climate 3
Warm, shady

A *warm* room is one kept at a temperature of 60°-70°F—a range preferred by many house plants. Ideally, for the comfort of people, the day temperatures are 65°-70°F and the night range between 60°-65°F or even lower, which the plants can tolerate.

A *shady* position, in our definition, receives no direct or filtered sunlight, but does not have "poor" light (which is too low for healthy plant growth). Plants that like some shade can be grown away from the window in a room that is well-lit, or in the window of a room that is not well-lit.

Conditions are ideal for this thriving Swiss cheese plant.

Light filtered by trees outside and curtains.

There is not enough light in this corner of the room for healthy plant growth.

Dark floor absorbs light, reducing brightness in the room.

Curtain serves to reduce light entering large window.

Staghorn fern thrives when suspended out of direct light.

Dark furnishings absorb light reflected by pale floor and walls.

Large pot catches the drips from watering.

Mini-climate 4
Cool, sunny

A *cool* room is one kept at a temperature of 50°-60°F. This is the range preferred by many temperate zone plants, although plants from warmer climates may also be able to thrive—and temporary flowering house plants often live longer—at these temperature levels.

A *sunny* position is one that gets direct, unobstructed sunlight for part of the day. A plant standing in or very near to a south-facing window is in a sunny position; those in east- or west-facing windows receive less sun each day.

The large leaves of this banana plant require strong direct sunlight, but this plant can tolerate temperatures as low as 50°F.

Cool, airy landing with high ceiling is ideal environment for large-scale feature plants.

Spacious, open-plan staircase forms part of very large, unenclosed area of cool air.

Very large, unshaded window provides plenty of light for this assortment of plants.

Mini-climate 5
Cool, filtered sun

A *cool* room is one kept at a temperature of 50°-60°F. This is the range preferred by many temperate zone plants, although plants from warmer climates may also be able to thrive—and temporary flowering house plants often live longer—at these temperature levels.

A room receiving *filtered sun* may face south, east or west (or south-east or south-west) but direct sunlight is baffled by translucent blinds or curtains, or a tall building or leafy tree outside a window.

Creeper outside window prevents strong light being reflected from white wall.

Heavy draped curtains may be partially drawn to keep room temperature down.

This thriving ivy is shielded from the window by the mass of the arrangement.

Suitable plants for these conditions include Japanese fatsia.

This plant can be given the amount of shade it requires by the Venetian blind.

White walls and bed linen contribute to the cool environment by reflecting heat.

Full-length blinds filter the sunlight entering the room.

Living rooms 1

For most people, the living room is the show-piece of the home and the room in which most entertaining takes place. A considerable amount of money may be spent on furnishings, fabrics and general decoration. Broadly speaking, living rooms may be traditional or modern, with elements of one style being adapted and combined with those of others. Plants provide a restful background and fresh colors, and should enhance the layout of the room without dominating it. Living rooms usually contain large items of furniture, and plants should be of an appropriate size to counterbalance them: one or two large ones usually look much better than a clutter of smaller ones. Arrangements

of cut or dried flowers and small-scale plants can be used for incidental groupings on coffee tables, side tables and shelves.

Position your plants away from radiators or open fires, in a place which provides adequate light for their specific needs, and where you can water them easily. It is very important that plants should not be in the way of people moving about, both for the convenience of the human inhabitants and the protection of the plants themselves. So, once you have decided on the type of plant and the scale you need, work its positioning into your basic plan making sure that plant and container are an integral part of your design concept.

Linear forms *below*
A classic modern interior of oriental simplicity, composed of linear forms —the table, sofas and pictures—and muted colors without patterns. The focal point of the room is the arrangement of dried twigs on the table, which is counter-balanced by the ornament and bonsai. The large rainbow plants (*Dracaena marginata*) soften what might otherwise be too spartan a room.

Black and white
The placement of the furniture in this severe, modern interior is governed by the position of the chimney breast and the view of the terrace. The plants used inside are very low-key, but nonetheless link the two spaces effectively. It is interesting that the designer felt that this uncompromisingly robust interior should be softened by a trailing tradescantia (*Tradescantia* sp.). The all-white flower arrangement is in keeping with the overall color scheme, and picks up the white of the floor and walls in an area where black predominates.

Pattern and color
A softer decorative look permeates this room with much use of fabric in the full drop of the curtains and the table covering. Bright colors and patterns call for large plant forms that will accompany, but not dominate, decoration. Behind the sofa stands a European fan palm (*Chamaerops humilis*) and part of a fishtail palm (*Caryota mitis*) can be seen in the foreground. The central feature is the low coffee table with its clutter of books and the large bowl, whose shape is cleverly echoed by the smaller bowls on the corner table, and contrasted with the curving leaves of an orchid in flower.

Living rooms 2

Rustic style

In this cottage living room the overall effect is cluttered and without a single dominant feature. Spectacular tropical species would be out of character, but small-leaved temperate plants are used to good effect, as are the bowl of pot-pourri and bird's nest in the foreground. Rustic wooden furniture, botanical prints and floral patterns are all in keeping with the gentle mood of this type of decoration.

Bold color contrast *left*

Compared to the room above, the overall impression here is one of severity, although all the furniture is, in fact, highly decorative. The strong color contrast of black, red and white is brought together in the patterned carpet, and given a final flamboyant touch with the addition of the vase of huge cut amaryllis (*Hippeastrum* sp.) which echo the red of the canvas.

Low-key *right*

The blinds in this room give it a soft lighting effect which creates a tranquil mood not disturbed by heavy patterns or assertive colors. The gentle green foliage of the bamboo (*Arundinaria* sp.) is in keeping with the relaxed atmosphere. The cut flowers and small house plant are additional features which serve as minor points of interest.

Size, shape and color co-ordination *right*
The large leaves of the African hemp (*Sparmannia africana*) are in accord with the geometric wall patterning behind the plant. The foliage of the foreground Kentia palm (*Howea belmoreana*) is similar to the leaf shape in the painting, and the soft colors of the room are repeated in the table arrangement of cut flowers.

Horizontal lines *below*
Downlighters pick out the colors of the simple furniture and patterned fabric, echoed by the flowers, plants and objects. The bold horizontal patterning of blinds and floor unify the diverse points of interest.

Living rooms 3

Part of creating a comfortable, inviting living space is building up one or more attractive seating areas which draw the visitor into the room. Whether these are in the corners of the room, at one end, or in alcoves, window bays and recesses, house plants can play a large part in making the most of them. Plants can highlight a fabric, either by forming a total contrast or by echoing colors and patterns in the curtains or soft furnishings. Alternatively, the shape and form of plants can enhance and soften these settings—gracefully overhanging a sofa or armchair perhaps, complementing a picture, or providing a solid background for a group of cane or wicker chairs in a corner.

Making a feature of the ceiling *right*
Distinctive roof supports are something of a feature in this room, and the shiny spotlights are certainly there to be noticed. So two trailing plants set up high enhance the effect and save space in the room.

Sofa in a window bay
above
A tall golden-feather palm (*Chrysalidocarpus lutescens*), arching its delicate fronds over the sofa, makes the whole area more inviting. Light filtered from the window gives the plant a strong silhouette. The two other house plants are a small parlor palm (*Chamaedorea elegans* "Bella") and white calla lily (*Zantedeschia aethiopica*).

Modern sofa setting
right
This cushion seating is backed by a window in a modern living room. The effect is clean and sharp but, at the same time, softened by the arrangement of creamy-white hydrangeas (*Hydrangea* sp.) on the left.

Making a plant grouping for a corner of a room

Here, I have set out to compose a little period piece to accompany the easy chair and draped curtain. The site is a corner of a living room decorated in neutral shades, next to an east-facing window. Since the room is not in constant use, and therefore not always heated, I needed plants suited to a cool room. When you are aiming to create a particular atmosphere like this, you may find that certain of your possessions suggest themselves as "props".

The setting and overall styling
below and right

This is an attractive corner, but the décor shades are muted and monotone, and something bright and colorful is needed to guide the eye towards the large window. An arrangement of plants or flowers will look well on the graceful occasional table. As the room is not used very often, an arrangement of potted plants will enhance the corner for longer than an arrangement of cut flowers. The arrangement needs to be large, without dominating the corner. To continue the period feel, I added a pair of Victorian dolls and a small footstool. The red of the footstool and the velvet cushion picks up the exact red of the cyclamen.

Making up the arrangement
I used a plastic tray in which to stand the various pots, so that the plants can be watered according to their individual needs. I planned the arrangement around the two cyclamen (*Cyclamen persicum* hybrids), making sure they were offset by the solid greenery of the Japanese fatsia (*Fatsia japonica*). Then I added a spiky green spider plant (*Chlorophytum comosum*) to provide outline interest, and lightened the whole effect with trailing stems of variegated ivy (*Hedera helix* hybrids) to mask the edge of the table. Finally, just for fun, I included a bunch of grapes, and these actually have the effect of "lifting" the green/red/beige scheme.

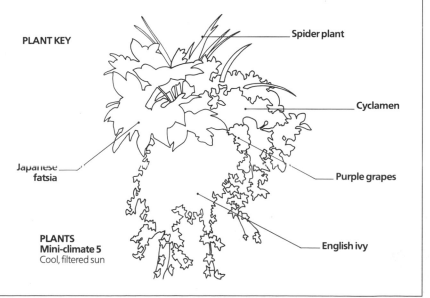

PLANT KEY

Spider plant

Cyclamen

Japanese fatsia

Purple grapes

English ivy

PLANTS
Mini-climate 5
Cool, filtered sun

Living rooms 4
Focal point

Sometimes, plants are allowed to become the dominant feature of a room. Whereas strong patterning and bold colors tend to obscure vegetation by competing with it visually, simple fabrics, plain colored walls and the long, low lines of modern furniture all serve to draw attention to house plants or flower arrangements.

Bold leaves *below*
A plant with small leaves would look weak in this airy setting, but the massive fiddle leaf fig (*Ficus lyrata*) looks superb and automatically becomes the focal point of the room. Such a sizeable plant easily draws attention from the large studio windows.

Small-scale setting *right*
This ponytail (*Beaucarnea recurvata*) is a fairly dominant plant which has been used here with a table and a lamp to make an interesting group. The pebbles on the table and floor help to link the treelike plant to its setting.

On a grand scale *right*
The imposing banquette is surmounted by an arching Kentia palm (*Howea belmoreana*), providing a magnificent central feature. The palm's graceful lines are echoed by the pair of white sails (*Spathiphyllum* "Clevelandii") on the console table, and combine with the panelled door and ornate coving to make this room evocative of past grandeur.

Splash of color *left*
Almost minimalist in style, this dark-colored furniture makes a restrained setting for an arrangement of larkspur (*Delphinium consolida*) in a glass vase. Thus the simple colorful display immediately becomes a focal point.

Contrasting textures *right*
Here, the arrangement is one of scale, line and textural contrast. The hard geometry of the dark-colored beams is emphasized by the soft hanging English ivy (*Hedera helix* hybrids) and the graceful clumps of the umbrella plant (*Cyperus alternifolius*).

Living rooms 5
Table-top ideas

In any style of living room there will usually be side tables and coffee tables that can be made into smaller focal points of interest. Plants and flowers should relate to other objects, such as ornaments, books or lamps, which may in themselves suggest the choice of a plant or group of flowers.

A question of scale *right*
A small plant would be swamped by this bold interior, but the magnificent painted nettle (*Coleus blumei*) is large enough to demand attention. The red markings of the foliage pick up the color of the sofa.

Mellow tones *above*
A basket of dried flowers and grasses blends in with the warm colors of leather-bound books and polished wood, bringing a touch of summer to a library setting.

Graceful lines *above*
The graceful curved neck of this decoy swan is echoed in the lines of the tulip stems and the shape of the central pot. The soft colors match those of the sofa.

Contrasting forms *above*
The basket of dried lavender and the cluster of spherical wooden objects combine with the dominant, oriental lamp base to form a pleasing group.

A dominant feature *above*
Mosslike baby's tears plants (*Soleirolia soleirolii*) arranged in a basket make a dominant central display that needs to be surrounded by low-key furnishings that do not vie for attention.

Imposing order *left*
In this eclectic mixture of furnishings, an eye-catching arrangement of Swiss cheese plant leaves (*Monstera deliciosa*) and foxtail lilies (*Eremurus* sp.) serves to unify the diverse features.

Living rooms 6

Although designed expressly for putting things on, shelves and mantelpieces do not usually promote the long-term well-being of plants. Lack of space and light means that arrangements of cut or dried flowers are usually the best choice, or, perhaps, flowering annual plants or bulbs.

Shelves of cacti *left*
Because of their simple, compact shapes, cacti look good ranged on shelves. Moreover, a set-up like this alcove—with an overhead light source, backing mirror and glass shelves—will help to maximize the impact of the group. The overhead lighting has the effect of highlighting any fluffy down or dramatic spikes on the cacti. Notice how glass shelves look green in cross section (due to refraction), which enhances the plant display—try for a similar effect with a collection of tumbling greenhouse plants, or a collection of ferns, making sure there is sufficient light.

Using dried flowers
above
Five bunches of dried flowers provide a lower-edge "frame" for this large over-mantel mirror. They form part of the "ordered clutter" of objects and ornaments around and on the marble mantelpiece. When displaying dried flowers for any length of time, blow the dust off them occasionally.

Using wild flowers *right*
Wild flowers are easy on the eye and, in general, have softer-hued flower heads than garden varieties. Too strong an arrangement of plants in this gothic setting would have been out of character, but two light, feathery bunches of wild flowers do not detract from the delicate tracery of the wall decoration. Beneath this shelf is a radiator, which should be turned off when any fresh flowers are displayed on the shelf. Wild flowers, especially, wilt very quickly if not kept in cool conditions. (Grow your own rather than picking from the wild.)

Making wreath decorations for mantelpieces

An open fireplace easily becomes the focal point of a room. But when there is no fire lit, a mantel decoration can counteract the empty void below.

The setting *right*
This dried wreath succeeds in echoing the style and natural colors of the fireplace and the remainder of the décor—the books, wooden decoy ducks and an old straw hat. The wreath is positioned off-center and is balanced by the objects on the left.

PLANT KEY

Old-man's beard stems

Bracken

Straw flower

Oats

Bells-of-Ireland

Wheat

Baby's breath

Lady's mantle

Yellow statice

Decoration for a special occasion *right*
This idea for a festive occasion includes fresh flowers, so do not light the fire, unless the blooms only need to last a few hours for a party. The two swags are made of white-painted magnolia (*Magnolia* sp.) leaves, pampas grass (*Cortaderia* sp.) and lemons, wired to a base of crumpled netting, which is filled with damp moss into which yellow chrysanthemums (*Chrysanthemum* sp.) have been pushed.

Living rooms 7
Plants and pictures

Various styles of painting will suggest different types of display; by using plants or flowers in conjunction with a picture, you can recreate a still life with fresh material or pick up the patterns, textures or colors in a painting. Each composition may be a little set piece on its own or, if you are working with a large painting, it may dominate the whole room.

Old and new *above*
Lilies (*Lilium auratum*) and Transvaal daisies (*Gerbera jamesonii*) in a modern vase make a humorous contrast with a traditional still life.

Linking textures *above*
There is a textural harmony between the painting, the table inlay and the mottled leaves of the leopard plant (*Ligularia* sp.).

Picking up a color *above*
It is color that unifies this triangular mantelpiece display—the yellow of the painted sun is echoed by that of the lilies (*Lilium* hybrids).

Using a dominant color *right*
Color again provides the association here, between the flowers in the painting and those in the vase. The vibrant yellow stands out in a monochromatic setting.

Dining rooms 1

It is not easy to be specific about current styles of interior decoration for any room, as there are so many styles about and the dividing lines between them are often not exact.

Styles for dining rooms show the same range as living rooms. One of the most popular current styles is based on fabrics inspired by eighteenth- and nineteenth-century prototypes and casual country furniture. Temperate plants, fresh garden flowers and dried flowers will all enhance this type of room. Offshoots of this style are the informal American colonial look and an eclectic ethnic style based on imports from the Far East and India. Another style of interior decoration has its origins in industrial high-tech, which first appeared in the late 1970s. It still has a utilitarian look, but one which has been adapted by popular chain stores to furnish a sophisticated urban market. Large, architectural plants used with this décor continue the austere effect. Another style currently in vogue is a softer look, full of pastel colors and the use of draperies, which recalls the 1920s.

Country style *above*
This dining room epitomizes country style in its furniture, floor covering and small-print curtain fabric. Large baskets of dried flowers are in keeping with the rustic mood and their subdued colors harmonize with the rich, dark colors of the antique furniture.

Softening sharp angles *right*
The wiry, angular shapes of the lamp and chairs in this eating area are reminiscent of popular furniture in the 1950s. Their harshness is softened by the large leaves of the avocado pear plant (*Persea americana*).

Hard-edged sophistication *above*
This glass table increases the impact of a flower arrangement, and the shape of the dining chairs is repeated in the curved glass bowls. Red tulips (*Tulipa* hybrids) contrast spectacularly with the furniture.

Using a mantelpiece *above*
A softer, period look with a froth of baby's breath (*Gypsophila paniculata*) as a central feature on the polished table. Delicate baby's tears plants (*Soleirolia soleirolei*) line the mantelpiece.

Dining rooms 2

Opulence on a small scale
right
This attic dining room, although small, has a baronial feel. The tapestry-covered dining chairs and gleaming silver table accessories are complemented by two large, bushy crotons (*Codiaeum variegatum pictum*). The predominant colors of the decoration —red and green—are repeated in the leaves of the plants.

Large-scale dining space
below
This interesting, airy setting is overhung by a footbridge on the upper level. At one end of the dining table, a luxuriant mass of the cut-leaved finger plant (*Philodendron bipinnatifidum*) and ferns is a fittingly dramatic backdrop. The plants look equally attractive viewed from above.

Successful decoration with two plants *left*
The spectacular palm dominating one corner of this dining room catches your eye immediately. But the smaller bushy foliage plant, cleverly placed on a lower level, has the effect of drawing the eye down and towards the table which, after all, is the focal point of the room.

Thematic table setting *below*
For a special occasion, display cut flowers or flowering house plants which match your china. Here, yellow and white flowers echo the colors of the table mats and plates, while a huge African hemp (*Sparmannia africana*) brings fresh greenery into the room.

Dining rooms 3

The focal point of a dining room must be its table. Floral centerpieces should be in the mood of the table setting but should not impede conversation across the table. Just a few flower heads floating in water will make an attractive display, particularly if they complement the colors of the food. Other arrangements in the room should not distract attention from the centerpiece.

An elegant still life *left*
A charmingly simple still life composition on a dining room side table which is not too demanding on the eye. The arrangement is enlivened by the addition of a regal lily (*Lilium regale*) in a narrow vase.

Echoing floral motifs *right*
Even without its centerpiece, this dining room setting conjures up a mood of summer with its vibrant colors and abundance of greenery. An ivy patterned wallpaper, a floral tablecloth and two weeping figs (*Ficus benjamina*) on either side of a fireplace set the scene for a stunning central arrangement of red trumpet honeysuckle (*Lonicera brownii*) mixed with English ivy (*Hedera helix* hybrids) in a basket.

Co-ordinating colors *right*
In certain situations artificial flowers are perfectly acceptable, and perhaps the dining table is one of them. The chance to recreate a summer arrangement in midwinter is always welcome. Here, the bright colors provide a strong contrast to the predominantly white table setting and furniture. The mixture of orange, white and purple flowers and green foliage picks up the colors in the floral pattern of the china perfectly.

Kitchens 1

Kitchens can be of two types: working galley kitchens and kitchens to live in. By definition, the worktop surfaces are practical and do not lend themselves to too much decoration—add to this the hazards of steam and constantly changing temperatures and you may not have ideal growing conditions. However, some plants will prefer the added humidity and warmth of the kitchen environment. Arrangements of dried flowers, and bowls of gourds, fruit and vegetables, can be most attractive as long as they do not impede the cook. Window-ledges can be utilized, but plants must be protected from the fall in temperatures at night if there is no double glazing. Plants can be displayed in hanging baskets, but only in places where it is easy to water them frequently.

Strong primaries *left*
Cut chrysanthemums (*Chrysanthemum* hybrids) make a bright addition to the edible strawberries, lemons, peppers and tomatoes which complement the strong primary color scheme of this streamlined kitchen unit. The location of the display makes imaginative use of the concealed, split-level lighting.

Period feel *below*
Something of a period mood has been created here with copper pans, wooden spoons and basketware—all visually strong in themselves. However, the white tulips (*Tulipa* hybrids) are the focal point.

Practical and decorative *left*
The typical type of clutter one might expect to find on the wide sill of a country kitchen. Drying herbs hang in a swathe above the window, their presence serving both a practical and a decorative use. The bowl of fruit and the cyclamen (*Cyclamen persicum* hybrids) on the sill itself contribute to the overall impression of a warm, welcoming room and a place of work.

Casual and homely *left*
This breakfast area is enlivened by an informal arrangement of garden flowers, foliage and grasses in a jug, and a heartleaf philodendron (*Philodendron scandens*) trails attractively over the shelves which house a collection of American blue-and-white spatterware. These plants like a warm and humid atmosphere, as their natural habitat is the tropical rain forest.

Square patterns *right*
A high-tech kitchen which has ingeniously utilized squared wire mesh for hanging utensils above the sink, and repeated the motif as a support for a mosaic of climbers against the window. These are positioned in such a way as to benefit from the light of the window whilst not interfering with the work of the cook. The square pattern is repeated in the wall and floor coverings, but the angular style of the kitchen is softened by the presence of the plants.

Utilizing a high ceiling
right
The ceiling of a large kitchen which does not get too steamy makes an ideal place to hang and dry summer flowers and herbs. When the ceiling is high, bunches of flowers can make the room seem less bare and are in no danger of getting in the way of the cook. In this country kitchen, baskets, rattan blinds and a bird cage complement the simple pine furniture and complete the styling.

Kitchens 2

In a compact kitchen, the chances are that you will not want any plants cluttering up your valuable worktops. Yet it seems a pity to do without greenery, and there are several ways of solving the problem practically and safely, while keeping plants off surfaces and away from kitchen appliances.

Making a feature of a plain wall *right*
People hang pans and utensils in the kitchen, and there is no reason why you cannot hang up plants. A plastic-coated grid attached to the wall makes an attractive base to which you can fix a selection of small potted herbs so that they are to hand when you are cooking.

Decorating an eating area
above
This kitchen eating area is en-livened by an Algerian ivy (*Hedera canariensis* hybrids). The simple white décor focuses attention on the green foliage.

A kitchen corner *below*
Several house plants enliven this kitchen, but none of them occu-pies a working surface. The luxuriant Boston fern (*Nephrolepis exaltata* "Bostoniensis") is sus-pended by a chain from the ceiling.

Decorating a kitchen dresser

A collection of blue-and-white china looks very appealing ranged on the dresser of a traditional country kitchen. But perhaps the scene is a little stark. Dresser shelves are quite narrow and normally used for display, rather than as functional shelves for much-used kitchen items. So a dresser is an ideal "showcase" for plants, provided you observe the rules of lighting and watering, and change the plants when necessary.

The setting *below*
The areas of white wall behind the dresser look rather austere and would benefit from some "filling in". But introducing a random collection of plants would interrupt the subtle styling of the kitchen.

PLANT KEY

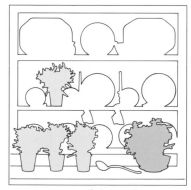

PLANTS   Christmas cherry
Mini-climate 4
Cool, sunny

Making up the arrangement
As a solution, I selected five plants of the same variety—the Christmas cherry (*Solanum capsicastrum*). Its orange berries provide a color contrast, without being too distracting to the eye, and complement the china collection.

The overall styling *above*
Within the country-style setting of this kitchen interior, the Christmas cherries, with their bright berries and small, pretty leaves, warm and soften what could easily be too severe a room-scheme.

Looking after the plants *left*
This useful little winter berrying plant, which has insignificant flowers earlier in the year, lasts up to two months. Given a coolish interior, it appreciates a degree of humidity and should be misted every day or so. Since the dresser does not offer the direct light these plants prefer, move them to a sunny position for several hours a day.

Bedrooms 1

Your bedroom is a highly personal part of your house and one where you can indulge your most imaginative ideas about decoration. An arrangement of fresh or dried flowers in a guest room is a thoughtful touch, too. Yet displays must still be practically planned. If space is a problem, consider fixing up a hanging arrangement in the form of a wreath or garland, or using a pedestal to support a plant or flower arrangement in one corner.

Balancing vibrant colors *below*
This unusual bedroom is decorated in bright colors and excitingly lit. A stylish combination of artificial white tulips in two large, yellow vases and a tall euphorbia (*Euphorbia pseudocactus*) help reinforce the whole effect.

Art-deco style bedroom *right*
A large house plant sits on a beautiful ceramic jardiniere, totally in keeping with the collection of art-deco paraphernalia and the floral design of the window blind. Place pedestals like this where they will not be knocked over.

Creating a romantic mood *left*
A nostalgic bedroom is reflected in this floor-length mirror decorated with garlands of dried flowers. The bed's brass corner poles are adorned with ribbons and bunches of artificial rosebuds.

Maintaining a spacious feel *below*
A magnificent weeping fig (*Ficus benjamina*) stands in a sunny corner of this airy bedroom. Although large, the plant is positioned well out of the way and adds to, rather than detracts from, the feeling of lightness and space.

Bedrooms 2

Complementing a picture *above*
The chest of drawers provides a solid support for a single cineraria (*Senecio cruentus* hybrids) which subtly reinforces the subject of the picture hanging directly above it.

A conservatory corner *above*
Sunlight flooding through a bedroom window illuminates this collection of plants. A large fuchsia (*Fuchsia* sp.) contributes to the "conservatory" feel.

A place for artificial flowers *left*
Occasionally, people may be physically averse to plants or fresh flowers in the room where they sleep. Instead, try an artificial, but informal, decoration such as this enchanting basket filled with artificial forget-me-nots. Country-style bedrooms can be enhanced by using painted or stencilled baskets as containers for flower arrangements.

A romantic bedroom
right
A vase of lilac (*Syringa* hybrids) seen through a mirror fills a softly pretty bedroom with fragrance. The lilac complements the lace-covered pillows and delicate pink-and-white wallpaper. Always place bedroom vases somewhere safe, where they will not be knocked over while you dress or make the bed. Use other fragrant flowers and plants as they come into season.

Co-ordinating color scheme *right*
In a carefully put-together period room, a tall vase of dried Chinese lanterns (*Physalis alkekengi* "Gigantea") stands on the mantelpiece, helping to make a focal point of the fireplace area and the cosy coal fire. The green and orange lanterns co-ordinate perfectly with the color scheme of the bold designs on the wardrobe, fabric and wallcovering.

Bathrooms 1

The relaxing surroundings of a bathroom can form a stylish setting for some of your more striking plants, and matching containers to the bathroom fittings ensures a successful display.

Provided that they have good light, bathrooms come nearest to providing the ideal growing conditions for a number of the most popular house plants. They are generally warm places and, two or three times a day, the air becomes saturated with moisture. Quite a high level of humidity can continue for some time after someone has taken a bath, while damp towels dry out and moisture on surfaces and fabrics gradually evaporates. Even if obscured glass is fitted to windows, there is little light loss; direct sunlight becomes bright, filtered light.

A "jungle-look" corner *above*
In this Victorian-style bathroom, an empty corner provides a good home for a large Swiss cheese plant (*Monstera deliciosa*), which offsets the white, antique bath. This plant loves warmth and humidity, so it is an ideal bathroom plant.

Oriental-style bathroom *left*
There is a Japanese feel about this bathroom, with its clean black and white surfaces. The fine, filigree foliage of an umbrella plant (*Cyperus alternifolius*), which needs to be grown in a constantly wet medium, is shown to perfect advantage on the windowsill.

A fragrant bathroom *right*
An elegant bathroom with potted gardenias (*Gardenia* sp.) standing on the bath surround. Their perfume will dominate the bathroom and they thrive in a moist atmosphere.

A temporary display *below*
Although you will need to change a plant such as this African lily (*Agapanthus campanulatus*) every three weeks or so (there being no natural light), it makes a beautiful addition to the bathroom.

Cut flowers in the bathroom *left*
The fresh pink, green and white color scheme of this bathroom is picked up by the cut flowers at the window and on the edge of the bath.

The small bathroom *right*
Mirrors are a superb device for increasing the apparent size of a small bathroom. Green plants used as decoration will have double the effect. Here, a pair of stick yuccas (*Yucca elephantipes*) add the final touch to a smart, masculine bathroom.

Bathrooms 2

Although space may be at a premium in the bathroom, different styles of plant decoration are possible. There is a "cluttered" look, with various small plants appearing among the soap and toothpaste; or, for a more dramatic effect, just one or two large plants can be used.

Using shelves *right*
Ferns like the warm and humid conditions of a bathroom, and small shelves above a basin surround make a suitable home for various potted specimens including a bird's nest fern (*Asplenium nidus*).

Country-style simplicity *above*
In this traditional, stencilled bathroom, a wall shelf-unit is balanced by a plant arrangement either side of the head of the bath. The rather bare, bleached feel of the room lends itself to plant decoration.

Real and painted *left*
Two exquisite viridiflora tulips (*Tulipa* hybrids) stand in an elegant vase against a mural which continues the floral theme of this bathroom.

A flower-filled bathroom *above*
The design of the blind fabric has been continued on the walls with hand-painted primroses and rose sprigs. Fresh flowers and potted plants add to the effect.

Displaying airplants in a bathroom window recess

Airplants make a fascinating display in a bathroom. Most bromeliads are native to the tropical regions of the Americas, where they cling to rocks or trees. Their roots are used merely for support—the plants survive on moisture in the air, so spray them regularly with water.

Making up the arrangement *right*
Single airplants are difficult to display well; the best approach is to mass them together. A collection of shells and coral provides decorative support for the plants and gives them an underwater look suitable for the bathroom.

The setting *below*
Airplants like the moist air in a bathroom and, despite their delicate appearance, are very tolerant. This well-lit window recess with glass shelves makes an ideal setting.

PLANT KEY

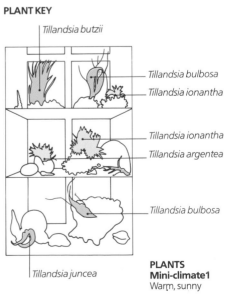

Tillandsia butzii

Tillandsia bulbosa

Tillandsia ionantha

Tillandsia ionantha

Tillandsia argentea

Tillandsia bulbosa

Tillandsia juncea

PLANTS
Mini-climate1
Warm, sunny

Details of the airplant arrangement *above left and right*
Mounted on coral, shells, pieces of wood, cork or minerals, airplants have a magical feel. Here, the delicate gray-green leaves contrast with the strong shapes of the shells and coral. The glass shelves allow light to filter between the plants and reflect the pearly sheen of the shells. Tuck or gently tie the plants into the shells, or use a special airplant fixative; in time they will probably attach their roots to the support.

Halls and entrances 1

Front doors and entrance halls are the first areas you see on entering the house. Decorated attractively, they can be warm and welcoming, drawing the visitor into the heart of the house. So first impressions are important, yet halls and lobbies often have poor light and fluctuating temperatures. You will need to plan displays for the hall using the most tolerant house plants. Cast-iron plants (*Aspidistra elatior*) and mother-in-law's-tongues (*Sansevieria trifasciata*) are good choices. Dried flowers and foliage are particularly useful for displaying in any hall or entrance with a lighting problem. People pass through the hall at standing height, so scale up plants accordingly and avoid using trailing plants in awkward places. Any plant which is constantly brushed against will inevitably become damaged.

Decorations for a large entrance hall *above*
The plain brick walls of this hall are softened by a mass of dried beech leaves (*Fagus sylvatica*) whose warm tones harmonize with the mellow brick. Two stick yuccas (*Yucca elephantipes*) stand either side of the door, and a bowl of gourds relieves the expanse of bare table-top.

Framing a doorway *left*
Two sturdy yuccas frame the doorway leading into the conservatory beyond. Tumbling light-green foliage makes an inviting transition between the two rooms.

An impressive focal point *right*
A magnificent staghorn fern (*Platycerium bifurcatum*) dominates the center of an entrance hall. A large pot standing underneath catches drips from watering and prevents people from walking too close to the plant and damaging it.

Halls and entrances 2

If you have a hall large enough to furnish, you will have the opportunity to go for maximum effect in your plant and floral arrangements. However, even in a hall which is little more than a passageway, there are several devices you can use to make sure your decorations do not go unnoticed by people passing through.

If space is a real problem, make up a swag using wire netting with dried flower heads entwined in it. Wreaths are also pretty and festive, especially at Christmas.

Using a mirror *above*
A huge mirror placed behind the side table doubles the effect of the two plants—a dragon tree (*Dracaena marginata*) and a glossy grape ivy (*Cissus rhombifolia*). Also, the mirror enlarges the apparent size of the hall and reflects light on to the plants.

Using a shelf *right*
A pretty marble shelf bracketed to the wall provides the perfect surface for an arrangement of dried roses and grasses. Two small vases containing more roses stand on either side of the central glass vase, and a tall mirror makes the most of the arrangement.

Scaling up to fill a space
left
Because it is likely to be cooler than a living room, the hall is often a good place to site an arrangement of fresh-cut flowers to help them last longer. Here, a large, informal arrangement of day lilies (*Hemerocallis* sp.) and fennel (*Foeniculum* sp.) helps to fill an area of bare whitewashed wall in a country cottage hall. The flowers, which stand on a beautiful black inlaid chest, pick up the warm colors in the furnishing fabric, helping to make the hall cosy and welcoming.

Making a winter arrangement for a hall

In a rather dull corner of this hall, in front of some pine doors opening to a seldom-used cupboard, I sited a winter arrangement of red and yellow cut flowers, including berries, early flowering shrubs and evergreen foliage to soften the effect. I used a mixing bowl and a large block of floral foam 6in higher than the container.

The setting *above*
This corner of the hall is well lit from the side and gives easy access for replacement of water. The honey-colored stripped pine makes a pleasing background for the arrangement whose triangular outline helps to soften the vertical lines of the area. As the pedestal is turned slightly to one side, emphasis is drawn towards the light source.

Making up the arrangement

A triangular arrangement
To outline the shape, I used bold Oregon grape sprays, and then I added the large chrysanthemums—yellow at the outer edge, deepening to bronze-red at the core. More sprays of jasmine, freesias and evergreen foliage added dimension.

FLOWER KEY

Crab apple

Chrysanthemum

Winter jasmine

Oregon grape

Freesia

Spider chrysanthemum

Cotoneaster

Daffodil

Japanese fatsia leaves

Persian ivy

Stairs and stairwells

The staircase may not be the first place you think of for displaying plants but, if you follow the principles outlined for halls and entrances, the results can be effective. Stairs and stairwells can be cold and drafty so select the hardier house plants.

The stairs themselves should normally be kept free of obstructions, but there may be space on a wide turn of the stairs for a large specimen plant or a collection of smaller ones. If the staircase turns round a central well, and receives some daylight, try placing a tall, upright plant or a climber in the otherwise redundant space.

Landing windowsills and skylights at the top of the stairs are two possible light sources which can help plants thrive. Large hanging baskets filled with easy-care plants such as trades-cantias (*Tradescantia* sp.), spider plants (*Chlorophytum* sp.) and Swedish ivies (*Plectranthus australis*), can be secured to the framework of a skylight. The plants will soon cascade impressively, several feet down the stairwell.

Making a feature of a landing *left*
This landing halfway up a flight of stairs is well lit and deep enough for a large display of plants. Furniture, pictures and ornaments are all of the period and the twin vases of tall pampas grasses (*Cortaderia* sp.) enhance the Victorian flavor, as does trailing greenery framing the lower portion of the window.

A landing on the grand scale *right*
This imposing period staircase leading on to a wide, sunny landing is a fine enough setting for the massive foliage of a banana plant (*Musa* sp.). The huge bay window means a selection of large plants can be housed on the landing, and the back-lighting from the sun shining through the different leaf shapes creates a dramatic effect.

Making use of a skylight
Suspended plants dominate this small Edwardian landing, which is toplit from the large skylight. The arrangement of green plants, which include spider plants (*Chloro-phytum* sp.) and ferns (*Nephrolepis* sp.), is reflected in a wall mirror, increasing the "cluttered" effect which is in keeping with the style of the period.

A cascade of greenery
This cool, wide stone staircase is filled with hanging plants, but has an open, spacious feel. A magnificent ladder fern (*Nephrolepis cordifolia*) dominates the foot of the stairs, while great swathes of grape ivy (*Cissus rhombifolia*) hang from the upper balcony and are silhouetted by the toplighting.

Flowers on a landing
A peaceful corner of the stairs is brought into focus by an informal arrangement of garden flowers, illuminated by sidelighting from the landing window. The flowers balance the picture above, while still maintaining the neutral tones of the rest of the interior.

Sunrooms and conservatories 1

Traditionally, the conservatory was a place in which to display plants that had been raised in the greenhouse, where they were returned when the display started to deteriorate. The modern sunroom is more a place in which people relax and enjoy the warmth, but it is also one that suits plants. Real fanatics may transform the room into something resembling a jungle, where greenery takes over, but fewer plants, well displayed, can be just as effective.

Rooms like these provide light and airy conditions, a moist atmosphere and space for plants to spread. With careful watering in winter, many plants can be grown in a room with a night temperature of 50°F, but somewhat higher during the day. However, most sunrooms are warmer than this.

Furnishing a dining area with plants *right*
This conservatory-like house extension has a tall, airy feel. This has been maintained by using a relatively small number of plants to furnish it, and soften the architectural lines. The majority of these sit on waist-level shelves fitted all round the outer edge of the room. A large rubber plant (*Ficus elastica*) stands in one corner. The conservatory is one place where large-leaved plants like this can be given their head and allowed to fill as much space as they want.

A warm sunroom *below*
This spectacular room needs to maintain a considerable temperature in winter to sustain the tropical plants growing here. Windows must be double-glazed to prevent heat loss through the large areas of glass. Huge plants are placed in pots, baskets and specially constructed brick troughs. The hanging platform which provides extra space for a suspended "island of greenery" is a most unusual, and practical, feature, since it can be lowered for watering and maintenance.

An elegant conservatory *below*
This pretty room with its distinctive glazing bars contains a selection of flowering plants, as well as a citrus tree. Color accents are provided by a poinsettia (*Euphorbia pulcherrima*) and a cactus (*Schlumbergera* sp.).

Plant-filled sunroom *above*
Here, the living space extends through sliding glass on to a sunroom floored with white decking. The large plants include a dumb cane (*Dieffenbachia* sp.) and a thriving chestnut vine (*Tetrastigma voinieranum*).

Sunrooms and conservatories 2

The sunroom windowsill *left*
This windowsill is flooded with light all day, and four attractively shaped fans are used to shade the cyclamen (*Cyclamen persicum* hybrids) and Kafir lily (*Clivia miniata*) from bright light. The small cacti (*Mammillaria* sp.) are happy in full sun.

Variety for a rustic-style sunroom *below*
At least ten different varieties of green plants decorate this sun-room. The green of their leaves contrasts vividly with the warm apricot wash on the walls. A bunch of dried flowers hangs upside-down above the riot of foliage.

Conservatory shelves *above*
An idea for making the most of a group of impatiens plants (*Impatiens* sp.) is to combine the plants with a collection of glass or china such as these colored glass vases.

Decorating a corner *right*
An array of plants and cut flowers establishes the conservatory theme in this well-lit corner. On the table stand lilies (*Lilium* hybrids), white sails (*Spathiphyllum* "Clevelandii") and English ivy (*Hedera helix* hybrids). A huge stone vase of flowering onion (*Allium giganteum*) and a basket of white chrysanthemums (*Chrysanthemum morifolium* hybrids) complete the arrangement.

A place for herbs indoors *left*
A well-lit, cool conservatory can be a home for potted herbs. There is attractive color variation in this studied arrangement of fennel (*Foeniculum vulgare*), chives (*Allium schoenoprasum*), feverfew (*Chrysanthemum parthenium*), parsley (*Petroselinum crispum*) and lady's mantle (*Alchemilla vulgaris*).

A green oasis *right*
Consider what your conservatory looks like from inside the house. This one, glimpsed through an arch, has a hanging curtain of greenery which makes a charming transition from the interior.

·6·
THE PLANT FINDER'S GUIDE

The first function of *The Plant Finder's Guide* is to provide a catalogue of the various forms of plant material that can be used in the house. There are sections dealing with cut flowers and foliage and all kinds of dried matter, as well as nearly 150 of the most popular house plants. Color photographs provide a visual guide, and advice is given on how to display your material. Additionally, the guide gives special care advice, by way of readily recognizable symbols.

In the case of house plants, the symbols indicate the preferred light, temperature, watering and humidity levels of each plant, plus the relative ease of its cultivation. The entries are classified according to the basic shape of each plant—a prime factor in determining its decorative use in the home—and information is given regarding the probable dimensions of mature specimens. Similarly shaped plants of the same genus are listed, where appropriate, and briefly described. The amount of light and heat needed by each plant is described in terms of its *mini-climate:* a system that enables you to see, at a glance, which plants are compatible. Using this, you can determine which upright plants, for example, would be suitable for a warm and sunny position, or for a warm and shady one—thus allowing you to choose easily between different plants that are suitable for a given position.

Choosing plants and flowers
Plants come in such an overwhelming variety of shapes, sizes and colors and, depending on their origins, need a variety of different conditions: in order to choose the right ones for your home, you need to be aware of both their decorative qualities and growing needs.

How to use The Plant Finder's Guide

For easy reference, *The Plant Finder's Guide* is divided into three separate guides: one for house plants, one for cut flowers and one for dried flowers.

The guide to house plants contains almost 150 color photographs of the most widely used indoor plants, each with a detailed entry. Most of the entries are arranged in eight different shape categories: upright, arching, weeping, rosette-shaped, bushy, climbing, trailing and creeping. Of course, plants change shape as they grow and these categories are generalizations only. Each category is then sub-divided according to the shape and size of the leaves: large-leaved plants are those with leaves over 6in in length; small-leaved plants have leaves less than 6in in length; and compound-leaved plants have leaves divided into two or more leaf segments. There are separate sections in the guide for flowering bulbs, and for cacti and succulents, which are arranged according to their own shape categories. At the end of the house plant section there is a photographic color guide to a selection of flowering house plants, running through the spectrum from white to violet, and there is also a seasonal guide, in the form of a chart, to indicate their flowering or fruiting periods.

Within *The guide to cut flowers*, the flower entries are arranged according to season and the foliage entries are organized according to color. Each entry describes how to use and prepare the material and, of the 100 entries, 85 have a color photograph.

The guide to dried flowers is separated into flowers themselves, arranged according to color, and into other dried material, arranged according to type. A total of 65 species have been photographed and each has an entry giving advice on how to use it and on the best method of drying.

Symbols give additional information in all three guides.

SAMPLE PAGES

The guide to house plants

The plants are classified by their pattern of growth and foliage characteristics. An introduction to each group describes the main characteristics of the plants contained within it. Every plant has a color photograph. A key to the symbols used in the guide is given.

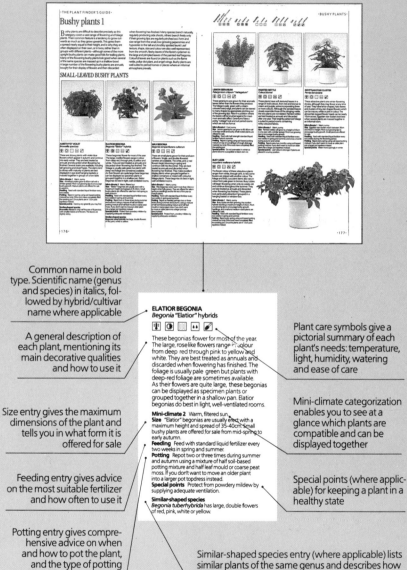

Common name in bold type. Scientific name (genus and species) in italics, followed by hybrid/cultivar name where applicable

A general description of each plant, mentioning its main decorative qualities and how to use it

Size entry gives the maximum dimensions of the plant and tells you in what form it is offered for sale

Feeding entry gives advice on the most suitable fertilizer and how often to use it

Potting entry gives comprehensive advice on when and how to pot the plant, and the type of potting mixture to use

Plant care symbols give a pictorial summary of each plant's needs: temperature, light, humidity, watering and ease of care

Mini-climate categorization enables you to see at a glance which plants are compatible and can be displayed together

Special points (where applicable) for keeping a plant in a healthy state

Similar-shaped species entry (where applicable) lists similar plants of the same genus and describes how they differ from the featured plant

---

How to use the symbols

The guide to house plants

Temperature

Cool with winter rest Keep plants cool from spring to autumn, 50°-60°F being ideal, and 45°-50°F in winter if possible.

Cool The plants, which thrive in a cool climate, prefer a year-long temperature around 50°-60°F, if possible.

Warm These plants, which prefer warmth, thrive between 60° and 70°F all year, but endure higher or lower ranges for reasonable periods.

Light

Sunny A sunny position is one near a south-, east- or west-facing window which receives unobstructed direct sunlight.

Filtered sun This is indirect sunlight, which shines through a translucent curtain or blind, or is baffled by a leafy tree outside a window.

Shady A shady position is one close to a north-facing window, or to the side of an east- or west-facing one which receives no direct or indirect sun.

Humidity

Low humidity The air surrounding the plant should be approximately 30-40 per cent saturated with water. Few plants tolerate low humidity.

Moderate humidity The air surrounding the plant should be approximately 60 per cent saturated with water.

High humidity The air surrounding the plant should be approximately 80 per cent saturated with water.

Watering

Water sparingly This involves barely moistening the whole mixture, and allowing it to dry out almost completely each time.

Water moderately This refers to moistening the entire mixture, but allowing the top inch or so to dry out before watering again.

The guide to cut flowers

Cut flowers and berries are classified according to their seasonal availability, and foliage is classified according to its color. An introduction to each section describes the variety of material available. A key to the symbols used in the guide is given.

The guide to dried flowers

Dried material is classified according to color or type. An introduction to each section describes the variety of material available and gives general suggestions on how to use it. Color photographs show examples. A key to the symbols used in the guide is given.

Common name in bold type. Scientific name (genus and species) in italics followed by hybrid/cultivar name of flower or foliage where applicable

Symbols show whether the flowers are fragrant, long-lasting, have useful foliage or are suitable for drying

Description of how to use the flowers/foliage and what to mix them with

Colors available (flowers only)

Advice on how to prepare and condition the flowers/foliage

Common name in bold type. Scientific name (genus and species) in italics followed by hybrid/cultivar name where applicable

Advice on decorative uses, and details of any other colors which are available

Symbols give the most suitable method of drying the material

ANEMONE
Anemone coronaria

These delicate flowers are available in a wide variety of shapes and sizes, although the ones pictured here are the most familiar. Their fragile flowers are made up not of petals but of sepals (these are usually green and are the leaf like structures which surround the flowers), and these form a cup shape round a deep-blue central disc. In the garden, anemones of different species can be found in spring, summer and autumn but, in florists' shops, they are available throughout the year. Although they can be mixed with other flowers, they look best massed in a glass vase. Pack them in tightly, as their stems have a tendency to bend and this can make a vase look untidy.

Colours available Red, blue, mauve, pink, white, yellow, magenta and scarlet. Many have a central disc ringed with another colour.

Preparation Cut the stems on a slant and make a 5cm slit with a sharp knife. Dip the cut ends in boiling water for a few seconds. Give a long, cool drink before arranging.

CELOSIA
Celosia argentea "Cristata"
The purple or pink blooms have a mossy texture and provide dramatic focal point for a large arrangement.

Water plentifully This means keeping all of the potting mixture moist at all times, not letting even the surface dry out.

Care

Easy Plants which are termed "easy" to care for are those which can be grown successfully with only the minimum of attention.

Fairly easy Plants in this category require the basic care plus some attention to their individual growing needs.

Challenging These plants must be provided with their very specific growing needs or they will not thrive.

The guide to cut flowers

Long lasting Flowers or leaves which remain attractive for a particularly long time when cut.

Useful foliage Flowers whose own leaves are suitable for using in any arrangement, with or without that particular flower.

Fragrant Flowers which have a pleasant scent.

Suitable for drying Flowers, or their seed heads, or foliage which can be successfully preserved and used in dried displays.

The guide to dried flowers

Air-dried This refers to plant material dried naturally, without the use of chemicals, and usually involves hanging material upside-down in bunches.

Glycerine method This method involves standing foliage stems, or immersing leaves, in a solution of glycerine which, when absorbed by plant cells, preserves them.

Silica/borax This process uses desiccants which absorb moisture from the plant material, retaining its lifelike appearance when dried.

Pressing This is a mechanical method which preserves leaves or flowers by means of compression but does not retain the original shape.

Upright plants 1

These are plants with a distinctly vertical habit of growth. They vary in size from the treelike crotons and large-leaved rubber plants to relatively low-growing species such as the pileas and calatheas. Some of the treelike plants in this category, such as the yucca, have a central unbranched stem with leaves at the top only. Others, such as the Norfolk Island pine and the false aralia, have a central, upright stem with branches at intervals along it. Not all upright plants have both stems and leaves. The mother-in-law's tongue is stemless, with the leaves rising directly out of the potting mixture. Many upright plants, which otherwise grow too tall for a domestic setting, can be made into shorter, rounder shrubs by pinching out the main growing shoot or tip and allowing side-stem growth

to develop; the rubber plant is a good example of this. Leaf shape differs widely within the group and leaf size varies from under 6in to over 2ft. Leaf color is also well represented; from the green-and-cream leaves of the spotted dumb cane to the red leaf markings of the croton. There are some beautiful flowering upright plants including the spectacular bird-of-paradise flower and the delicate flowering maple. With this range of form and size you can find plants for very different situations: imposing specimen plants, such as the Norfolk Island pine, which look best displayed on their own; plants of more modest size which contrast well with low-growing, creeping or trailing plants, and spiky-leaved plants which mix well with the rounded shapes of some cacti.

SMALL-LEAVED UPRIGHT PLANTS

CALAMONDIN ORANGE
Citrofortunella mitis

These ornamental orange trees bear fragrant flowers, unripe green fruits and ripe orange fruits all at the same time. The oranges produced are small and bitter but are excellent for making marmalade. The plants will fruit when still quite young and are best as specimen plants or arranged in formal groups.

Mini-climate 4 Cool, sunny.
Size Orange trees take several years to reach a maximum height of 3-6ft with a similar spread. Small specimens bearing fruit are offered for sale.
Feeding Feed every two weeks with a tomato-type fertilizer all year except in winter.
Potting Repot in spring using soil-based potting mixture but only if the roots have completely filled the existing pot. If you don't want to move an older plant into a larger pot topdress instead.
Special points Susceptible to scale insects. Prune to keep plants shapely and compact.

Similar-shaped species
Citrus limon will produce lemons of up to 3in in diameter.
Citrus sinensis is the only species which produces sweet fruit. Its stems have sharp spines.

ALUMINIUM PLANT
Pilea cadierei

The raised, silver leaf markings give the foliage of these attractive plants a quilted look. This effect is caused by pockets of air under the upper surface of the leaf. Group them with other attractively marked plants, or mass dwarf varieties together in a shallow bowl or in a bottle garden or terrarium.

Mini-climate 2 Warm, filtered sun.
Size Aluminium plants will reach a height of about 1ft in one year. A dwarf variety is available, which reaches a maximum height of about 6in.
Feeding Feed with standard liquid fertilizer every two weeks in spring and summer.
Potting Repot every spring using a mixture of two-thirds peat moss and one-third coarse sand or perlite. Once plants are in 3in pots topdress instead.

Similar-shaped species
Pilea spruceana has triangular, quilted, bronze-green leaves with a silver stripe down the middle.

FLOWERING MAPLE
Abutilon hybridum "Canary Bird"

Flowering maples are pretty, woody plants which can be trained when young. They have maplelike leaves from whose leaf-joints come the bell-shaped flowers. The flowers of the hybrids are red, pink, yellow or white. Flowering maples are long-lasting, making them suitable for use as feature plants, especially in front of a window.

Mini-climate 1 Warm, sunny.
Size Flowering maples may reach a height and spread of 3ft in three years. Pinch out growing tips to maintain bushy growth.
Feeding Feed with standard liquid fertilizer every two weeks in summer.
Potting Repot every spring using soil-based potting mixture. Once plants are in 10in pots topdress instead.
Special points Water more sparingly in winter and cut back any untidy stems in spring.

Similar-shaped species
Abutilon pictum "Thompsonii" has green and yellow variegated leaves and flowers which may be composed of one color, two colors or two shades of the same color.

Temperature 50°-60°F spring to autumn; 45°-50°F in winter · 50°-60°F · 60°-70°F
Light sunny · filtered sun · shady
Humidity low · moderate · high
Watering sparingly · moderately · plentifully
Care easy · fairly easy · challenging

LARGE-LEAVED UPRIGHT PLANTS

TI PLANT
Cordyline terminalis

These plants have large leaves patterned in red or green. The patterns of leaf coloring vary from plant to plant and ti plants look impressive when massed together to form a tapestry of color in a warm room containing richly colored fabrics.

Mini-climate 2 Warm, filtered sun.
Size Ti plants can grow to a height of 4ft with a spread of 1½ft. Small plants are offered for sale.
Feeding Feed with standard liquid fertilizer every two weeks from April to September.
Potting Repot every two years in spring using soil-based potting mixture. If you don't want to move an older plant into a larger pot topdress instead.
Special points Water more sparingly in winter. Clean leaves with a damp sponge.

RUBBER PLANT
Ficus elastica

The shiny, dark-green leaves are oval in shape with a pronounced point at their tip. The growth point is covered in a pink sheath for protection. Rubber plants have a strong shape and look best displayed as specimen plants in a modern setting.

Mini-climate 3 Warm, shady.
Size Rubber plants can grow up to 6ft in height. Plants of all sizes are offered for sale.
Feeding Feed with standard liquid fertilizer every two weeks in spring and summer.
Potting Repot in spring using soil-based potting mixture but only if the roots have completely filled the existing pot. If you don't want to move an older plant into a larger pot topdress instead.
Special points Clean older leaves regularly with a damp sponge. Do not clean young leaves.

Similar-shaped species
Ficus lyrata has huge puckered leaves which are shaped like a violin.

BELGIAN EVERGREEN
Dracaena sanderana

Also known as "ribbon plants", these are the most dainty of the dracaenas. They are slender, upright plants with narrow, cream-striped leaves. Because they rarely branch, three or four specimens should be planted together in a pot to create an interesting spiky mass of leaves.

Mini-climate 2 Warm, filtered sun.
Size Belgian evergreens are slow-growing but will reach a maximum height of 3ft. Small plants, usually three to a pot, are offered for sale.
Feeding Feed with standard liquid fertilizer every two weeks from mid-spring to early autumn.
Potting Repot every two or three years in spring using soil-based potting mixture. Once plants are in 4½-5in pots topdress instead.
Special points Water more sparingly in winter.

SPOTTED DUMB CANE
Dieffenbachia maculata

Spotted dumb canes are bold feature plants with handsome, variegated leaves. Older plants tend to lose their lower leaves giving a solitary plant a bizarre look; but several plants grouped together make a dramatic display in a modern setting.

Mini-climate 3 Warm, shady.
Size Spotted dumb canes will grow to a height of 5ft and a spread of 2ft. Plants of all sizes are offered for sale.
Feeding Feed with standard liquid fertilizer every two weeks from early spring to mid-autumn.
Potting Repot every spring using soil-based potting mixture in clay pots. Once plants are in 8in pots topdress instead.
Special points The sap is poisonous and can cause severe inflammation of the mouth.

Similar-shaped species
Dieffenbachia amoena has 1½ft long, pointed leaves which are dark green with herringbone markings in cream.
Dieffenbachia "Exotica" has 10in long dark-green leaves marked with white and pale green.

Upright plants 2

LARGE-LEAVED UPRIGHT PLANTS continued

CROTON
Codiaeum variegatum pictum

Crotons are striking, highly colored, tropical shrubs with many variations in leaf shape, size and color. Young leaves have a green color; reds, oranges and purples develop with age. Crotons naturally drop their lower leaves with age but will retain them longer in a humid atmosphere. Mass plants with different colored leaves for a vivid display.

Mini-climate 1 Warm, sunny.
Size Crotons rarely grow larger than 3ft tall, with a similar spread. Small and medium-sized plants are offered for sale.
Feeding Feed with standard liquid fertilizer every two weeks from spring to autumn.
Potting Repot every spring using soil-based potting mixture. When plants are in 8-10in pots topdress instead.
Special points Stand plants on trays filled with moist pebbles to increase humidity.

AFRICAN HEMP
Sparmannia africana

Also known as "indoor limes", these plants have large, apple-green leaves, covered in fine, white hairs. A plant blooming in a cool room can produce clusters of small, white flowers nearly all year round. African hemp plants look best displayed on their own as feature plants in both modern and traditional settings.

Mini-climate 4 Cool, sunny.
Size African hemps grow to about 5ft in height with a spread of 3ft wide in two years. Small plants are offered for sale.
Feeding Feed with standard liquid fertilizer every two weeks.
Potting Repot in spring using soil-based potting mixture but only if the roots have completely filled the existing pot. Once plants are in 12in pots topdress instead.
Special points Water more sparingly in winter.

SILVERED SPEAR
Aglaonema crispum "Silver Queen"

The beautiful foliage of these plants is green only at the margins and main veins; the rest of the leaf is silvery-white and cream. As plants age they lose some of their lower leaves and develop a short, trunklike stem. They are excellent as part of a bold, leafy arrangement, particularly if contrasted with dark-green foliage plants.

Mini-climate 2 Warm, filtered sun.
Size Silvered spears reach a maximum height of 3ft with a spread of about 2ft.
Feeding Feed with standard liquid fertilizer once a month from spring to autumn.
Potting Repot every spring using soil-based potting mixture. Once plants are in 6in pots topdress instead.

BIRD-OF-PARADISE
Strelitzia reginae

These plants have spectacular orange-and-blue crested flowers which emerge in succession over a period of several weeks from a beak-shaped bud. Birds-of-paradise are unusual specimen plants for a modern interior; a large-scale setting is best as leaves and flowers become very big.

Mini-climate 1 Warm, sunny.
Size Birds-of-paradise will grow to 3ft in height with a spread of 2ft. Young plants are offered for sale but will not flower until they are five years old.
Feeding Feed with standard liquid fertilizer every two weeks in spring and summer and once a month in autumn and winter.
Potting Repot every spring using soil-based potting mixture. Once plants are in 12in pots topdress instead.
Special points Clean leaves with a damp sponge.

Temperature 50°-60°F spring to autumn; 45°-50°F in winter / 50°-60°F / 60°-70°F
Light sunny / filtered sun / shady
Humidity low / moderate / high
Watering sparingly / moderately / plentifully
Care easy / fairly easy / challenging

CAST-IRON PLANT
Aspidistra elatior

As their name suggests, cast-iron plants will tolerate a certain amount of neglect. They were much used by the Victorians as specimen plants, but despite these associations, cast-iron plants can be used to great effect, either massed together or grouped with other, smaller plants. They are ideal plants for filling difficult, darker spaces.

Mini-climate 5 Cool, filtered sun.
Size Cast-iron plants have a maximum height and spread of 3ft. Small plants are offered for sale.
Feeding Feed with standard liquid fertilizer every two weeks in spring and summer.
Potting Repot every three years using soil-based potting mixture but only if the roots have completely filled the existing pot. If you don't want to move an older plant into a larger pot topdress instead.

TREE IVY
Fatshedera lizei

Also known as "aralia ivies", these plants have palmate, glossy-green leaves and can be displayed as upright feature plants, either alone or to give height to a group of smaller plants. They will also climb and can be trained, if tied to supports, to cover staircases and balconies and to frame windows.

Mini-climate 5 Cool, filtered sun.
Size Tree ivies can grow upright to a height of 3ft with a similar spread. If allowed to wander over a support their growth will be unlimited.
Feeding Feed with standard liquid fertilizer every two weeks.
Potting Repot every spring using two-thirds soil-based potting mixture and one-third peat-moss. If you don't want to move an older plant into a larger pot topdress instead.

PEACOCK PLANT
Calathea makoyana

The leaves of peacock plants look as if they have been hand painted with dark-green patterns. They look best in a mixed group of foliage plants. Smaller plants can be used in bottle gardens and larger terraria.

Mini-climate 3 Warm, shady.
Size Peacock plants can grow to a height of 3ft with a spread of about 2ft. Plants of all sizes are offered for sale.
Feeding Feed with standard liquid fertilizer every two weeks during spring and summer and once a month during autumn and winter.
Potting Repot every spring using a mixture of two-thirds soil-based potting mixture and one-third leaf mold or peat. Once plants are in 6in pots topdress instead.
Special points Stand plants on trays filled with moist pebbles to increase humidity.

COMPOUND-LEAVED UPRIGHT PLANTS

FALSE ARALIA
Dizygotheca elegantissima

Also known as "finger aralias", these plants are elegant, open shrubs made up of many narrow leaflets. Leaf color changes with age from bronze to a very deep green and the leaf texture becomes coarser. The dark tracery of the palmate leaves makes a delicate background to set off bolder foliage, or several plants can be grouped together to create a lacy mass of leaves.

Mini-climate 2 Warm, filtered sun.
Size False aralias reach 7ft in height with a spread of 2ft. Pinch out growing tips to encourage bushy growth. Plants of all sizes are offered for sale.
Feeding Feed with standard liquid fertilizer every two weeks in spring and summer.
Potting Repot every two years in spring using soil-based potting mixture. If you don't want to move an older plant into a larger pot topdress instead.
Special points Stand plants on trays filled with moist pebbles to increase humidity.

Upright plants 3

COMPOUND-LEAVED UPRIGHT PLANTS continued

NORFOLK ISLAND PINE
Araucaria heterophylla

Also known as "Christmas tree plants", these pines are at their best when four years old. Because of their starkness, they seldom look well mixed with other plants, but a most striking effect can be created by grouping several of these conifers together to give a Japanese look.

Mini-climate 5 Cool, filtered sun.
Size Norfolk Island pines are slow-growing: a ten-year old plant rarely exceeds 6ft in height and 4ft width.
Feeding Feed with standard liquid fertilizer every two weeks in spring and summer.
Potting Repot every two or three years in spring using soil-based potting mixture. Once plants are in 9-10in pots topdress instead.
Special points Water more sparingly during the winter rest period.

SILK OAK
Grevillea robusta

Silk oaks are treelike evergreen shrubs with finely divided, fernlike leaves. The leaves are bronze when they first appear, turning green later. They look good grouped with other plants and, when they are large enough, displayed as specimen plants.

Mini-climate 4 Cool, sunny.
Size Silk oaks are fast growing and will reach 5ft high in two or three years. Encourage bushy growth by pinching the main shoot when young. Young plants are offered for sale.
Feeding Feed with standard liquid fertilizer every two weeks during spring and summer.
Potting Repot every spring using lime-free soil-based potting mixture. If you don't want to move an older plant into a larger pot topdress instead.
Special points Water more sparingly in winter.

UMBRELLA PLANT
Cyperus alternifolius "Gracilis"

The radiating grasslike bracts of these plants resemble the spokes of an open umbrella. The tall stems are very brittle and should be handled with care. Umbrella plants have a Japanese look and suit stark modern interiors.

Mini-climate 2 Warm, filtered sun.
Size Umbrella plants will reach a height of 4ft given suitably wet conditions.
Feeding Feed with standard liquid fertilizer once every month.
Potting Repot in spring using soil-based potting mixture with added charcoal, but only if the roots have completely filled the existing pot. Ensure plants are repotted at the same soil level. If you don't want to move an older plant into a larger pot topdress instead.
Special points Stand permanently in a water-filled saucer to keep the roots saturated.

SPIKY-LEAVED UPRIGHT PLANTS

BOAT LILY
Rhoeo spathacea "Variegata"

These plants are also known as "Moses-in-the-cradle", referring to the boat-shaped cups which encase the small, white, three-petalled flowers. The long, rather stiff leaves are beautifully colored, having yellow and cream stripes on their upper surface and purple on their lower surface. Boat lilies are best displayed on their own so that the unusual flower-cups can be seen.

Mini-climate 2 Warm, filtered sun.
Size Boat lilies reach a maximum height of 1ft with a spread of 1½ft. Plants of this size are offered for sale. Maintain as an upright plant by pinching off basal shoots.
Feeding Feed with standard liquid fertilizer every two weeks in spring and summer.
Potting Repot every second year in spring using soil-based potting mixture. If you don't want to move an older plant into a larger pot topdress instead.

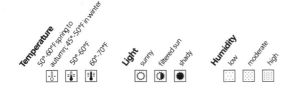

EUROPEAN FAN PALM
Chamaerops humilis

Also known as "dwarf fan palms", these handsome, low-growing palms have wide, fan-shaped fronds. These are made up of rigid, sword-shaped segments with split ends. There is no recognizable stem, except in very mature plants, the fronds being held upright on long leaf stalks. These are ornamental plants with an oriental look to them to be used as specimens or in groups depending on their size.

Mini-climate 2 Warm, filtered sun.
Size European fan palms are slow-growing, but will reach 5ft in height with a similar spread when mature. Plants of all sizes are offered for sale.
Feeding Feed with standard liquid fertilizer once a month in spring, summer and autumn.
Potting Repot every two years in spring using soil-based potting mixture. Once plants are in 12in pots topdress instead.
Special points Stand plants outside in a sheltered place in summer. Water more sparingly in winter.

MOTHER-IN-LAW'S TONGUE
Sansevieria trifasciata "Laurentii"

The upright leaves of this plant emerge in a cluster from an underground stem. The thick, leathery leaves are marbled with dark green and have golden bands along their margin. Display large plants as specimens or group them with other spiky-leaved plants in a modern setting.

Mini-climate 2 Warm, filtered sun.
Size The leaves of mother-in-law's tongues can grow to a height of about 3ft. Plants of all sizes are offered for sale.
Feeding Feed with half-strength standard liquid fertilizer once a month.
Potting Repot in spring or early summer, using a mixture of one-third coarse sand or perlite and two-thirds soil-based potting mixture, but only when a mass of roots appears on the surface. If you don't want to move an older plant into a larger pot topdress instead.
Special points Water more sparingly in winter.

RAINBOW PLANT
Dracaena marginata "Tricolor"

The name "rainbow plant" is derived from the leaf markings, which form stripes of green, cream and pink. In mature plants, the topknot of leaves emerges from the bare, woody stem, giving plants a palmlike look. Three or four specimens planted in the same pot make a good display in a modern setting.

Mini-climate 2 Warm, filtered sun.
Size Rainbow plants will grow to 5ft with a spread of 1½ft. Lower-growing plants are offered for sale, but there is more demand for older plants with bare stems.
Feeding Feed with standard liquid fertilizer every two weeks in spring and summer, and once a month in autumn and winter.
Potting . Repot every spring using soil-based potting mixture. If you don't want to move an older plant into a larger pot topdress instead.
Special points Water more sparingly in winter.

STICK YUCCA
Yucca elephantipes

These plants have a very distinctive appearance. Many are specially grown from logs which, when planted, produce roots and leaves. The leaves are long and narrow, and can appear in clumps at any point of the upright stem. Yuccas have a strong shape and should be displayed on their own, or with other spiky-leaved plants in a modern setting.

Mini-climate 1 Warm, sunny.
Size Yuccas up to 6½ft in height with a spread of 1½ft are offered for sale. The spread increases as more leaves are produced. Plants can also be bought which are virtually stemless; these are known as "tip yuccas".
Feeding Feed with standard liquid fertilizer once every month.
Potting Repot every spring using soil-based potting mixture. If you don't want to move an older plant into a larger pot topdress instead.
Special points Water more sparingly in winter.

Arching plants 1

The overall shape of the plants in this category is determined by the way the stems, leafstalks or fronds branch out in an arch from the base of the plant. Because of this, most of the arching plants take up a great deal of space when fully grown and are best displayed on their own. Indeed, the largest arching plants, with their strong architectural shapes, make striking additions to the modern interior. Also in this category are three plants, the ponytail, West Indian holly and weeping fig, whose leaves hang downwards to give a "weeping" effect.

There is a great variety of leaf shape and texture in this category, ranging from the smooth, lance-shaped leaves of the white sails to the deeply cut leaves of some philodendrons and the delicate leaflets of the ferns and palms.

The diversity of leaf shape among arching plants compensates for the lack of colorful foliage in the group, and some species, such as the wax plant and white sails, produce very attractive flowers.

The graceful lines of the Boston and hare's foot ferns are produced by the arching fronds and are best appreciated when viewed at eye-level, as is the flat-topped button fern: display them in an urn, a tall terracotta pot or hanging basket. Plants such as the bamboo palm, the Kentia palm and the coconut palm can grow to quite a size and older plants are dominant enough to become the focal point of a room. Arching plants are among the most elegant of plants and should ideally be displayed in a position where they can be seen from all angles.

SMALL-LEAVED ARCHING PLANTS

FUCHSIA BEGONIA
Begonia foliosa miniata

These delicate-looking begonias have small, oval leaves with a glossy texture. The leaves are borne on long, thin stems which begin to arch over as they get longer. Small, waxy, succulent-looking, shell-pink flowers appear in clusters between autumn and spring. The plants need some kind of support if they are to be seen to best effect. Display with green foliage groups in an informal setting.

They are attractive if allowed to trail from a hanging basket.

Mini-climate 1 Warm, sunny.
Size Fuchsia begonias can grow to about 3ft in height, with a spread of about 20in. Pinch out growing tips to maintain bushy growth. Small plants are offered for sale.
Feeding Feed with standard liquid fertilizer once every two weeks during the flowering period.
Potting Repot every spring using an equal-parts mixture of soil-based and peat-based potting mixture. If you don't want to move an older plant into a larger pot topdress instead.
Special points Water more sparingly in winter.

BUTTON FERN
Pellaea rotundifolia

These unusual-looking ferns have low, spreading fronds making them one of the few ferns with an almost horizontal outline. The pinnae of the fronds are also most unfernlike, consisting of leathery, button-shaped leaflets arranged in a row, one on either side of a stiff midrib. These leaflets weigh the fronds down to give an arching appearance. Button ferns make excellent infill plants to hide foreground pots in groups of plants. Display with plants of varying leaf texture in a modern setting for best effect. They can also be used in bottle gardens and terraria.

Mini-climate 3 Warm, shady.
Size The individual fronds of button ferns grow to a maximum of 1ft long, giving the plant a wide but very flat shape.
Feeding Feed with standard liquid fertilizer every two weeks.
Potting Repot in spring using fern potting mixture in a shallow pot, but only if the roots have completely filled the existing pot. If you don't want to move an older plant into a larger pot, prune the roots to curb growth.
Special points Button ferns can be placed outside in a sheltered shady spot in summer. Stand plants on trays filled with moist pebbles to increase humidity.

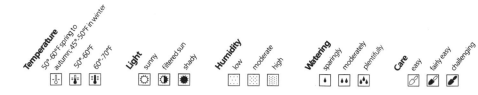

LARGE-LEAVED ARCHING PLANTS

FINGER PLANT
Philodendron bipinnatifidum·

The leaves of these plants are heart-shaped in outline with deeply cut edges. The leaves are borne on stout stalks radiating from a central stem and unlike most of the other philodendron species these plants do not climb. They make dramatic feature plants for a large room.

Mini-climate 3 Warm, shady.
Size Finger plants can reach a height and spread of about 3-6ft. Plants of all sizes are offered for sale.
Feeding Feed with standard liquid fertilizer every two weeks in spring and summer.
Potting Repot in spring using half soil-based potting mixture and half leaf mold, but only if the roots have completely filled the existing pot. Once plants are in 12in pots topdress instead.
Special points Destroy any scale insects you find.

WHITE SAILS
Spathiphyllum "Clevelandii"

The striking arumlike flower heads of the white sails are produced from May to August. Each flower lasts for six weeks or more, turning from white to an attractive pale green. Their elegant shape makes them ideal specimen plants for the modern interior.

Mini-climate 3 Warm, shady.
Size Mature white sails can reach a height and spread of 3ft. Plants in flower are offered for sale.
Feeding Feed with standard liquid fertilizer every two weeks from early spring to late summer.
Potting Repot every two years in spring using peat-based potting mixture. Once plants are in a 6-8in pot root prune instead.
Special points Stand plants on trays filled with moist pebbles to increase humidity.

COCONUT PALM
Cocos nucifera

These most striking looking plants grow directly from the nut which sits on top of the potting mixture. From the nut sprout the upright stalks which bear the once-divided, arching fronds. These fronds are heavily ribbed. The coconut palm makes a striking specimen plant for a stark modern interior.

Mini-climate 2 Warm, filtered sun.
Size Coconut palms can reach more than 5ft in height. Large plants are offered for sale.
Feeding Feed with half-strength liquid fertilizer every two weeks in spring and summer.
Potting Repotting is unnecessary.
Special points Coconut palms only last about two years in the home as they resent root disturbance.

COMPOUND-LEAVED ARCHING PLANTS

HARE'S FOOT FERN
Polypodium aureum "Mandaianum"

These plants derive their common name from the furry rhizome from which the fronds arise. The fronds are carried on long, arching stems and each bears up to ten silvery blue-green leaflets. Each leaflet has a ruffled edge. Since their color is so attractive, hare's foot ferns should be displayed as feature plants when they are large enough. Smaller plants mix well with other ferns.

Mini-climate 3 Warm, shady.
Size The fronds of the hare's foot fern can grow to about 2ft in length giving the plant a large spread. Plants of all sizes are offered for sale.
Feeding Feed with half-strength standard liquid fertilizer once a week from spring to autumn.
Potting Repot in spring using half soil-based potting mixture and half leaf mold in a shallow container, but only if the rhizomes have completely filled the existing pot. Once plants are in 8in pots root prune instead.
Special points Stand plants on trays filled with moist pebbles to increase humidity.

Arching plants 2

COMPOUND-LEAVED ARCHING PLANTS continued

KENTIA PALM
Howea belmoreana

These slender palms were great favorites in the 19th century, adding soft grace to large rooms. The arching fronds are borne on upright stems giving the plant an elegant look. Always specimen plants, Kentia palms can be difficult to place due to their large size but seem to thrive in a range of conditions found in the home.

Mini-climate 2 Warm, filtered sun.
Size Kentia palms can grow to 10ft with a spread of 8ft. Medium and large plants are offered for sale.
Feeding Feed with standard liquid fertilizer once a month from spring to autumn.
Potting Repot every second year in spring using soil-based potting mixture. Once plants are in 12in pots topdress instead.
Special points Clean leaves with a damp sponge.

Similar-shaped species
Howea forsterana is very similar and can only be told apart by the greater, flat-topped spread and wider gaps between the frond leaflets of this species.

DWARF COCONUT PALM
Microcoelum weddellianum

These compact palms have shiny fronds which are deeply divided into many threadlike leaflets arranged in a herringbone fashion. Although the fronds look feathery they are quite tough to the touch. Dwarf coconut palms have no true trunk; the fronds arise from a short, thickened base. They are not as arching as the larger types and are therefore suitable for use on table tops or shelves.

Mini-climate 2 Warm, filtered sun.
Size Dwarf coconut palms reach a maximum height and spread of 3ft. Small plants are offered for sale all year.
Feeding Feed with standard liquid fertilizer once a month in summer.
Potting Repot every two years in spring using soil-based potting mixture. If you don't want to move an older plant into a larger pot topdress instead.

BAMBOO PALM
Rhapis excelsa

Also known as "little lady palms", these plants have stems which cluster together giving the plant a crowded look. The leaves are composed of five to nine, often blunt-tipped segments giving an overall fan-shaped look. Each segment is deeply cut. Display the bamboo palm with other dark-green foliage plants. Older plants lose their lower leaves making them suitable for displaying on their own.

Mini-climate 2 Warm, filtered sun.
Size Bamboo palms are slow-growing taking several years to reach a height of 5-10ft tall with a similar spread. Medium and large plants are offered for sale.
Feeding Feed with standard liquid fertilizer once a month during the active growing period.
Potting Repot every second year in spring using soil-based potting mixture. Once plants are in 12in pots topdress instead.

BOSTON FERN
Nephrolepis exaltata "Bostoniensis"

These lush but graceful ferns have swordlike fronds which are available in several forms: some with crested fronds, others with very finely divided leaf sections. Boston ferns make elegant specimen plants, used either on a pedestal or in a hanging basket, and suit almost any type of setting.

Mini-climate 3 Warm, shady.
Size Boston ferns have fronds that are often 3ft long and can grow to 6ft. Plants of all sizes are offered for sale.
Feeding Feed with standard liquid fertilizer every two weeks when actively growing, otherwise feed once a month.
Potting Repot in spring using fern potting mixture but only if the roots have completely filled the existing pot. If you don't want to move an older plant into a larger pot topdress instead. Or divide it.
Special points Stand plants on trays filled with moist pebbles to increase humidity.

Similar-shaped species
Nephrolepis cordifolia is smaller; its fronds will grow up to 2ft long.

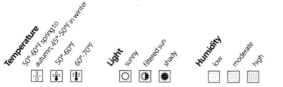

PARLOR PALM
Chamaedorea elegans "Bella"

These palms have dainty, deeply divided fronds arching from the central stem. The fronds are fresh green when young and darken with age. Mature plants produce small sprays of tiny, yellow, beadlike flowers. Parlor palms thrive in the conditions of a bathroom, and small plants add interest to bottle gardens and terraria.

Mini-climate 2 Warm, filtered sun.
Size Parlor palms are dwarf palms reaching a height of about 3ft after several years, with a spread of 1½ft. Young plants are offered for sale.
Feeding Feed with standard liquid fertilizer once a month from spring to autumn.
Potting Repot in spring using soil-based potting mixture but only if the roots have completely filled the existing pot. Once plants are in 6-8in pots topdress instead.
Special points Water more sparingly in winter.

Similar-shaped species
Chamaedorea erumpens forms a clump of slender stems, knotted at intervals like bamboo and with sections of bare stem. They can grow to about 6-8ft in height.

WEEPING ARCHING PLANTS

WEST INDIAN HOLLY
Leea coccinea

These plants have deep-green, holly-shaped leaves which are often tinged with a coppery-red. The plant has a very open appearance as the leaves are twice divided. West Indian hollies can be used as specimen plants or as a foil for low-growing foliage plants.

Mini-climate 2 Warm, filtered sun.
Size West Indian hollies reach a maximum height of about 5ft with a similar spread. Plants of about 1ft tall with a similar spread are offered for sale.
Feeding Feed with standard liquid fertilizer every two weeks from spring to autumn.
Potting Repot every spring using soil-based potting mixture. If you don't want to move an older plant into a larger pot topdress instead.
Special points Water more sparingly in winter.

WEEPING FIG
Ficus benjamina

These plants are the most elegant of the ornamental figs with their graceful, gray-barked arching stems bearing the dangling, pointed leaves. The arrangement of the leaves gives the plant an open appearance, good for both modern and period interiors.

Mini-climate 3 Warm, shady.
Size Weeping figs have a maximum height of 5ft with a spread of about 4ft if given enough room. Medium-sized and large plants are offered for sale.
Feeding Feed with standard liquid fertilizer every two weeks in spring and summer.
Potting Repot in spring using a soil-based potting mixture but only if the roots have completely filled the existing pot. If you don't want to move an older plant into a larger pot topdress instead.
Special points Water more sparingly in winter.

PONYTAIL
Beaucarnea recurvata

These are most bizarre-looking plants, having a ponytail-like tuft of narrow, green leaves sprouting from the top of a fat or long, woody stem. The swollen base adds to the unusual appearance of the plant. Ponytails are ideal plants for displaying in a modern interior and will thrive in any centrally heated room.

Mini-climate 2 Warm, filtered sun.
Size Ponytails reach a maximum height of 5ft with a spread of 2ft. Small and medium-sized plants are offered for sale.
Feeding Feed with standard liquid fertilizer every month during summer.
Potting Repot every three or four years in spring using soil-based potting mixture. Ponytails thrive in small pots.
Special points Can easily be killed by overwatering.

Rosette-shaped plants 1

This category is made up of plants whose leaves radiate from a central growing point and overlap each other, forming a circular cluster of leaf bases, usually at potting mixture level. Plants can be small and low-growing, or tall with large leaves: the shape of the cluster varies from the flat-leaved rosette of low-growing plants, such as African violets and earth stars, to the tall, arching rosette of the bird's nest fern and the blue-flowered torch. Another variation is the spiky-leaved rosette formed by the variegated pineapple plant and the scarlet star. These plants look good displayed on their own as they have such strong shapes. Flat-leaved rosette-shaped plants should be massed and placed where they can be seen from above.

Many of the plants in this category are from the brome-liad family and originate from tropical America. They are striking, exotic-looking plants which often have bold and unusual flower spikes, or leaves which become suffused with strong color prior to, and during, the flowering period. The leaves of many bromeliads, such as the urn plant and the bird's nest bromeliad, form a cup-shaped central reservoir which should be kept topped with fresh water if the plant is to remain in good condition.

Many bromeliads are epiphytic; in their native tropical environment they grow on trees—using them only as a means of support, not as a source of nutrients. An effective way to display them, therefore, is on a natural-looking support such as a dried branch covered in moist sphagnum moss, or attach them to a large piece of cork or bark.

ARCHING ROSETTE-SHAPED PLANTS

URN PLANT
Aechmea fasciata

When three or four years old, these plants produce a drumstick-shaped inflorescence which rises from the center of the rosette. This flower head comprises many spiny, pink bracts through which peep short-lived, pale-blue flowers. The head remains attractive for about six months. The leathery leaves are marked with white cross-banding on a gray-green background. Display large plants as specimens, or grow small plants on a dried branch covered with sphagnum moss.

Mini-climate 1 Warm, sunny.
Size The leaves of urn plants reach 2ft long and the flower spikes grow 6in above the leaves. Small plants grown from offsets and mature plants are offered for sale.
Feeding Feed with half-strength standard liquid fertilizer once a month in spring and summer. Apply feed to the center of the rosette as well as the roots.
Potting Repot in spring using bromeliad potting mixture but only if the roots have completely filled the existing pot. Once plants are in 6in pots topdress instead.
Special points Keep the center of the rosette filled with fresh water. Change the water once a month.

FLAMING SWORD
Vriesea splendens

These bromeliads have exotically marked leaves; they are shiny green banded with deep purple. The leaves form an upright vase, from the center of which a bright-red spike of bracts emerges when the plants are several years old. Small, yellow flowers poke through the red bracts. Several plants massed make a spectacular display; alternatively, include the flaming sword with strong foliage plants or use small specimens on a dried branch covered with sphagnum moss.

Mini-climate 2 Warm, filtered sun.
Size Flaming swords can reach a height and spread of about 1½ft. The flower spike can reach 2ft in height. Plants of all sizes are offered for sale.
Feeding Feed with half-strength standard liquid fertilizer once a month. Ensure the feed gets on the leaves, roots and the central cup.
Potting Repot in spring using bromeliad potting mixture but only if the roots have completely filled the existing pot. Once plants are in 6in pots topdress instead.
Special points Keep the center of the rosette filled with fresh water except when the flower bud first appears. Change the water once a month.

Similar-shaped species
Vriesea fenestralis is a little larger with paler green leaves covered in brown markings.
Vriesea psittacina has shorter leaves which are plain green with mauve shading towards the center of the rosette.
Vriesea saundersii has a squat rosette of gray-green leaves with a dull rose-pink underside and a yellow flower spike.

Temperature 50°-60°F spring to autumn; 45°-50°F in winter | 50°-60°F | 60°-70°F

Light sunny | filtered sun | shady

Humidity low | moderate | high

Watering sparingly | moderately | plentifully

Care easy | fairly easy | challenging

QUEEN'S TEARS
Billbergia nutans

These plants have tough leaves with toothed edges. There may be many plants in the same pot, as production of offsets is prolific. During the short flowering season in May and June, the foliage is interspersed with trailing, bright-pink bracts which are very attractive. These bracts open to display the small yellow, green and purple flowers. Queen's tears are best displayed at eye-level as feature plants.

Mini-climate 1 Warm, sunny.
Size The leaves of queen's tears reach about 2ft in length. Spread depends on the number of offsets produced. Small plants are offered for sale.
Feeding Feed with standard liquid fertilizer once every two weeks during spring and summer.
Potting Repot every spring using bromeliad potting mixture. Once plants are in 6in pots topdress instead.
Special points The rosette of leaves should be cut away at the base after flowering to allow the offsets around it to develop.

BLUE-FLOWERED TORCH
Tillandsia cyanea

These are medium-sized bromeliads with stiff, arching, grassy leaves arranged in a loose rosette. When mature, the plants produce a fleshy spear-shaped flower head, made up of pinky-green overlapping bracts. This unusual flower head is flat and wide and will remain decorative for some months. Three-petalled, bright violet-blue flowers appear in succession from between the bracts. Display blue-flowered torches as feature plants.

Mini-climate 1 Warm, sunny.
Size The leaves of blue-flowered torches reach about 1ft in length. Offsets give the plant a large spread. Small plants are offered for sale.
Feeding Feed with half-strength standard liquid fertilizer once a month. This can be applied to the leaves as a foliar feed.
Potting Repot every spring using bromeliad potting mixture. Once plants are in 4in pots topdress instead.
Special points Place in a sheltered part of the garden in summer to encourage flowering.

BIRD'S NEST FERN
Asplenium nidus

These plants have shiny, apple-green fronds arranged in an upward-spreading rosette at whose base is a circle of young leaf fronds. These slowly unroll from the fibrous core of the plant. Large bird's nest ferns are too bold in shape to display with other ferns and look best either arranged on their own, or included in a mixed group of large-leaved foliage plants.

Mini-climate 3 Warm, shady.
Size The fronds of bird's nest ferns can reach 1 ½ ft long. Young plants are offered for sale.
Feeding Feed with standard liquid fertilizer once a month.
Potting Repot in spring using fern potting mixture but only when a mass of roots appears on the surface of the potting mixture. If you don't want to move an older plant into a larger pot root prune instead.
Special points Stand plants on trays filled with moist pebbles to increase humidity.

SPIKY-LEAVED ROSETTE-SHAPED PLANTS

VEITCH SCREW PINE
Pandanus veitchii

These plants get their name from the way the leaf bases spiral round the stem but, despite their name, they are unrelated to the pine family. The long, arching leaves are a rich dark green edged in cream and have a fine-toothed edge which can rasp the skin. Use these handsome specimens in a modern setting for a dramatic effect.

Mini-climate 1 Warm, sunny.
Size Screw pines can reach a height and spread of about 3ft. Plants of all sizes are offered for sale.
Feeding Feed with standard liquid fertilizer every two weeks during spring and summer and once a month during autumn and winter.
Potting Repot every spring using soil-based potting mixture. If you don't want to move an older plant into a larger pot topdress instead.
Special points Thick, stiltlike aerial roots form after two years and lift the plant base away from the potting mixture. These roots should be encouraged to grow into the potting mixture for improved anchorage.

Rosette-shaped plants 2

SPIKY-LEAVED ROSETTE-SHAPED PLANTS continued

VARIEGATED PINEAPPLE
Ananas comosus "Variegatus"

These plants are prized for their stiff, spiny leaves, which curve gracefully outward, giving them a symmetrical shape. When five or six years old they produce striking pink flower heads, followed by a pink fruit, which is unlikely to ripen and be edible. Large plants displayed in an urn suit formal interiors.

Mini-climate 1 Warm, sunny.
Size Variegated pineapple plants grow to a maximum height of about 3ft with a spread of up to 6ft. Fruiting plants are offered for sale.
Feeding Feed with standard liquid fertilizer every two weeks during spring and summer.
Potting Repot in spring every two years using bromeliad potting mixture. Once plants are in 6-8in pots topdress instead.
Special points In direct sunlight, a rich-pink hue enhances the variegation of the leaves.

Similar-shaped species
Ananas bracteatus striatus is the variegated form of the wild pineapple and has boldly striped leaves which become pink if grown in bright light.
Ananas nanus is much smaller with plain, dark-green leaves and produces small, inedible fruits. It can be bought in fruit in a 4in pot.

FLAT-LEAVED ROSETTE-SHAPED PLANTS

SCARLET STAR
Guzmania lingulata

These winter-flowering bromeliads have centers made up of bright-orange or scarlet bracts filled with small, yellow flowers. The arching leaves are soft, glossy and bright-green in color. These are strongly colored plants which suit bold, modern interiors. Mass several plants in a shallow glass bowl or display in pairs for a symmetrical arrangement.

Mini-climate 2 Warm, filtered sun.
Size The scarlet star reaches about 10in in height and has a spread of up to 1ft.
Feeding Feed with half-strength standard liquid fertilizer once a month. Ensure the feed gets onto the leaves and roots and into the central cup.
Potting Repot in spring using bromeliad potting mixture but only if the roots have filled the existing pot.
Special points Empty the central cup and fill with fresh water every month.

EARTH STAR PLANT
Cryptanthus bivittatus

These small plants have some of the most beautifully colored foliage found in the bromeliads. The sharply pointed leaves have two distinctive cream stripes running along their length, which turn pink or even a strong red if placed in the direct sun. Clusters of small white flowers are hidden by the leaves. These stemless plants can be massed in shallow bowls or terraria.

Mini-climate 1 Warm, sunny.
Size Earth stars are slow-growing and will reach 6-8in across by the time they flower.
Feeding Feed occasionally by splashing with half-strength standard liquid fertilizer.
Potting Repotting is hardly ever necessary.
Special points Some time after flowering has finished cut away the parent plant to allow the offsets around its base to develop.

BLUSHING BROMELIAD
Neoregelia carolinae "Tricolor"

These flat-topped bromeliads have striking foliage; young leaves are a soft green striped with ivory white. As the plants mature the leaves become suffused with pink, and just before flowering the center becomes bright red. Display within a group of bold foliage plants for best effect.

Mini-climate 2 Warm, filtered sun.
Size Mature blushing bromeliads grow to about 8in in height with a spread of about 1½ft.
Feeding Feed with half-strength standard liquid fertilizer once a month. Apply on to the leaves, into the cup and on to the potting mixture.
Potting Repot in spring using bromeliad potting mixture but only if the roots have completely filled the existing pot. Once plants are in 5in pots topdress instead.

Temperature 50°–60°F spring to autumn; 45°–50°F in winter 50°–60°F 60°–70°F

Light sunny filtered sun shady

Humidity low moderate high

Watering sparingly moderately plentifully

Care easy fairly easy challenging

AFRICAN VIOLET
Saintpaulia sp. and hybrids

These plants have an impressive range of flower colors from white and pink to purple, magenta and violet. The flowers are held in clusters above the rosette of furry leaves. With this range of color African violets can be used in both modern and period interiors. One of the most effective ways to display them is massed in a shallow bowl. Miniature varieties can be displayed in a terrarium.

Mini-climate 2 Warm, filtered sun.
Size African violets will form a flat rosette of about 8in diameter. Flowering plants are available all year. Named varieties run into thousands.
Feeding Feed with specially prepared African violet liquid fertilizer, used at one-quarter strength, at each watering throughout the year.
Potting Repot only when the roots have completely filled the existing pot. Use a mixture of equal parts peat moss, perlite and vermiculite in half pots or shallow pans.
Special points Avoid wetting the hairy leaves when watering and feeding as they will become stained.

BIRD'S NEST BROMELIAD
Nidularium innocentii

These plants form low, spreading rosettes of straplike, dark-green leaves. The center of the rosette becomes very dark red, sometimes almost black, at flowering time. The small, white flowers form a clump in the center of the water-filled vase and last only a short time, although the colored center remains attractive for some months. Bird's nest bromeliads can be grouped with other bold-leaved plants.

Mini-climate 2 Warm, filtered sun.
Size Bird's nest bromeliads grow to a height of about 8in with a spread of 16in. Three or four year old plants about to flower are offered for sale.
Feeding Feed with half-strength standard liquid fertilizer once a month. Apply on to the leaves, into the cup and on to the potting mixture.
Potting Repot in spring using bromeliad potting mixture but only if the roots have completely filled the existing pot. Once plants are in 4in pots topdress instead.
Special points Some time after flowering has finished cut away the parent plant to allow the offsets around its base to develop.

Similar-shaped species
Nidularium fulgens is of similar size with dark-spotted, spiky-edged leaves.

CAPE PRIMROSE
Streptocarpus "John Innes" hybrids

These small plants have primrose-like leaves and large, tubular flowers on long stalks. Flowers may be white, pink, red, mauve or blue. Attractive twisted seed pods appear but these are best cut off to encourage more flowers. These plants can be treated as annuals and discarded when flowering has finished. Like primroses and African violets, Cape primroses should be massed together in a shallow bowl placed on a low table.

Mini-climate 5 Cool, filtered sun.
Size Cape primroses grow to about 1ft in height with a spread of 1½ft. Small plants in bud are offered for sale.
Feeding Feed with half-strength, high-phosphate liquid fertilizer every two weeks from early spring to late autumn.
Potting Repot every spring using an equal-parts mixture of sphagnum peat moss, coarse grade perlite and vermiculite. Add half a tablespoon of limestone chips to every cup of mixture. Once plants are in 6in pots root prune instead.

GLOXINIA
Sinningia speciosa hybrids

The large, downy leaves have a bold pattern of veins on them but are eclipsed by the large, showy flowers. They are borne in a cluster on top of the rosette of leaves. Trumpet-shaped with frilled edges they can be white, pink, red or purple, and are often margined in white. Although gloxinias can be treated as annuals they have a tuber which can be dried off in autumn and repotted in spring. Gloxinias are best in period rooms, displayed either singly or in a group.

Mini-climate 2 Warm, filtered sun.
Size Gloxinias can attain a height and spread of about 1ft. Plants in bud are offered for sale.
Feeding Feed with high-phosphate liquid fertilizer once a month during the flowering period.
Potting Repot the tubers in spring using equal parts of peat-based potting mixture, vermiculite and perlite. Repotting once the plant is flowering is unnecessary.

Similar-shaped species
Sinningia pusilla is very small, no higher than 1in or so, but has relatively large, pale-lavender flowers. Many attractive named varieties exist.

Bushy plants 1

Bushy plants are difficult to describe precisely as this category covers a vast range of flowering and foliage plants. Their common feature is a tendency to grow outwards as much as they grow upwards. This gives them a spread nearly equal to their height, and is why they are often displayed on their own, or in twos, rather than in groups with different plants—although some of the more upright bushy plants can make good foils for trailing plants. Many of the flowering bushy plants look good when several of the same species are massed in a shallow bowl. A large number of the flowering bushy plants are annuals, bought for their display of flowers and then discarded when flowering has finished. Many kinds branch naturally, regularly producing side shoots, others branch freely only if their growing tips are regularly pinched out. Form and size range from the small, low-growing peperomias and hypoestes to the tall and shrubby spotted laurel. Leaf texture, shape, size and color are also well represented; from the smooth, fleshy leaves of the florist's cyclamen to the large and pimpled leaves of the painted-leaf begonia. Colorful leaves are found on plants such as the painted nettle, polka-dot plant, and angel wings. Bushy plants are well suited to period décor or places where an informal atmosphere prevails.

SMALL-LEAVED BUSHY PLANTS

AMETHYST VIOLET
Browallia speciosa

Also known as "bush violets", these are showy plants with violet-blue or white flowers that appear in early summer to autumn, depending on climate and when the seeds were started. They are usually treated as annuals and discarded when flowering has finished. Several strains are available, including the "Troll" and "Bells" series. The stems tend to droop so display plants at eye level in hanging baskets or massed on a low table.

Mini-climate 1 Warm, filtered sun.
Size Amethyst violets grow to 10-12in tall with a similar spread. Pinch out growing tips to encourage bushy growth. Seedlings can be bought in spring, or grow your own from seeds sown early indoors under fluorescent tubes.
Feeding Feed with standard liquid fertilizer every two weeks.
Potting Repotting is unnecessary.
Special points Destroy any greenfly you may find.

Similar-shaped species
Browallia viscosa is only half the size of *B.speciosa*, with smaller leaves and flowers. The leaves are slightly sticky.

ELATIOR BEGONIA
Begonia "Elatior" hybrids

These begonias flower for most of the year. The large, roselike flowers range in color from deep red, through pink, to yellow and white. They are best treated as annuals and discarded when flowering has finished. The foliage is usually pale green but plants with deep-red foliage are sometimes available. As their flowers are quite large these begonias can be displayed as specimen plants or grouped in a shallow pan. Elatior begonias do best in light, well-ventilated rooms.

Mini-climate 2 Warm, filtered sun.
Size "Elatior" begonias are usually erect with a maximum height and spread of 14-16in. Small bushy plants are offered for sale from mid-spring to early autumn.
Feeding Feed with standard liquid fertilizer every two weeks in spring and summer.
Potting Repot two or three times during summer and autumn using a mixture of half soil-based potting mixture and half leaf mold or coarse peat moss. If you don't want to move an older plant into a larger pot topdress instead.
Special points Protect from powdery mildew by supplying adequate ventilation.

Similar-shaped species
Begonia tuberhybrida has large, double flowers of red, pink, white or yellow.

WAX BEGONIA
Begonia semperflorens-cultorum

These are small plants grown for their profusion of flowers. Single- and double-flowered varieties are available. The white, pink or red flowers begin blooming in spring and continue well into the winter. They are best treated as annuals and discarded when flowering has finished. They make excellent display plants when grouped in shallow containers or mixed with colorful foliage plants. These begonias do best in light, well-ventilated rooms.

Mini-climate 1 Warm, sunny.
Size Wax begonias never reach more than 1ft in height when fully grown. They are offered for sale in spring as seedlings and for the rest of the year as mature plants.
Feeding Feed with standard liquid fertilizer every two weeks in spring and summer.
Potting Repot as needed, perhaps two or three times during summer and autumn, using a mixture of half soil-based potting mixture and half leaf mold or coarse peat moss. If you don't want to move an older plant into a larger pot top-dress instead.
Special points Protect from powdery mildew by supplying adequate ventilation.

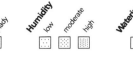

Temperature 50°–60°F spring to autumn, 45°–50°F in winter | 50°–60°F | 60°–70°F **Light** sunny | filtered sun | shady **Humidity** low | moderate | high **Watering** sparingly | moderately | plentifully **Care** easy | fairly easy | challenging

LEMON GERANIUM
Pelargonium crispum "Variegatum"

These geraniums are grown for their aromatic leaves rather than the flowers they produce. The foliage is pale green with a cream-colored wavy edge, and plants can be trained to many shapes by appropriate pinching out of the growing tips. Place in a position where the leaves will be brushed against for maximum aromatic effect. Geraniums have a pretty, "cottage" look and suit period rooms which are not too formal.

Mini-climate 4 Cool, sunny.
Size Lemon geraniums can grow to 2-3ft tall or be kept small and bushy. Small rooted plants are offered for sale.
Feeding Feed with half-strength standard liquid fertilizer twice in summer.
Potting Repot in spring using soil-based potting mixture on top of a small layer of rough drainage material, but only if the roots have completely filled the existing pot.
Special points Do not overwater in winter as plants become susceptible to black stem rot.

PAINTED NETTLE
Coleus blumei

These plants have soft-textured leaves in a range of vivid colors, from red and bronze to cream and purple, some incorporating three or more colors. Although the serrated leaves closely resemble those of the stinging nettle, the two plants are not related. Painted nettles are best treated as annuals and discarded after one year. Their brightly patterned foliage is suited to period rooms containing richly colored fabrics.

Mini-climate 1 Warm, sunny.
Size Painted nettles will grow to a height of 18in in one year with a similar spread. Pinch out growing tips to encourage bushy growth.
Feeding Feed with standard liquid fertilizer every two weeks in spring and summer, and once a month during autumn and winter.
Potting Repot every two months using soil-based potting mixture. If you don't want to move an older plant into a larger pot topdress instead.
Special points Leaf color is stronger if plants are placed in a sunny position.

EGYPTIAN STAR CLUSTER
Pentas lanceolata

These attractive plants are winter-flowering shrubs, although they may flower at any time of year. They have lance-shaped, hairy leaves and clusters of tiny, star-shaped flowers which can be mauve, white or pink in color. The almost flat-topped flower heads can be nearly 4in across. Egyptian star clusters look best when several plants are massed in an informal room.

Mini-climate 1 Warm, sunny.
Size Egyptian star clusters reach between 1ft and 1½ft in height. Pinch out growing tips to encourage bushy growth. Small plants are offered for sale.
Feeding Feed with standard liquid fertilizer every two weeks during the flowering period.
Potting Repot every spring using soil-based potting mixture. If you don't want to move an older plant into a larger pot topdress instead.
Special points Water more sparingly in winter.

IMPATIENS
Impatiens wallerana hybrids

The flower color of these ubiquitous plants ranges from white, through pink, to red; some flowers are striped with another color. The foliage and thick, succulent stems also vary in color from pale green to bronze. Impatiens will begin flowering when only six weeks old and continue throughout the summer. They are best treated as annuals and discarded when flowering has finished. These plants look particularly attractive if grouped in a hanging basket or window-box.

Mini-climate 1 Warm, sunny.
Size Impatiens are fast-growing, some hybrids reaching a maximum height of 14in. Pinch out growing tips to encourage bushy growth. Seedlings and small and medium-sized plants are offered for sale, or start seeds indoors.
Feeding Feed with standard liquid fertilizer every two weeks in spring and summer.
Potting Repot every spring using soil-based potting mixture but only if the roots have completely filled the existing pot. Once the plants are in 5in pots topdress instead.

Bushy plants 2

SMALL-LEAVED BUSHY PLANTS continued

CHINESE HIBISCUS
Hibiscus rosa-sinensis

Large, funnel-shaped flowers and glossy, dark-green leaves make Chinese hibiscuses spectacular plants. Flowers can be red, pink, white, yellow or orange and appear singly, usually in spring and summer. Use in a bright, sunny setting for an oriental look, either individually or by grouping several plants of different colors together.

Mini-climate 1 Warm, sunny.
Size Chinese hibiscuses are fast-growing, quickly reaching 5ft in height. Plants with opening buds are usually offered for sale in spring.
Feeding Feed with high-potash liquid fertilizer every two weeks in spring and summer, and once a month in autumn and winter. If flowers are not produced freely, increase the frequency of feeding (not the strength of the fertilizer).
Potting Repot every spring using soil-based potting mixture. If you don't want to move an older plant into a larger pot topdress instead.
Special points Water more sparingly in winter.

GERMAN VIOLET
Exacum affine

Also known as "Persian violets", these are small, bushy plants with fragrant blue flowers with yellow eyes and shiny, olive-green leaves. They bloom in summer and the flowers can last for up to two months. They are best treated as annuals and discarded when flowering has finished. To display German violets, mass them in a large bowl, as they make an eye-catching show in any setting—traditional or modern.

Mini-climate 2 Warm, filtered sun.
Size German violets will quickly grow stems up to 1ft long. Young plants are rarely available so grow your own from seeds sown early indoors.
Feeding Feed with standard liquid fertilizer every two weeks while the plant is in flower.
Potting Repot using soil-based potting mixture but only if the plant was bought in a very small pot. Further repotting is unnecessary.
Special points Stand plants on trays filled with moist pebbles to maintain high humidity.

REGAL GERANIUM
Pelargonium domesticum hybrids

These geraniums have large flower heads that range in color from white to red, many are bicolored or tricolored. The flowering season is short, lasting only from spring to midsummer, but the showiness of the flowers compensates for this. Very much at home in indoor window-boxes, they look equally good as specimen plants.

Mini-climate 4 Cool, sunny.
Size Regal geraniums can be grown as single-stemmed plants of up to 2ft tall, or as small bushy shrubs. Plants of all sizes are offered for sale.
Feeding Feed occasionally with standard liquid fertilizer during spring and summer.
Potting Repot every spring using a soil-based potting mixture. Once plants are in 6in pots topdress instead.
Special points Cut off faded flower heads to encourage new growth.

Similar-shaped species
Pelargonium hortorum has ball-like clusters of flowers almost all year round.

PRAYER PLANT
Maranta leuconeura erythroneura

Prayer plants, also known as "red herringbone plants", are so-called because of the way pairs of leaves close together at night. They are remarkable for their beautiful leaves marked with deep-red, raised veins. The red midrib is surrounded by a pale-green stripe on the olive-green leaf. Prayer plants are amongst the showiest of plants and should be displayed in a prominent position. They can also be trained to grow up short, moss-covered poles.

Mini-climate 3 Warm, shady.
Size Prayer plants will grow to a maximum of 6-12in tall with a 16in spread. Small plants are offered for sale.
Feeding Feed with standard liquid fertilizer every two weeks during spring, summer and autumn.
Potting Repot every spring using soil-based potting mixture in half-pots or other shallow containers. If you don't want to move an older plant into a larger pot topdress instead.

Temperature			Light			Humidity			Watering			Care		
50°-60°F spring to autumn, 45°-50°F in winter	50°-60°F	60°-70°F	sunny	filtered sun	shady	low	moderate	high	sparingly	moderately	plentifully	easy	fairly easy	challenging

CINERARIA
Senecio hybridus

Cinerarias have large, daisy-shaped flowers clustered in the center of the fleshy leaves. The flowers can be of orange, red, magenta, pink, blue or purple, often with a circle of white surrounding the central disc. The leaves are furry to touch and are often tinged with blue on their undersides. Cinerarias are best treated as annuals and discarded when flowering has finished. A bold display can be made with several cinerarias of the same color massed in a china dish or basket. They suit both traditional and modern rooms.

Mini-climate 4 Cool, sunny.
Size Budding cineraria plants up to 1ft tall and of similar spread are offered for sale throughout winter and spring.
Feeding Feeding is not required for these temporary pot plants.
Potting Repotting is unnecessary.
Special points To keep plants in a decorative state for as long as possible, ensure that the potting mixture does not dry out too much. Water is easily lost through the large leaves and the plant will collapse if the roots dry out. Destroy any aphids or whitefly you may find.

POINSETTIA
Euphorbia pulcherrima

With their flamboyant red, pink or creamy-white bracts, poinsettias are welcome at Christmastime. The bracts remain decorative for two months. After this they should be cut hard back and kept for their foliage alone, as it is not easy to get these plants to bloom for a second year. The poinsettia is essentially a specimen plant; the common red form is particularly striking, but can look good when mixed with dark-green foliage plants.

Mini-climate 1 Warm, sunny.
Size Poinsettias are available in many sizes, ranging from 1 to 5ft. They are offered for sale in winter.
Feeding Feed with standard liquid fertilizer once every month.
Potting Repotting of first year plants is unnecessary. If keeping the plant for a second year, repot in the same pot with fresh soil-based potting mixture.
Special points Poinsettias have a sap which can cause irritation of the skin in some people.

POLKA-DOT PLANT
Hypoestes phyllostachya

These are pretty plants with unusual foliage. The leaves, which range from olive-green to very dark green, are spotted with pale-pink dots. They are best treated as annuals and discarded after one year. New forms, as they are quite small, look more dramatic if several plants are grouped together, either in separate pots or planted in a shallow pan.

Mini-climate 2 Warm, filtered sun.
Size Polka-dot plants can grow quite tall but will become straggly, so it is advisable to limit growth to 1ft tall by pinching out the growing tips. Small, bushy plants of 3-5in tall are offered for sale.
Feeding Feed with standard liquid fertilizer every two weeks from early summer to mid-autumn.
Potting Repot in spring but only if the roots have completely filled the existing pot. Once plants are in 5in pots topdress instead.
Special points Spray leaves occasionally with tepid water to discourage red spider mites.

AZALEA
Rhododendron simsii

Azaleas produce clusters of brightly colored flowers atop a mass of shiny, green leaves. Flower color ranges from white to magenta, including almost every shade of red and pink. Some flowers are bicolored. They are best treated as annuals and discarded when flowering has finished. Mass azaleas in a shallow bowl and place in a prominent position in a hallway or other cool place.

Mini-climate 5 Cool, filtered sun.
Size Azaleas vary in size according to age and variety. Budding plants are offered for sale in winter and spring. After flowering, trim back new growth to maintain bushiness.
Feeding Feed with standard liquid fertilizer once every two weeks from spring to autumn.
Potting Repot as necessary using one part soil-based potting mixture, two parts peat moss, and one part coarse sand.
Special points To keep plants in a decorative state for as long as possible, keep the potting mixture permanently moist and display in a cool place.

Bushy plants 3

SMALL-LEAVED BUSHY PLANTS continued

FLORIST'S CYCLAMEN
Cyclamen persicum hybrids

Florist's cyclamens flower in late autumn, winter and early spring. Many varieties are available, with the color of the swept-back flowers ranging from white, through red, to purple. Some varieties have frilled or perfumed flowers. Although usually treated as an annual, if the tubers are dried off in the late spring and rested during the summer months, cyclamens can last for many years. Cyclamens do not mix well with other plants. They are ideal for colorful displays in entrance halls or period rooms where conditions are not excessively hot.

Mini-climate 5 Cool, filtered sun.
Size Cyclamens rarely grow larger than 8-10in tall. Budded plants are offered for sale from September until Christmastime.
Feeding Feed with standard liquid fertilizer every two weeks when in flower.
Potting Repotting of first year plants is unnecessary. Repot a rested tuber in soil-based potting mixture in September. Use the same pot each year.
Special points Never pour water directly onto the tuber; instead stand the pot in water for ten minutes.

CHRISTMAS CHERRY
Solanum capsicastrum

Marble-sized, orange-red berries make these small, shrubby plants an autumn favorite. The berries will last for several months if kept in a sunny but cool place; hot, dry air considerably shortens their lives. Placed on a low table or in a window-box, the Christmas cherry adds color and interest to a group of foliage plants.

Mini-climate 4 Cool, sunny.
Size Christmas cherries reach a height of 1½ft. Plants bearing berries are offered for sale.
Feeding Feed with standard liquid fertilizer every two weeks.
Potting Repot in spring using soil-based potting mixture. To keep for a second fruiting season cut away half the growth and move them outside in 5in pots for the summer.
Special points Mist-spray daily to increase humidity and aid pollination when in flower. The berries are not edible, so keep the plants away from small children.

EMERALD RIPPLE PEPEROMIA
Peperomia caperata

These small plants have very distinctive, deeply ridged, heart-shaped leaves. The low-growing form of the leaves is offset by the vertical, white flower spikes which emerge from the rosette of leaves. Peperomias look good when included in foliage groups with plants of contrasting sizes and textures.

Mini-climate 2 Warm, filtered sun.
Size Emerald ripple peromias are compact plants, rarely growing taller than 6in with a similar spread. Young plants and a miniature form for use in bottle gardens are offered for sale.
Feeding Feed with half-strength standard liquid fertilizer once a month from mid-spring to autumn.
Potting Repot in spring using a peat-based potting mixture but only if the roots have completely filled the existing pot.
Special points Do not overwater peperomias as they are liable to rot.

CHRISTMAS PEPPER
Capsicum annuum

An increasingly popular plant bearing brightly colored fleshy berries which appear in autumn and remain decorative until after Christmas. The most familiar berries are orange-red in color but white, yellow, green and purple-berried varieties are also available. They are best treated as annuals and discarded when the fruiting has finished. They make colorful Christmas displays and are striking massed as a table decoration.

Mini-climate 1 Warm, sunny.
Size Christmas peppers are available at 12-14in height and spread.
Feeding Feed with standard liquid fertilizer every two weeks in the fruiting season.
Potting Repotting is unnecessary.
Special points To keep plants in a decorative state for as long as possible, stand plants on trays filled with moist pebbles to increase humidity. The fruits are edible but very hot.

Temperature 50°-60°F spring to autumn 45°-50°F in winter / 50°-60°F / 60°-70°F   Light sunny / filtered sun / shady   Humidity low / moderate / high   Watering sparingly / moderately / plentifully   Care easy / fairly easy / challenging

FLORIST'S CHRYSANTHEMUM
Chrysanthemum morifolium hybrids

Also known as "pot chrysanthemums", these plants are offered for sale with flowers of every color but blue. The flowers and foliage have a distinctive scent. They will remain in flower for about six weeks, and are best treated as annuals and discarded when flowering has finished. Several plants grouped together in a shallow basket or pan on a low table look particularly attractive.

Mini-climate 5 Cool, filtered sun.
Size Florist's chrysanthemums have been specially cultivated to reach no more than 1ft in height. They are offered for sale in flower throughout the year.
Feeding Feeding is not required for these temporary plants.
Potting Repotting is unnecessary.
Special points When buying chrysanthemums make sure the flower buds show color as tightly closed green buds often fail to open.

POISON PRIMROSE
Primula obconica

This is one of the prettiest flowering plants, blooming between Christmas and summer. The long-stalked clusters of flowers are white, pink, salmon or mauve with a distinctive green eye. Poison primroses are best treated as annuals and discarded when flowering has finished. Use singly or massed in a shallow pan or basket in any cool area.

Mini-climate 5 Cool, filtered sun.
Size Poison primroses rarely grow taller than 1ft with a spread of 10in. Plants in flower are offered for sale.
Feeding Use liquid fertilizer every two weeks.
Potting Repotting is unnecessary.
Special points Leaves can cause painful skin rash.

Similar-shaped species
Primula malacoides is a very delicate plant with small white, rose pink or lilac flowers.

CUPID'S BOWER
Achimenes grandiflora

Also known as "magic flowers", these plants have hairy, upright, green or red stems and dull-green leaves which are also hairy. Flowers can be pink, purple or yellow in color, with white throats. The flowering period lasts from summer to autumn. These are very useful infill plants for an indoor window-box.

Mini-climate 1 Warm, sunny.
Size Cupid's bowers grow to 1 ½ft in height. Tubers or small plants are offered for sale in spring.
Feeding Feed with phosphate-rich liquid fertilizer at one-eighth strength when watering during the flowering period.
Potting Repot every spring using an equal-parts mixture of peat moss, coarse sand or perlite and vermiculite. Divide older plants every spring.
Special points Dry off and rest in winter.

LARGE-LEAVED BUSHY PLANTS

JAPANESE FATSIA
Fatsia japonica

An evergreen shrub which has been used for over a century as an indoor and outdoor plant. It has attractive, shiny, fingered leaves whose color and texture contrast with the stem which becomes gnarled and woody with age. The plant can be moved outside in summer, where the leaves become a deeper shade of green. Japanese fatsias can look extremely decorative in an architectural setting.

Mini-climate 5 Cool, filtered sun.
Size Japanese fatsias are fast-growing shrubs, reaching 1.5m in height and spread in two years. Small plants are offered for sale.
Feeding Feed with standard liquid fertilizer every two weeks during spring and summer.
Potting Repot every spring using soil-based potting mixture. Clay pots are best because fatsias tend to be top-heavy. If you don't want to move an older plant into a larger pot topdress instead.

Bushy plants 4

LARGE-LEAVED BUSHY PLANTS continued

SPOTTED LAUREL
Aucuba japonica "Variegata"

Also known as "Japanese laurels", these plants were much used by the Victorians in their shrubberies and greenhouses. The modern hybrids are more cheerful, having leaves strongly variegated with yellow. Spotted laurels can be used in window-boxes and in foliage arrangements for cool rooms as they tolerate a certain amount of neglect, poor light and drafts.

Mini-climate 5   Cool, filtered sun.
Size   Spotted laurels can reach 3-4ft in height. Plants of about 8in high are offered for sale.
Feeding   Feed with standard liquid fertilizer once a month in summer.
Potting   Repot every spring using soil-based potting mixture. Once plants are in 8in pots topdress instead.
Special points   Clean leaves regularly with a damp sponge. Plants can be put outside in summer.

ANGEL WINGS
Caladium hortulanum hybrids

Angel wings send up long, fleshy stalks bearing the paper-thin, heart-shaped leaves. The variety of leaf colors and patterns is immense—besides green leaves with red veining, white and cream leaves veined with pink or green are also available. Angel wings are highly ornamental, especially if several different leaf colors are grouped together.

Mini-climate 3   Warm, shady.
Size   The mainly green-leaved angel wings grow to a maximum height of 8-10in. Varieties with colored leaves may reach 1½-2ft high. Plants in full leaf are offered for sale.
Feeding   Feed with half-strength liquid fertilizer every two weeks in spring and summer.
Potting   Repot a rested tuber in spring using peat-based potting mixture. Make provision for good drainage. Use 5in pots and cover the tuber with about 1in of potting mixture.

SAFFRON SPIKE
Aphelandra squarrosa "Louisae"

These are dual-purpose flowering and foliage plants. For about six weeks the plant has unusual flower heads of overlapping yellow bracts. When flowering has finished, pinch off the dead blooms and use the saffron spike as a foliage plant. The leaves are large and glossy and marked with large, white veins. Mix with plain-leaved plants for a contrasting display in a modern living-room.

Mini-climate 2   Warm, filtered sun.
Size   Saffron spikes grow to about 1ft in height with a similar spread. Plants already in flower are offered for sale.
Feeding   Feed with standard liquid fertilizer every week from spring to early autumn.
Potting   Repot every spring using soil-based potting mixture. Once plants are in 6in pots topdress instead.

FLAMINGO FLOWER
Anthurium scherzeranum hybrids

The exotic flower heads consist of a bright scarlet bract encircling a tail-like flower spike. They last for several weeks and can appear at any time between February and July. When in flower, groups of several plants make an attractive display; when not in flower, the leaves harmonize with those of other tropical plants suitable for shady spots.

Mini-climate 3   Warm, shady.
Size   Flamingo flowers grow to about 2ft in height. Small plants are often offered for sale.
Feeding   Feed every two weeks with standard liquid fertilizer.
Potting   Repot every spring using a mixture of one-third soil-based potting mixture, one-third coarse peat moss, and one-third coarse sand. Once plants are in 7in pots topdress instead. Cover any exposed roots in peat moss.
Special points   Water more sparingly in winter. Stand plants on trays filled with moist pebbles to increase humidity.

Temperature 50°-60°F spring to autumn, 45°-50°F in winter | 50°-60°F | 60°-70°F Light sunny | filtered sun | shady Humidity low | moderate | high Watering sparingly | moderately | plentifully Care easy | fairly easy | challenging

PAINTED-LEAF BEGONIA
Begonia rex-cultorum

Also known as "rex begonias", these are among the most handsome begonias, grown for the beautifully colored leaves rather than their flowers, which tend to be insignificant. The heart-shaped leaves, which can be up to 1ft in length, bear striking patterns made up of variations of red, black, silver and green. Leaf texture also varies: some hybrids have smooth leaves; this one has a rippled or pimpled surface.

Mini-climate 3 Warm, shady.
Size Painted leaf begonias can grow up to 1ft in height with a 3ft spread. Young plants 2-3in high are offered for sale.
Feeding Feed with standard liquid fertilizer every two weeks in spring and summer.
Potting Divide overcrowded rhizomes and repot in spring every three years using peat-based potting mixture in a shallow container.
Special points Water very sparingly in winter. Destroy any powdery mildew you may find.

Similar-shaped species
Begonia masoniana has a deep-red, cross-shaped pattern in the middle of its pale-green leaves.

COMPOUND-LEAVED BUSHY PLANTS

DELTA MAIDENHAIR FERN
Adiantum raddianum

Delta maidenhair ferns have delicate, pale-green fronds borne on black, wiry stalks. They mix well with both foliage and flowering house plants and are useful for softening the outline of many arrangements. They also look very attractive on their own. Small plants can be planted in terraria.

Mini-climate 3 Warm, shady.
Size These ferns grow to 1ft in height with a similar spread. Plants of all sizes are offered for sale.
Feeding Feed with standard liquid fertilizer once a month during spring and summer.
Potting Repot in spring using fern potting mixture but only when a mass of roots appears on the surface of the potting mixture.
Special points Stand plants on trays filled with moist pebbles to increase humidity.

Similar-shaped species
Adiantum raddianum microphyllum has minute, dark-green, wedge-shaped leaflets.
Adiantum hispidulum is very small and has fingerlike fronds.

ASPARAGUS FERN
Asparagus setaceus

Asparagus ferns have light, feathery foliage made up of tiny branchlets on wiry stems. Taller growing kinds may be trained up thin canes to form a delicate column shape. Trained around east- or west-facing windows they can give a charming "cottage" effect. They can also be included in fern groups in a hanging basket.

Mini-climate 2 Warm, filtered sun.
Size Asparagus ferns can produce stems up to 4ft long. Small plants are offered for sale.
Feeding Feed with standard liquid fertilizer every two weeks in spring and summer, and once a month in autumn and winter.
Potting Repot every spring using soil-based potting mixture. If you don't want to move an older plant into a larger pot topdress instead.

Similar-shaped species
Asparagus asparagoides is a vigorous climbing vine with leaflet-like branchlets up to 2in long.
Asparagus falcatus is similar but has sickle-shaped spines on its stems.

CRETAN BRAKE FERN
Pteris cretica

Also known as "table ferns", these plants form clumps of striped fronds which grow from short, underground rhizomes. Each frond is hand-shaped, the individual pinnae looking like fingers. Cretan brake ferns mix well with other plants, especially if used as pot hiders at the front of plant groupings. They are ideal for a north-facing conservatory or plant window collection.

Mini-climate 3 Warm, shady.
Size Cretan brake ferns grow to 14in in height with a similar spread. Small plants of about 5in in height are offered for sale.
Feeding Feed with half-strength standard liquid fertilizer once a month.
Potting Repot in spring using fern potting mixture but only if the roots have completely filled the existing pot. If you don't want to move an older plant to a larger pot topdress instead.

Similar-shaped species
Pteris tremula looks like bracken. It is fast-growing, with fronds up to 2ft long and 1ft wide.

Climbing plants 1

Climbing plants usually have stems that are too weak to grow unaided in an upright position, but will grow in any direction provided they have a support to cling to. Many climbing plants can be displayed equally effectively as trailers, and vice-versa. The species, which bear aerial roots, such as the philodendrons and the Swiss cheese plant, usually produce quite thick stems and their fleshy leaves can be large and weighty, so they are best grown on a stout moss-covered pole. Some climbing plants naturally scramble through other plants, gaining some support by sending out tendrils or by just "leaning" on their neighbors. Others which produce curly leaf tendrils can be trained on canes, wire hoops and trellis work. Although the tendrils may look thin and frail they are usually very strong. Climbing plants can also be trained to frame windows, mirrors or archways or used to create a foliage screen dividing areas in a room. Many have attractive foliage, such as the scalloped leaves of the kangaroo vine and the yellow-and-green variegated leaves of the Cape ivy and Algerian ivy. A number of climbers have flowers, including the Cape leadwort whose blooms are a striking sky-blue and the jasmine, with its small but heavily scented white flowers. Most spectacular of all are the large, showy flowers of the passion flower.

SMALL-LEAVED CLIMBING PLANTS

ALGERIAN IVY
Hedera canariensis

Also known as "Canary Island ivies", these plants have slightly lobed dark-green leaves with patches of gray-green variegation. They are vigorous climbers and can easily be trained up any kind of support. They make good specimen plants when very large and are most suitable for use in cool places such as halls and stairways.

Mini-climate 5 Cool, filtered sun.
Size Algerian ivies are fast-growing with an unpredictable maximum height and spread; certainly 6ft. Leaves can be as much as 6in long and 6in wide. Plants of all sizes are offered for sale.
Feeding Feed with standard liquid fertilizer every two weeks when actively growing.
Potting Repot in spring using soil-based potting mixture but only if the roots have completely filled the existing pot. Once plants are in 4½-6in pots topdress instead.
Special points Water more sparingly in winter.

CAPE IVY
Senecio macroglossus

These plants are very similar to the English ivies, but their leaves are smoother, softer and more fleshy. The leaves are borne on purple stems and are green marked with pale-cream streaks and patches. In some cases, where variegation is very strong, all the leaves on a shoot may be predominantly cream-colored. Cape ivies should be trained around hoops of bamboo cane or wire, or planted in small hanging baskets.

Mini-climate 1 Warm, sunny.
Size Cape ivies grow up to 3ft in height and spread. Pinch out growing tips to maintain bushy growth. Small plants are offered for sale.
Feeding Feed with standard liquid fertilizer every two weeks during spring and summer.
Potting Repot every spring using a mixture of one part coarse sand to three parts soil-based mixture. Once plants are in 6in pots topdress instead.
Special points Water more sparingly in winter. Destroy any aphids you may find.

GRAPE IVY
Cissus rhombifolia

These plants have deeply toothed leaves. New leaf growth appears to be silver due to a fine covering of hairs on both surfaces. Older leaves have undersides covered in fine, brown hairs. Trained up a simple framework of bamboo canes, grape ivies can become quite large feature plants relatively quickly. They also make an excellent display in large hanging baskets.

Mini-climate 2 Warm, filtered sun.
Size Grape ivies grow to 6ft in height in around two years and can reach 10ft in ideal conditions. Pinch out growing tips regularly to encourage bushy growth. Plants of all sizes are offered for sale.
Feeding Feed with standard liquid fertilizer every two weeks in spring and summer.
Potting Repot every spring using soil-based potting mixture. Once plants are in 6-7in pots topdress instead.

Temperature 50°-60°F spring to autumn, 45°-50°F in winter | 50°-60°F | 60°-70°F
Light sunny | filtered sun | shady
Humidity low | moderate | high
Watering sparingly | moderately | plentifully
Care easy | fairly easy | challenging

PASSION FLOWER
Passiflora caerulea

These exotic-looking plants have beautiful flowers. Each consists of five pinkish-white petals and five pinkish-white sepals encircling a ring of purple-blue filaments. These filaments encircle the golden anthers. The flowers may appear at any time during the summer and autumn. The foliage is dark-green and stems should be trained over a wire support to make an attractive shape. Passion flowers make striking specimen plants for conservatories or large, bright windowsills.

Mini-climate 1 Warm, sunny.
Size Passion flowers have a maximum height and spread of about 20ft. Plants of all sizes are offered for sale.
Feeding Feed with standard liquid fertilizer every two weeks during spring, summer and autumn.
Potting Repot every spring using soil-based potting mixture. Once plants are in 8in pots topdress instead.
Special points To keep plants in a decorative state for as long as possible, prune heavily in spring.

WAX FLOWER
Stephanotis floribunda

These plants have dark-green, glossy leaves carried on woody stems, which twine readily round any support, and delightfully scented, waxy, white flowers. The flowers grow in clusters of ten or more and each is tube-shaped, flaring out into five pointed lobes. They appear from spring until autumn. Wax flowers may be trained to climb a trellis or, if space is more limited, round a hoop of wire or cane inserted into the pot.

Mini-climate 1 Warm, sunny.
Size Wax flowers are vigorous growers. Height and spread is variable, but is usually about 10ft. Pinch out growing tips to encourage bushy growth. Plants of all sizes are offered for sale.
Feeding Feed with standard liquid fertilizer every two weeks during spring and summer.
Potting Repot every second year in spring using soil-based potting mixture. Once plants are in 8in pots topdress instead.
Special points Stand plants on trays filled with moist pebbles to increase humidity. Water more sparingly in winter.

PLUSH VINE
Mikania ternata

These small plants have soft, slaty-green foliage covered in fine, purple hairs. The underside of the leaves and the stems are purple. Plush vines can be used in much the same way as ivies—either as trailers or climbers—although they do not grow as tall. Their unusual coloring provides a contrast to light-green plants in a mixed foliage arrangement.

Mini-climate 2 Warm, filtered sun.
Size Plush vines have a maximum height and spread of about 10ft. Small plants are offered for sale.
Feeding Feed with standard liquid fertilizer every two weeks from spring to autumn.
Potting Repot in spring using soil-based potting mixture. Discard the plant after the second repotting.
Special points Do not wet the hairy foliage.

BLACK-EYED SUSAN VINE
Thunbergia alata

Black-eyed Susan vines have attractive bright-orange flowers with a characteristic deep chocolate-brown "eye". The large, round blooms are produced from spring to late autumn. Black-eyed Susan vines look particularly good when trained to climb up strings in front of a window.

Mini-climate 4 Cool, sunny.
Size Black-eyed Susan vines may reach over 6ft in height. Buy young plants or grow your own from seed.
Feeding Feed with standard liquid fertilizer every two weeks.
Potting Repot in spring using soil-based potting mixture but only if the roots have completely filled the existing pot. Once plants are in 6in pots top-dress instead.
Special points To keep plants in a decorative state for as long as possible, pinch out any faded flowers.

Climbing plants 2

SMALL-LEAVED CLIMBING PLANTS continued

KANGAROO VINE
Cissus antarctica

Relatives of the grapevine, these are scrambling foliage plants whose glossy, dark-green leaves have marked veining and a scalloped edge. They can be used in many different ways: either trained up poles, used as specimen plants or displayed in hanging baskets.

Mini-climate 2 Warm, filtered sun.
Size Kangaroo vines grow to 6ft tall with a spread of 2ft in about two years. Plants of all sizes are offered for sale.
Feeding Feed with standard liquid fertilizer every two weeks in spring and summer.
Potting Repot every spring using soil-based potting mixture. Once plants are in 6-8in pots topdress instead.
Special points Stand plants on trays filled with moist pebbles to increase humidity. Mist-spray plants in hanging baskets.

CAPE LEADWORT
Plumbago auriculata

These plants produce clusters of up to 20 pale-blue flowers from spring to autumn. A narrow, darker blue stripe runs down each of the five petals which flare from a 1½in long tube. Training these plants round a trellis produces an attractive display, or they can be trained to cover a wall.

Mini-climate 1 Warm, sunny.
Size The stems of the Cape leadwort can reach over 3ft in length, but should be pruned every spring as the plants can become very straggly. Plants of all sizes are offered for sale.
Feeding Feed with tomato-type liquid fertilizer once every two weeks from spring until autumn.
Potting Repot every spring using soil-based potting mixture. Once plants are in 8in pots topdress instead.
Special points Water more sparingly in winter.

WHITE-SCENTED JASMINE
Jasminum polyanthum

Clusters of white, scented flowers are produced by these attractive plants in winter and spring. Jasmine are most delicate-looking, but are very vigorous climbers, easily trained round wire hoops or any other fine support. If planted in a conservatory border, they can be trained to cover a wall.

Mini-climate 4 Cool, sunny.
Size White-scented jasmine can reach 20ft if grown in a border, 3ft if grown in a pot. Spread depends upon the support used. Plants in flower are offered for sale in winter.
Feeding Feed with standard liquid fertilizer once a month in summer and autumn.
Potting Repot every spring using soil-based potting mixture. Once plants are in 8in pots topdress instead.
Special points Place plants outdoors in summer.

GOLDEN TRUMPET
Allamanda cathartica

These climbing plants produce bright, buttercup-yellow flowers over a period of many weeks during the summer. The oval leaves which are carried on long stems are a glossy dark-green color. If grown in a conservatory border, or in a tub, golden trumpets can be trained to cover a wall. For the smaller room, they can be grown in pots and trained over a wire framework of any shape.

Mini-climate 2 Warm, filtered sun.
Size Golden trumpets are fast-growing and can attain a maximum height and spread of 7ft. Plants should be cut back by as much as two-thirds in winter. Small plants are offered for sale in summer.
Feeding Feed with standard liquid fertilizer every two weeks in summer.
Potting Repot every spring using soil-based potting mixture. If you don't want to move an older plant into a larger pot topdress instead.
Special points Water more sparingly in winter.

Temperature			Light			Humidity			Watering			Care		
50°-60°F spring to autumn; 45°-50°F in winter	50°-60°F	60°-70°F	sunny	filtered sun	shady	low	moderate	high	sparingly	moderately	plentifully	easy	fairly easy	challenging

PAPER FLOWER
Bougainvillea buttiana

Armed with sharp spines, these plants are woody-stemmed. The small, creamy-white flowers are insignificant in themselves but are surrounded by large, decorative, papery bracts which can be white, yellow, orange, pink, red or purple. These are produced in clusters of between 10 and 20, mainly during spring and summer. Although they are naturally climbing plants, paper flowers can be trained to remain bushy indoors. They are best grown in very sunny rooms or conservatories, since they require a large amount of light to encourage them to flower.

Mini-climate 1 Warm, sunny.
Size Paper flowers can reach a maximum height and spread of about 6ft. Pinch out growing tips to encourage bushy growth. Small plants are offered for sale.
Feeding Feed with standard liquid fertilizer every two weeks in summer.
Potting Repot every spring using soil-based potting mixture with extra peat moss mixed in. Once plants are in 8in pots topdress instead.
Special points Water more sparingly in winter. Destroy any mealy bugs you may find.

LARGE-LEAVED CLIMBING PLANTS

BURGUNDY PHILODENDRON
Philodendron "Burgundy"

These large-leaved philodendrons have bright-red leaf stalks and undersides to their leaves. They will flourish if trained around a moss-covered pole. Large specimens look best displayed on their own.

Mini-climate 3 Warm, shady.
Size Burgundy philodendrons are slow-growing; they eventually reach a height of 6ft.
Feeding Feed with standard liquid fertilizer every two weeks in spring and summer.
Potting Repot in spring using half soil-based potting mixture and half peat moss, but only if the roots have filled the existing pot. Once plants are in 6-10in pots topdress instead.

Similar-shaped species
Philodendron hastatum has deep-green leaves.

ARROWHEAD PLANT
Syngonium podophyllum "Imperial White"

These climbing plants are unusual in that the shape of the leaves changes as the plant matures. Young leaves have three deeply-cut lobes but, in older specimens, the leaves have five lobes. Arrowhead plants can be trained to climb up thin stakes, or up a moss-covered pole, or they can trail from a hanging basket.

Mini-climate 2 Warm, filtered sun.
Size The stems can grow up to 6ft. The spread depends on the support system used.
Feeding Feed with standard liquid fertilizer every two weeks from spring to autumn.
Potting Repot in spring using an equal-parts mixture of soil-based potting mixture and leaf mold, but only if the roots have completely filled the existing pot. If you don't want to move an older plant into a larger pot topdress instead.

SWISS CHEESE PLANT
Monstera deliciosa

These plants have undivided, heart-shaped leaves when young; the characteristic split edges and holes appear with age. Train Swiss cheese plants up a moss-covered pole so that the pencil-thick aerial roots can be guided into the moss; never cut these roots off as they take in nutrients. The scale of a mature plant makes it a good foil for large pieces of furniture.

Mini-climate 3 Warm, shady.
Size Swiss cheese plants can reach heights in excess of 8ft. Plants of all sizes are offered for sale.
Feeding Feed with standard liquid fertilizer every two weeks in spring and summer.
Potting Repot every spring using two-thirds soil-based potting mixture and one-third leaf mold. Once plants are in 8in pots topdress instead.
Special points Clean older leaves regularly.

Trailing plants 1

Most of these plants look best displayed with their stems hanging downwards, although some, such as ivies and philodendrons, can be trained to climb as well. Trailing plants are best displayed in hanging baskets, on pedestals, or on shelves, so that the tumbling foliage can be appreciated. They can also be used to soften the outline of any arrangement or to disguise the edges of a hanging basket, shelf or table. Within the group there is a wonderful range of leaf textures, from the light, feathery fronds of the emerald fern to the bold, fleshy fronds of the staghorn fern, and the delicate, dripping foliage of the strawberry geranium. A dramatic hanging display can be made using the large foliage of the staghorn fern contrasted with the heart-shaped leaves of the heartleaf philodendron. For color there are the red flowers of the columneas and the light-blue or white flowers of the Italian bellflower. The leaves of trailing plants can also provide color and different textures: for example, the furry, purple foliage of the purple velvet plant and the beautiful, silver-marked foliage of the pothos vine.

SMALL-LEAVED TRAILING PLANTS

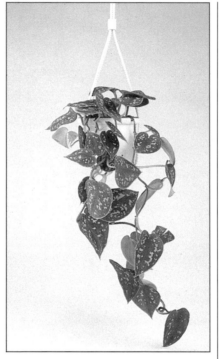

HEARTLEAF PHILODENDRON
Philodendron scandens

These small-leaved philodendrons are the easiest members of this genus to grow. The acutely pointed leaves are fleshy and attractively bronzed when they first appear, but become dark green and leathery with age. These plants can be trained up a support, such as a moss-covered pole, as well as being left to trail. They make good fillers for the front of groups, and are ideal for warm rooms which don't get too much sun.

Mini-climate 3 Warm, shady.
Size These philodendrons are fast-growing; maximum size is unpredictable but a 6ft length and a 20in spread can be reached. Pinch out growing tips to encourage bushy growth. Small plants are offered for sale.
Feeding Feed with standard liquid fertilizer every two weeks in spring and summer, and once every month in autumn and winter.
Potting Repot every spring using half soil-based potting mixture and half leaf mold or peat moss. Once plants are in 10-12in pots topdress instead.
Special points Stand plants on trays filled with moist pebbles to increase humidity.

POTHOS VINE
Scindapsus pictus "Argyraeus"

The most striking feature of these plants is their matt olive-green colored leaves covered with silver spots. The heart-shaped leaves are carried on thick stems which occasionally produce aerial roots. Mass several small plants together or put a large specimen in a hanging basket near a sunny window. Pothos vines also make attractive feature plants when trained up moist, moss-covered poles.

Mini-climate 1 Warm, sunny.
Size Pothos vines are slow-growing, but mature plants can reach 5ft in height with a similar spread. Pinch out growing tips in spring to encourage bushy growth. Plants of 4-6in in height are offered for sale.
Feeding Feed with standard liquid fertilizer every two weeks from spring to autumn.
Potting Repot in spring using soil-based potting mixture but only if the roots have completely filled the existing pot. Once plants are in 6in pots topdress instead.
Special points Water more sparingly in winter.

DEVIL'S IVY
Epipremnum aureum

These plants, also known as "Solomon Island's ivies", have yellowish-green, angular stems with aerial roots and large, bright-green leaves boldly and irregularly marked with yellow. Devil's ivy is impressive in hanging baskets, on high shelves, or when trained up moss-covered poles. Large specimens have large leaves and are best displayed on their own in a warm room.

Mini-climate 2 Warm, filtered sun.
Size The stems of devil's ivy grow to a maximum of 6½ft long with a 3ft spread. Pinch out growing tips to encourage bushy growth. Young, small-leaved plants are offered for sale.
Feeding Feed with standard liquid fertilizer every two weeks in spring and summer.
Potting Repot every spring using soil-based potting mixture. If you don't want to move an older plant into a larger pot topdress instead.
Special points Water more sparingly in winter.

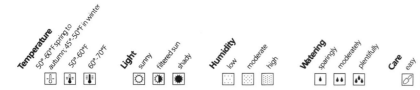

Temperature: 50°-60°F spring to autumn, 45°-50°F in winter | 50°-60°F | 60°-70°F
Light: sunny | filtered sun | shady
Humidity: low | moderate | high
Watering: sparingly | moderately | plentifully
Care: easy | fairly easy | challenging

WANDERING JEW
Zebrina pendula

Also known as "inch plants", wandering Jews are highly decorative with attractive leaf coloring. The oval leaves have a striped, iridescent upper surface and a deep-purple underside. In spring and autumn, clusters of small, purple-pink flowers are produced. Wandering Jews make a fine display when massed in hanging baskets, but also look attractive trailing over the edge of a bowl in a mixed planting.

Mini-climate 1 Warm, sunny.
Size The stems of wandering Jews grow to 16in long with a spread of 1ft. Pinch out growing tips to encourage bushy growth. Small plants are offered for sale.
Feeding Feed with standard liquid fertilizer once every two weeks.
Potting Repot in spring using soil-based potting mixture but only if the roots have completely filled the existing pot. Discard the plant after the second or third repotting. Start new plants from cuttings.
Special points Remove stems with poorly colored leaves should they appear.

MINIATURE WAX PLANT
Hoya bella

These are spreading plants with drooping stems and dull green, fleshy leaves. The pure white, strongly scented flowers are grouped in star-shaped clusters of eight to ten, each flower having a curious purple center. Flowers appear through the summer. Miniature wax plants are best displayed in hanging baskets as the centers of the drooping flowers can only be seen from below. They look good in a sunny conservatory or modern interior.

Mini-climate 1 Warm, sunny.
Size Miniature wax plants grow to 1ft in height, the branches then begin to trail and produce a maximum spread of 1½ft.
Feeding Feed with high-potash liquid fertilizer every two weeks from spring to early autumn.
Potting Repot every spring using soil-based potting mixture making provision for good drainage. Once plants are in 5-6in pots topdress instead.
Special points Destroy any mealy bugs you may find.

COLUMNEA
Columnea banksii

These plants have striking scarlet flowers borne amongst the small, waxy leaves on long trailing stems. The flowers may be produced at any time of year and a large plant may have up to 100 flowers at any one time. Use large plants as specimens in plain containers or hanging baskets in a warm room.

Mini-climate 2 Warm, filtered sun.
Size The trailing stems of columneas reach a maximum length of 4ft. Young plants are offered for sale in spring.
Feeding Feed with one-quarter strength high-phosphate liquid fertilizer at every watering.
Potting Repot every spring using a mixture of equal parts peat moss, perlite and vermiculite. If you don't want to move an older plant into a larger pot prune the roots instead.
Special points Maintain high humidity throughout the year.

TRADESCANTIA
Tradescantia albiflora "Albovittata"

Tradescantias are very similar to zebrinas. The silver-and green-striped leaves are almost transparent. Mass plants in a hanging basket or allow a large specimen to trail from a shelf. They are useful for inclusion at the front of mixed arrangements in a suitably sunny room. Tradescantias will also climb.

Mini-climate 1 Warm, sunny.
Size Tradescantias are fast-growing, the stems reaching 1ft long. Pinch out growing tips to encourage bushy growth.
Feeding Feed with standard liquid fertilizer every two weeks from spring to autumn.
Potting Repot in spring using soil-based potting mixture but only if the roots have completely filled the existing pot. Discard the plant after the second repotting. Start new plants from cuttings.
Special points Remove any dried or poorly colored leaves.

Similar-shaped species
Tradescantia fluminensis "Variegata" has leaves which are a deep olive-green striped with cream and pink and covered with soft, velvety hairs.
Tradescantia sillamontana has peppermint-green leaves with long, white, woolly hair.

Trailing plants 2

SMALL-LEAVED TRAILING PLANTS continued

PICKABACK PLANT
Tolmiea menziesii

These plants, which are also known as "mother-of-thousands", derive their common names from the way that a number of mature leaves produce small plantlets on their upper surfaces. These weigh down the long leafstalks to give a trailing appearance. The fresh-green leaves and slender leafstalks are covered with soft hair. These are excellent plants to display in hanging baskets. They are easily kept in any cool place.

Mini-climate 5 Cool, filtered sun.
Size Pickaback plants are fast-growing and reach a height of about 1 ft with a similar spread. Small plants are offered for sale.
Feeding Feed with standard liquid fertilizer every two weeks during spring and summer.
Potting Repot in spring using soil-based potting mixture but only if the roots have completely filled the existing pot. Discard the plant after the second or third repotting.
Special points Water more sparingly in winter.

SPIDER PLANT
Chlorophytum comosum "Vittatum"

These cultivars have a distinctive white or cream stripe down the center of each leaf. The narrow leaves arch over but the true trailing effect is produced by long stems bearing numerous plantlets. Well-grown spider plants make striking feature plants when displayed from a height, either on pedestals or in hanging baskets.

Mini-climate 5 Cool, filtered sun.
Size The leaves of spider plants can grow up to 2ft long. The spread depends on the number of plants growing in the same pot. Plants of all sizes are offered for sale.
Feeding Feed with standard liquid fertilizer every two weeks.
Potting Repot in spring using soil-based potting mixture but only if the roots have completely filled the existing pot. If you don't want to move an older plant into a larger pot topdress instead.
Special points Allow a 1in space at the top of the pot for the development of the fat roots.

STRAWBERRY GERANIUM
Saxifraga stolonifera

These plants produce many plantlets on threadlike stems. The mother plants are small and low-growing and the plantlets hang down from the center of the plant giving a trailing effect. Strawberry geraniums are best displayed in hanging baskets so that the red undersides to their leaves may be seen. Display in cool places, such as hallways, and ensure the delicate trailing stems are not brushed against.

Mini-climate 5 Cool, filtered sun.
Size Strawberry geraniums are fast growing, but reach no more than 8in high. The trailing stems grow to 2ft long.
Feeding Feed with standard liquid fertilizer once a month.
Potting Repot every spring using soil-based potting mixture. Discard the plant after the second repotting.
Special points Water more sparingly during the winter rest period.

ENGLISH IVY
Hedera helix hybrids

There are many hybrids of the English ivies, all forming low-growing bushy trailers, but with many variations in leaf shape and color.
Ivies may be used in a variety of ways: to infill the fronts of groups, as trailers in hanging baskets, or displayed along shelves. They can also be trained to climb.

Mini-climate 5 Cool, filtered sun.
Size Ivies can grow very large and straggly so pinch out growing tips to encourage bushy growth. Plants of all sizes are offered for sale.
Feeding Feed with standard liquid fertilizer every two weeks in spring and summer and once a month in autumn and winter.
Potting Repot in spring using soil-based potting mixture but only if the roots have completely filled the existing pot. If you don't want to move an older plant into a larger pot topdress instead.
Special points Water more sparingly during the winter rest period.

Temperature 50°-60°F spring to autumn; 45°-50°F in winter 50°-60°F 60°-70°F Light sunny filtered sun shady Humidity low moderate high Watering sparingly moderately plentifully Care easy fairly easy challenging

EMERALD FERN
Asparagus densiflorus "Sprengeri"

These plants have arching stems which begin to trail with age. Each frond is covered in tiny branchlets, giving the plants a delicate, fernlike appearance; in fact they are not true ferns but related to the lilies. Use them to soften the outline of arrangements, or group with true ferns in a hanging basket. Emerald ferns thrive in most conditions and have a fresh, informal look which makes them suitable for most types of setting.

Mini-climate 2 Warm, filtered sun.
Size The fronds of emerald ferns can grow up to 3ft in length. Small plants are offered for sale.
Feeding Feed with standard liquid fertilizer every two weeks in spring and summer, and once a month in autumn and winter.
Potting Repot in spring using soil-based potting mixture but only if the roots have completely filled the existing pot. If you don't want to move an older plant into a larger pot topdress instead.
Special points To keep plants in a decorative state for as long as possible, faded stems should be cut out as they appear.

PURPLE VELVET PLANT
Gynura aurantiaca

The tooth-edged leaves of these plants are covered in fine, purple hair and are at their most colorful when the leaves first open. The stems are upright at first but sprawl as they get longer. The downy leaves are seen to full advantage when the plants are massed in hanging baskets and viewed against a sunny window. A large plant looks good displayed in a room containing richly colored fabrics.

Mini-climate 1 Warm, sunny.
Size The trailing stems of purple velvet plants can reach over 3ft in length. Small, compact plants are offered for sale.
Feeding Feed with standard liquid fertilizer once every month.
Potting Repot in spring using soil-based potting mixture. Discard the plant after the second repotting.
Special points Water more sparingly in winter. Unpleasantly scented orange flowers are produced and should be removed before they open.

ITALIAN BELLFLOWER
Campanula isophylla

Italian bellflowers produce clusters of delicate-looking white or pale-blue flowers in early August and continue flowering until November. The flowers are normally so numerous that they completely hide the pale-green foliage. They are best treated as annuals and discarded when flowering has finished. Italian bellflowers are useful plants for massing in hanging baskets or window-boxes. They look good in conservatories or informal rooms.

Mini-climate 4 Cool, sunny.
Size The slender stems of Italian bellflowers reach a maximum length of 1ft. Pinch out growing tips to encourage bushy growth. Small plants are offered for sale in summer from some house plant specialists.
Feeding Feed with standard liquid fertilizer every two weeks during the flowering season.
Potting Repot every spring using soil-based potting mixture. When plants are in 5in pots topdress instead.
Special points Mist-spray plants in hanging baskets every day throughout summer and autumn.

LARGE-LEAVED TRAILING PLANTS

STAGHORN FERN
Platycerium bifurcatum

These are most unusual ferns. All plants have two types of frond: small fronds which clasp the plant's support and large, drooping fronds which give the fern its distinctive appearance. The fronds are dark green and covered with a fine, white, felty scurf. Staghorn ferns make striking specimen plants, particularly when displayed from a height.

Mini-climate 3 Warm, shady.
Size The fronds of the staghorn fern reach up to 3ft. Small plants are offered for sale.
Feeding Feed with standard liquid fertilizer once a month during active growth. Add feed to a bucket of water used to soak the pot or bark.
Potting Only small plants should be in pots—use fern potting mixture. Older plants should be grown on a piece of bark. Wrap the root ball in sphagnum moss and tie to the bark.
Special points Mist-spray regularly to maintain high humidity.

Creeping plants

These are plants with stems that grow just over the surface of the potting mixture. This ground-hugging habit creates a carpeting effect when they are allowed to spread. Creeping plants can be used successfully as ground cover around upright plants and to break up the hard lines of large containers. Some creeping plants, such as the little club moss, send roots down into the potting mixture whenever they touch it, virtually creating new plants; while others, such as the Swedish ivy, do no more than rest on the surface of the mixture.

Plants in this group tend to be small-leaved and most are small in overall size. Some will spread to become quite large with age, but will only do this if they are given adequate space. Certain species, like the versatile creeping fig, have a naturally creeping habit but can also be trained to climb up a support or trail from a hanging basket, as can the larger Swedish ivy.

Some of the plants in this category have unusual leaf-markings: the eyelash begonia has reddish-brown markings on lime-green leaves; the nerve plant has exotic, carmine-red leaf veins on a dark-green background; and the little nerve plant has silver leaf veins. The bead plant has pea-sized orange berries which remain decorative for several months. The colorful leaves and berries of the creeping plants compensate for the lack of flowers; any flowers which do appear are small and insignificant. Many of the creeping plants are particularly well suited to the humid atmosphere of bottle gardens and terraria.

SMALL-LEAVED CREEPING PLANTS

BABY'S TEARS
Soleirolia soleirolii

These pretty plants produce masses of tiny, bright-green leaves on thin stems, and will quickly carpet all available space in the pot. A number of these mossy mounds make an attractive display if they are arranged in a wicker basket They also look good filling in the front of foliage displays. Do not use them in bottle gardens or terraria as they quickly fill all the available space.

Mini-climate 4 Cool, sunny.
Size Baby's tears plants will not exceed 2in in height, but their spread is only limited by the size of the container in which they are grown. Trim the plant with a pair of scissors to maintain a neat shape. Small and medium-sized plants are offered for sale all year.
Feeding Feed with half-strength standard liquid fertilizer every two weeks in summer.
Potting Repot in spring using soil-based potting mixture. Discard the plant after the second repotting.
Special points Keep potting mixture damp at all times to prevent the leaves from turning brown.

BEAD PLANT
Nertera granadensis

The attractive bead plants have tiny, green leaves, but are prized for the profusion of pea-sized, bright-orange berries that develop from the insignificant, greenish-yellow flowers. The berries appear in late summer and last several months. They are best treated as annuals and discarded when the berries begin to die off. Bead plants make colorful table displays and are also suitable for growing in dish gardens, bottle gardens and terraria as long as they are kept small.

Mini-climate 4 Cool, sunny.
Size Bead plants form a low mound up to 3in high, with a maximum spread of around 6in. Small plants are offered for sale.
Feeding Feed with standard liquid fertilizer every two months while the berries are growing.
Potting Repot every spring using a mixture of two-thirds soil-based potting mixture and one-third peat moss. If you don't want to move an older plant into a larger pot topdress instead.
Special points Water more sparingly in winter. Bead plants can be placed outside, in a sheltered spot, in summer.

LITTLE CLUB MOSS
Selaginella martensii

These unusual plants have decorative, medium-green leaves which are packed round the branches like the scales of a fish. The creeping stems of little club mosses form a dense mat of foliage with a pleasant, soft texture. Roots are put down into the potting mixture at intervals. A terrarium or bottle garden is the best environment in which to display these small plants as they will thrive in the humid atmosphere.

Mini-climate 2 Warm, filtered sun.
Size The creeping stems of little club mosses may grow to 6in in length. Small plants are offered for sale.
Feeding Feed with one-quarter strength standard liquid fertilizer every two weeks.
Potting Repot every spring using a mixture of two-thirds peat-based potting mix and one-third coarse sand. Once plants are in 6-8in pots simply remove plants from their pots, clean and refill them with fresh mixture and replace the plants.
Special points Touch the plants as little as possible as this can damage the foliage.

Similar-shaped species
Selaginella apoda has shorter stems which branch more profusely, bearing fleshy, pale-green leaves.
Selaginella pallescens has white-edged leaves which grow on erect stems of up to 1ft long.

EYELASH BEGONIA
Begonia "Tiger Paws"

Eyelash begonias derive their name from the short, coarse hairs which grow around the edge of each lopsided, heart-shaped leaf. The attractive foliage is bright lime-green in color, marked with a bronze-red pattern which gives the leaves a patched or blotchy appearance. The stalks are also speckled with red and arise from a rhizome which creeps across the surface of the potting mixture. Arrange these begonias together in a basket or mix them with other foliage plants.

Mini-climate 2 Warm, filtered sun.
Size Eyelash begonias grow to about 6in in height with a 1ft spread. Small plants are offered for sale all year.
Feeding Feed with standard liquid fertilizer every two weeks during spring and summer.
Potting Repot every spring using an equal combination of soil-based potting mixture and leaf mold. If you don't want to move an older plant into a larger pot topdress instead. Discard the plant after several repottings.
Special points Stand plants on trays filled with moist pebbles to increase humidity. Protect from powdery mildew by supplying adequate ventilation.

NERVE PLANT
Fittonia verschaffeltii

These plants have oval, olive-green leaves which are covered by a network of fine, carmine-colored veins creating a mosaic effect. Yellow flower spikes may occasionally be produced. These plants are suitable for displaying together on a low table; they also look good in the forefront of a foliage group and are ideal for bottle gardens or terraria.

Mini-climate 3 Warm, shady.
Size Nerve plants reach a height of 6in with a spread of about 1ft. Pinch out growing tips to encourage bushy growth. Small plants are offered for sale all year.
Feeding Feed with half-strength standard liquid fertilizer every two weeks in spring and summer.
Potting Repot every spring using peat-based potting mixture in half-pots or other shallow containers. Once plants are in 4½in pots simply remove plants from their pots, clean and refill them with fresh mixture and replace the plants.
Special points Stand plants on trays filled with moist pebbles to increase humidity.

Similar-shaped species
Fittonia verschaffeltii argyroneura "Nana" has smaller leaves with silver veins and reaches a maximum spread of only 6in.

SWEDISH IVY
Plectranthus australis

Swedish ivies have fleshy, dark-green foliage borne on succulent, pink stems which lie flat on the potting mixture before they grow over the edge of the pot. The occasional pale-lavender flowers are insignificant and can be removed as they develop. Especially attractive in hanging baskets, the Swedish ivy also provides excellent ground cover for indoor window-boxes and other large groupings.

Mini-climate 1 Warm, sunny.
Size Swedish ivies are fast-growing; their stems quickly reach 3ft in length, with a height of 8in. Pinch out the growing tips to encourage bushy growth. Small plants are offered for sale.
Feeding Feed with standard liquid fertilizer every two weeks from spring to autumn.
Potting Repot in spring using soil-based potting mixture but only if the roots have completely filled the existing pot. If you don't want to move an older plant into a larger pot topdress instead.
Special points Water more sparingly in winter.

Similar-shaped species
Plectranthus oertendahlii has bronze-green leaves covered in soft hairs. The leaves have prominent white veins and are rosy-purple underneath.

CREEPING FIG
Ficus pumila

These plants have small, heart-shaped, slightly wrinkled leaves borne on long, wiry stems which spread out across the surface of the potting mixture. Creeping figs look good in shallow hanging baskets. Alternatively, they can be used as ground cover in indoor window-boxes. Small plants make good fillers in bottle gardens.

Mini-climate 5 Cool, filtered sun.
Size The stems of the creeping fig can reach 2ft in length. Spread depends on the mode of growth. Small plants are offered for sale.
Feeding Feed with standard liquid fertilizer every two weeks.
Potting Repot in spring using peat-based potting mixture but only if the roots have completely filled the existing pot.
Special points Stand plants on trays filled with moist pebbles to increase humidity. Never allow the potting mixture to dry out as the leaves will shrivel and never recover.

Bulbs

Bulbs and corms are the food storage organs of plants which have a distinct dormant period when all top growth dies down and no further growth takes place. Bulbs are made up of tightly packed modified leaves surrounding an embryo shoot and usually a complete embryo flower. Corms consist of modified stem bases covered in thin, papery scales and do not contain the young plant, but a bud from which the shoots and roots appear. Many bulbs and corms are "hardy", in that they need a period of wintering. Hardy bulbs are bought in their dormant state during autumn and early winter and, when potted up and provided with the right growing conditions, they start to come into flower in a matter of a few weeks. These special cold, dark conditions are known as "wintering" and it is during this period that roots are produced. To produce good flowers, the wintering recommendations for each bulb should be

adhered to, as it is essential that adequate roots are established before flowering is induced. It should be noted that the care symbols for each entry refer to conditions applicable when the plant is in full flower. Some corms, such as crocuses, need to be kept cool right up to the stage when the flower buds start to show color, and their early development cannot be enjoyed in the home. Some spring bulbs, such as tulips, daffodils and hyacinths, especially those treated by the grower, can be potted up and most of their growth and development watched and enjoyed. The size of the plants produced ranges from the tiny crocus to the tall and elegant amaryllis.

Hardy bulbs and corms provide temporary house plants, but tender bulbs, such as the amaryllis, can be brought into flower season after season providing they are given a rest period in autumn.

DAFFODIL AND NARCISSUS
Narcissus sp. and hybrids

These bulbs have bright, graceful flowers, many of which are scented, with colors ranging through all shades of orange, yellow, cream and white. Many different shapes are available: trumpets, clusters, double-flowered and many other forms. The common name daffodil is used for most members of the genus, although some kinds are often called narcissi, especially those whose flowers have short trumpets. The flowers bloom naturally in late winter and early spring, but can be forced to flower earlier indoors. Many of the bulbs—including *N.* "Cragford" and *N.* "Paper-white"—can be forced in bowls filled with moist pebbles.

Mini-climate 4 Cool, sunny
Size Daffodils grow from 6-18in high, according to variety. Bulbs are sold in the autumn, the best quality being double-nosed bulbs, each bulb produces two or three flowers.
Feeding Feeding is unnecessary.
Potting Plant in early autumn in a peat-based potting mixture. Use about three bulbs of tall varieties in a 6in pot or several bulbs of miniature varieties to a smaller, squat pot. Allow the tips of the bulbs to show.
Special points Soak the pots of bulbs well before starting their "wintering" of eight to ten weeks. Forced daffodils—except for paper-whites—can be planted later in the garden.

AMARYLLIS
Hippeastrum hybrids

These plants have spectacular trumpet-shaped blooms up to four on a bare stem. Straplike leaves may be present or appear after the flowers. The flowers, which are produced in spring, can be white, red, orange or yellow, and are often striped or patterned. For a dramatic display, mass several plants together in a large bowl.

Mini-climate 1 Warm, sunny.
Size The flower stems of the amaryllis grow to 20in long, with flowers as much as 6in in diameter. Ordinary bulbs are offered for sale in autumn. Specially prepared bulbs, which will flower at Christmastime, are also offered for sale.
Feeding Feed with standard liquid fertilizer every two weeks from the time the flowers fade until mid-summer. Switch to high-potash fertilizer to ripen the bulb and to ensure flowering the following year. Stop feeding from early autumn.
Potting Plant new bulbs by themselves in 4½-6in pots using soil-based potting mixture. Bury only half of the bulb in the mixture. Repotting should only be necessary every three or four years or more.
Special points These tender bulbs should not be "wintered". During the autumn rest period, leave the bulbs in their pots and water very sparingly. Stand them outside in a sunny spot during summer and early autumn to help induce flowering the following year.

MINIATURE IRIS
Iris reticulata

These lovely little bulbs produce flowers early in the season, sometimes even before the leaves have developed, although the leaves eventually become taller than the flowers. The flowers are the typical iris shape and may be light or dark blue or mauve in color, with bright-yellow markings. Each bloom rarely lasts more than two days, even if they are displayed in a cool place. However, their delicate fragrance makes it worth displaying them so that they can be appreciated close-up.

Mini-climate 4 Cool, sunny.
Size The flower stalks of miniature irises grow to about 6in in height, with leaves which are slightly longer. The tiny bulbs are sold dry in autumn or sometimes planted up and in leaf in winter.
Feeding Feeding is unnecessary.
Potting Plant the bulbs in the autumn in a shallow container using bulb fiber. Good drainage is essential as these tiny bulbs rot very easily. Plant them 2in deep and close together—about 12 in a 12in pot.
Special points Bulbs should be "wintered" for six weeks. Miniature irises can be planted out in the garden when flowering has finished.

Temperature 50°-60°F spring to autumn, 45°-50°F in winter 50°-60°F 60°-70°F **Light** sunny filtered sun shady **Humidity** low moderate high **Watering** sparingly moderately plentifully **Care** easy fairly easy challenging

CROCUS
Crocus hybrids

The most commonly seen indoor crocuses are large-flowered Dutch hybrids which have green-and-white striped leaves and white, yellow, bronze, purple or striped blooms. These are cup-shaped and appear during winter and early spring. It is best to mass one variety of crocus in a shallow bowl.

Mini-climate 4 Cool, sunny.
Size Crocuses grow to about 5in in height. Dry corms are offered for sale in late summer. Pre-planted pots are offered for sale at Christmastime.
Feeding Feeding is unnecessary.
Potting Plant several corms together in early autumn, using soil-based potting mixture or bulb fiber. Plant the corms just below the surface of the potting mixture.
Special points Corms must be "wintered" for ten weeks and only brought into a warm room when the flower buds are seen.

TULIP
Tulipa hybrids

Tulips have an extraordinary variety of shapes, colors and patterns; even the leaves can be plain or variegated. The flowers are produced during late winter and early spring. It is best to plant just one variety of tulip in a pot rather than mixing the colors in the same container.

Mini-climate 4 Cool, sunny.
Size Tulips grow to about 30in tall. Dwarf varieties grow to 8-12in tall. Most tulip bulbs are "rounds", producing only one flower. Specially prepared bulbs which will flower earlier are also offered for sale.
Feeding Feeding is only necessary if the bulbs are to be planted outside the following season. Feed every ten days from the time the buds appear.
Potting Plant in early autumn using either peat-based potting mixture or bulb fiber. Five or six bulbs should be planted close together, with just the tips exposed above the potting mixture.
Special points Prepared bulbs should be "wintered" for eight weeks, ordinary bulbs for ten weeks.

GRAPE HYACINTH
Muscari sp.

The tiny bulbs of the grape hyacinth produce long narrow stalks topped with an elongated cluster of tiny blue or white flowers. Each individual flower is bell-shaped, and rimmed with a frilled white edge. The clusters of flowers open from the bottom upwards. The narrow leaves are strap-shaped and in the case of one species at least, are produced in autumn. Plant several bulbs in small pots and display them along a windowsill.

Mini-climate 4 Cool, sunny.
Size Grape hyacinths reach a height of about 6in with leaves of nearly the same length. Bulbs already in leaf are offered for sale.
Feeding Feeding is unnecessary.
Potting Plant about twelve bulbs in a 6in pot in soil-based potting mixture or bulb fiber. Leave the tips of the bulbs above the potting mixture.
Special points These bulbs should be "wintered" for ten weeks.

HYACINTH
Hyacinthus orientalis hybrids

Hyacinth flowers appear in spring and may be single or double, red, pink, yellow, blue or white. Their color and distinctive scent make them really welcome in the home. A group known as Roman hyacinths may produce two or even three flower stalks, but these are less tightly packed with the bell-shaped flowers. Bulbs of the same color should be massed in a shallow bowl for the best effect. They can also be cut and used in flower arrangements, combined with carnations, freesias and catkins, for example.

Mini-climate 5 Cool, filtered sun.
Size The single flower stalks are 6-12in tall. Bulbs are sold according to size, in the autumn, and the size of the flower spike depends on the size of the bulb. Specially prepared bulbs which flower slightly earlier are offered for sale.
Feeding Feeding is unnecessary.
Potting Plant the bulbs "shoulder to shoulder" in soil-based potting mixture or bulb fiber. Leave the tips of the bulbs above the potting mixture. Hyacinths can also be grown in gravel, or water alone.
Special points Prepared bulbs should be "wintered" for six weeks, ordinary bulbs for ten weeks.

Cacti and succulents 1

Cacti and succulents add a different range of shapes and textures to a collection of house plants. Most of the cacti have abandoned leaves and developed their unusual body shapes to prevent excessive loss of water. Some are ribbed or segmented and they may be covered with decorative spines, bristles or hairs. One species, the old man cactus, is so closely covered with white hair that it resembles a ball of wool. Desert cacti (usually covered in spines), such as mammillarias and rebutias, have the added attraction of striking flowers. The jungle cacti (often without spines), such as the orchid and Christmas cacti, have stems which are notched at intervals and respectively produce brightly colored flowers in early spring and mid-winter. Many cacti are relatively small

reaching only a few inches in height; but others, such as the old man cactus, can grow to 10ft tall.

Succulents are those plants which have fleshy stems or leaves that store water. They come in a range of shapes and sizes as diverse as those of the cacti. Succulents may be upright and treelike in shape, or have thin trailing stems, or be spherical or columnar in outline. Some are just a few inches high; others can grow to 6ft tall and make large, striking plants. Leaf shape varies from the thick, succulent leaves of the Chinese jade and the silver crown to the thin, narrow leaves of the crown-of-thorns. Leaf color also varies from the green of the lace aloe and kalanchoe to the silvery-mauve of the rosary vine or the green and white of the queen agave.

UPRIGHT PLANTS

SILVER CROWN
Cotyledon undulata

These most unusual plants have fleshy, fan-shaped leaves with undulating edges and a dense covering of fine, silver-white scurf. Although orange-yellow flowers may appear on older plants in summer, it is for their leaves that they are grown. Mass several plants in a bowl on a low table.

Mini-climate 4 Cool, sunny.
Size Silver crowns are slow-growing reaching a height of about 20in in three years. Plants of all sizes are offered for sale.
Feeding Feed with standard liquid fertilizer once a month from spring to early autumn.
Potting Repot every spring using two-thirds soil-based potting mixture and one-third coarse sand, making provision for good drainage. Once plants are in 6in pots topdress instead.
Special points Avoid handling the plants as the meal will rub off. Water more sparingly in winter.

Similar-shaped species
Cotyledon orbiculata grows taller and has gray-green leaves edged with red, with just a little meal. Orange flowers appear in summer.

CROWN-OF-THORNS
Euphorbia milii

These succulent shrubs have horizontal branches bearing many sharp spines and relatively few leaves. The clusters of yellow or red "flowers" are in fact bracts which last for months, appearing in greatest profusion from February to September. Their interesting form and colorful bracts make them excellent specimen plants for the modern interior.

Mini-climate 1 Warm, sunny.
Size Crown-of-thorns can grow to about 3ft in height with a similar spread. Plants of all sizes are offered for sale.
Feeding Feed with standard liquid fertilizer once a month from spring to autumn.
Potting Repot young plants every second year in spring using half soil-based potting mixture and half coarse sand, making provision for good drainage. If you don't want to move an older plant into a larger pot topdress instead.
Special points These plants "bleed" a white latex if damaged: this latex should not be allowed to touch the eyes or the mouth.

KALANCHOE
Kalanchoe blossfeldiana hybrids

These attractive succulents flower in late winter and early spring, and remain in flower for about three months. The small flowers are grouped in closely packed flower heads borne on long stems. Each head has between 20 and 50 flowers. Color ranges from pink, through red, to orange and yellow. The fleshy leaves are dark green and often edged in red. Kalanchoes are best treated as annuals and discarded when flowering has finished. Use them massed on a low table for a splash of winter color.

Mini-climate 1 Warm, sunny.
Size Kalanchoes reach a maximum height of about 14in tall. A dwarf form is available and reaches 8in in height. Plants in flower are offered for sale all year but are particularly common around Christmastime.
Feeding Feed with standard liquid fertilizer once a month whilst in flower.
Potting Repotting is unnecessary.
Special points To keep plants in a decorative state for as long as possible remove flowers as they fade.

Temperature 50°-60°F spring to autumn; 45°-50°F in winter | 50°-60°F | 60°-70°F
Light sunny | filtered sun | shady
Humidity low | moderate | high
Watering sparingly | moderately | plentifully
Care easy | fairly easy | challenging

OLD MAN CACTUS
Cephalocereus senilis

The common name of these cacti is derived from the long, fine, white hair that shrouds the fleshy columnar body and hides the sharp spines. Flowers are only produced on older plants. Old man cacti look best massed with other cacti in a cactus garden.

Mini-climate 4 Cool, sunny.
Size Old man cacti are slow-growing and unlikely to grow taller than 10-12in. Plants of all sizes are offered for sale.
Feeding Feed with tomato-type fertilizer once a month from spring to mid-autumn.
Potting Repot in spring using three parts soil-based potting mixture and one part coarse sand, but only if the plant has completely filled the existing pot. If you don't want to move an older plant into a larger pot topdress instead.
Special points Do not water during the winter rest period. The long hairs may be washed in a weak solution of detergent to keep them clean.

PERUVIAN APPLE CACTUS
Cereus peruvianus "Monstrosus"

These cacti have bright-green columnar bodies which are twisted and contorted into most unusual shapes. They are in fact mutations of the true species. The yellow spines are short and inconspicuous. Large but short-lived white, scented flowers are produced in summer on older specimens. Their sculptural quality can be quite spectacular when several plants are grouped in a modern interior.

Mini-climate 4 Cool, sunny.
Size The Peruvian apple cactus is slow-growing and each mutation varies in maximum height and spread. Small plants are offered for sale.
Feeding Feed with tomato-type fertilizer once a month from spring to early autumn.
Potting Repot every spring using two-thirds soil-based potting mixture and one-third coarse sand. If you don't want to move an older plant into a larger pot topdress instead.

RABBIT'S EARS CACTUS
Opuntia microdasys

These arresting cacti are made up of flattened, oval segments which fit on top of one another. These segments are densely covered in tufts of tiny, yellowish spines. Yellow flowers are produced very occasionally. Rabbit's ears cacti have a spectacular outline and larger ones can be used as specimen plants. Group smaller plants in a cactus garden.

Mini-climate 4 Cool, sunny.
Size Rabbit's ears cacti can reach a maximum height of about 3ft and spread of about 2ft. Plants of all sizes are offered for sale.
Feeding Feed with tomato-type fertilizer once a month from spring to autumn.
Potting Repot in spring using two-thirds soil-based potting mixture and one-third coarse sand, but only if the plants have completely filled the existing pot.
Special points The tiny spines can be very painful if they touch the skin. Water more sparingly during the winter rest period.

CHINESE JADE
Crassula arborescens

These succulents have fleshy, almost round leaves which are gray in color and rimmed with red. They are borne on thick, branching, woody stems which are symmetrical in shape when the plant is mature. Small Chinese jades can be used as "trees" in dish gardens or miniature oriental gardens.

Mini-climate 4 Cool, sunny
Size Very young Chinese jades are offered for sale; they will eventually reach 3ft or more in height, when the stems will resemble gnarled tree trunks.
Feeding Feed with standard liquid fertilizer once a month from spring to early autumn.
Potting Repot every spring using three parts soil-based potting mixture and one part coarse sand. Once plants are in 8in pots topdress instead.
Special points Water more sparingly in winter.

Similar-shaped species
Crassula ovata has shiny, jade-green succulent leaves and symmetrical branches.

Cacti and succulents 2

SPHERICAL PLANTS

FISH-HOOK CACTUS
Ferocactus latispinus

These cacti are noted for their fierce-looking spines which are grouped in clusters. Spines within individual clusters vary in size, shape and color, with one being broader and more prominently hooked than the others. Really mature plants can produce violet-colored flowers in summer. Large plants make good specimens—otherwise mix them with cacti of contrasting shapes in a cactus garden.

Mini-climate 4 Cool, sunny.
Size Fish-hook cacti can reach a maximum of 1 ft in height and 8in across. Plants of all sizes are offered for sale.
Feeding Feed with tomato-type fertilizer once a month from spring to autumn.
Potting Repot in spring using a combination of two-thirds soil-based potting mixture and one-third coarse sand, but only if the plant has completely filled the existing pot.
Special points Do not water during the winter rest period or plants will rot.

BISHOP'S CAP
Astrophytum myriostigma

These spherical cacti are divided into wide segments, each covered with a silvery meal instead of thorns. They look rather like de-spined sea urchins. The bright-yellow flowers resemble daisies and appear from the top of the plant in summer. Bishop's caps look good in cactus gardens or massed in a shallow bowl with a gravelly surround.

Mini-climate 4 Cool, sunny.
Size Bishop's caps are slow-growing, reaching about 10in in height with a spread of 5in. Plants of all sizes are offered for sale.
Feeding Feed with tomato-type fertilizer once a month from spring to autumn.
Potting Repot in spring using two-thirds soil-based potting mixture and one-third coarse sand, but only if the plant has completely filled the existing pot.
Special points Water more sparingly during the winter rest period.

GOLDEN PINCUSHION
Mammillaria rhodantha

These spherical cacti have bright-green bodies covered in small knobs which bear long, yellow-orange spines. They are arranged in circular groups over the whole body. Pink, daisylike flowers appear in a ring around the top of the body in summer. Display the golden pincushion in a cactus garden or group with other cacti.

Mini-climate 4 Cool, sunny.
Size Golden pincushions grow to about 4in in height and 3in in spread. Small plants are offered for sale.
Feeding Feed with tomato-type liquid fertilizer once a month from spring to autumn.
Potting Repot in spring using two-thirds soil-based potting mixture and one-third coarse sand, but only if the plant has completely filled the existing pot.
Special points Water more sparingly during the winter rest period.

RED CROWN
Rebutia minuscula

These small, white-spined cacti are almost completely round and quickly become surrounded by many offsets. They flower when very young and are crowned with red, funnel-shaped flowers from spring through the summer. The flowers open in the morning and close in the afternoon. Group flowering red crowns together for a spectacular display in a modern setting.

Mini-climate 4 Cool, sunny.
Size Red crowns are fast-growing and can make clumps 6in across in a year or two.
Feeding Feed with tomato-type fertilizer once a month from spring to mid-autumn.
Potting Repot in spring using three parts soil-based potting mixture and one part coarse sand, but only if the roots have completely filled the existing pot.
Special points Do not water during the winter rest period or plants will rot.

Temperature 50°-60°F spring to autumn, 45°-50°F in winter   50°-60°F   60°-70°F   **Light** sunny   filtered sun   shady   **Humidity** low   moderate   high   **Watering** sparingly   moderately   plentifully   **Care** easy   fairly easy   challenging

ROSE PINCUSHION
Mammillaria zeilmanniana

The spherical body of the rose pincushion is densely covered in regularly arranged yellow and brown spines. The numerous flowers are produced in summer and form a ring at the top of the body. They are reddish-purple in color. Allow the rose pincushion to form large clumps.

Mini-climate 4 Cool, sunny.
Size Individual rose pincushions grow to 2in in height but will form clumps of 10in across in around five years. Small plants are offered for sale.
Feeding Feed with tomato-type fertilizer once a month from spring to autumn.
Potting Repot in spring using two-thirds soil-based potting mixture and one-third coarse sand, but only if the plant has completely filled the existing pot.
Special points Water more sparingly during the winter rest period.

GOLDEN BARREL CACTUS
Echinocactus grusonii

These cacti are armed with stout, golden-yellow spines arranged in rows on the ribbed stems. Older plants develop the typical pattern of raised vertical ribs. Golden barrel cacti can be displayed with other cacti or foliage plants.

Mini-climate 4 Cool, sunny.
Size Golden barrel cacti grow quickly to 3-4in across, then it takes many years for the plant to double its size, though they can eventually reach a diameter of 8in. Small plants are offered for sale.
Feeding Feed with tomato-type fertilizer once a month from spring to autumn.
Potting Repot in spring using two-thirds soil-based potting mixture and one-third coarse sand, but only if the plant has completely filled the existing pot. When repotting is not necessary topdress instead.
Special points Do not water during the winter rest period or plants will rot.

OLD LADY CACTUS
Mammillaria hahniana

These globular cacti get their name from the white, silky hairs which cover and hide the grayish-green body and the sharp spines. When the cacti are about four years old, crimson flowers appear in early May. Group several old lady cacti together for a dramatic display or use in a cactus garden.

Mini-climate 4 Cool, sunny.
Size Old lady cacti grow to 4in tall with a spread of 3in. Small plants are offered for sale.
Feeding Feed with tomato-type fertilizer once a month from spring to autumn.
Potting Repot in spring using two-thirds soil-based potting mixture and one-third coarse sand, but only if the plant has completely filled the existing pot.
Special points Water more sparingly during the winter rest period.

SPIKY-LEAVED PLANTS

LACE ALOE
Aloe aristata

These stemless succulents are made up of many fleshy leaves arranged in tight rosettes. The triangular leaves are dark green and covered with raised white spots. The small orange-red flowers are borne on a long stalk which appears from the center of the rosette in summer and last only a few days. Offsets are readily produced from the base of mature plants. Group plants together and place them so that they are seen from above for maximum effect.

Mini-climate 1 Warm, sunny.
Size Lace aloes reach a maximum height of 6in. Spread is only limited by the size of the pot.
Feeding Feed with standard liquid fertilizer once a month from spring to autumn.
Potting Repot every spring using soil-based potting mixture. If you don't want to move an older plant into a larger pot topdress instead.
Special points Water more sparingly in winter. Avoid trapping water in the rosette of leaves.

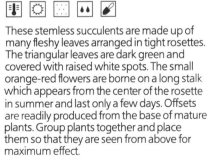

Cacti and succulents 3

FLAT-LEAVED ROSETTE-SHAPED PLANTS

PAINTED LADY
Echeveria derenbergii

These pretty succulents have tightly packed bluish-gray leaves with a coating of silvery scurf and red margins. Yellow and orange bell-shaped flowers borne on spikes are produced in winter and early spring. They make good, small specimen plants for the kitchen windowsill all year round.

Mini-climate 4   Cool, sunny.
Size   Painted ladies form cushions 4-6in across. Young single plants are offered for sale.
Feeding   Feed with half-strength standard liquid fertilizer once a month from spring to autumn.
Potting   Repot every second spring using four parts soil-based potting mixture and one part coarse sand. If you don't want to move an older plant into a larger pot topdress instead.
Special points   Water more sparingly in winter.

MOLDED WAX PLANT
Echeveria agavoides

These succulents have triangular fleshy leaves which are light green with brown tips. Yellow flowers tipped with red are produced in spring. Molded wax plants should be viewed from above for best effect—place them on a low table, or use in a succulent garden.

Mini-climate 4   Cool, sunny.
Size   Molded wax plants grow to about 3½in tall with a spread of about 6in. Plants of all sizes are offered for sale.
Feeding   Feed with half-strength standard liquid fertilizer once a month from spring to autumn.
Potting   Repot plants every second spring using four parts soil-based potting mixture and one part coarse sand. If you don't want to move an older plant into a larger pot topdress instead.
Special points   Water more sparingly in winter.

QUEEN AGAVE
Agave victoriae-reginae

These succulents have three-dimensional scalelike leaves. Each fleshy leaf is dark green with a white margin and bears a sharp black spine at its tip. Queen agaves are the most attractive of agaves and should be displayed so that they can be seen from above.

Mini-climate 4   Cool, sunny.
Size   Queen agaves are slow-growing, reaching a maximum height of 8in, but they can attain a spread of about 1½ft. Small plants are offered for sale.
Feeding   Feed with standard liquid fertilizer once a month during spring and summer.
Potting   Repot every second year in spring using two-thirds soil-based potting mixture and one-third coarse sand. If you don't want to move an older plant into a larger pot topdress instead.
Special points   Water more sparingly in winter.

TRAILING PLANTS

CLAW CACTUS
Schlumbergera truncata

These jungle cacti have flattened, segmented stems which are notched at intervals. Bright-magenta, pink or white flowers are produced in late autumn. The stems are erect at first but begin to trail as more segments are produced. They make good specimen plants for hanging baskets or shelves.

Mini-climate 2   Warm, filtered sun.
Size   The stems of claw cacti can grow to about 2ft in height and spread. Plants of all sizes are offered for sale.
Feeding   Feed with tomato-type fertilizer once a month from early November to the end of flowering.
Potting   Repot every second year in spring using two-thirds peat-based potting mixture and one-third coarse sand. Once plants are in 8-10in pots repot every year.
Special points   Water more sparingly during the rest period following flowering..

Similar-shaped species
Schlumbergera "Bridgesii" is very similar but blooms later and has less sharply defined notches.

ROSARY VINE
Ceropegia woodii

These small, tuber-forming succulents have trailing threadlike stems bearing heart-shaped leaves. These fleshy leaves, which appear in pairs at intervals along the stems, are marbled with silvery-gray and have purple undersides. Small, tube-shaped flowers appear amongst the leaves in summer. Several rosary vines displayed together in a small hanging basket in a warm room make an unusual display. Position them where they will not be brushed

against. Alternatively, the stems may be coiled in the pot so the flowers stand upright.

Mini-climate 1 Warm, sunny.
Size Rosary vine stems do not usually grow longer than 3ft. Cut back any bare stems to encourage leafy growth. Small plants are offered for sale.
Feeding Feed mature plants with standard liquid fertilizer once a month in spring and summer.
Potting Repot young plants every spring using an equal-parts combination of soil-based potting mixture and coarse sand. Older plants thrive in 3-4in half pots. Hanging baskets should have a 1in layer of drainage material at the bottom.
Special points Water more sparingly in winter.

RAT'S TAIL CACTUS
Aporocactus flagelliformis

These cacti have long streamers of narrow, fleshy stems covered with many rows of fine, prickly spines. Striking crimson-pink flowers appear in spring; each bloom lasts several days and the flowering season extends for up to two months. Display them in hanging baskets or on shelves, and position them where they will not be brushed against, as the spines are very difficult to remove from the skin. They can also be displayed in a cactus garden, with their long stems trailing through an arrangement of rocks.

Mini-climate 4 Cool, sunny.
Size Rat's tail cacti are fast-growing and their stems can reach 3ft long (occasionally much more) in three or four years. Plants of all sizes are offered for sale.
Feeding Feed with tomato-type fertilizer once a month from late December to the end of flowering.
Potting Repot every spring after flowering using soil-based potting mixture. Once plants are in a 6-10in pot topdress instead.
Special points Water more sparingly during the rest period following flowering.

Similar-shaped species
Aporocactus mallisonii has stouter stems and flowers ranging from soft pink to deep crimson.

DONKEY'S TAIL
Sedum morganianum

These most unusual-looking plants have trailing stems which are densely packed with small, fat, succulent leaves. Each stem takes on the appearance of a rope as it is so thick. The individual leaves are a pale green, covered with a fine white bloom. Pink flowers may appear at the end of each "rope" in spring, but these plants do not flower readily in the house. Ideal plants for hanging baskets, donkey's tails should be displayed in a place where they will not be brushed against, as the leaves drop off very easily.

Mini-climate 1 Warm, sunny.
Size The stems of donkey's tails can grow to a maximum of 3ft in length. Plants of all sizes are offered for sale.
Feeding Feeding is not necessary.
Potting Repot every spring using a combination of one-third coarse sand and two-thirds soil-based potting mixture. Donkey's tails grow best in half-pots or hanging baskets where they have room to spread. Once the plants have grown too big for an 8in pot, discard the plant and grow a new one from a cutting.
Special points Water more sparingly in winter.

The color guide to flowering house plants

Whites, creams and yellows

We all respond to the colors found in nature; bring them inside and they cannot fail to enhance almost any type of setting. Concentrate on related or contrasting schemes: combine plants in various shades of the same color for a subtle effect, or use exciting complementaries for a bold effect. Before you buy any flowering plants to decorate your home, always think about the location you have chosen for them and make sure that, however beautiful their color, they will enhance and harmonize with your existing color scheme.

The most colorful part of a plant is not always the flower itself: in some plants, such as the poinsettia and flamingo flower, it is the bract, or petal-like leaf, which surrounds the flowers; in others, such as the bead plant and Christmas pepper, it is the berries and fruits which appear after the flowers have faded.

WHITE SAILS
Spathiphyllum "Clevelandii" (see p.169)
White arumlike flower heads which turn pale green with age. The color of this plant suits any kind of interior decoration.

PRIMROSE
Primula obconica (see p.181)
Pure white flowers with green centers, also available with pink, red and mauve flowers. Use either singly, or massed in a bowl using different shades from white through to mauve.

ITALIAN BELLFLOWER
Campanula isophylla (see p.191)
Star-shaped white flowers, also available in several shades of blue. Use plants of one color, or mix blue and white together, and place on a high shelf or in a hanging basket.

WAX BEGONIA
Begonia semperflorens-cultorum (see p.176)
Small white flowers, also available with pink and red flowers. Arrange plants of the same color together or mix them with exotic-colored leaves.

MADAGASCAR PERIWINKLE
Catharanthus roseus
White flowers with carmine-red centers, also available with pink or all-white flowers. Use in groups with other plants or mass in a bowl or basket.

YELLOW ELATIOR BEGONIA
Begonia "Elatior" hybrids (see p.176)
Primrose-yellow double flowers, also available in many other colors. Mass plants of one color for a bold effect.

CHRISTMAS PEPPER
Capsicum annuum (see p.180)
The bright fruits may be orange, red or yellow and will change color as they ripen. Use massed to make a colorful winter table decoration.

WHITE ELATIOR BEGONIA
Begonia "Elatior" hybrids (see p.176)
Cream-colored double flowers, also available in many other colors.

YELLOW TUBEROUS BEGONIA
Begonia tuberhybrida (see p.176)
Deep-yellow flowers, also available with white, pink, red or orange flowers.

BLACK EYED SUSAN VINE
Thunbergia alata (see p.185)
Bright orange-yellow flowers with a black central eye. Leave them to ramble through other plants or train them up a support to create a cascade of color.

See below left
AFRICAN VIOLET
Saintpaulia hybrids (see p.175)
Pure white flowers and white flowers edged with purple, also available in many shades of pink, blue and purple. Mass plants of one color, or in various shades of the same color, in a shallow bowl on a low table.

YELLOW CHRYSANTHEMUM
Chrysanthemum morifolium hybrids (see p.181)
Pale yellow daisylike flowers, available in many other colors.

WHITE TUBEROUS BEGONIA
Begonia tuberhybrida (see p.176)
Ivory-colored flowers, also available with pink, red, yellow or orange flowers. Display individually or in groups of one, or several, colors.

GOLDEN CHRYSANTHEMUM
Chrysanthemum morifolium hybrids (see p.181)
Dense golden flowers, available in many other colors.

YELLOW FLOWERING MAPLE
Abutilon hybridum (see p.162)
Bell-shaped, creamy-yellow flowers, available in many other colors. Group several different colors together or display as feature plants when full grown.

WHITE CHRYSANTHEMUM
Chrysanthemum morifolium hybrids (see p.181)
Dense creamy-white flowers, available in many other colors. Mass in a large basket and display so they can be seen from above.

See following page

Oranges and reds

CHRISTMAS PEPPER
Capsicum annuum (see p.180)
The bright fruits may be orange, red or yellow and
will change color as they ripen. Use massed to make a
colorful winter table decoration.

WHITE ELATIOR BEGONIA
Begonia "Elatior" hybrids (see p.176)
Cream-colored double flowers, also
available in many other colors.

BEAD PLANT
Nertera granadensis (see p.192)
Beadlike, deep-orange berries cover the plant.
Make a formal display on a table, or low shelf.

YELLOW KALANCHOE
Kalanchoe blossfeldiana hybrids (see p.196)
Long-lasting deep-yellow flowers, also available with
orange, pink and red flowers. Mass plants together
on a sunny windowsill for winter color.

PINK KALANCHOE
Kalanchoe blossfeldiana
hybrids (see p.196)
Long-lasting pink flowers
also available in yellow,
red and orange.

ORANGE KALANCHOE
Kalanchoe blossfeldiana
hybrids (see p.196)
Long-lasting orange flowers,
also available in yellow, pink
and red.

**GOLDEN
CHRYSANTHEMUM**
*Chrysanthemum
morifolium* hybrids
(see p.181)
Dense golden flowers,
available in
many other colors.

RED KALANCHOE
Kalanchoe blossfeldiana hybrids (see p.196)
Long-lasting scarlet flowers, also
available with yellow, orange and
pink flowers.

CHINESE HIBISCUS
Hibiscus rosa-sinensis
hybrids (see p.178)
Large deep-red flowers with a protruding stamen, also
available with white, yellow, pink or orange flowers.
Use either singly or in a group with different-colored forms.

PINK IMPATIENS
Impatiens wallerana hybrids (see p.177)
Deep-pink single flowers, also available with white, red, orange or bicolored flowers. Mass plants of the same color together in a hanging basket or window-box.

SCARLET STAR
Guzmania lingulata (see p.174)
Scarlet bracts surround small white flowers. Put plants together in a container or use them in a symmetrical arrangement. They may also be cut and wired for use in large floral arrangements.

BEDDING GERANIUM
Pelargonium hortorum hybrids (see p.179)
Tight clusters of scarlet flowers, also available with white, mauve or pink flowers. Display in a row along a windowsill or group with foliage geraniums.

GLOXINIA
Sinningia speciosa hybrids (see p.175)
Red trumpet-shaped flowers, also available with white or violet flowers. Mass plants together and display on a low table.

PINK ELATIOR BEGONIA
Begonia "Elatior" hybrids (see p.176)
Deep-pink double flowers, also available in many other colors.

RED FLOWERING MAPLE
Abutilon hybridum (see p.162)
Scarlet bell-shaped flowers, available in many other colors. Group several different colors together or display as a feature plant when full grown.

See following page

Pinks, mauves and purples

PINK IMPATIENS
Impatiens wallerana hybrids (see p.177)
Deep-pink single flowers, also available
with white, red, orange or bicolored
flowers. Put plants of the same
color together in a hanging basket
or window-box.

FLAMINGO FLOWER
Anthurium andraeanum hybrids (see p.182)
A salmon-colored, shield-shaped bract surrounds
the central flower spike, also available with white or red flower
heads. Group plants together for an exotic display.

**RED WAX
BEGONIA** *Begonia semperflorens-cultorum* (see p.176)
Scarlet flowers with yellow centers, also available with pink or white
flowers. Mass plants of the same color together or mix with exotic-colored leaves.

PINK NEW GUINEA IMPATIENS
Impatiens "New Guinea" hybrids (see p.177)
Pinky-orange flowers and strongly variegated leaves, also available
with white, pink, orange
and bicolored flowers.

SHRIMP PLANT
Justicia brandegeana
White flowers emerge from
pink, shrimp-shaped
bracts. Show plants
together in a shallow
basket for a subtle
color effect.

PINK ELATIOR BEGONIA
Begonia "Elatior"
hybrids (see p.176)
Deep-pink double flowers,
also available in many
other colors.

CAPE LEADWORT
Plumbago auriculata (see p.186)
Clusters of small, blue flowers, also
available with white flowers.
Use trained round a window or
up a support.

PINK WAX BEGONIA
Begonia semperflorens-cultorum (see p.176)
Strong-pink flowers with yellow eyes,
also available in red and white.

ITALIAN BELLFLOWER
Campanula isophylla (see p.191)
Star-shaped, bluish-mauve flowers, also available in other shades of blue and white. Use plants of one color, or mix blue and white together, and place on a high shelf or in a hanging basket.

PURPLE AFRICAN VIOLET
Saintpaulia hybrids (see p.175)
Intense violet-colored flowers with yellow centers, also available with pink, blue or white flowers. Mass plants of one color, or several shades of the same color, in a shallow bowl on a low table.

GLOXINIA
Sinningia speciosa hybrids (see p.175)
Purple blooms banded with white, also available with white or red flowers. Put plants of the same color together on a low table.

PINK AFRICAN VIOLET
Saintpaulia hybrids (see p.175)
Deep-pink flowers with yellow centers, also available with blue, purple or white flowers.

PASSION FLOWER
Passiflora caerulea (see p.185)
Curious white-petalled flowers with purple fringed filaments, also available with pink and purple petals. Train round a sunny window or up a support.

URN PLANT
Aechmea fasciata (see p.172)
Short-lived, pale-blue flowers emerge from pink bracts. Use as feature plants or in a bold arrangement.

GERMAN VIOLET
Exacum affine (see p.178)
Tiny lilac-colored flowers with gold centers, also available with white flowers. Mass several plants in a large bowl or group with golden flowers for counterpoint.

PINK IMPATIENS
Impatiens wallerana hybrids (see p.177)
Sugar-pink single flowers, available with white, red, orange or bicolored flowers.

The seasonal guide to flowering house plants

Key

Winter / Spring / Summer / Autumn

Plant	Jan	Feb	Mar	Apr	May	Jun	Jul	Aug	Sep	Oct	Nov	Dec	Comments
Egyptian star cluster (see p.177)	■								■	■	■	■	Can flower at other times
Christmas cherry (see p.180)	■								■	■	■	■	Fruit
Tulip (see p.194)	■	■										■	Can flower at other times
Claw cactus (see p.201)										■	■		Can flower at other times
Poinsettia (see p.178)	■	■	■							■	■		
Hyacinth (see p.194)	■	■	■									■	
Daffodil and narcissus (see p.195)	■	■	■									■	
Crocus (see p.194)	■	■	■										
Scarlet star (see p.174)	■	■	■										
Florist's cyclamen (see p.180)	■	■	■	■						■	■		
White-scented jasmine (see p.186)	■	■	■	■									
Kalanchoe (see p.196)	■	■	■	■							■		Can flower at other times
Miniature iris (see p.194)	■	■	■	■									
Amaryllis (see p.194)	■	■	■	■	■								
Primrose (see p.181)	■	■	■	■	■	■							Can flower at other times
African hemp (see p.164)		■	■	■									
African violet (see p.175)		■	■	■	■	■	■	■	■	■			Can flower continuously
Powder-puff cactus (see p.198)		■	■	■	■								
Rat's tail cactus (see p.201)		■	■	■									
Azalea (see p.179)		■	■	■									Can flower at other times
Grape hyacinth (see p.195)		■	■	■									
Saffron spike (see p.182)		■	■	■	■								
Rose pincushion (see p.198)		■	■	■	■								
Regal geranium (see p.179)		■	■	■	■	■							
Bird-of-paradise (see p.164)		■	■	■	■	■							Only mature plants will bloom
Wax begonia (see p.176)		■	■	■	■	■	■	■					Can flower continuously
Columnea (see p.189)		■	■	■	■	■	■	■	■	■			Can flower continuously
Crown-of-thorns (see p.196)		■	■	■	■	■	■	■	■	■			Can flower continuously
Cineraria (see p.178)			■	■	■								
Red crown (see p.198)			■	■	■	■							
White sails (see p.169)			■	■	■	■							Can flower at other times
Wax flower (see p.185)			■	■	■	■							
Bishop's cap (see p.198)			■	■	■	■	■						
Chinese hibiscus (see p.178)			■	■	■	■	■	■	■				Can flower at other times
Flaming sword (see p.173)			■	■	■	■	■	■	■				Only mature plants will bloom
Paper flower (see p.186)			■	■	■	■	■	■	■	■			
Impatiens (see p.177)			■	■	■	■	■	■	■	■			Can flower continuously
Cape leadwort (see p.186)			■	■	■	■	■	■	■	■			
Calamondin orange (see p.162)				■	■	■	■	■					Can flower at other times
Bird's nest bromeliad (see p.174)				■	■	■	■	■	■				Only mature plants will bloom
Cape primrose (see p.175)				■	■	■	■	■	■	■			
Black-eyed Susan vine (see p.185)					■	■	■	■	■	■			
Gloxinia (see p.175)						■	■	■					
Blue-flowered torch (see p.172)						■	■	■					Only mature plants will bloom
Flowering maple (see p.162)						■	■	■					
Urn plant (see p.172)						■	■	■					Can flower at other times
Cupid's bower (see p.181)						■	■	■					
Flamingo flower (see p.182)						■	■	■					Can flower at other times
Elatior begonia (see p.176)						■	■	■					
Queen's tears (see p.173)						■	■	■					Can flower at other times
German violet (see p.178)						■	■	■					
Miniature wax plant (see p.189)						■	■	■					
Passion flower (see p.185)						■	■	■	■	■			
Bead plant (see p.192)						■	■	■	■				Fruit
Golden trumpet (see p.186)						■	■	■	■	■			
Blushing bromeliad (see p.174)						■	■	■	■	■			Only mature plants will bloom
Christmas pepper (see p.180)						■	■	■	■	■	■	■	Fruit
Amethyst violet (see p.176)							■	■	■	■			
Italian bellflower (see p.191)							■	■	■	■			
Florist's chrysanthemum (see p.181)								■	■	■			Can flower continuously

THE CUT-FLOWER GUIDE

Displays of cut flowers can transform a room with their shapes, colors and scents, and bring the freshness of the garden indoors at any time of the year. Arrangements need not be lavish; a few flowers arranged in an appropriate container can look just as effective as a large, complicated display.

On the following pages you will find a seasonal guide to the flowers and berries that are most useful to the flower arranger. Foliage is another essential ingredient of flower arrangements and, since much of it is available from spring to autumn, it has been grouped according to its color. Many of the types of foliage and flowers shown mix well together for striking seasonal arrangements. The entry for each featured plant contains advice on how to prepare the cut stems, and suggests how it can be used in arrangements.

Spring flowers 1

A quick appraisal of late winter and early spring color is of a ubiquitous dull brown, but on closer inspection you will find many interesting colors and textures. Quite early in the year the garden becomes infused with spots of white, lemon and pale green. As the season moves properly into spring, the colors intensify—and, against the fresh green of the new foliage, you see the many yellows of daffodils, followed by the subsequent rainbow colors of other cultivated bulbs and flowering trees.

Many garden shrubs also flower early; the sprays of the bright yellow forsythia, the white spiraea blossoms and the green clusters of European cranberry bush flowers can be cut and used to extend the outline of a simple spring arrangement. Later in the season, fruit blossoms, such as apple and pear, come into their own too, along with the earliest of the perennial material from the garden. These early perennials include some types of iris, violets, spurges, lilacs and rhododendrons.

LILY-OF-THE-VALLEY
Convallaria majalis

These delicate, bell-shaped flowers are easily grown in a shady spot in the garden. As they grow from a creeping rhizome, they quickly spread. Processed roots for forcing are sold by a few bulb dealers in winter. They look best arranged in bunches, with their own dark-green foliage, in a small glass vase. The heady scent of the flowers adds to their attraction. The white flowers are also very beautiful when mixed with other white flowers in a bridal bouquet.

Colors available White and pale pink.

Preparation Cut the stems on a slant and make a 2in slit with a sharp knife. Strip any foliage from the floral stems and give a drink in warm water for about an hour before arranging in deep water.

Daffodils **1** "Golden Ducat" **2** "Pheasant's Eye" **3** "Mrs Backhouse" **4** "Inglescombe" **5** "Cheerfulness" **6** "Mary Copeland"

DAFFODIL
Narcissus sp. and hybrids

This group of hardy spring bulbs includes many different species and hybrids. Daffodil is the common name used for most members of the genus, although some kinds are referred to as narcissi, especially those whose flowers have short center trumpets. Dwarf species are available, while the tallest varieties are nearly 2ft in height. The bulbs must be planted in the autumn but then reappear each spring. Use the flowers in country-style spring arrangements. They also go well with forsythia or catkins and look good when massed in a simple container for a bold color effect.

Colors available Daffodils are available in a wide range of combinations of white, cream, yellow, orange and peach.

Preparation Cut the stems on a slant and make a 2in slit with a sharp knife. Pass the cut ends through a flame to seal them. Give a deep drink for about an hour before arranging in shallow water.

FRITILLARY
Fritillaria sp. and hybrids

Fritillarys are not easily grown in the garden, but ones raised in a cool greenhouse can be bought from florists' shops. The size and shape of the fritillary flower depend upon the species—some have clusters of large flowers at the top of a tall stalk, others have small bell-

shaped flowers which are borne singly on drooping stems. The leaves resemble those of a tulip in shape, although some plants can have very long, narrow leaves. Fritillarys are amongst the first long-stemmed flowers to bloom in spring and the clustered flowers look good in large arrangements. The smaller species have drooping heads, so look better arranged in a simple vase on their own.

Colors available Red, orange, yellow, white, maroon and purple. The flowers of the smaller species are usually checkered or spotted with another color.

Preparation Cut the stems with a sharp knife to avoid bruising. Give a deep drink in cool water before arranging.

Lilacs **1** "Katherine Havemeyer" **2** "Maud Notcutt" **3** "Massena"

LILAC
Syringa sp. and hybrids

Lilacs are woody shrubs, easily grown in the garden, which flower profusely in late spring. Forced lilac is also readily available in florists' shops in winter and early spring. It should only be bought on long stems, as short-stemmed flowers do not last as well. The tiny, highly fragrant flowers are arranged in elongated clusters and the full blossom heads look good mixed with other pastel-colored flowers, such as pale-colored poppies and peonies, in a simple vase. The yellow and white varieties can be used in soft-yellow and cream spring arrangements.

Colors available Purple, pink, white, whitish-green and yellow.

Preparation Cut the stems on a slant and make a 2in slit with a sharp knife. Strip any foliage from the floral stems and dip into boiling water before giving a deep drink in cold water overnight. Arrange on long stems in deep water.

Lily-of-the-valley

Additional features
Long-lasting · Useful foliage · Fragrant · Suitable for drying

Lilies

LILY
Lilium hybrids

Lilies are amongst the loveliest of flowers, having an extremely elegant shape. Despite their fragile appearance, most lilies can be grown in the garden, usually among perennials. They should be arranged simply, with nothing to detract from the flower itself. Ivory-colored lilies are useful for wedding bouquets or church decoration.

Colors available Lilies are available in all colors except blue. Many flowers have two or more colors and most have dots or stripes of another color.

Preparation Cut the stems on a slant and make a 2in slit with a sharp knife. Strip any foliage from the floral stems and give a deep drink overnight in cold water before arranging.

TULIP
Tulipa sp. and hybrids

The vast range of color and shape makes the tulip useful for many different types of arrangement. Apart from the traditional single, cuplike form, tulips may be double, feathered, vase-shaped or shaped like a lily. Tulip stems have a tendency to twist and bend once they are cut so they are not suitable for very formal arrangements. Tulips mix well with many types of flowers and have colors to suit most arrangements. Possibly the best way of displaying them is to mass flowers of the same color in a vase with their own foliage.

Colors available Tulips are available in most colors, ranging from the almost black to pure white. Many are streaked with another color.

Preparation Cut off any white ends to the stems and all foliage, and roll the bunch in newspaper. Place the bundle in deep warm water for a few hours. This will straighten any curved stems. Prick each stem just below the head with a pin and arrange in water containing a teaspoonful of sugar.

Rhododendrons

RHODODENDRON
Rhododendron sp. and hybrids

Rhododendrons are large, robust flowers. Use flowers on long stems to give a focal point to large, textured arrangements; shorter-stemmed flowers can be used in small vases of snowdrops or primroses. The heads can be floated in shallow dishes of water.

Colors available White, pink, red and purple.

Preparation Cut the stems on a slant and make a 2in slit with a sharp knife. Strip any foliage from the floral stems and leave overnight in hot water. Arrange in fresh water containing a little household bleach.

Tulips

"White Triumphator"

"Aster Neilson"

"Dyanito"

"Blue Parrot"

"West Point"

"Flying Dutchman"

"Black Parrot"

"Greenland"

"May Blossom"

"Captain Fryatt"

"China Pink"

Spring flowers 2

Freesias

FREESIA
Freesia hybrids

❋ ✄ 🗑

Freesias are very delicate in appearance and can become "lost" in very large, fussy arrangements. Their elongated shape is best seen when a small spray is displayed on its own in a vase, although the large white freesias can be used in bridal bouquets. The double variety lasts longer than the single variety.

Colors available White, yellow, mauve, pink, red and orange.

Preparation Cut the stems on a slant and make a 2in slit with a sharp knife. Give a deep drink before arranging in deep water.

SPURGE
Euphorbia sp.

❋ ✄

These small shrubby plants should be included in every flower arranger's garden, as they last well when cut and add an unusual range of colors, shapes and textures to country-style flower arrangements. The large

inflorescences are made up of tiny flowers surrounded by papery bracts and look good contrasted with feathery grasses or foliage.

Colors available Orange, red, yellow and green.

Preparation Cut the stems on a slant and make a 2in slit with a sharp knife. Scald the ends in boiling water or pass them briefly over a flame to staunch the flow of latex from the cut stem. Give a deep drink in cold water before arranging.

IRIS
Iris sp. and hybrids

✄ 🗑

These are very useful flowers, particularly if you grow them in your garden, as the foliage is as decorative as the flowers. The flowers are amongst the first to appear in spring. There are many varieties available, giving an enormous range of shapes, colors and sizes. Some irises grow very tall and have large flower heads suitable for large-scale flower arrangements. The smaller, early irises can be arranged with some of their own foliage and a few tulips.

Colors available Mauve, purple, yellow, brown, orange, gray and white. The flowers are usually spotted or striped with another color.

Preparation Cut the stems on a slant and make a 2in slit with a sharp knife. Strip any foliage from the floral stems and give a deep drink in cool water.

MIMOSA
Acacia dealbata

✄ 🗑 🌲

These delicate, fluffy flower heads mix well with all kinds of spring flowers. They can be used in formal bouquets, but look equally lovely massed in a terracotta pot with a few golden daffodils and their own foliage. The

feathery, gray-green leaves make good background material in many arrangements and the strong, heady scent adds to the attractiveness of this plant.

Colors available Yellow.

Preparation Keep wrapped in plastic to exclude air for as long as possible before arranging. Just prior to arranging, remove the plastic and dip flower heads in cold water for a few moments. Cut the stems on a slant and make a 2in slit with a sharp knife. Dip the stems in boiling water for a few seconds, then give a deep drink in warm water until the heads are dry.

Stocks **1** "Parma Violet" **2** "Yellow of Nice" **3** "Princess Alice"

STOCK
Matthiola incana

🗑 🌲

Stocks are widely available in both gardens and florists' shops. Those grown under glass are available for many months of the year.

Spurges

Euphorbia wulfenii

Euphorbia robbiae

Euphorbia griffithii "Fireglow"

Euphorbia characias

Euphorbia polychroma

Additional features
Long-lasting Useful foliage Fragrant Suitable for drying

Their short spikes are packed with small, round flowers which can act as the focal point, or as filler material, in informal country-style arrangements.

Colors available White, yellow, crimson, mauve, purple, pink and orange.

Preparation Cut the stems on a slant and make a 2in slit with a sharp knife. Strip any foliage from the floral stems. Dip in boiling water for a few minutes before giving a deep drink in cold water. Arrange in deep water.

POLYANTHUS
Primula vulgaris

These small, bushy plants have tubular flowers which flare out into a round face with a prominent, colored eye. The variety of colors is immense, as new hybrids are being produced all the time. They can be grown in the garden but, for instant color, it is often easier to buy them in florists' shops in early spring. Choose polyanthus with short stems, as the longer ones wilt very easily. Simple bunches bound with their own foliage look good in plain containers. Alternatively, they can be used with other similarly colored flowers, such as hellebores or heaths, in a miniature arrangement.

Colors available Polyanthus are available in all colors including blue. Many varieties have a yellow ring surrounding the eye.

Preparation Cut the stems short with a sharp knife. Dip the ends in boiling water for a few minutes and then give a deep drink. Prick each stem just below the head to allow any air bubbles to escape. This helps the water to rise freely up the stem.

BABY'S BREATH
Gypsophila paniculata

These delicate sprays of flowers were once looked upon as foils for other, more robust flowers. They do add a pretty, hazy effect to arrangements of roses and carnations, but a generous amount massed in a glass vase or urn can look very striking in a modern setting. Baby's breath is commonly used in bouquets.

Colors available White and pink.

Preparation Cut stems on a slant and make a 2in slit with a sharp knife. Strip any foliage from the floral stems and give a deep drink in hot water before arranging. Spray the arrangements with setting spray as the flowers fall easily. Change the water regularly to prevent fouling.

Baby's breath

Peruvian lily

PERUVIAN LILY
Alstroemeria pelegrina

These elegant, eye-catching flowers are hard to grow in the garden but are available in florists' shops for most of the year. They have stiff, upright stems at the top of which are the groups of flowers, making them ideal for massing in a vase, with just a few of their own leaves, for a striking display.

Colors available White, pink, red, orange and lilac. Some may be marked with red-purple dots.

Preparation Cut the stems on a slant and make a 2in slit with a sharp knife. Strip any foliage from the floral stems and give a deep drink in cool water before arranging.

CALLA LILY
Zantedeschia aethiopica

It is possible to grow these beautiful flowers outside in a sheltered spot, but the best specimens come from the greenhouse. They have thick, fleshy flowers borne on erect stalks. The heart-shaped leaves are a rich green and just a few blooms, displayed with their own foliage in a round glass bowl, make an elegant display. The strong shape of calla lilies makes them a good focal point in any green group; they are also useful for formal displays which need to be seen from a distance.

Colors available White, yellow, green and pink

Preparation Cut the stems on a slant and make a 2in slit with a sharp knife. Give a deep drink in warm water before arranging. Soak the leaves in a starch solution for twenty-four hours to make them last longer.

Flowering fruit trees 1 *Prunus serrulata* **2** *Prunus serrulata* "Ukon" **3** *Pyrus calleryana* "Chanticleer" **4** *Malus eleyi* **5** *Prunus serrulata* "Shirotae" **6** *Prunus serrulata* "Kwanzan"

FLOWERING FRUIT TREES
Prunus sp. and *Malus* sp.

This is a large group of ornamental and fruiting trees which bear delicate clusters of flowers in early spring. Masses of flowers make excellent background material for displays of pink tulips or yellow daffodils. A Japanese effect can be created by displaying a few stems of a white-flowered variety in a red and black setting.

Colors available Red, pink and white.

Preparation Cut the stems on a slant and make a 2in slit with a sharp knife. Give a cool drink before arranging in deep water.

PANSY
Viola wittrockiana

Pansies are pretty flowers whose round heads are usually marked with appealing, facelike blotches. Their small, delicate size suits them to table-top or miniature arrangements in small containers. Many are subtly scented.

Colors available Pansies are available in all colors, including blue and black. There are many plain-colored varieties and many marked types.

Preparation The soft stems should be cut with a sharp knife to avoid bruising them. Dip the heads in water for a few minutes before arranging.

Other spring flowers

Crocus	Honesty
Hawthorn	Blazing star
Rosemary	Azalea
Bluebell	Wallflower
Forsythia	Magnolia
Clematis	Arctic poppy
Spirea	Buttercup
Kafir lily	Primrose
Alyssum	Love-in-mist
Jasmine	Broom
Hyacinth	Jew's mallow
Cowslip	Quince

Summer flowers 1

S ummer brings flowers and foliage in abundance, of every shape, size, color and texture. The overall colors of summer move from the pale yellows, pastel pinks, peaches and white of the carnations and foxgloves, to the deeper tones and warmer colors of peonies and sweet Williams. Many summer flowers, such as the poppy, sweet pea and rose, are available in a wide range of colors, and can be used in many different arrangements. Moreover, flowers are often accompanied by an equally wide range of different shaped and colored foliage—of which the hostas, ivies and privets must be among the most useful.

While much available material is herbaceous or perennial, there is an equally large range of flowering shrub material: use these branches either on their own or with cut flowers for bigger, grander displays, choosing from weigela, viburnum or mock orange, amongst many others.

Summer arrangements should make use of this abundance of material, and flowers should be arranged *en masse*. Most summer flowers have a heady fragrance which makes them doubly welcome in the home.

LADY'S MANTLE
Alchemilla vulgaris

These plants are easily grown in the garden but are not commonly seen in florists' shops. Lady's mantle is very versatile: the blooms can be used in both formal and informal arrangements, and the lovely, yellow-green heads mix well with almost every color of flower and foliage. They also look good massed on their own or arranged with feathery grasses and foliage in a simple glass or dull metal container. The round, umbrella-like leaves are soft and downy and contrast beautifully with red or bronze leaves in an arrangement.

Colors available Yellow-green.

Preparation Cut the stems on a slant and make a 2in slit with a sharp knife. Strip any foliage from the floral stems and arrange in deep water immediately. This will prevent air bubbles forming in the stem.

Peonies **1** *Paeonia lactiflora* **2** *Paeonia officinalis* "Rubra-plena" **3** *Paeonia officinalis*

PEONY
Paeonia sp.

The most commonly seen peony is the large-flowered, deep-magenta variety. Although very beautiful, it needs to be used thoughtfully as it can be dominating in flower arrangements; it looks good arranged with red or yellow-green foliage. There are many other kinds of peony, all of which can be used as focal points in arrangements. Red peonies mix well with other red flowers, and the delicate pinks look ravishing with the salmon-pink spikes of foxgloves or gladioli. Larger peonies can be used in large arrangements that are meant to be seen from a distance.

Colors available Shades of pink, red, magenta, yellow and white.

Preparation After cutting, peonies can be left out of water for several days if placed in a cold room. If put in plastic bags in a cold room they will keep fresh for some weeks. Prior to arranging, cut the stems on a slant and make a 2in slit with a sharp knife. Give a long, warm drink before arranging.

FOXTAIL LILY
Eremurus sp.

These long spikes are covered in densely packed, small, star-shaped flowers. The flowers open from the bottom of the stem upwards and, as the stems can range in height from 2-6ft, they can look majestic arranged in a long, narrow vase with some stiff, lance-shaped leaves.

Colors available White, yellow, pink and orange.

Preparation Cut the stems on a slant and make a 2in slit with a sharp knife. Give a deep drink in cool water before arranging.

CARNATIONS AND CLOVE PINKS
Dianthus caryophyllus hybrids

Carnations and pinks present a great challenge to the grower, as they hybridize very easily and new hybrids are always appearing on the market. These new hybrids may be bigger, smaller, more fragrant, have brighter colors, or be formed with a new mixture of colors—the range to choose from is vast. Although pinks and carnations look very similar, they can be told apart by the fact that carnations have larger flowers, wider leaves and longer stems than the pinks. Carnations and pinks are very formal flowers, especially the shop-bought ones with very straight stems. They can be used in all kinds of summer arrangements, but do look good on their own in a simple, tall-necked vase. Use the delicate pink or white flowers with gray foliage such as eucalyptus or artemisia.

Colors available Available in almost every color except blue. Many are marked with another color.

Preparation Cut the stems on a slant between the nodes (bumps on the stems). Make a 2in slit with a sharp knife and strip any foliage from the floral stems. Give a long deep drink before arranging them in warm water.

"Purple Frosted"

"Crowley Sim"

Lady's mantle

Additional features
Long-lasting Useful foliage Fragrant Suitable for drying

Sword lilies **1** "Albert Schweitzer" **2** "White Angel" **3** "Madam Butterfly"

SWORD LILY
Gladiolus hybrids

With their elegant shape, gladioli are extremely useful for all types of arrangement. They are also easy to grow in the garden. There are many varieties of gladiolus, varying in size, color and floret type, although all the florets face the same way on the flower spike. Arrange the smaller, soft-colored gladioli with pink roses or other small flowers. Three or four spikes of the tall, bright-red gladioli look good in a long, elegant vase in a prominent position.

Colors available A wide range of colors including red, orange, yellow, pink and white.

Preparation Cut the stems on a slant and make a 2in slit with a sharp knife. Cut stems under water and, to make the blooms last longer, cut off a small piece of the stem every four or five days. If you don't want to use these flowers immediately, keep them in a cold place for about a week.

POPPY
Papaver sp. and hybrids

The popular conception of the poppy is of a bright-red, large-petaled flower. There are, however, many hybrids and cultivars available in a wide range of colors and sizes. Poppies have very delicate petals so they are not really suitable for formal arrangements. They are very short-lived, usually lasting only one day. Use the bright-red flowers with dark-green foliage. All the pastel shades mix well with other muted flowers—lilacs, roses and delphiniums.

Colors available Many shades of red, pink, orange, yellow, cream and white.

Preparation Cut the stems with a sharp knife. Dip the ends in boiling water or pass them over a flame to seal them and prevent the sap from clouding the water. Give a long, deep drink before arranging.

Sweet Williams

SWEET WILLIAM
Dianthus barbatus

Fragrant varieties of sweet William are available in florists' shops and are very easy to cultivate in the garden. Their round, flat heads consist of many small flowers tightly packed together. The bright colors mix very well with other summer flowers in informal arrangements, and they look particularly attractive when massed together in a wicker basket.

Colors available Flowers are usually a mixture of two or more of the following colors: red, pink, crimson and white, arranged in rings of color around the center of the flower.

Preparation Cut the stems on a slant and make a 2in slit with a sharp knife. Strip any foliage from the floral stems. Give a long, cool drink before arranging.

Carnations and clove pinks

"Zebra"

"Portrait"

"Joker"

"Allwood's Cream"

"Fragrant Ann"

"Arthur Sim"

"Comoco Sim"

"Inchmery"

Summer flowers 2

Chinese delphinium

DELPHINIUM
Delphinium sp. and hybrids

Delphiniums are popular as both florists' flowers and garden plants, and many new hybrids are coming on to the market, extending the range of colors and sizes available. The long spikes are laden with small, fragrant flowers and are good for arrangements in tall vases. Use the tall, white varieties for large-scale decorations. If you don't have room for large arrangements, there are shorter hybrids available in all the colors, and these can look

Foxgloves

 Digitalis purpurea

D. purpurea "Alba"

D. grandiflora "Ambigua"

very attractive massed together with some of their own feathery foliage.

Colors available Many shades of blue and mauve. Also pink, white and cream.

Preparation Cut the stems on a slant and make a 2in slit with a sharp knife. Give a long drink in cool water before arranging. To make the flowers last longer for a special occasion, it is worth filling the hollow stems with water and plugging the ends with cotton wool.

FLOWERING ONION
Allium sp.

These members of the onion family bear numerous tiny flowers in often large, ball-like clusters. Use as focal points in an arrangement of large-headed flowers.

Colors available Yellow, purple, pink and white.

Preparation Cut the stems on a slant and make a 2in slit with a sharp knife before arranging in deep water. Add a teaspoonful of bleach to the water to remove the onion smell.

FOXGLOVE
Digitalis sp. and hybrids

These beautiful, mostly biennial, flowers on tall, stately plants have always been popular in gardens or in semi-wild sites where they selfsow freely and tolerate all soil types. Grow your own from seed as they are rare in florists' shops. They are useful in arrangements as they retain their petals for some considerable time after cutting. Their delicate colors mix well with other pastel-colored flowers and their elongated form can outline large, formal arrangements. Foxgloves are also handsome arranged informally in a basket or terracotta pot.

Colors available Mauve, purple, white, cream, red, yellow and gold. Most are spotted with another color within the bell.

Preparation Cut the stems on a slant and make a 2in slit with a sharp knife. Strip any foliage from the floral stems and give an overnight drink in warm water before arranging.

Rose hybrids **1** "Message" **2** "Goldgleam" **3** "Pascali" **4** "Margaret Merrill"

HYBRID ROSES
Rosa hybrids

The variety of roses available is never-ending as new cultivars appear each year. The only drawback has been the loss of fragrance from some introductions. Hybrid tea, floribunda and miniature roses all have compact bushes with mainly high-centered double flowers. Some varieties have attractive hips. Roses of one color, massed in a basket, are lovely. So is one flower in a bud vase. Use the foliage as background material.

Colors available Roses are available in just about every shade of every color except blue.

Preparation Cut the stems on a slant and make a 2in slit with a sharp knife. Strip any foliage from the floral stems and dip stems in boiling water for a minute. Give a long drink in cold water before arranging.

Yarrow "Coronation Gold"

FERN LEAF YARROW
Achillea filipendulina

These informal-looking, flat-headed flowers are available in a range of sizes as well as colors. They are easily grown in the garden and commonly found along roadsides and in hedgerows. Use large, bright-gold heads as

Additional features

Long-lasting · Useful foliage · Fragrant · Suitable for drying

focal points in large arrangements and smaller, pale-yellow or white heads in arrangements of white flowers, such as roses, or with varie-gated plantain lily leaves. As the petals do not fall and the flowers dry well, they can be included in dried-flower arrangements whilst still fresh.

Colors available Many shades of yellow and gold, and white.

Preparation Cut the stems on a slant and make a 2in slit with a sharp knife. Strip any foliage from the floral stems and give a deep drink before arranging.

TRANSVAAL DAISY
Gerbera jamesonii

These large, brightly colored, daisy-shaped flowers have soft, furry petals and soft, gray-green stems which are leafless. They can be greenhouse-grown and are becoming more readily available in florists' shops. The yellow and orange flowers look good arranged with white spider chrysanthemums and eucalyptus leaves, and can also be used to effect in autumnal dried-flower arrangements, as their color complements the warm tones of the dried material. Contrast the round heads with iris spikes, gladioli, or delphiniums of the same color.

Colors available Purple, crimson, red, pink, white, yellow and orange.

Preparation Cut the stems on a slant and make a 2in slit with a sharp knife. Dip the ends of the stems in boiling water, then give a long drink in cool water before arranging.

Transvaal daisies

African lily

AFRICAN LILY
Agapanthus africanus

These evergreen plants have smooth, lance-shaped leaves and tall, succulent stems. The individual flowers are small and borne in a ball-shaped cluster at the top of the stem, giving a large inflorescence. They can be grown in tubs outdoors in a sheltered spot and wintered indoors in cold regions. African lilies can be used in large arrangements and make a lovely, cool, summer arrangement if their round heads are mixed with tall, white, spiky flowers such as irises or gladioli.

Colors available Blue and white.

Preparation Cut the stems on a slant and make a 2in slit with a sharp knife. Arrange in deep water.

Sweet peas

SWEET PEA
Lathyrus odoratus

These delicate flowers are well known for their sweet scent which can quickly fill a room. They are easily grown in the garden, where their climbing stems will need to be supported if they are to bloom profusely. They are often found in florists' shops during summer. There are usually four or five blooms to a stem and a large bunch of flowers of the same color can be very eye-catching. Sweet peas also look lovely arranged informally with roses of the same color. This gives a very fragrant display.

Colors available A wide range of shades of red, pink, purple, apricot and white.

Preparation Sweet peas should be handled as little as possible. Cut long stems with a sharp knife and give a deep drink in cool water for several hours before arranging.

Other summer flowers

Bells-of-Ireland	Snapdragon
Gentian	Lupine
Angelica	Candytuft
Cornflower	Marigold
Columbine	Clarkia
Brodiaea	Loosestrife
Zinnia	Lavender
Anthemis daisy	Hollyhock
Marguerite daisy	Petunia
Geranium	Clary
Bellflower	Perennial phlox
Mock orange	Day daisy

Autumn flowers and berries 1

The colors of autumn flowers are deeper than those of spring and summer. Purples, reds, browns and golds predominate among both flowers and foliage. Deep-yellow sunflowers and coneflowers, and fiery red-hot pokers provide rich and vibrant colors, while the many types of dahlia offer a splendid range of hues and shapes. When the flowers are over, the fruits, berries and vegetables of autumn can be used in arrangements. Vegetables, such as globe artichokes, can add interesting texture and color to a display. Berries and fruits, such as rose hips and crab apples,

add rich color to arrangements and can look very attractive displayed informally by themselves or with some foliage. Autumn foliage is well worth using as the supply of home-grown flowers diminishes. Some foliage changes color, turning to shades of red, orange, coppery-brown and deep purple. Towards the end of the season it may be worth investing in some flamboyant imported material. One or two of the large South African nodding pincushion heads are enough to prolong the displays of autumnal flowers for a little longer, adding variety in shape and color.

CONEFLOWER
Rudbeckia sp. and hybrids

These pretty, daisy-shaped flowers have lovely, rich coloring. The round face is centered by a dark cone. Single and double flowers are available, and flowers of different colors massed in a terracotta pot bring the colors of autumn indoors. Coneflowers look equally good with red or yellow foliage.

Colors available   Yellow, orange and brown, often ringed with red. The centers are dark brown.

Preparation   Cut the stems on a slant and make a 2in slit with a sharp knife. Strip any foliage from the floral stems and dip the cut ends into boiling water for a few minutes. Give a deep drink before arranging.

CAPE LILY
Crinum powellii

These elegant plants have clusters of trumpet-shaped flowers borne at the top of a thick, succulent stem. The flowers are produced in succession and should be picked off as they fade. Use the Cape lily in large, formal arrangements where a certain elegance is required. The white variety is ideal for wedding displays. It also looks good arranged in a simple, white, porcelain vase with sprays of delicate flowers, such as twigs of lime from which all the foliage has been removed.

Colors available   Pink and white.

Preparation   Cut stems on a slant and make a 2in slit with a sharp knife. Give a long drink before arranging. The hollow stems can be filled with water and the ends plugged with cotton wool to make the flowers last longer.

Cape lily

Crab apple "John Downie"

CRAB APPLE
Malus sp.

The fruits of the crab apple tree are small and round and usually inedible when raw. More often found in the garden or hedgerow than in florists' shops, the attractive coloring of the fruits and the coppery tones of the autumn foliage make them useful for autumn groups. Mix them with flowers of autumnal shades, such as dahlias, red-hot pokers or coneflowers, or with woody shrubs such as the flowering maple or spindle tree. The undried fruits are suitable for dried arrangements, although they will begin to shrivel after a time.

Colors available   The fruits and leaves take on the shades of autumn—reds, yellows and oranges. The spring blossoms are red, pink or white.

Preparation   Scrape the stems and make a 2in slit with a sharp knife. Give a long drink in deep water before arranging.

ST JOHN'S WORT
Hypericum inordorum

A popular garden shrub which is very easy to grow. Although common in gardens, it is not often seen in florists' shops. St John's wort is a semi-evergreen shrub: the leaves are retained in the winter but, instead of remaining green, turn a greenish-red and are aromatic if crushed. The yellow flowers are very delicate but will last until October, when they are followed by

the clusters of oval berries. The sprays are most useful as background material in all kinds of arrangements and the berries fit into arrangements of autumn fruits and flowers.

Colors available   Summer flowers are yellow and foliage green; autumn berries are red and the foliage a greenish-red.

Preparation   Cut the stems on a slant and make a 2in slit with a sharp knife. Strip any foliage from the floral stems. Give a deep drink before arranging in cool water.

FLOWERING MAPLE
Abutilon hybridum

These woody shrubs are common in mild climate gardens, but are usually grown as house plants in cold winter regions. The delicate papery flowers are a wide-funnel shape and hang down from the leaf axils. The woody branches and pale green, often mottled leaves, interspersed with the colorful flowers look good arranged on their own in a plain vase or with other delicate material.

Colors available   The flowers are combinations of red, yellow, mauve and pale blue.

Preparation   Cut the stems on a slant and make a 2in slit with a sharp knife. Strip any foliage from the floral stems and give a deep drink before arranging.

Flowering maple

Additional features

Long-lasting Useful foliage Fragrant Suitable for drying

Globe artichoke

Spindle tree

SPINDLE TREE
Euonymus sachalinensis

The berries of this shrub are most unusual—they are round and fleshy, suddenly bursting open into a flowerlike shape to reveal a mass of bright-orange seeds. The foliage is deep green, fading to a green speckled with white and yellow. Branches are best used at the back of an arrangement.

Colors available The berries may be red, pink or white, with bright-orange seeds.

Preparation Scrape the ends of the stems and make a 2in slit with a sharp knife before arranging.

MICHAELMAS DAISY
Aster novi-belgii

Michaelmas daisies have upright main stems which bear shorter stems topped with the flower. Due to their ragged appearance, they do not mix well with other flowers. For best effect, mass flowers of one color and place in a large copper pan, then position the arrangement so it reflects the autumn sun.

Colors available White, purple and pink.

Preparation Cut the stems on a slant and make a 2in slit with a sharp knife. Strip any foliage from the floral stems and dip the ends into boiling water for a few seconds, then give a deep drink for twelve hours.

Michaelmas daisy hybrids **1** "Ada Ballard" **2** "Blandie"

GLOBE ARTICHOKE
Cynara scolymus

Globe artichokes are most useful in all stages of their development. Apart from being good to eat, the flower buds are made up of fresh-green, overlapping bracts which add textured interest to the base of autumnal groups. The tufts of purple flowers emerge later. The seed heads and the beautiful, fernlike foliage are also most useful.

Colors available The flower buds are pale green; the flowers are purple.

Preparation The flower heads need no special preparation. The leaves last much longer if the stems are held in boiling water for thirty seconds and then the whole leaf submerged in cold water for an hour.

STRAW FLOWER
Helichrysum bracteatum

These flowers, which are most often seen dried, can also be used in fresh flower arrangements. The daisylike flower heads are surrounded by papery bracts giving the illusion of being dried, when in fact they are quite fresh. The colors of the flowers are ideally suited to informal autumn arrangements and look good with almost all types of flowers. Mass the flowers in baskets, then use them to fill alcoves or unused fireplaces. As the petals do not fall, allow the flowers to dry out, to provide a dried arrangement.

Colors available. Yellow, red, orange, magenta, purple and combinations of these colors.

Preparation Cut the stems with a sharp knife, and dip in boiling water. Allow a long drink in cool water before arranging.

Straw flowers

Autumn flowers and berries 2

Sunflower

SUNFLOWER
Helianthus annuus

Sunflowers are favorites in the garden as they are so easy to grow, and most rewarding as they reach such a size. The large heads can easily unbalance an arrangement of small flowers, so use them as a focal point with large flowers, or mix them with foliage and berries.

Colors available Golden-yellow petals with dark-brown central discs.

Preparation Cut stems on a slant and make a 2in slit with a sharp knife. Dip the ends of the stems into boiling water and give a long drink before arranging.

Bear's breeches

BEAR'S BREECHES
Acanthus spinosissimus

These unusual, tall spikes are formed by small flowers enclosed in leafy bracts all the way up the succulent stem. The spikes give a good outline to large, formal and informal arrangements of autumn flowers and foliage. They can also be contrasted with large, round flowers such as sunflowers and dahlias. The spiky foliage is very attractive, especially arranged in a vase with pink flowers.

Colors available Purple-pink flowers hidden amongst purple-green, leafy bracts.

Preparation Cut the stems on a slant and make a 2in slit with a sharp knife. Dip the cut ends in boiling water and give a deep drink in cold water for several hours. Leaf stalks should also be dipped in boiling water for a few moments. The whole leaf should then be submerged in a weak solution of starch for about twelve hours.

DAHLIA
Dahlia hybrids

Dahlias are popular, easily grown garden flowers which are becoming more readily available in florists' shops. They come in many sizes, shapes and colors. All the various shapes have a different name—"cactus", "pompom", "quilled" and "fancy", to name but a few, and the range is ever expanding as growers experiment with new crosses and hybrids. Dahlias mix well in all types of arrangements as they have an attractive, round shape and a predominant "face", so that you know which way to place them in an arrangement. Use the peach- and apricot-colored flowers with autumn foliage arrangements and the vibrant reds in a vase of red roses or red-hot pokers. Mix the whites with other white flowers and deep-green foliage for a striking effect, or mass dahlias of the same color but different shapes for a textured, informal arrangement.

Colors available Dahlias are available in many different colors, and many shades of the same color, as new hybrids produce increasingly subtle tones. The only color not yet produced is blue.

Preparation Cut the stems on a slant and make a 2in slit with a sharp knife. Strip any foliage from the floral stems and dip the ends in boiling water for a few minutes. Give a cool drink overnight before arranging in deep water. For special occasions or formal arrangements, when the flowers have to look good for as long as possible, arrange in deep water containing a commercial preservative.

Dahlias

"Rokesley Mini"

"Authority"

"Little Conn"

"Glorie van Heernstede"

"Super"

Additional features
Long-lasting
Useful foliage
Fragrant
Suitable for drying

Rose hips **1** *Rosa* sp. **2** *R. moyesii* **3** *R. rugosa*

European cranberry bush berries

ROSE HIPS
Rosa hybrids

Autumnal hedgerows were once full of the bright-red hips of wild roses, but the supply of these is decreasing. Hips will form on all garden roses, but are often not given the chance as the plants are pruned back. They are, however, very beautiful and come in many different shapes and sizes, according to the type of rose. Rose hips look good in all autumn arrangements, especially those incorporating dark-red flowers and foliage. Hips can also be used to add a splash of color to arrangements of dried foliage and seed heads.

Colors available Rose hips may be many different shades of red, depending on the time of cutting.

Preparation Cut the stems on a slant and make a 2in slit with a sharp knife. Strip any foliage and thorns from the stems. Dip the cut ends into boiling water for a minute before giving a long drink.

FLOWERING TOBACCO
Nicotiana alata

Other kinds are grown commercially for their leaves which are used in tobacco production. The garden varieties are cultivated for their colorful flowers which are heavily scented. The flowers are tubular, flaring out into a star-shaped face. Their myriad colors make them useful in all kinds of informal arrangements. Use the vibrant colors with red flowers or foliage, or make a truly autumnal arrangement using the orange- and yellow-colored varieties. The lime-green flowers can add interest to a vase of delicate green foliage.

Colors available White, red, orange, yellow, crimson, lime-green, cream and pink.

Preparation The stems are very soft and should be cut with a sharp knife. Place in warm water before arranging in deep water.

RED-HOT POKER
Kniphofia uvaria

These easily grown garden plants are not often seen in florists' shops. They make good cut flowers, although their large size makes them a little difficult to arrange. Their colors are ideally suited to autumnal arrangements

and they add spiky interest to large, informal displays. The succulent stems of red-hot pokers tend to grow on, even when cut; this causes the stems to twist, so you will have to rearrange the flowers if you want to retain a particular shape.

Colors available The heads of red-hot pokers are green when they first appear, but then turn red. Hybrids are now available in cream-and-yellow and cream-and-pink.

Preparation Cut the stems on a slant and make a 2in slit with a sharp knife, then give a long drink in cool water before arranging.

Red-hot poker

EUROPEAN CRANBERRY BUSH BERRIES
Viburnum opulus "Xanthocarpum"

The translucent, golden berries which appear in autumn are as useful as the white flowers which appear in spring. The berries are held in small clusters on branches which retain their leaves even when quite dry. This makes them useful for background sprays in arrangements of fresh or dried materials.

Colors available Berries are yellow in this cultivar. Spring flowers are white, in flat clusters. Foliage is bright green.

Preparation Scrape the stems and cut on a slant. Make a 2in slit with a sharp knife and dip the cut ends into boiling water for a few moments. Give an overnight drink in cool water before arranging.

NODDING PINCUSHION
Leucospermum nutans

These spectacular flower heads are members of the protea family and are imported from South Africa. The heads have a rounded shape covered with yellow spikes with red bulbous tips. Nodding pincushions add a focal point to large arrangements of fresh or dried materials.

Colors available Yellow-red.

Preparation Cut the stems on a slant and make a 2in slit with a sharp knife. Give a deep drink before arranging in cool water.

Other autumn flowers

Japanese anemone	Red valerian
Clematis	Chinese lantern
Hydrangea	Fleabane
Marigold	Montbretia
Sedum	Ageratum
Statice	Forget-me-not
Monkshood	Rose mallow
Cotoneaster	Verbena
Lilyturf	Autumn crocus
Shasta daisy	Scabiosa

Winter flowers and berries

In winter, evergreens come into their own, producing masses of beautifully textured foliage and glowing berries. The term evergreen covers a multitude of foliage colors, including many variegated types, as well as textures—so that you can make up quite a bright arrangement using only evergreen foliage throughout the winter.

Towards the end of winter, many of the deciduous shrubs become covered with the palest of flowers—many of which have a deep scent which is released when twigs are cut and brought into the warmth. Winter camellias flower in white, red, and pink at this time in mild climate regions. Also come the snowdrops, followed by the yellow winter aconites, some crocuses, and the earliest of the daffodils. The choice of blooms is increased with commercially grown anemones, lilac, early carnations and roses. Orchids are imported at this time of year too. All these flowers are plentiful in the shops, if somewhat expensive so, for larger arrangements, rely on evergreens or well-shaped bare twigs. You will find that some of these may burst into leaf in the warmth of the house.

ENGLISH HOLLY
Ilex aquifolium

The glossy, dark-green leaves with their wavy, spined edges and clusters of red berries are a familiar sight in winter, both in gardens and florists' shops. This holly can grow as bushes or as trees, and is as colorful in the garden as it is in the home. Traditional winter arrangements using holly include Christmas wreaths and garlands, but it is also useful as background material to deep-red flowers.

Colors available Holly leaves may be deep green or variegated. Berries may be bright red, orange-red or yellow according to the variety.

Preparation When cutting, use a pair of pruners. Holly lasts a short time if kept out of water.

English holly

Wattle

WATTLE
Acacia longifolia

This delicate-looking shrub is related to the spring-flowering mimosa and has very similar yellow flowers. However, unlike the mimosa, the gray-green leaves of this wattle are undivided and willowlike in shape. The fragrant flowers contrast well with the foliage and the sprays are a welcome addition to winter arrangements of flowers and foliage.

Colors available Yellow ball-like flowers and gray-green foliage.

Preparation Keep wrapped in plastic to exclude air for as long as possible before arranging. Just prior to arranging, remove the plastic and dip flower heads in cold water for a few moments. Cut the stems on a slant and make a 2in slit with a sharp knife. Dip the stems in boiling water for a few seconds, then give a deep drink with warm water until the heads are dry.

ANEMONE
Anemone coronaria

These delicate flowers are available in a wide variety of shapes and sizes, although the ones pictured here are the most familiar. Their fragile flowers are made up not of petals but of sepals (these are usually green and are the leaflike structures which surround the flower), and these form a cup shape round a deep-blue central disc. In the garden, anemones of different species can be found in spring, summer and autumn but, in florists' shops, *Anemone coronaria* is the species available in winter. Although they can be mixed with other flowers, they look best massed in a glass vase. Pack them in tightly, as their stems have a tendency to bend and this can make a vase look untidy.

Colors available Red, blue, mauve, pink, white, yellow, magenta and scarlet. Many have a central disc ringed with another color.

Preparation Cut the stems on a slant and make a 2in slit with a sharp knife. Dip the cut ends in boiling water for a few seconds. Give a long, cool drink before arranging.

Anemones

CHINCHERINCHEE
Ornithogalum thyrsoides

Imported in winter, these flowers are a useful addition to the range available at this time of year. The tightly packed flowers will open from the bottom upwards and the spike is soon a mass of small, white, star-shaped flowers. They look good when used with colorful sprays of holly or cotoneaster at Christmas.

Colors available White.

Preparation Some chincherinchees come with wax sealing their ends. Cut this off and make a 2in slit with a sharp knife. Give a deep drink of warm water and then put them in cool water for several days to allow all the flowers to open.

Additional features
Long-lasting · Useful foliage · Fragrant · Suitable for drying

Orchid

ORCHID
Dendrobium sp. and hybrids

These exotic flowers are imported from the Far East. They come in many different sizes and shapes, all with the usual "lip" surrounded by a ring of sepals and petals. The flowers need to be seen close up to be appreciated, so these orchids are best displayed very simply, either on their own or with the bare, red stems of the dogwood, in an uncluttered setting.

Colors available Red, orange, yellow, white and purple. The flowers are usually marked or patterned with another color.

Preparation These orchids are usually bought in sprays or branches of flowers rather than as single flowers. They will last over a long period if the water is changed daily.

Chrysanthemums

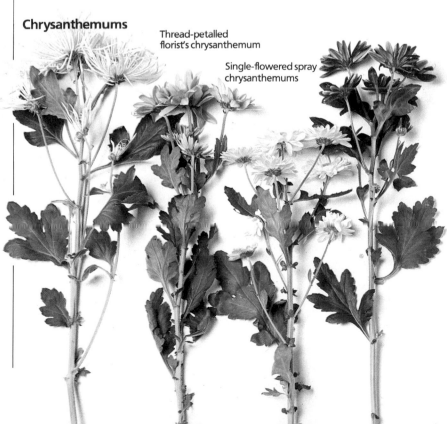

Thread-petalled florist's chrysanthemum

Single-flowered spray chrysanthemums

WINTER-FLOWERING JASMINE
Jasminum nudiflorum

These shrubs are easily grown in the garden, and cut stems are available in florists' shops. In summer, the bush is covered in dark-green leaves, but during the winter it is covered with tubular, yellow flowers. Display a few sprays in a plain terracotta container or mix with early flowering daffodils.

Colors available Yellow.

Preparation Cut the stems on a slant and make a 2in slit with a sharp knife. No other treatment is required before arranging.

CHRYSANTHEMUM
Chrysanthemum hybrids

At a time when substantial, brightly colored flowers are not abundant, these flowers are a great addition to winter flower arrangements. Chrysanthemums grow in gardens in autumn but are now commercially forced and can be bought in florists' shops throughout the year. They are available as single heads and sprays in many different shapes and sizes. The single blooms are easier to arrange as focal points in a vase. The sprays are a little more difficult, as there are many flowers on each stem. These should be massed together in a large vase, or the individual flowers can be picked off and used in miniature arrangements.

Colors available Chrysanthemums are available in a wide range of colors—red, orange, rust, pink white, yellow, lime-green, peach and cream. Many of the daisy-shaped flowers have a central disc of a different color.

Preparation Cut the stems at a slant and make a 2in slit with a sharp knife. Dip the cut ends in boiling water for a few seconds. Immerse the whole stem in cool water and give a long drink before arranging in deep water.

Cotoneaster

COTONEASTER
Cotoneaster "Cornubius"

The dark-green, lance-shaped leaves of this evergreen shrub are deeply veined and slightly matt, giving them an attractive texture. The red berries are borne in large clusters. Use small sprays in seasonal table decorations or in place of holly in wreaths and garlands. This cotoneaster can also be used as colorful background material in large arrangements.

Colors available Deep-green leaves, red berries in winter, cream flowers in summer.

Preparation Cut the stems on a slant and make a 2in slit with a sharp knife. Give a long cool drink before arranging.

WINTER ACONITE
Eranthis hyemalis

These little flowers appear in gardens in early spring. The yellow flowers resemble buttercups in shape and are ringed by lime-green sepals. Display them with their own foliage in a miniature arrangement.

Colors available Yellow.

Preparation Cut the stems on a slant and make a slit with a sharp knife. Arrange in cool water.

Other winter flowers

Snowdrop	Mahonia
Hellebore	Toadflax
Winter sweet	Algerian iris
Cymbidium	Cyclamen
Chionodoxa	Squill
Winter camellia	Hepatica
Witch hazel	Hyacinth
Grape hyacinth	Snowflake
Skimmia	Lenten rose
Firethorn	Heath
Barberry	Snowberry

Foliage 1

Foliage plays as great a part in flower arranging as flowers themselves. Individual leaves or sprays can either be used as background or filler material in mixed arrangements, or the foliage can be used on its own to make an attractive display. While the choice of foliage available in florists' shops may be limited, gardens and woods can provide an enormous variety of leaves with a fascinating range of colors, shapes and textures with which to experiment. Plain-green leaves range from the forest-green of the pittosporum to the apple-green of the plantain lily; or leaves may be variegated with white, cream or yellow—they may be completely colored, like the golden-yellow leaves of the spindle tree, or marked only at the margins, like the variegated holly. Silver and gray foliage looks particularly attractive with yellow or pink flowers and can be used on its own—many different textures massed together in a monochromatic arrangement look very striking. Red and bronze leaves are usually associated with autumn, but many leaves have this color all year round. When planning arrangements, try to utilize the natural outline of the leaves or sprays as an integral part of a design. Use spikes of leaves as outline material, soft, arching ivies and ferns to add curves—either within the arrangement or trailing down from an arrangement placed on a pedestal—and bold leaves, such as those of the plantain lily and bergenia, to make a dramatic, modern display. Arrangements made up entirely of foliage can be just as attractive as arrangements of flowers.

To prepare cut foliage for display, condition it first by soaking it in water—overnight for older leaves and about two hours for younger leaves. Do not soak silver or gray foliage as it has a tendency to become soggy. Wash evergreen foliage in a solution of mild detergent to restore its shine. All foliage can be pressed; individual entries state which items can be air-dried or dried in glycerine.

GREEN FOLIAGE

VIBURNUM
Viburnum rhytidophyllum

These deep-green leaves have a distinctive wrinkled texture caused by the heavy veining on the upper surface. They mix very well with pansies and white or red dahlias, and can be used to vary texture in an all-green display. The evergreen leaves dry particularly well in air or glycerine.

SOFT SHIELD FERN
Polystichum setiferum

The leaves of this handsome fern have a soft texture and a good, bright-green color. They are finely divided and gently arching, providing an excellent foil for cut flowers. They mix well with teasel and driftwood in a modern arrangement. Soft shield fern is an evergreen that does not dry well.

MAGNOLIA
Magnolia grandiflora

These shiny, green leaves have a leathery texture and a rust-colored, feltlike underside. They can be used as a background for deep-red flowers. The evergreen leaves do not dry well.

PLANTAIN LILY
Hosta plantaginea

The leaves of this plant are large and broad and are a bright-green color. Their size and deeply grooved, glossy texture make them ideal for modern arrangements, and they combine well with large flowers such as lilies or poppies. Other kinds of hosta have especially attractive foliage.

COTONEASTER
Cotoneaster horizontalis

Tiny, delicate, dark-green leaves are arranged on stiff stems. The leaves have a glossy upper surface, and are gray and hairy beneath. The long, narrow spikes of leaves are suitable for establishing the outline of an arrangement; the tiny leaves complement larger and more dominant elements with their delicate appearance. This foliage is evergreen but turns red in autumn. These leaves can be air-dried or dried in glycerine.

JAPANESE ANGELICA
Aralia chinensis

The oval-shaped leaves are a rich-green color, and there is also a yellow-and-green variety. The number of leaflets on each spray makes them useful as filler material in all types of arrangement. They are deciduous leaves that can be air-dried.

BERGENIA
Bergenia sp.

The large, dark-green leaves of the bergenia have a smooth, shiny texture with bold ribbing. They are good for focal interest and are suitable for large-scale modern arrangements. These plants are perennial and are grown in colonies in part shade.

PITTOSPORUM
Pittosporum tobira

These attractive, tear-drop shaped leaves are a lustrous green and have a prominent central vein. Their thick, leathery texture contrasts well with rough or hairy leaves. As the leaves are small, pittosporum makes a good background material to cut flowers. This plant is an evergreen and can be used all year round.

Green foliage 1 Viburnum **2** Soft shield fern
3 Magnolia **4** Plantain lily **5** Cotoneaster
6 Japanese angelica **7** Bergenia **8** Pittosporum

Green-and-yellow foliage

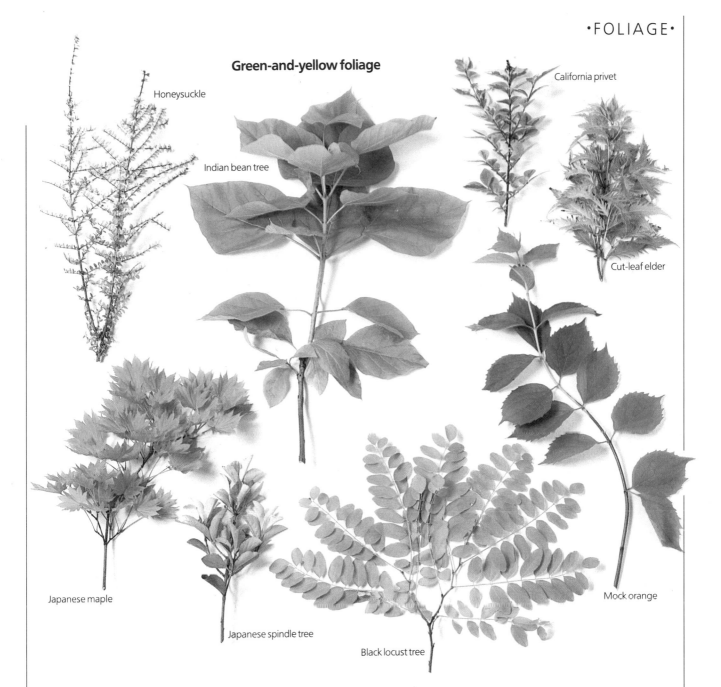

Honeysuckle

Indian bean tree

California privet

Cut-leaf elder

Mock orange

Japanese maple

Japanese spindle tree

Black locust tree

GREEN-AND-YELLOW FOLIAGE

HONEYSUCKLE
Lonicera nitida "Baggesen's Gold"

The rows of tiny, golden and pale-green leaves are borne in upright spikes. This shrubby form of honeysuckle can be used for outline, or as filler material in flower and foliage arrangements, and looks good with yellow roses. The evergreen leaves can be used fresh or air-dried at any time of year.

INDIAN BEAN TREE
Catalpa bignonioides

With its large, heart-shaped, pale yellow-green leaves, this foliage is useful for large-scale arrangements—though it does exude a pungent smell if crushed. Beanlike seed pods are produced in autumn. The leaves are at their best during summer. They do not dry well.

CALIFORNIA PRIVET
Ligustrum ovalifolium "Aureum"

This variety of privet is a pale-green color with wide borders of deep yellow. Other varieties of privet may be green or white and green. The leaves have a soft texture. The evergreen leaves are borne in bushy spikes, and are useful in many types of arrangement, but do not dry well.

CUT-LEAF ELDER
Sambucus racemosa "Plumosa Aurea"

These unusual golden-yellow and green leaves have deeply serrated margins. The leaves are borne in sprays which are useful for giving a soft outline shape to a large arrangement. The cut-leaf elder produces berries in autumn, but the leaves are at their best in spring or summer. They do not dry well, but are very useful for fresh arrangements.

JAPANESE MAPLE
Acer japonicum "Aureum"

Deeply serrated margins give these large leaves a beautiful shape. The fresh, bright coloring and unusual "fan" shape make them a suitable focal point for a foliage display and are seen at their best in simple displays. The yellow leaves turn a rich crimson in autumn. They are especially attractive when pressed.

JAPANESE SPINDLE TREE
Euonymus japonica "Ovata-aurea"

The small, oval leaves are golden-yellow or yellow-green in color and have an attractive glossy texture. They grow in dense sprays and make good filler material in arrangements of small, yellow flowers. These are evergreen leaves that do not dry well.

BLACK LOCUST TREE
Robinia pseudoacacia

When they first appear, the leaves are golden-yellow, turning into a pale yellow-green in the summer. The "Frisia" variety has golden-yellow leaves throughout the season. The small leaflets are arranged in very regular pairs on thin branchlets. Display these leaves so that the natural fan shape and interesting texture can be used to best effect.

MOCK ORANGE
Philadelphus coronarius "Aureus"

When young, the foliage of this plant is bright golden-yellow, becoming dark green with age. The round leaves have a pointed tip and roughly toothed margins, and are at their best in spring. Use them to complement large flowers of any color.

Foliage 2

GREEN-AND-WHITE FOLIAGE

TARTARIAN DOGWOOD
Cornus alba "Elegantissima"

This mid-green foliage is irregularly edged with white and grows on red stems. The plain-green varieties often turn red or orange in autumn. All provide useful color for flower or foliage groups, mixing especially well with white flowers. The leaves are at their best in autumn. They do not dry well.

EUROPEAN ELDER
Sambucus nigra "Albo-variegata"

These slender, dark-green, pointed leaves are finely edged with pale yellow. They exude a disagreeable odor if bruised, but are an ideal background to a vase of yellow flowers. The leaves are at their best during spring and summer. They do not dry well.

COMMON PRIVET
Ligustrum vulgare "Aureo-variegatum"

These long, elegant leaves grow on densely packed branches which have an elongated overall shape. The smaller leaves are more prominently yellow, so a good color range is present on each stem. These evergreen leaves air-dry well.

ENGLISH HOLLY
Ilex aquifolium "Golden Queen"

The sharp, spiky, dark-green leaves have white or silver edging. Holly is an evergreen foliage traditionally used in Christmas garlands and wreaths. It can also be usefully combined with hellebores, red or white carnations, or ivy. Holly lasts longer if arranged without water and air-dries well.

GREATER PERIWINKLE
Vinca major "Variegata"

These leaves are oval in shape and are mid-green edged with white. They are arranged in pairs on slender, curving stems which can be allowed to trail or twine. Use these evergreen leaves as trailing material in a pedestal arrangement.

ENGLISH IVY
Hedera helix "Argento-variegata"

These small, heart-shaped leaves are mid-green with irregular, white edging. Ivies are evergreen trailers but can also be used to twine up through an arrangement. They contrast well with snowdrops and catkins in a winter arrangement, and can also be used effectively with freesias or foxgloves in shades of yellow for a fresh-looking display. The leaves are suitable for drying in glycerine.

Green-and-white foliage

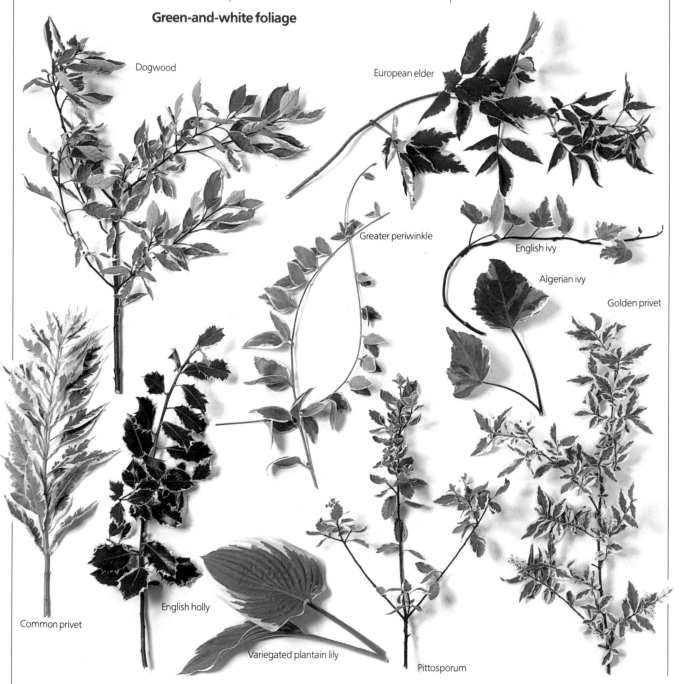

Dogwood

European elder

Greater periwinkle

English ivy

Algerian ivy

Golden privet

Common privet

English holly

Variegated plantain lily

Pittosporum

ALGERIAN IVY
Hedera canariensis "Variegata"

These large, leathery leaves are dark green edged with white. The heart-shaped leaves grow on red stems and look good in displays of large flowers, such as daffodils or yellow Transvaal daisies. Whole stems of these evergreen leaves can trail from arrangements. The leaves are suitable for drying in glycerine.

VARIEGATED PLANTAIN LILY
Hosta sp.

These large, broad leaves have a prominent pale-yellow margin. Their size and deeply grooved, glossy texture make them ideal for modern arrangements. They also combine well with large flowers, such as roses, or with ferns in a foliage display. They are at their best in spring.

PITTOSPORUM
Pittosporum tenuifolium "Garnettii"

These pale-green leaves have narrow, irregular yellow margins and are borne on black stems. They have an open appearance and make excellent filler material at any time of year. The leaves can be dried in glycerine.

GOLDEN PRIVET
Ligustrum ovalifolium "Albo-marginatum"

These glossy, mid-green leaves have wide, irregular, creamy-white borders. The spikes of leaves are good filler material, and a useful addition to a green foliage arrangement at any time of year.

GRAY FOLIAGE

EUCALYPTUS
Eucalyptus gunnii

The distinctive young foliage of this evergreen plant encircles the thin gray stems. (The leaves become elongated as they get older.) The color varies between blue-green and silvery-white. Eucalyptus leaves look good with pink or blue flowers in a modern setting, or with grasses and ferns in a dried arrangement. The fragrance is also attractive. These leaves can be used throughout the year but look best when still young. They can be dried in glycerine.

SEA KALE
Crambe maritima

The leaves of this spring vegetable are large, fleshy and brittle, and have a distinctive blue-green color. They have a crinkly outline that provides an interesting contrast with more formal shapes, or they can be used to good effect in more abstract arrangements of leaves of different textures. They are at their best in summer. They do not dry well.

COMMON WORMWOOD
Artemisia "Powis Castle"

A sprig of common wormwood resembles a tiny tree in shape. The delicate silver-gray leaves are deeply dissected into slender filaments which have a silky texture and provide an unusual outline for small groups. These are evergreen leaves which may prove difficult to dry.

GROUNDSEL
Senecio "Sunshine"

Two distinct colors and textures are displayed by these small, oval leaves. They have a dark-green, leathery upper surface and a pale-green and densely felted lower surface. They look good in both flower and foliage arrangements as both sides of the leaves can be displayed to effect. Although the leaves are evergreen, they are at their best in winter. They do not dry well.

WHITE WILLOW
Salix alba

These two-tone leaves are deep-green above and silky-white beneath. The leaves are long and narrow and borne in pairs on the woody stems. Used thoughtfully, the sprays of leaves can add interest to both flower and foliage groups. The leaves are at their best in summer. They do not dry well.

MULLEIN
Verbascum sp.

These large, pale-gray leaves have a soft texture and gentle shape that combines well with other soft-textured foliage. They look attractive when mixed with flowers, particularly with pale-pink, blue or green flowers for a pastel-colored arrangement. The evergreen leaves are at their best in summer. They do not dry well.

SENECIO
Senecio maritima

A fine, white down covers both surfaces of these deeply dissected leaves and gives them an attractive, silvery appearance. The leaves have a soft texture and they are ideal for adding an interesting shape to a small arrangement. They mix particularly well with pink roses and statice. The leaves are evergreen and are at their best in summer. They do not dry well.

ORNAMENTAL OATS
Helicotrichon sempervirens

These long, thin and slightly arching leaves are an intense blue-gray color. They provide dramatic definition and contrast and go well with bright-blue flowers, such as irises, delphiniums and larkspur in a stark, modern arrangement. Although evergreen, the leaves are at their best in summer.

BALLOTA
Ballota pseudodictamnus

The very unusual leaves of this plant grow densely on slim, upright stems. They are heart-shaped with slightly scalloped edges and are "woolly-gray" in color; they provide excellent textural variation for a fresh or dried all-foliage arrangement. The leaves are evergreen but are at their best in spring and summer. They do not dry well.

SAGEBRUSH
Artemisia "Douglasiana"

The linear leaves are borne on tall spikes and have a pale-gray underside with a slightly darker upper surface. The long, slender shape of the stems provides graceful lines and strong definition for mixed groups, whether used as focal point or as a background for pink or blue flowers such as roses, larkspur or cornflowers. These leaves are at their best in summer and are suitable for air-drying.

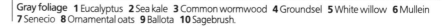

Gray foliage **1** Eucalyptus **2** Sea kale **3** Common wormwood **4** Groundsel **5** White willow **6** Mullein **7** Senecio **8** Ornamental oats **9** Ballota **10** Sagebrush.

Foliage 3

BRONZE FOLIAGE

ORNAMENTAL GRAPE VINE
Vitis vinifera "Purpurea"

These crimson-red leaves turn to a richer claret-red in the autumn. Pretty red-and-green variegated types are also available. The butterfly shape of the leaves is an attractive feature and as such should be arranged thoughtfully. The ornamental grape vine is useful in autumnal arrangements, mixing well with yellow and orange flowers and foliage of autumnal shades. The leaves do not dry well.

COPPER BEECH
Fagus sylvatica "Purpurea"

The delicate oval leaves have toothed edges and are a rich-copper color. They blend well with other foliage, provide an excellent backing for large displays, and look especially striking when arranged with white or red flowers. Use older foliage, as young foliage is green. The leaves are at their best in spring and dry well in glycerine.

JAPANESE BARBERRY
Berberis thunbergii "Atropurpurea"

Small, rich dark-bronze leaves grow in clusters on long tapering stems. They turn bright red in autumn, as does the variety which is mid-green for the rest of the year. This excellent and colorful outline foliage can be combined effectively with wood and pine cones in modern arrangements. The leaves are at their best in autumn and air-dry well.

NEW ZEALAND FLAX
Phormium tenax "Purpureum"

These straplike, stiff, leathery leaves may be red or green, and some varieties may be striped with yellow. They can grow to 10ft long, but at this length become rather unusable. The young, shorter leaves provide elegant lines for arrangements. The leaves have good color all year but do not dry well. They can, however, be used in short-term dried arrangements whilst still fresh.

NORWAY MAPLE
Acer platanoides "Goldsworth Purple"

Apart from the deep purple-crimson of this foliage, there are white-margined, pale-green and red varieties. The bold, pointed outline of maple leaves makes them suitable for large arrangements, and they make excellent filling material, combining well with large flowers such as yellow tulips or chrysanthemums. The leaves are at their best in autumn and can be dried in glycerine.

SMOKE TREE
Cotinus coggygria

These elliptical leaves grow in dense clusters. They are green with red veins, and assume a rich-red color in autumn. The delicate mass of flower stems emerging from these clusters creates an unusual "smoky" effect which can be used effectively in Japanese-style arrangements. They also mix well with orange flowers. The leaves are at their best in autumn. They do not dry well.

PURPLE-LEAVED FILBERT
Corylus maxima "Atropurpurea"

These large, round leaves grow on slim arching stems and are deep-purple in color. They make good foliage for large arrangements and combine well with round flowers of red, purple or mauve. They are at their best in autumn, but may prove difficult to dry.

STONECROP
Sedum maximum "Atropurpureum"

The green-and-red fleshy leaves are matched by clusters of tiny flowers of similar shades. Use them to instil texture and color in an arrangement of fresh or dried flowers of autumnal shades. They are at their best during late summer and can easily be air-dried.

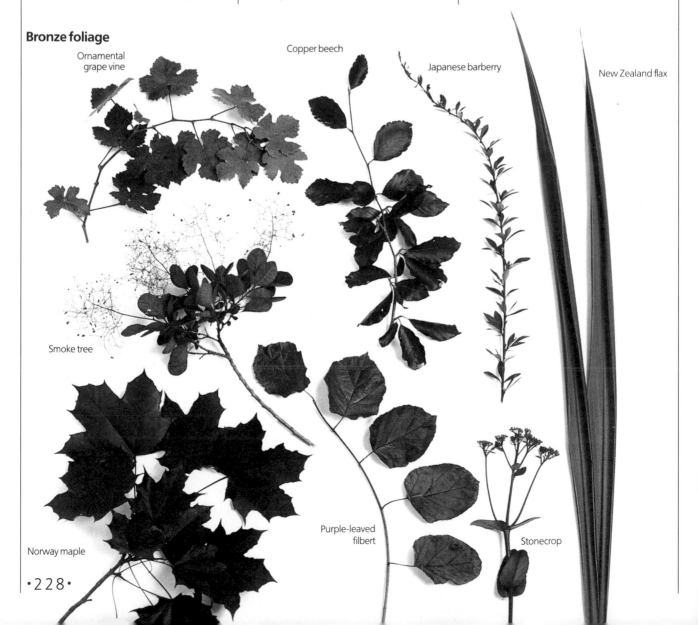

Bronze foliage

Ornamental grape vine

Copper beech

Japanese barberry

New Zealand flax

Smoke tree

Purple-leaved filbert

Stonecrop

Norway maple

THE
DRIED-FLOWER
GUIDE

Dried flowers have a charm that is independent of season, and create an appealing palette of pale and bright colors and of brittle and soft forms.

Flowers are not the only suitable materials; many other sorts of dried matter can be used, offering a great variety of shapes, textures and colors. The soft, neutral colors of grasses and cereals are a useful foil to flowers. The rich colors of autumnal foliage can be mixed with flowers and grasses, and both familiar and exotic seed heads offer unusual shapes and textures.

On the following pages you will find a selection of dried flowers (arranged according to their color), foliage, cereals, grasses, seed heads and fruits, all of which can be used to make attractive and long-lasting displays. Advice is offered on how to use each item of dried material and, for each entry, the most effective method of drying is given.

Dried flowers 1
Whites and yellows

This range of colors, from the muted tones of the greenish-whites to the brilliant snow-whites and vibrant yellows, adds freshness and light to any arrangement. They mix well with other colors, and can be used either to evoke the brilliance of summer sunshine, when used with other brightly colored dried flowers, or to reflect the mellow tones of autumn, when combined with flowers, foliage and grasses in shades of orange and brown. Their colors blend well with wicker baskets, terracotta and frosted glass.

Methods of drying

Air-drying Glycerine Silica/borax Pressing

LADY'S MANTLE
Alchemilla vulgaris
The delicate, yellow-green flowers blend well with grasses, cereals and seed heads.

TUMBLEWEED
Amaranthus albus
These green spikes look good in both flower and foliage arrangements.

WHITE BUTTON FLOWERS
Chrysanthemum hybrids
When the petals have been removed the central parts of the flowers can be dyed to any color.

STATICE
Limonium sinuatum
The yellow, white, purple, pink or red flowers look attractive massed in a terracotta container.

TANSY
Tanacetum vulgare
The bright-yellow, buttonlike flowers add a splash of color to an arrangement.

EVERLASTING
Helipterum roseum
White flowers with yellow centers add delicate color to small arrangements and wreaths.

STRAW FLOWER
Helichrysum bracteatum
The yellow, white, orange or red daisylike flowers should be wired before drying.

〰

EVERLASTING
Helipterum humboldtianum
These attractive bright-yellow flowers add color to winter arrangements.

〰

PEARL EVERLASTING
Anaphalis margaritacea
Clusters of ivory-white flower heads that may be sprayed or dyed for display.

〰

GOLDEN MARGUERITE
Anthemis tinctoria
These versatile yellow flowers can be dyed or sprayed to any color.

〰

YARROW
Achillea filipendulina
The flat-headed yellow or white flowers provide focal point in a group.

〰

BABY'S BREATH
Gypsophila paniculata
The white or pink flowers are often used in bouquets and wreaths, but also look good on their own.

〰

Dried flowers 2
Pinks, reds and oranges

The colors in this group range from pale, delicate pinks to deep reds and flame oranges. Red flowers are perhaps the boldest and most eye-catching of all, but they attain a more subtle appeal when toned with brown, yellow or blue. Shades of pink add a light and delicate quality to an arrangement, and are seen at their best when contrasted with white and green. Deep, rich-orange flowers are especially lovely if used with the yellows and reds of autumnal foliage.

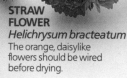

STRAW FLOWER
Helichrysum bracteatum
The orange, daisylike flowers should be wired before drying.

ROSE
Rosa sp.
Mass roses in low baskets or tall containers to create an intense focal point of color.

FALSE SAFFLOWER
Carthamus tinctorius
Red-orange flowers and gray-green leaves provide a stiff outline shape for arrangements.

MARSH ROSEMARY
Limonium suworowii
The long, narrow clusters of rose-pink flowers add unusual lines to any group.

CELOSIA
Celosia argentea "Cristata"
The purple or pink blooms have a mossy texture and provide a dramatic focal point for a large arrangement.

CHINESE LANTERN
Physalis alkekengi
The orange and green flower pods can be used in mixed autumnal arrangements, but also can stand on their own.

Methods of drying

Air-drying Glycerine Silica/borax Pressing

BOTTLE BRUSH
Callistemon citrinus
The bright-orange heads shine forth in both flower and foliage arrangements.

STATICE
Limonium sinuatum
The pink, purple, yellow, white or red flowers look attractive when massed together in a terra-cotta container.

EVERLASTING
Helipterum roseum
Pink flowers with yellow centers add delicate color to small arrangements and wreaths.

FLOWERING ONION
Allium sp.
The flowers may be pink, blue or yellow. Mass them together in a tall container.

LARKSPUR
Delphinium consolida
Pink, mauve, blue or white flowers add height to arrangements of delicate flowers and are excellent for small wreaths.

GLOBE AMARANTH
Gomphrena globosa
These delicate, cloverlike flowers should be wired before drying.

STRAW FLOWER
Helichrysum bracteatum
The pink, daisylike flowers should be wired before drying.

JOE PYEWEED
Eupatorium purpureum
Use these delicate rose-pink flowers as filler material in larger flower arrangements.

ROCK CRESS
Arabis alpina "Rosea"
The tiny pink flowers can be used in bouquets and wreaths, but also look good on their own in a delicate container.

Dried flowers 3
Blues and purples

These dried flowers have colors ranging from cool and pale silvery-blue to the rich, warm tones of mauve and deep purple. The cool colors can be bright and stimulating when mixed with the complementary colors of yellow and orange; they can also be juxtaposed with white or used in a monochromatic arrangement. Mauve and purple flowers can add a touch of richness to a room if arranged with red flowers and foliage.

Methods of drying

Air-drying | Glycerine | Silica/borax | Pressing

DELPHINIUM
Delphinium elatum
Use single spikes to give height to an arrangement.

BLAZING STAR
Liatris spicata
These long spikes of tiny flowers can be used for outline in an arrangement.

LARKSPUR
Delphinium consolida
Blue, mauve, pink or white flowers add height to arrangements of delicate flowers and are excellent for small wreaths.

HYDRANGEA
Hydrangea macrophylla
Dense clusters of blue, white or pink flower heads can be used in wreaths and garlands, or in wide-necked glass bottles filled with other dried flowers.

STATICE
Limonium sinuatum
The purple, red, yellow, white or pink flowers look attractive massed in a terracotta container.

ASTILBE
Astilbe japonica
The feathery plumes look good in arrangements of flowers or grasses. The ornamental foliage can be pressed.

DOCK
Rumex acetosa
These rust-purple plants make excellent filling material, or can be used to make a rustic group if massed in a rush basket.

LAVENDER
Lavandula angustifolia
The fragrant purple flowers may be used in small bouquets, wreaths, pot-pourris and herbal pillows.

IMMORTELLE
Xeranthemum annuum
These purple, lilac, white or pink flowers should be wired together in bunches for use in arrangements.

GLOBE THISTLE
Echinops ritro
The rounded blue heads mix well with yellow flowers.

SEA HOLLY
Eryngium maritimum
The silver-blue stems and heads can be used to add texture to an arrangement.

THRIFT
Armeria maritima
The ball-like, silver-pink flowers provide focal point in a group.

GLOBE AMARANTH
Gomphrena globosa
These delicate, cloverlike flowers should be wired before drying.

Dried foliage, cereals and grasses

Foliage, cereals and grasses should be considered essential dried-flower arranging materials. Certainly, very few arrangements are produced without one or more of these ingredients to add some variation in shape, color or texture. But they are more than a mere foil to brightly colored flowers; with a little imagination they can provide an attractive display by themselves.

BRISTLE BENT
Agrostis curtisii
This gray-green grass has a dense flower head and is suitable for many arrangements, including wreaths.

HARESTAIL GRASS
Lagurus ovatus
This delicate grass can be used with flowers or with leaves, seed heads and other grasses.

QUAKING GRASS
Briza media
The delicate, nodding flower heads add lightness to small arrangements.

GREVILLEA
Grevillea triternata
These interesting fernlike leaves have an unusual spiky quality that adds variety to an arrangement.

REED MACE
Typha latifolia
The hard-edged spikiness of this relation of the bullrush is useful in large groups.

PLATYLOBIUM
Platylobium angulare
The unusual foliage can be used as background material in arrangements of delicate flowers.

EUCALYPTUS
Eucalyptus sp.
The red or brown leaves add strong shape and color to foliage arrangements.

PAMPAS GRASS
Cortaderia selloana
A useful background material for large groups, pampas grass looks attractive when displayed on its own in an urn.

Methods of drying
Air-drying Glycerine Silica/borax Pressing

BEECH
Fagus sylvatica
These attractive, copper-colored leaves provide an excellent background for large displays.

BROME GRASS
Bromus sp.
This wild grass adds an attractive feathery texture to any dried arrangement.

BARLEY
Hordeum vulgare
This grass provides traditional arrangements with an interesting variation in shape and texture.

OATS
Avena sp.
This pale-green grass can be mixed with other grasses and foliage or used in flower arrangements.

BENT GRASS
Agrostis sp.
This pale grass adds a delicate lightness to grass or foliage arrangements.

BRACKEN
Pteridium aquilinum
All ferns add a delicate outline to dried-flower groups.

Dried seed heads and fruits

Dried material is not restricted solely to flowers, grasses and foliage; seed heads and fruits add to the already extensive range. Many plants have attractive seed heads which are only revealed when the flower itself has died. These are extremely useful, providing exciting variations of shape, color and texture. Fruits can be wired for use in an arrangement or can be placed to create interest around the base of a container.

ORNAMENTAL GOURD
Cucurbita pepo ovifera
Many colors, shapes and textures are available. Dried gourds can be waxed or varnished and can be massed in a bowl or mixed with real fruits. Gourds retain their shape by varnishing.

POPPY
Papaver sp.
A great assortment of differently shaped pods is available. The heads can be wired and used in wreaths.

PROTEA
Protea sp.
These heads are for large, dramatic arrangements. Several heads massed together in a rush basket look effective.

COTTON
Gossypium sp.
These fluffy, white tufts are an unusual and interesting addition to displays of grasses or foliage.

BANKSIA
Banksia menziesii
These deep-brown seed heads are excellent for inclusion in modern abstract arrangements.

Methods of drying

Air-drying Glycerine Silica/borax Pressing

BEECH NUTS
Fagus sylvatica
These rich-brown nuts can be contrasted with delicate grasses in an arrangement or wired for use in wreaths.

SCABIOUS
Scabiosa caucasica
These delicate heads can be used in autumn foliage arrangements, or mixed with dried flowers for a light effect.

CHILLI PEPPER
Capsicum annuum
These red, orange or yellow fruits add outline shape and vivid color to autumn foliage arrangements. Wire the heads for use in wreaths.

CARDOON BALLS
Cynara cardunculus
The handsome, fluffy heads provide height and texture for large arrangements.

MAIZE
Zea mays
The whole stems can be used in large seed pod and foliage arrangements or the heads can be wired for smaller arrangements.

LOVE-IN-A-MIST
Nigella damascena
The rosebud-shaped heads may have red or purple streaks. The frilly foliage around the heads adds a misty look to delicate arrangements.

TEASEL
Dipsacus fullonum
Distinctively shaped heads which may be cut in half to provide a starlike "flower". The heads can be wired for use in wreaths.

·7·
PLANT CARE

Outdoors, plants are able to fend very much for themselves, needing only occasional assistance on our part. In the indoor garden, however, plants depend on us to meet all their needs: we decide what level of light and humidity they are given, the quantity and regularity of watering and feeding, how big a root-run they should be allowed, and what the minimum winter temperature should be. Successful gardeners and those whose house plants thrive are said to have green fingers or, at the very least, a green thumb. Certainly, some people seem to have a built-in feel for what plants need, and how they should be cared for, while others fail totally with their charges. There is, however, no mystery about growing plants successfully; good results can be achieved by anyone who is prepared to understand the needs of particular plants and establish a routine for looking after them. Always remember that you are dealing with living things; unhealthy specimens are a sorry sight and act as a reproach to us for failing to give them enough attention. Caring for plants is more likely to be a joy—as opposed to a chore—if you choose them carefully. Decorative qualities are, of course, important, but you should also be confident of your ability to look after the plant and be sure that it is capable of flourishing under the conditions you have to offer in your house or apartment.

Potting up your own plants
Plant care need be neither complicated nor time-consuming. Potting up young plants, such as these variegated bedding geraniums (*Pelargonium* hybrids), is quick and easy, and should result in healthy growth if you use the correct size of pot and the right kind of potting mixture.

Requirements for healthy plants

The plants we grow in our homes come from temperate, sub-tropical and tropical areas where widely differing growing conditions exist. For example, some are exposed to direct sunlight, others are protected from the fierce rays of the tropical sun by neighboring plants or are given some shade from overhanging trees, while still more grow on the forest floor in considerable shade. This diversity of natural habitat explains why different plants require different conditions when grown indoors.

Having said this, however, the ability to adapt to unfamiliar conditions is a major reason for the popularity of many common house plants. Most generally dislike widely fluctuating temperatures, although a drop of 5°-10°F at night is natural when the thermostat is lowered at bedtime and is preferred by most indoor plants; those that produce flowers require this change to form buds. Such a drop is similar to nature's pattern: temperatures fall as the sun goes down. A warmer house during daytime also follows nature's pattern—as the sun rises, the environment becomes warmer.

There is much pleasure and fulfillment to be derived from growing and looking after house plants. Maintaining healthy and attractive plants does not involve complicated or time-consuming procedures but just sensible and sensitive attention to the plants' basic needs. To thrive, plants need adequate light at the preferred intensity and for the right duration, a comfortable temperature, and the right level of atmospheric humidity. They have to be watered when they start to dry out a little, and some need a dormant period during the winter when the water supply needs to be curtailed—allowing the plant to rest and often encouraging flower-bud production. Food must be provided, the right kind of growing medium made available and, as the roots fill the pots, plants will need potting on. These and other needs are described in the sections that follow.

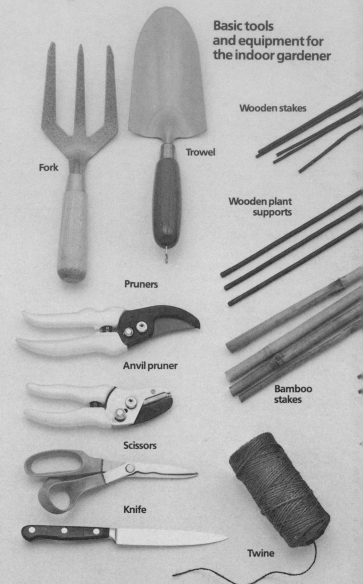

Basic tools and equipment for the indoor gardener

Fork

Trowel

Wooden stakes

Wooden plant supports

Pruners

Anvil pruner

Bamboo stakes

Scissors

Knife

Twine

Photosynthesis

This is the process undertaken by the parts of plants containing the green pigment chlorophyll, in which light energy is used to produce carbohydrates from water and carbon dioxide. During daylight hours, carbon dioxide is taken from the air through the pores (stomata) of the leaves—situated mainly on the leaf undersides. Photosynthesis occurs through the action of light on the chlorophyll in the leaves. The light energy is used to split water molecules into oxygen and hydrogen. The hydrogen is then combined with the carbon dioxide taken in through the stomata to form carbohydrates, such as glucose, which provide the plant with food. Certain minerals are required for these complex chemical reactions to occur, and these are taken up, with water, by the roots.

The essential processes
Photosynthesis occurs during the day, or whenever light is available to the green parts of a plant. This diagram shows the movements of carbon dioxide, oxygen, water and minerals during this process. Photosynthesis cannot take place in the dark and the flow of oxygen and carbon dioxide is reversed as the plant respires or "breathes".

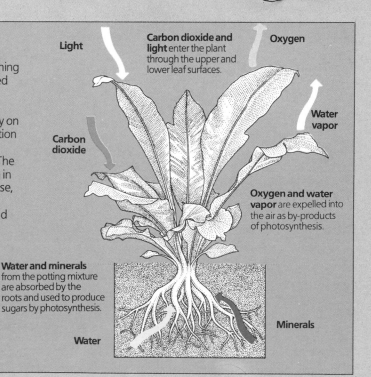

Light

Carbon dioxide and light enter the plant through the upper and lower leaf surfaces.

Oxygen

Carbon dioxide

Water vapor

Oxygen and water vapor are expelled into the air as by-products of photosynthesis.

Water and minerals from the potting mixture are absorbed by the roots and used to produce sugars by photosynthesis.

Water

Minerals

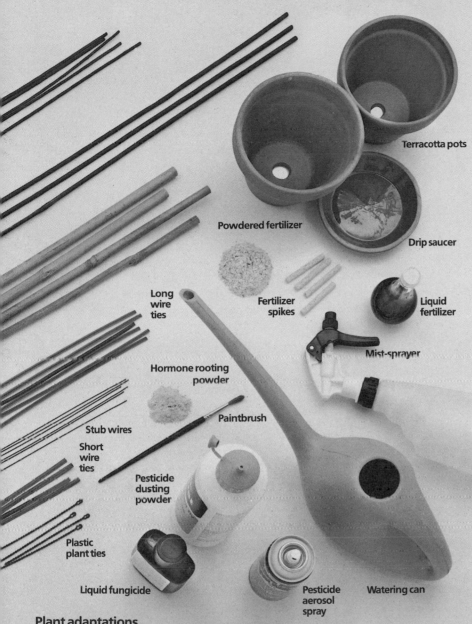

Terracotta pots

Powdered fertilizer

Drip saucer

Long wire ties

Fertilizer spikes

Liquid fertilizer

Hormone rooting powder

Mist-sprayer

Paintbrush

Stub wires

Short wire ties

Pesticide dusting powder

Plastic plant ties

Liquid fungicide

Pesticide aerosol spray

Watering can

Signs of ill-health

Slow or sluggish growth
If symptom occurs during summer months:—
Are you overwatering? (see p.251)
Are you underfeeding? (see p.252)
Does the plant need repotting? (see p.257)
If symptom occurs during winter months:—
Is this a natural rest period?

Wilting
Is the potting mixture very dry? (see p.251)
Are you overwatering? (see p.251)
Is there adequate drainage? (see p.255)
Is the location too sunny? (see p.245)
Is the temperature too high? (see p.246)

Drooping leaves and wet soil
Are you overwatering? (see p.251)
Is there adequate drainage? (see p.255)

Brown leaf tips/spots on leaves
Are you overwatering? (see p.251)
Is the plant too close to the sun or another
source of heat? (see p.246)
Is the humidity level too low? (see p.247)
Is the plant standing in a draft? (see p.246)
Are you overfeeding? (see p.252)
Have you splashed water on the leaves?
(see p.249)

Falling flowers, leaves and buds
Are you overwatering? (see p.251)
Are you underwatering? (see p.251)
Is the temperature inconsistent? (see p.246)
Is the light inconsistent? (see p.245)
Is the humidity level too low? (see p.247)

Variegated leaves turning green
Is the plant getting enough light? (see p.245)

Rotting at the leaf axils
Has water lodged in the axil? (see p.249)

Leaves turn yellow
If growth is straggly:—
Are you overwatering? (see p.251)
Is the plant getting enough light? (see p.245)
Is the temperature too high? (see p.246)
Are you underfeeding? (see p.252)
Does the plant need repotting? (see p.257)
If leaves fall off the plant:—
Are you overwatering? (see p.251)
Is the plant standing in a draft? (see p.246)
Is the humidity level too low? (see p.247)
Is the temperature too low? (see p.246)

Plant adaptations

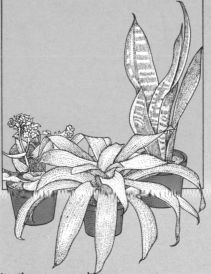

Thin, delicate-looking leaves
These usually indicate that plants come from tropical regions where they are protected from the extremes of great heat or cold.

Leathery or waxy leaves
These usually indicate that plants come from hot, dry areas, since such plants store water more effectively, reducing the amount of water lost through transpiration.

Spines or fuzzy hair
These usually indicate that plants come from desert areas as they help to baffle hot desert sunshine—the spines take the place of leaves and the stem becomes thick and succulent.

Light

Light is essential to all plants. Without enough light, growth suffers, and leaves become small and pale. Healthy growth depends on the process of photosynthesis, triggered off by the action of light on the green pigment chlorophyll. This pigment is present in red, bronze, purple and gray leaves as well as green ones; the other color is just an overlay to the green beneath. Variegated-leaved plants, however, are at a disadvantage as the yellow, cream or white sections on their leaves contain no chlorophyll. For this reason, variegated-leaved plants generally need brighter light if their strong leaf color contrast is to be maintained.

Indoor light levels

Plants in their native habitats have adapted to a wide range of different light levels. Indoors, you should try to provide the light intensity preferred by each plant as far as possible. To do this, you need to assess the amount of light present in various parts of any particular room. This can be difficult because the human eye is not a good judge of light intensity; it compensates for different light levels to give the impression of even overall lighting. The only really accurate way of measuring light intensity is to use a small hand-held photographic light-meter, or a camera with a built-in meter, which both give a good indication of light levels. You will probably be surprised at how low the levels of light are indoors: on a south-facing windowsill your plants will only get about half as much light as they would if they were growing outside, due to reflection from the glass. And as little as 3ft into the room there is only about three-quarters as much light as at the window. Having said this, however, most popular house plants are extremely tolerant, their adaptability being the main reason for their popularity.

Day length

In addition to intensity, light duration or day length is an important factor in determining how much light a plant receives. Most plants need about 12 to 16 hours of daylight to sustain active growth. Foliage house plants fall into two main groups: those that stop growing in the late autumn and need resting during the winter, and those that will continue to grow throughout the winter and remain attractive. Foliage plants from the tropics which, in the wild, receive around 12 hours of sunlight each day throughout the year, will only continue to grow all the year round in more temperate regions if they are given as much light as possible in winter, by using supplementary artificial light, and when kept in a warm room. Plants from more temperate regions stop growing (or slow down their growth very considerably) with the onset of winter and a shorter day.

In general, flowering plants need more light than foliage plants in order to initiate flower bud production and to allow the buds to develop properly. In many plants, flower production is triggered off by day length. These plants fall into two groups: long-day plants and short-day plants. Long-day plants flower when they have received more than 12 hours of light a day over a certain period. (It does not matter whether the light is natural or artificial—African violets (*Saintpaulia* hybrids) can be induced to flower at any time of year under artificial light.) Short-day plants flower

Light intensity and orientation

Levels of light intensity striking a house from all points of the compass. The lightest area corresponds to the strongest light, and the darkest area to the weakest, (assuming the sun is shining from the south). By finding out the orientation of your house, you will be able to place plants in appropriately lit positions.

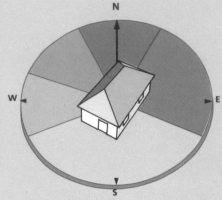

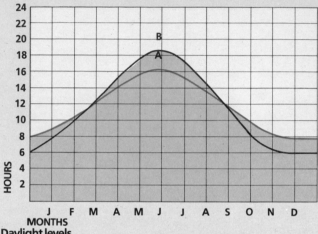

Daylight levels
In northern regions (B) plants receive more but less intense daylight in summer and less adequate light in winter than those further south (A).

when they receive less than 12 hours light a day over a certain period. Poinsettias (*Euphorbia pulcherrima*), chrysanthemums (*Chrysanthemum* hybrids), azaleas (*Rhododendron simsii*) and claw cacti (*Schlumbergera* sp.) are short-day plants which flower naturally in the autumn, but chrysanthemums can now be bought all through the year because growers can simulate the short day and initiate flower production by covering the plants in black plastic for the requisite number of hours each day. Many plants appear to have no strong preference with regard to day length, and flower through most or all of the year. These are known as day-neutral plants.

How plants seek light

All plants turn their leaves towards the source of light, apart from stiff-leaved species such as mother-in-law's tongue (*Sansevieria* sp.), many palms and dracaenas, and rosette-shaped bromeliads. Rooms with white or pale-colored walls will reflect light back on to plants, whereas those decorated in darker colors absorb light and will cause plants to turn towards the window. To counteract this natural tendency, and to promote balanced, upright growth, you should turn your plants frequently.

Suitable light levels for different plants

In *The Plant Finder's Guide*, the light preference of each featured plant is indicated by one of three symbols. These stand for sunny, filtered sun and shady, and are described in detail on the following page.

Sunny

A sunny position is one that gets direct sunlight for all, or part of, the day. South-facing windows will receive sunlight for most of the day, east-facing windows receive sunlight for several hours in the morning, and west-facing ones for several hours in the afternoon. The strength of the sunlight will depend on latitude and on the orientation of the room. South-facing rooms receive more intense light, but in summer it reaches less far into the room than in east- or west-facing rooms. In lower latitudes, or at the coast where light is brighter due to reflection from the sea, some form of shading may be necessary at a large south-facing window in summer to prevent possible leaf scorching and too-frequent drying out of the potting mixture. This type of bright light is for plants such as desert cacti, succulents from open bush or savanna, hard-leaved bromeliads from the tree-tops and certain sun-loving flowering plants.

Filtered sun

Filtered sun is direct sun that has been filtered through a translucent curtain or blind, or baffled by a tree or building outside. This level of light is also found between 3 and 5ft from a window which receives sun for all, or part of, the day. Although no direct sun falls here, the general level of brightness is high. Filtered sun is about a half to three-quarters as intense as direct sunlight. If you are in any doubt about the amount of light your plant needs, place it in filtered light, as few plants like direct, hot summer sunlight. In general, too little light is less harmful than too much light. Palms, tropical rain forest plants, and shrubs, including dracaenas, ti plants (*Cordyline terminalis*), and false aralias (*Dizygotheca elegantissima*), and soft-leaved bromeliads, such as scarlet stars (*Guzmania lingulata*) and flaming swords (*Vriesea splendens*), prefer this kind of light, as it is similar to the dappled light they receive in their native forest.

Shady

This position is one that receives no direct or indirect sunlight, yet does not have poor light. This level of light is found in, or just a little distance from, a well-lit north-facing window. It is also found in shaded areas within sunny rooms—for instance, along side walls—where the plant is well out of reach of direct sunlight, yet no more than 5-6ft from a sunny window. Shady positions receive about a quarter as much light as sunny ones. This amount of light suits plants from low-down in the jungle canopy where they are shielded from the rays of direct sun. However, day length in tropical jungles is considerably greater than that in northern hemispheres in winter, and you may need to move shade-loving plants nearer to the source of light during our winter. No flowering plants, or foliage plants with variegated leaves, will be happy in a shady position. Without sunlight, they will lose most of their leaves, and those that remain will lose their variegation.

Levels of light intensity in a room

Different levels of light in a typical room, in the northern hemisphere, on a summer day when direct sunlight is not obscured by clouds. In lower latitudes the light would be brighter, but would extend less far into the room. Obviously, the amount of light entering a room will be affected by local factors such as the number and size of the windows, and the presence of nearby buildings and trees.

Curtains absorb light, reducing the levels on either side of the windows.

Blind for shading plants on the windowsill from hot summer sun.

East- or west-facing windows get good light all day and direct light for a few hours.

South-facing windows receive direct sun for much of the day.

Bird's nest fern
Asplenium nidus

Belgian evergreen
Dracaena sanderana

Stick yucca
Yucca elephantipes

Poor light	Shady	Filtered sun	Sunny
An area more than 6ft away from the source of light. No plant will thrive here, even though the area seems bright to the human eye.	A moderately-lit area 5-6ft away from a sunny window, usually along a side wall, or near a well-lit north-facing window.	A well-lit position 3-5ft inside a south-, east- or west-facing window, or one receiving direct sunlight filtered by a tree or curtain.	A position which receives direct sunlight for most, or part of, the day. The strength of the sunlight will depend on latitude.

Temperature and humidity

Temperature

House plants have a preferred temperature range in which they thrive, and usually another that they will tolerate. Most popular house plants are from tropical and sub-tropical areas and do best in a temperature range of 60°-70°F. (Seeds usually germinate best when temperatures reach 64°F or more; and tip-cuttings and divided sections root well at 64°-75°F.) Other types of plants—mainly temperate evergreens and flowering species—prefer cooler conditions in the range of 50°-60°F. These are the two temperature ranges described by the mini-climates in *The Plant Finder's Guide* as "warm" and "cool". Although these are the conditions to which the plants are best suited, they will almost certainly be tolerant of slightly higher or lower temperatures for at least part of the time.

Plants that grow naturally in cool places will grow faster when given higher temperatures. Some may adapt and thrive, perhaps growing more quickly than is convenient indoors, although the blooming period of certain short-term flowering plants is greatly reduced if they are given higher temperatures than they need. It is rare that plants from a warm place do well in much cooler conditions.

In general, a fall in temperature of 5°-10°F at night is natural in the wild and advisable indoors. Some plants, such as cacti, can tolerate a much sharper fall, but fluctuations of more than 15°-18°F between daytime and night-time temperatures should be avoided in the house.

Winter- and spring-flowering bulbs must have their "wintering" at around 40°-50°F—a period when root growth is encouraged and active top growth discouraged. In addition, many house plants, especially evergreen species, require a winter rest period, away from the steady winter warmth of most domestic rooms. If possible, it is best to set aside a specific room which can be kept reasonably cool for several months.

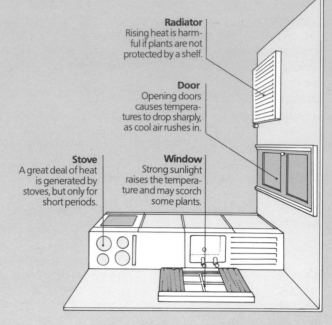

Radiator
Rising heat is harmful if plants are not protected by a shelf.

Door
Opening doors causes temperatures to drop sharply, as cool air rushes in.

Stove
A great deal of heat is generated by stoves, but only for short periods.

Window
Strong sunlight raises the temperature and may scorch some plants.

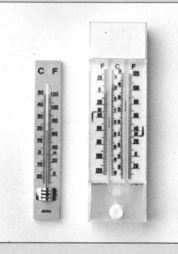

Variable temperatures *above*
This typical kitchen does not have a uniform temperature, and this factor should be borne in mind when positioning plants.

Monitoring temperatures *left*
It is always a good idea to monitor temperatures. The photograph shows a simple thermometer and a minimum/maximum thermometer which measures the daily fluctuation in temperature by recording the highest and lowest levels reached.

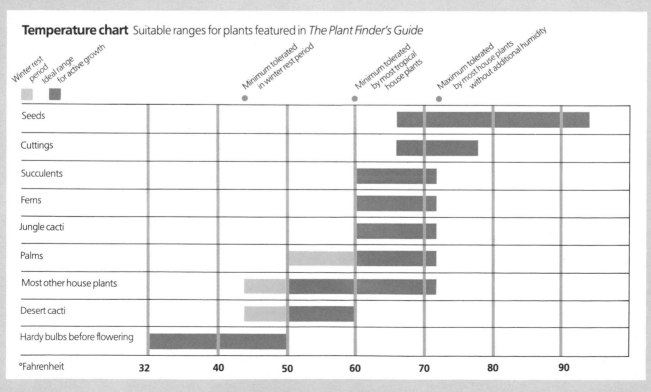

Temperature chart Suitable ranges for plants featured in *The Plant Finder's Guide*

Legend: ▨ Winter rest period ▪ Ideal range for active growth

Markers: Minimum tolerated in winter rest period · Minimum tolerated by most tropical house plants · Maximum tolerated by most house plants without additional humidity

Plant	32	40	50	60	70	80	90
Seeds					■■■■■■■■■■		
Cuttings					■■■■■■■		
Succulents				■■■■■			
Ferns				■■■■■			
Jungle cacti				■■■■■			
Palms			▨▨	■■■■			
Most other house plants			▨▨▨	■■■■■			
Desert cacti			▨▨	■■■			
Hardy bulbs before flowering	■■▨▨▨▨						

°Fahrenheit

Humidity

Humidity is the amount of water vapor contained in the air. It is affected by changes in temperature: warm air is capable of carrying more moisture than cold air, and it will cause water to evaporate from all available sources, including the leaves of plants. The amount of water in the air is measured on a scale of "relative" humidity—that is, the amount of water in the air compared to saturation point at a given temperature. 0 per cent equals absolutely dry air and 100 per cent equals absolutely saturated air. A relative humidity of at least 40 per cent is a requirement for most plants. To maintain this degree of humidity, a greater amount of water will need to be present in warm air than in colder air.

Cacti and succulents are used to a level of around 30-40 per cent, but the average tolerant house plant does best with a level of around 60 per cent. The thin-leaved jungle plants, such as delta maidenhair ferns (*Adiantum raddianum*) and painted nettles (*Coleus blumei*), however, enjoy a level nearer 80 per cent. These three figures correspond to the "low", "medium" and "high" humidity categories given in *The Plant Finder's Guide*. The relative humidity level of the average living room with the heating switched on, but with no humidifying device, is only around 15 per cent so the air in bathrooms and steamy kitchens makes them better homes for most plants than living rooms.

Signs of humidity deficiency

There are a number of signs which indicate that a plant is suffering from a lack of humidity: its leaves may begin to shrivel or show signs of scorching—watch out for the drying out of leaf tips on plants with long, narrow leaves, such as spider plants (*Chlorophytum comosum*) and palms; buds may fall off; or flowers may wither prematurely.

Plants lose moisture from the tiny pores (stomata) of the leaves. These open during the day to take in carbon dioxide from the air but, at the same time, water from the tissues of the leaves escapes; this process is known as transpiration. Low levels of humidity mean that plants lose more moisture through transpiration. House plants grown in warm rooms, therefore, suffer all the disadvantages: the warm air encourages them to grow, but "sucks" moisture from their leaves and causes water in the potting mixture to be taken up more quickly, making more frequent watering necessary. You can alleviate this condition by increasing the humidity.

How to increase humidity

Portable humidifiers powered by electricity can be bought to increase the level of humidity throughout the room. These are effective—keeping humidity levels between 30 and 60 per cent in heated homes—benefiting people and furniture as well as plants. Growing several plants in proximity helps to make the air around them more humid, as moisture transpired by one plant increases the humidity for its neighbor. Arrangements of plants in bowls and large containers therefore offer good growing conditions. Other methods of increasing humidity include mist-spraying and standing plants on trays filled with moist pebbles.

The ultimate solution for those plants which must have a very high level of humidity is to grow them in closed or almost-closed containers such as bottle gardens and terraria.

Ways of increasing humidity

Mist-spraying *left*
A hand-spray fitted with a fine mist nozzle, used once or twice a day, temporarily places a thin film of moisture over the leaf and stem surfaces. Spraying also washes off room dust and discourages certain insect pests.

Pebble-filled trays *right*
Stand pots on a tray lined with moist pebbles. The water evaporates into the surrounding air.
Burying pots in peat *below*
Bury pots up to their rims in a larger outer container filled with moist peat or vermiculite (see pp.48-9).

Lining baskets *right*
Line hanging baskets with sphagnum moss and wet it thoroughly by regular spraying (see pp.54-5). Periodically dunk the whole basket base in a bowl of water.

Temperature/humidity ratio
Water in grams

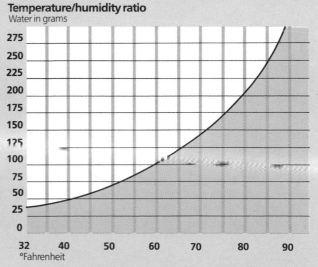

°Fahrenheit

The higher the temperature the greater the amount of water the air can hold. If this water is not supplied artificially, moisture is "sucked" out of plants. Therefore, if the temperature is high, additional humidity must be supplied, unless the atmosphere is naturally very humid.

Watering 1

In the wild, water appears as rain, mist or fog and is taken up mainly by the root system. Plants in the home are reliant on us to meet all their watering needs. Water is essential to all plants; without it they will die. The length of time this takes may vary from one day for young seedlings to several months in the case of a succulent plant, but death will always occur eventually. Water acts as a transport medium, in the way blood does for animals, and it is also essential for the process of photosynthesis, which supplies the plant's food. Water from the potting mixture is passed by the roots to all parts of the plant, carrying with it the nutrients vital for the food-manufacturing process. It charges stems and leaves and makes them sturdy and plump (turgid); without it they cannot stay erect. Any shortage of water results in stems and leaves going limp and drooping, flowers fading quickly, and buds falling before they can open. A temporary drought often means that leaves shrivel and go brown at the edges and the tips, making the plants look unattractive.

When to water

Knowing when to water can be difficult but, as a general rule, you should water potted plants when they need it. This may seem to be an over-simplification, but it is accurate. The real problem is to judge when that is. Drooping leaves and limp stems are obvious signs that more water is needed, but you should not wait for such an advanced stage to be reached. There are more subtle signs: some plants' leaves take on a paler, translucent look when water is needed; on others, the flower buds dry and shrivel. Each plant has its own watering needs, dependent on its size, its natural environment and, most importantly, the time of year; actively growing plants need a lot of water, the same plants can manage with much less during the winter rest period. Never water routinely just because someone tells you to water every so many days. It is far better to test the potting mixture first, as this will indicate whether or not the plant needs watering. "Weighing" the pot in your hand regularly can also give an indication of the amount of water in the potting

mixture; a mixture that is saturated with water weighs more than one that is dry. This method is reliable, but it takes a little practice to gauge whether or not the plant needs water, and is not always practical with larger plants in bigger pots. Moisture gauges are available which record on a dial the exact moisture content of the potting mixture. Readings such as "wet", "moist" or "dry" can be seen at a glance and allow you to act accordingly. Quite simple small indicator "sticks" or probes can be bought which are pushed into the mixture and change color according to the moisture content. Generally, play safe and, if in doubt whether to water, wait a day or two before taking the decision.

How to water

Most plants prefer to be given a really thorough drink, and like the dose to be repeated only when a given amount of the potting mixture has dried out. To water frequently in dribbles is bad practice. To give too little often means that the water never reaches the lower layers of the mixture which become compacted around the roots; and to give too much often results in a water-logged potting mixture. Waterlogging forces air out of the potting mixture and, as roots rot, produces the same wilting appearance as underwatering does.

Type of water to use

Tap water is safe to use on most plants, even though it can have a high lime content. It is always best to apply it when it is tepid, or at least at room temperature; stand a can filled with water overnight in the same room as the plant, to allow the water to reach room temperature and some of the chlorine to dissipate. Ideally, the water should be as lime-free as possible. Rain water is good if you live in the country but, if collected in towns, it is liable to be polluted by chemicals. Water can be boiled (and allowed to cool) for the real lime-haters such as azaleas (*Rhododendron simsii*); distilled water is also lime-free, but rather expensive for use on anything but the most precious of plants. Do not use water from an ordinary domestic water-softener, as this is full of chemicals and can cause serious damage.

Watering checklist
Plants needing plenty of water

● Plants which are actively growing.

● Plants with delicate-looking, thin leaves, e.g., angel wings (*Caladium hortulanum* hybrids).

● Plants in very warm rooms, especially those near windows in summer.

● Plants with many large leaves that clearly transpire a lot of water.

● Plants that have filled their pots with a mass of healthy roots.

● Plants that are grown in relatively small pots, e.g., African violets (*Saintpaulia* hybrids).

● Plants grown in dry air.

● Plants from bogs and marshy areas, e.g., umbrella plants (*Cyperus* sp.).

● Plants grown in free-draining potting mixes, including peat-based mixtures.

● Plants in clay pots.

● Plants with budding leaves and blossoms.

Plants needing less water

● Plants which are resting and those without buds or flowers.

● Plants with thick, leathery leaves, e.g., rubber plants (*Ficus elastica*).

● Plants grown in cooler rooms, especially in winter.

● Plants which are succulent and therefore naturally adapted to store water for future use, e.g., cacti; they transpire much less than leafy plants.

● Plants that have recently been repotted and whose roots have not yet penetrated all of the mixture.

● Plants that are given a high level of humidity, e.g., ferns, and those grown in a shady position or in bottle gardens and terraria.

● Plants grown in water-retentive potting mixtures, including soil-based mixtures.

● Plants grown in plastic and glazed clay pots.

● Plants that have thick, fleshy roots or water-storing sections on their roots, e.g., spider plants (*Chlorophytum comosum*), asparagus ferns (*Asparagus setaceus*) and the ponytail (*Beaucarnea recurvata*).

Methods of applying water

Topwatering *left*
Pour water on to the surface of the potting mixture; this gives more control over the amount of water the plant receives and flushes away any excess mineral salts that may have accumulated.

Watering from below *right*
Stand the pots in saucers filled with water. This method forces mineral salts to the upper layer of the potting mixture, but these can be flushed away with an occasional topwatering.

Bromeliad watering
Pour the water into the "cup" with a narrow-spouted watering can.

How much water to give

It is very important to choose the right amount of water, since damage to plants can occur by both underwatering and overwatering. Overwatering is probably more fatal to plants than underwatering (see also pp.250-1). In *The Plant Finder's Guide*, three symbols have been used to indicate the correct amount of water to give each plant shown; these recommend watering plentifully, moderately or sparingly. A detailed explanation of the three main instructions is given below. Although the illustrations show topwatering, details of how to water from below are also given.

Watering sparingly
Give enough water at each watering to barely moisten the potting mixture throughout. Do this in several stages, adding a little water each time. Never give so much water that it appears in any quantity through the drainage hole in the bottom of the pot. When watering from below, put no more than ¼in in the saucer at a time. Repeat if necessary.

1 Test the potting mixture with a stake. It is time to water when approximately two-thirds of the mixture has dried out.

2 Add just enough water to the surface of the potting mixture to allow percolation without water appearing in the saucer.

3 Test again with the stake. Add a little more water if you find any dry patches. Never leave water in the saucer.

Watering moderately
This involves moistening the mixture all the way through, but allowing the top ¼-1in to dry out between applications. When watering from below, stand pots in ¼in of water and repeat until the surface of the potting mixture becomes moist.

1 When the potting mixture feels dry to the touch, give the plant a moderate amount of water.

2 Pour on enough water to moisten, but not saturate, all of the potting mixture.

3 Stop adding water when drops start appearing from the drainage hole. Pour away any excess water from the saucer.

Watering plentifully
This involves keeping all of the potting mixture moist and not letting even the surface of the mixture dry out. Give enough water at each watering to let some flow through the drainage holes at the bottom of the container. If watering from below, keep re-filling the saucer until no more water is taken up. Half an hour is usually sufficient.

1 When the potting mixture feels dry to the touch, give the plant plenty of water.

2 Flood the surface of the potting mixture with water until it flows through the drainage hole.

3 Empty the saucer once the excess water has drained through the potting mixture.

Watering 2

Going away on vacation can present problems if you have a collection of healthy house plants and no-one to look after them. An absence of just a few days should not cause any harm to your plants; if they are given a thorough watering and moved into a cool room, they should quite happily survive. Increasing the humidity can also help at this time (see p.247). For longer periods, some form of self-watering system is required so that your plants do not suffer.

Certain of the methods shown below are better suited to plants in plastic pots; others are suited to plants in clay pots, as they need a larger, more constant supply of water. Automatic methods of watering are not suitable for plants in containers without drainage holes because of the risk of waterlogging the potting mixture. Happily, such containers are usually glazed and, therefore, water loss is much less than with porous clay pots. Plants in these kinds of containers should be well watered before departure on vacation, placed out of direct sun or strong light and stood on trays filled with moist pebbles or even a thick wad of wet newspaper—either of which will improve the humidity and allow a plant to survive a drought period.

Capillary mats
Place the capillary mat on a draining board or a shelf next to the bath and let at least half of it trail into the sink, or bath, which should be filled with water. As the mats are made of thick felt or felt rubber, the water will be carried up to the plants. The plants then take up what water they need by capillary action. Use capillary mats for plants in plastic pots; the thinness of a plastic pot and the many holes in its base allow the easy passage of water. Clay pots are too thick—the pot tends to absorb the water, rather than passing it to the plant.

Covering with transparent material *right*
Plants can be put into large plastic bags or into purpose-made domes. The processes of respiration and photosynthesis produce water vapor which condenses on to the sides of the bag or container. Do not use this method for long periods, as the plant may begin to rot.

Temporary wicks *left*
Simple wicks for short-term use can be made using water-absorbent materials such as oil-lamp wicks, cotton shoe-laces or old tights. Place one end in a reservoir of water and the other firmly in the potting mixture. Capillary action should do the rest.

Making a "self-watering" wick

This type of wick, made in a similar way to a temporary wick, is actually embedded in the potting mixture and is suitable for permanent or long-term use. It enables the plants to take up their water needs automatically, by capillary action, and saves the grower time and effort. Some growers "wick" their plants throughout the year. However, regular checks should be made to ensure that the plant is not being overwatered or underwatered by the wick. If this happens, remove the wick immediately.

These wicks are suitable for plants in either clay or plastic pots. The reservoir can be any container which will safely support the plant pot and should be covered by a lid (pierce a hole for the wick) to prevent the water from evaporating.

1 Carefully remove the plant from its pot, taking care not to damage the root ball in any way as you do so.

2 Make a wick using a strip of cotton or nylon material. Push it through one of the holes in the bottom of the pot.

3 Carefully push one end of the wick up into the root ball using a thin cane or a pencil.

4 Lower the plant back into the pot. Stand the pot over a reservoir, ensuring that the "tail" extends into the water.

Possible watering problems

If the watering instructions given in *The Plant Finder's Guide* are followed, your plants should receive the right amount of water for healthy growth. However, there are problems which arise if plants are underwatered, or overwatered—particularly during the winter rest period.

Watering in winter

At some time during the twelve month season, most plants need a period of rest. Many should be fed and watered more sparingly than during the rest of the year, others need no food or water at all. The rest period is brought on naturally by the reduced amount of light available to plants (so it coincides with winter), and to give too much water at this time stimulates growth which is not supported by adequate light. This results in poor, and often moldy growth, browning of leaves and early leaf fall.

Underwatering

Underwatering can still occur if you apply water "little and often", as the plant may need a large dose of water to thoroughly soak its roots. Should the potting mixture get over-dry (this happens particularly readily with peat-based potting mixtures), it can shrink appreciably, leaving a gap between root ball and pot sides. Any water applied to the plant just runs quickly away. The only solution is to soak the pot in a bowl or bucket of water until the mixture has swollen up again and the gap closed. The symptoms of under-watering are easily recognized and can often be arrested in time to save the plant. Plants particularly susceptible to problems if underwatered are those with succulent-looking stems, such as painted nettles (*Coleus blumei*), impatiens (*Impatiens* sp.), and all primroses and most ferns.

Overwatering

The symptoms of overwatering can take much longer to show themselves than those of underwatering. Again, watering "little and often" can lead to overwatering. Many plants need to start to dry out before they are re-watered and, if the potting mixture is kept permanently wet, the mixture soon becomes waterlogged. A warning sign that your mixture is waterlogged is the presence of green moss on the surface, since it will only grow in a constantly wet medium. Waterlogging leads eventually to plant death. The first indication that something is wrong with the plant is when a few leaves fall or become yellow, or when the plant makes poor growth. The lack of air and excess of water in the potting mixture cause the roots to become rotten, and cut off the supply of water and food to the plant. To save an overwatered plant, carefully remove it from the pot and check the roots; if they feel soft and come away easily, they are rotten and best removed. Replace the plant in the pot with some fresh potting mixture containing at least 25 per cent sand to aid drainage. Plants particularly susceptible to problems if overwatered include many of the cacti or succulents, whose bodies or leaves are adapted to store water.

Some plants, however, thrive on plenty of water. Their natural habitat is the swamp or bog and, consequently, their potting mixture should always be kept saturated.

Reviving a parched plant

If a plant does become parched and dried-out, it is often best to cut back the top growth and wait for next year's growth. If, however, you rescue it just in time, you could try the following emergency treatment.

Dried-out root ball

Root ball problems

Often, the root ball has shrunk away from the sides of the pot so that any water given runs away. Alternatively, the potting mixture often becomes compacted so that water cannot penetrate it.

Compacted root ball

1 This plant has clearly wilt-ed, as the drooping leaf and flower stalks can no longer support themselves.

2 Begin reviving the plant by using a fork to break up the dried-out potting mixture. Do not injure the roots.

3 Immerse the pot in a bucket filled with water until the air bubbles cease to rise from the potting mixture. Use a mist-sprayer on the leaves.

4 Allow any excess water to drain away, and put the plant in a cool place. Within a few hours the plant should begin to revive.

Danger signs

Too little water

- Leaves rapidly become wilted and limp.
- Leaf growth slows.
- Lower leaves become curled or yellow in color.
- Lower leaves fall prematurely.
- Leaf edges become brown and dried-out.
- Flowers fade and fall quickly.

Too much water

- Leaves develop soft, rotten patches on their surface.
- Leaf growth is poor.
- Leaf tips become brown.
- Leaves become curled or yellow in color.
- Plant remains wilted.
- Young and old leaves fall at the same time.
- Roots rot away.

Feeding

Plants are capable of manufacturing their own food but, in order to do so, they must have a supply of light, minerals and water. Minerals are present in garden soil and in most potting mixtures, and manufactured fertilizers are made up of a mixture of the minerals that plants need to carry out the essential processes in photosynthesis. The plant does all the work of converting the raw materials to form the food it needs for healthy growth (see p.242). When plants are bought ready potted, sufficient minerals should already be in the potting mixture to last the plant several weeks. Soil-based potting mixtures come from a variety of sources and some may be rich in nutrients. Their main advantage is that they release minerals over a period of several months, so plants grown in these mixtures will last longer without supplementary feeding than those grown in peat-based potting mixtures. However, the loam content of soil-based mixtures may vary considerably in its nutrient value.

Peat-based potting mixtures were introduced because of their convenience and efficiency for both nurserymen and gardeners. They contain a mixture of peat moss and sand to which is added perlite and vermiculite. The mixture has no food value, but some manufacturers add nutrients to the base and, by looking at the list of ingredients on the packet, you can check whether or not they are present. The nutrients that are added are of the slow-release kind and should feed plants for around eight weeks. However, some nutrients are soon leached away from the mixture by regular watering, or are used up quickly by the plants, so it is advisable to start giving supplementary feeds to plants grown in peat-based potting mixture about six weeks after purchase, or eight weeks after repotting.

Signs of a hungry plant

A hungry plant has an unhealthy "washed-out" look. Hunger signs are very slow—or a lack of—growth; weak stems; small, pale or yellowing leaves; lower leaves falling before they should, and few or no flowers. Ideally, plants should not be allowed to reach these extremes before you notice that they need feeding.

How often to feed

The Plant Finder's Guide recommends the feeding frequency for each featured plant. Fertilizer should only be applied during the active growth period, since feeding during the rest period will result in pale, spindly growth.

Feeding checklist

Too little fertilizer
- Slow growth, with little resistance to disease or attack by pests.
- Pale leaves, sometimes with yellow spotting.
- Flowers may be small, poorly colored or absent.
- Weak stems.
- Lower leaves dropped early.

Too much fertilizer
- Wilted or malformed leaves.
- White crust on clay pots and over the surface of the potting mixture.
- Winter growth is lanky while summer growth may be stunted.
- Leaves may have brown spots and scorched edges.

"Each-time feeding" is practiced by many specialist growers. It involves feeding at every watering with a considerably reduced strength of feed (half or quarter strength). This is a way of keeping a constant but weak supply of food always available—which is particularly important to plants that are grown in relatively small pots, and in peat-based potting mixture. It also prevents an unnecessary and harmful reserve of nutrients building up. New plants or recently repotted plants will not need feeding for some time: those in soil-based potting mixture should not need feeding for about three months; plants in soilless mixture (peat-based etc.) will need feeding after about six weeks.

The feeding tips given in *The Plant Finder's Guide* assume that you are looking for the maximum of strong and vigorous growth. In some cases, you may feel that you would like to keep a plant at about its present size, but in a healthy state. Three feeds of standard liquid fertilizer spread over the active growth period (roughly, mid-March, mid-June and mid-September) would keep most plants healthy without encouraging rampant growth.

Feeding guidelines

- Fertilizer is not medicine for an ailing plant; feeding will often only make matters worse. If a plant looks unhealthy, examine it for possible causes, including pests and disease, before dosing it with fertilizer.

- Overfeeding can do as much damage as underfeeding. Feed only at the strength (or much less) given in the instructions on the label.

- Feed no more frequently than recommended on the label or in *The Plant Finder's Guide*.

Effects of fertilizers

Fertilizer	Supplied as	Effect	Use
N Nitrogen	Nitrates N	Manufacture of chlorophyll. Active leaf and shoot growth.	All foliage house plants, especially at start of growing season.
P Phosphorus	Phosphate P_2O_5	Healthy root production. Flower bud production.	All house plants, especially those grown for their flowers.
K Potassium	Potash K_2O	Healthy formation of leaves; flower and fruit production.	All flowering house plants, bulbs and plants grown for their berries.
Trace elements	Iron, zinc, copper, manganese, magnesium	Essential processes such as photosynthesis and respiration.	All house plants.

Types of fertilizer

Fertilizers can be bought in many different forms: as liquids, soluble powders and crystals, pills or tablets and "spikes" or "pins". Liquid fertilizers, bought in concentrated form, are very convenient, as the bottles are easy to store and the contents need only to be diluted with water. Water soluble powders and crystals are also easy to handle and only need a thorough stirring in the prescribed amount of water to be dissolved completely. "Spikes" and "pins" are cards impregnated with chemicals that release foods when watered. These are often called slow-release fertilizers, as they work over a period of three to six months, slowly giving up their stored nutrients. Their disadvantage is that they tend to produce "hot-spots"—concentrations of food around the pill or "spike"—which can burn nearby roots. In addition to fertilizers applied to the potting mixture, there are foliar feeds: fertilizers that are diluted with water and then sprayed on to the leaves of plants which do not readily absorb nutrients through their roots. Foliar feeds also have an immediate tonic effect on any plant that looks starved. Always follow the instructions given on the packet, as an excessive amount of fertilizer can damage roots and leaves.

What fertilizers contain

Balanced growth relies on three essential elements. Nitrogen (supplied as nitrates) is vital for producing energy-forming chlorophyll, and healthy leaf and stem growth. Phosphorus (supplied as phosphates) allows healthy roots to develop.

Potassium (supplied as potash) is essential for fruiting and flowering and the general sturdiness of the plant. The packaging of fertilizers always indicates the relative chemical contents (shown as percentages) of the three main foods and may mention other ingredients, such as iron, copper and manganese, often under the general heading of "trace elements". The three most important elements may be spelled out fully, as nitrogen, phosphorus and potassium, or be given the codes N, P and K. Sometimes, only the percentage numbers appear, but the coding is always arranged in the same order to avoid confusion.

What to feed

Fertilizers suitable for use with house plants are usually ones with an even balance of the essential nutrients. These are known as standard or balanced fertilizers and will promote generally good growth in most plants. There are, however, specialist fertilizers for more specific purposes. High-nitrate fertilizers encourage healthy leaf growth and are suitable for foliage plants. High potash fertilizers are often called "tomato-type" fertilizers because they are used for tomatoes when they start to flower and fruit; these are useful for encouraging flowering and fruiting house plants that have reached a similar stage. High-phosphate fertilizers build up a strong, healthy root system and encourage the formation of flower buds, although foliage growth is slower. It is good practice to use a different fertilizer when the plant is flowering from the one used when it is not.

Methods of feeding

The method of feeding depends upon the type of plant you have and the form of fertilizer you have chosen to use. If you are using liquid fertilizer, or powders and crystals which have to be mixed with water, apply when watering the plant in the normal way. Before giving any type of food, ensure the potting mixture is already moist—to add food to dry soil is to risk root damage by "burning" with high concentrations of minerals. Foliar sprays are best applied with a mist-sprayer, used outside or in the bathtub to avoid inhalation and marking furnishings.

This type of food is rapidly absorbed, and will act very quickly on a plant with unhealthy foliage. Fertilizer pills are a very convenient form of feeding, as they can be inserted into the mixture and left to release their food gradually. Spikes, on the other hand, can be easily removed if you feel that a plant would benefit from a period without the stimulus of the fertilizer. Feeding mats are also now available; these are placed underneath the pot and the nutrients they contain are absorbed into the potting mixture.

Slow-release fertilizer spikes
As they tend to produce "hot-spots" of concentrated fertilizer, push the spike in at the edge of the potting mixture. Water well to help dissolve the food.

Foliar sprays
Always dilute to the correct concentration before spraying over both sides of the foliage with a mist-sprayer.

Liquid fertilizers
Add to the water you would give the plant at its normal watering time. These can be applied either from above or from below.

Slow-release fertilizer pills
These should be pushed deep into the potting mixture with the blunt end of a pencil. Try to avoid damaging the roots when pushing the pill in.

Pots and potting mixtures

Types of pot

Most house plants are sold in plastic pots, as this is the cheapest way of packaging them, but many other kinds are available including traditional, unglazed clay pots, and purpose-made ceramic and china pots. Almost any domestic container can be used to display plants effectively (see pp.28-31), but they may not all provide ideal conditions for healthy growth. All purpose-made containers will have one or more drainage holes to allow any excess water to drain away. It is possible to grow plants directly in bowls and other containers without drainage holes, but they need to be lined with drainage material and greater care is required when watering to prevent roots from rotting.

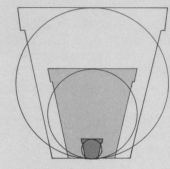

Pot shape *left*
In all pots, from the smallest available, with a diameter of 1½in to one of the largest, with a diameter of 12in, the depth is equal to the diameter of the rim.

Shards and gravel
These increase the drainage of a pot, and a layer is especially important in pots without drainage holes.

Gravel

Shards

Plastic pots
Plants grown in plastic pots need less frequent watering; plastic pots usually have several holes in their base.

Clay pots
Plants grown in clay pots dry out more quickly; the smaller sized clay pots have only one drainage hole in the base.

The depth of the pot
Measured from the top of the lip to the base, this is equal to the diameter.

The diameter of the pot
Measured at the rim, this is equal to the depth.

Standard pot dimensions

Always wider at its rim than at its base, and as deep as it is wide. Pots are usually round in shape, although square pots are also available and are useful for grouping several plants together.

2in

3in

4in

Half-pots *below*
Half-pots are less deep than broad, and come in a range of sizes up to 12in in diameter. Use them for seed sowing, rooting cuttings, and for plants with a shallow root system.

Drip saucers *right*
Made in a similar material, and a little larger than the base of the pot.

Pots with a built-in saucer base *below*
Made of a decorative plastic, these pots are supplied as hanging pots with a built-in drip tray.

Potting mixtures

Garden soil is usually not recommended for pots in the home. It is full of bugs, disease spores and weed seeds and its chemical content and physical make-up are uncertain. House plants should be grown in ready-prepared potting mixtures or a do-it-yourself mixture based on one of the standard prepared mixes. The contents of these have been very carefully tested as to their suitability to particular plants, and the ingredients have been sterilized to kill off unwanted visitors. The range of potting mixtures may seem large but a few basic potting mixtures will provide for the different needs of all the house plants featured in this book; details are given in *The Plant Finder's Guide*. There are two main mixtures, soil-based and peat-based. Soil-based mixtures have a heavy texture suitable for large plants; although sterilized, the soil contains some micro-organisms which break down organic matter into essential minerals, thus maintaining soil fertility. Peat-based mixtures are lighter and cleaner to handle but they often contain no built-in nutrients, so regular feeding is necessary.

Types of potting mixture

Potting mixtures are usually packaged in plastic bags of various sizes; the larger they are the more economical they become. The basic mixes are loam (soil) or peat. Specialized mixtures contain added ingredients. Additives for the mixes can be bought separately for home-made potting mixtures.

Bromeliad potting mixture *right*
Spongy and very porous, which suits the shallow root system of the bromeliads.

Bulb fiber *below*
Clean, light and drains well. Good drainage is essential to prevent the bulbs from rotting.

Soil-based potting mixture *left*
A heavy mixture. Suitable for large, top-heavy plants.

Charcoal *below*
Absorbs excess minerals and waste, keeping the mixture "sweet".

Peat-based potting mixture *right*
A lightweight, standardized mixture, containing very few nutrients.

Fern potting mixture *above*
Contains perlite or sand, and charcoal to keep it well drained.

Perlite *below*
Gives potting mixture an open texture for aeration and drainage.

Vermiculite *left*
Absorbs and retains nutrients and water.

Aggregate
Made of clay pellets, it has excellent water-retentive properties and is used for hydroculture and to provide drainage.

Sphagnum moss
Has excellent water-retaining properties.

Potting mixture recipes

Soil-based potting mixture
Best for large, established plants. A suitable home-made mixture consists of one-third sterilized fibrous loam, one-third medium-grade peat moss, leaf mold or tree bark and one-third coarse sand or fine perlite. A balanced fertilizer should also be added.

Peat-based potting mixture
A suitable mixture consists of one-third peat moss, one-third medium-grade vermiculite, and one-third coarse sand or medium-grade perlite. Add two tablespoonfuls of dolomite limestone powder to every two cups of the mixture to counteract the acidity of the peat.

Bromeliad potting mixture
A very open mixture, high in humus and almost lime free. A suitable mixture consists of half coarse sand or perlite and half peat moss. Specialist growers add other ingredients to the above mixture, including chunky pieces of partly composted tree bark (available in small bags) and pine needles (sometimes available locally) all ensure that excess moisture drains away swiftly.

Fern potting mixture
A high-humus mixture which should have good drainage. A suitable mixture consists of three-fifths peat-based potting mixture and two-fifths coarse sand or medium-grade perlite. Add one cup of charcoal granules to every quart of the mixture (to help sweeten it) and add a balanced granular or powdered fertilizer (according to the instructions on the pack).

Bulb fiber
Use only for indoor bulbs; it does not contain enough nutrients for other pot plants. A suitable mixture consists of six parts peat moss, two parts crushed oyster shell and one part charcoal.

Useful additives

Humus (leaf mold)
Retains nutrients and gives an open texture.

Manure
Used as a dried powder, cow manure is nutrient rich.

Peat moss
Holds water and added fertilizer very well.

Tree bark
Holds water and added fertilizer very well.

Dolomite limestone powder
Acts to reduce the acidity of potting mixtures.

Eggshell/oystershell
Reduces the acidity and assists drainage of potting mixtures.

Limestone chips
Reduces the acidity and assists drainage of potting mixtures.

Coarse sand
Opens up potting mixtures for better aeration and drainage.

Rockwool
Holds moisture and allows air to penetrate.

Repotting and potting on

Plants in gardens have a free root run. Their roots spread as far as they need to in search of water and food. With a few exceptions (bromeliads and other epiphytic plants), most wild plants have roots that run under the surface of the soil, where some moisture and food is usually present and where the soil temperature (which is cool) stays fairly constant. By contrast, the roots of house plants are confined within a relatively small container. Young, healthy plants quickly fill their pots with roots, and then find that there is nowhere else for them to go but through the hole in the bottom of the pot, or over the surface of the potting mixture. When this happens, the mixture dries out quickly and needs very frequent watering and feeding. "Potting on", or planting in a larger pot, is then necessary.

Sometimes it is not obvious just by looking at plants that they need potting on, so you must take them out of their pots and examine the root ball and root system. Look to see whether the roots have penetrated all the available potting mixture; if they have, it is time to move the plant into a larger pot—usually the next size up; if not, return the plant to its original container. Some plants thrive in small pots, in which case the roots of the plants should be checked and the plant put back in the same pot with some fresh potting mixture. This is known as "repotting", but the same term is often used to describe moving a plant to a larger pot.

When the maximum pot size has been reached, or if the plant is very large, the potting mixture can be revitalized by removing the top few inches and replacing it with fresh mixture containing added fertilizer. This is called "topdressing".

As repotting and potting on can be a messy business, it is best to deal with several plants at the same time, protecting furniture and the floor with newspaper. Have ready all the materials you will need—potting mixtures, pots, fertilizers and drainage materials. Make sure all the pots are clean, and soak any new clay pots until the air bubbles stop rising; this will ensure the pot will not absorb water from the potting mixture.

Removing plants from their pots

This can be an awkward business if plants are large, an unusual shape, or have sharp spines. Cover the area where you are working with newspaper, and water the plant an hour before the operation; this will help it slide out of the pot more easily, avoiding root damage and spilling of dry potting mixture. Repot the plant as quickly as possible to avoid drying of the roots.

Removing a plant from a small pot

1 Place the palm of one hand on the surface of the mixture with the main stem between your fingers.

2 Turn the pot upside-down and gently tap the pot edge on the side of a table.

3 The plant and its root ball should then slide out easily into your hand.

Removing a plant from a large pot

1 Gently run the blade of a blunt knife or spatula around the edge of the potting mixture.

2 Lay the pot on its side and tap it with a block of wood to loosen the potting mixture. Rotate the pot slowly, tapping it on all sides. Support the plant with one hand whilst doing this.

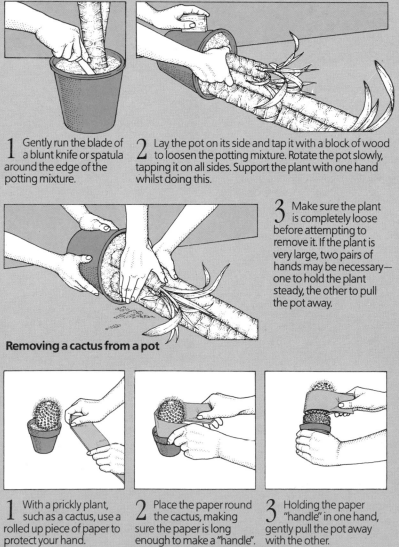

3 Make sure the plant is completely loose before attempting to remove it. If the plant is very large, two pairs of hands may be necessary— one to hold the plant steady, the other to pull the pot away.

Removing a cactus from a pot

1 With a prickly plant, such as a cactus, use a rolled up piece of paper to protect your hand.

2 Place the paper round the cactus, making sure the paper is long enough to make a "handle".

3 Holding the paper "handle" in one hand, gently pull the pot away with the other.

Potting on

The term "potting" refers specifically to the transfer of cuttings and seedlings to their first pot, while "potting on" is used to describe transferring a plant to a larger pot. It should be done at the beginning of the growing season. Do not pot on during, or just prior to, a rest period as no new root growth will be produced to penetrate the extra potting mixture; this will then become waterlogged and cause the existing roots to rot. Never pot on if the plant is unhealthy in any way (apart from being potbound), as this can cause unnecessary shock. Do not feed plants which have just been potted on for the first four to six weeks; instead let them send out new roots into the potting mixture in search of food.

A potbound plant

The earliest recognizable stage of a plant becoming potbound is when new roots start to cover the root ball. The roots will eventually become densely matted and form a thick spiral in the base of the pot. Potting on at this stage is essential.

Mass of new roots visible on surface of the root ball.

Roots begin to spiral at base.

Roots in a mass at the base of the pot, as they grow out of the drainage hole.

1 Remove any moss or other green surface growth from the top of the root ball.

2 Line the new pot with drainage material and ensure the plant will sit at the same level.

3 Prepare a mold by filling the space between the new pot and the old with potting mixture.

4 Insert the plant, fill in any gaps round the sides of the root ball and firm in gently to ensure it is supported.

Repotting

Plants do not always need potting on. If they are not potbound, or thrive better in a smaller pot, they may simply need repotting—taking them out of their pots and returning them to clean pots of the same size with some fresh potting mixture. Often, it is enough to gently tease away some of the old potting mixture and to supply the plant with a little fresh mixture which is high in nutrients. If the plant is growing too fast, or is already too big, the roots may need pruning to allow room for the new potting mixture.

1 Remove the plant from the pot gently. Watering about an hour before will help the plant to slide out.

2 To allow room for the new potting mixture, you may need to prune the roots by cutting slices off the root ball.

3 Place the plant in a clean pot of the same size. Fill in round the edges with new potting mixture and firm down.

Topdressing

Eventually, with well-established plants that have been potted on several times, it will not be practical to move them into larger pots. You must then find a way of providing them with extra nourishment. Topdressing each spring is the best way of doing this. The method also suits house plants, such as the amaryllis (*Hippeastrum* hybrids), which resent root disturbance and flower best when thoroughly pot-bound. Always use new potting mixture to which a slow-release fertilizer high in nutrients has been added.

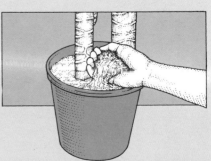

1 Gently scrape away the top few inches of the potting mixture, with an old kitchen fork or similar implement, taking care not to damage the roots.

2 Refill the pot to its original level using fresh potting mixture of a suitable type. Firm this down to ensure the plant is properly anchored in the pot.

Growing plants in artificial light

The use of artificial light is becoming more widespread among indoor gardeners, either as a substitute or supplement for natural light, or to allow plants to be grown in places where the light level is otherwise too low for healthy plant growth or regular flower production.

Incandescent bulbs can scorch plants if placed too close to them, and do not produce enough light for a plant's growing needs if placed the right distance away to avoid scorch. Incandescent floodlights are more effective, as they concentrate a beam of light by means of built-in reflectors, but this is still only sufficient for display purposes.

Fluorescent tubes are the most satisfactory and economical way of providing artificial light for plants in the home. They are available in several different colors; the coating on the outside of the tube determines the color of the light. If you are using a fitting with two tubes, a combination of "natural white" and "daylight" gives the closest approximation to natural light. Plants require the violet/blue and red wavelengths: "daylight" bulbs are high in blue but low in red; "warm white" and "natural white" are high in red, but low in blue. The simplest units consist of a reflector which holds one or two tubes and is supported on legs, enabling plants to be positioned underneath the lights. Multi-layered units are also available which have lights under each shelf to illuminate the plants immediately below. Alternatively, you can provide lights for plants in a bookcase or shelf-unit, or in the space between a kitchen countertop and wall-hung cabinets. It is important that any home-constructed units be fitted by a competent electrician.

Plants vary in their light needs (see pp.244-5) in natural conditions, and equally so under artificial light tubes. If they are too close, the foliage will be scorched, if too distant they will become etiolated and flowering species will produce fewer blooms than they should. Plants grown for their flowers, such as African violets (*Saintpaulia* hybrids), need to be 7-8in from the tubes, but most foliage plants are better placed 1ft away. Pots can be lifted nearer to the tubes by standing them on blocks of wood or upturned empty pots, and those that prefer least light should be stood at the ends of the tubes. Cuttings can be raised very well under artificial lights, as long as they are positioned the right distance away from them.

To grow plants exclusively under lights, the tubes must be kept on for around 12-14 hours per day for foliage plants and 16-18 hours per day for flowering plants, unless they are short-day types—such as poinsettias (*Euphorbia pulcherrima*)—which require less light. Electric timer switches can be installed so that the lights will come on when it is most convenient. When using units to provide additional light in winter, plants should have as much normal daylight as possible, and then the tubes should be illuminated for around 5 or 6 hours in the evening.

Decorative and functional lighting *left*
This small light fixture is equipped with a special bulb which should provide the light needed to keep this Boston fern (*Nephrolepis exaltata* "Bostoniensis") healthy in a position which would otherwise be too dark for it. The light also serves a decorative purpose, casting an interesting shadow on to the wall behind.

Types of bulbs *below*
Fluorescent light tubes, in a range of lengths and wattages, are the most efficient means of artificially lighting your plants. Incandescent bulbs provide effective display lighting and have the advantage of maneuverability.

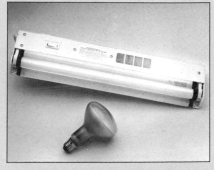

Simple but effective strip lighting *right*
A single, 6ft long fluorescent bulb suspended from the ceiling provides uncomplicated artificial lighting for the plants below. This type of bulb generates more light per watt than any other form of lighting and wastes less of its energy as heat. The attractive foliage of the plants is shown off to full advantage under the fluorescent light, which also fulfills their light needs.

Providing extra light *right*
A simple unit, like this one suspended from a wooden beam, is quick and easy to install. It can light a large number of plants in places which would otherwise be too dark for healthy plant growth.

Self-contained unit *below*
An illuminated unit filled with flowering plants can be a source of great pleasure through the dark months of winter. African violets (*Saintpaulia* hybrids), which naturally come into bloom in September, can be encouraged to flower all through the winter in this way.

Hydroculture

Hydroculture is the practice of growing plants in containers filled with water to which nutrients are added. Traditionally, the method was called hydroponics and can still be seen in its simplest form when hyacinth bulbs (*Hyacinthus orientalis* hybrids) are placed in bulb glasses filled with water; the bulbs sense the water is there and root down into it.

During the 1970s, growers started to market house plants growing in purpose-made, watertight containers filled with a special aggregate to support the roots of the plant, and chemically charged water to meet the plant's food needs. The special containers ranged in size from those suitable for housing a single plant to large, floor-standing models popular with establishments such as banks, libraries, hospitals and municipal offices, who liked the idea of bold, low-maintenance displays of plants. The beauty of hydroculture is that the plants need very little attention and virtually no expertise is required to cultivate them successfully (see also pp.72-3). Other advantages include vigorous and healthy growth, and freedom from soil-borne diseases and pests.

The basic materials for hydroculture are the aggregate, usually packed in plastic bags, and the container, which may be used on its own or have a liner. The aggregate must be clean and inert and can be grit, pea-gravel, perlite or, more commonly, a purpose-made granule composed of expanded clay. One name given to a particular aggregate is hydroleca—"hydro" meaning water, and "leca" standing for "lightweight expanded clay aggregate". This consists of lightweight pellets of varying sizes and fairly random shape that have been fired in a rotary kiln at extremely high temperatures. As a result, most of the clay has been forced to the outside wall of the pellet, leaving a honeycombed center. The great advantage of the pellets is that their outside cases conduct water from the reservoir sitting at the bottom of the container, thus moistening all the pellets. Another important feature is that there is plenty of air circulating between the upper pellets, where most of the plant's roots are.

Feeding methods

To feed plants grown in hydroculture, fertilizer is put into the water, but it can be put there in several different ways. The simplest way is to use a standard liquid fertilizer in the water used for filling the reservoir. The danger with this method is that nutrients which are not used immediately by the plants tend to crystallize out of the liquid on to the pellets and roots of the plant, and ought really to be washed out of the base periodically, which is rather a messy business. It is much simpler to use a specially designed hydroculture fertilizer bonded into a pad or disc, or packed in a sachet which is placed in the water. The advantage of these pads or discs is that they do not release multi-chemical fertilizer all the time, but only when the water lacks the particular element, and so no harmful build-up of chemicals is possible.

Containers for hydroculture

There are two main types of container that can be used—the single container and the double container. The single container may be made of any kind of watertight material (other than untreated metal that would affect the chemicals

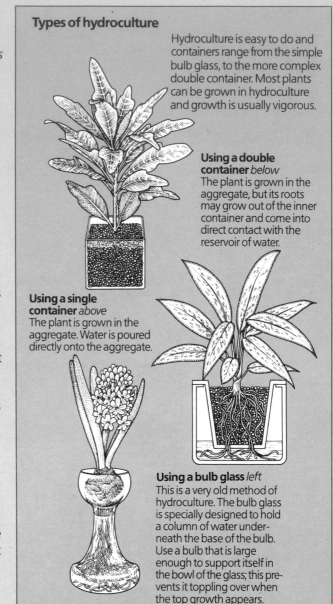

Types of hydroculture

Hydroculture is easy to do and containers range from the simple bulb glass, to the more complex double container. Most plants can be grown in hydroculture and growth is usually vigorous.

Using a double container *below*
The plant is grown in the aggregate, but its roots may grow out of the inner container and come into direct contact with the reservoir of water.

Using a single container *above*
The plant is grown in the aggregate. Water is poured directly onto the aggregate.

Using a bulb glass *left*
This is a very old method of hydroculture. The bulb glass is specially designed to hold a column of water underneath the base of the bulb. Use a bulb that is large enough to support itself in the bowl of the glass; this prevents it toppling over when the top growth appears.

put into the water and would probably rust), ideally with a broad base to give stability. Glass is probably the best material to use. Apart from looking attractive, a glass container allows you to keep a check on the water level and the amount of roots in the container.

The double container has a similar watertight outer container into which fits a smaller container. The small container hangs on the rim of the larger container and holds the aggregate and plant. The inner container is usually made of plastic and has holes or large slits in its sides and base to allow air and water to circulate around the pellets and the roots of the plant.

In both cases, the water should only be in the lower regions, never in the upper ones. With the single container, the bottom quarter or third of the aggregate should be submerged; with the double container, it is normally enough that the inner container, filled with the aggregate, be in direct contact with the reservoir of water. A water gauge will indicate when more water is needed.

Potting up rooted cuttings in hydroculture

Cuttings that have made roots in water can be planted in hydroculture containers in much the same way as cuttings are planted in potting mixture. Hold the cuttings upright and gently trickle the aggregate around the roots, then tap the container gently to settle the aggregate. Never bury the cuttings deeper than you would if planting them in a potting mixture, and shade the planted cuttings for a few days until they have settled down in their new home. When they have made strong root growth, carefully transfer the pots to their permanent position.

Rooting cuttings in hydroculture *right*
Cuttings of such plants as ivies (*Hedera* sp.), tradescantias (*Tradescantia* sp.), and wandering Jews (*Zebrina pendula*) can be rooted in "nursery beds"—small pots, filled with aggregate, which stand in deep saucers of water to which a little ordinary fertilizer at quarter strength has been added.

Potting on in hydroculture

A plant grown in hydroculture grows quickly but produces a much more compact root system than a plant grown in a potting mixture, so annual potting on is unnecessary. However, the plant will eventually need potting on as the roots grow to fill the container. Potting on in aggregate is a similar process to potting on in potting mixture, but much less messy and time-consuming. Always remember to pot on in a similar type of container—either single or double. If potting on in a double container, the size of the outer container needs to be increased as well as the size of the inner container to maintain the size ratio.

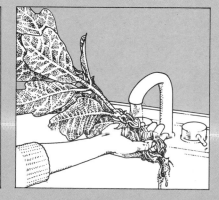

1 Cover the bottom of the new container with a layer of clean aggregate. Remove the plant from the old container. Do not pull the plant out as this will tear the roots.

2 Hold the plant over the new container of aggregate, making sure it is at the same level as before. Spread the roots out and trickle in the new aggregate.

3 Once the plant is properly anchored, fill with enough water to cover the bottom third of the new container, or until the water gauge indicates that it is "full".

Transferring a plant from potting mixture to hydroculture

It is not normally recommended that you transfer a well-developed or mature plant out of potting mixture into hydroculture because of the trauma it would suffer. However, it is possible. Because of the shock, it will be necessary to give the plant warmth and high humidity for 10-12 weeks to aid its recovery. A heated propagator provides the best conditions, but a warm greenhouse is also suitable, provided that the air around the plant is made very humid by the use of a plastic, tentlike cover and the temperature maintained at a constant level. During this time, all of the old, soil-adapted roots will die and new, succulent ones adapted to the semi-aquatic life will be made.

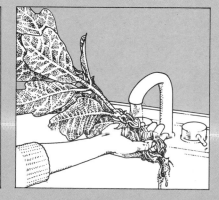

1 Using both hands, remove the mature plant from its pot, taking care not to damage the root ball. It is not advisable to use a rare or treasured specimen.

2 Supporting the plant with one hand, carefully tease apart the root ball, removing as much of the potting mixture as is possible without tearing the roots.

3 To remove the final traces of the potting mixture, wash the roots thoroughly under a gently running tap. Make sure the water is not too cold, as this will cause further trauma to the plant.

Pruning and training

House plants may need to be pruned periodically, or trained to the shape you wish them either to maintain or take on. They may become too big for the space available, or odd branches can start to grow in places where you do not want them, giving the plant an unbalanced look. Messy, tangled growth needs to be thinned out, and branches and stems induced to grow in a particular direction. Some plants need their growing points nipped out frequently to avoid unwanted leggy shoots and encourage a close, bushy shape. New growth on certain climbing plants will need to be supported as it is not capable of supporting itself.

The correct way to prune
Always cut just above the bud where you want the new shoot to form. Slope the cut downwards, away from the bud, and do not leave a long "snag", as this will be liable to rot.

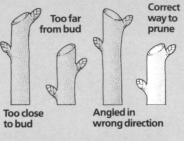

Too far from bud

Correct way to prune

Too close to bud

Angled in wrong direction

When to prune
Spring is the best time for pruning nearly all plants, as it is the season when new, active growth begins, but overlong stems can normally be cut back in the autumn if they get in the way or overcrowd the plant.

Some plants only make flower buds on the new season's growth and you can therefore cut away a lot of old growth in the spring, confident that you are not harming the prospect of flowers in the coming season. However, when cutting back woody-stemmed plants, it is usually safest to cut back into the previous year's growth and not beyond.

Whatever tool you use for pruning, it is important that it is sharp, to avoid bruising or otherwise damaging the remaining stem. A razor blade, scalpel or scalpel-like knife is excellent for soft-stemmed plants, and a finely pointed pair of scissors will allow you to get into the leaf axils of really bushy plants. For woody stems, pruners are essential.

Deadheading
Deadheading involves cutting away any dead or faded flowers on the plant. This encourages the plant to put more effort into producing new flowers rather than producing seeds, as would happen naturally.

Cutting back
Cutting back is probably the most drastic form of pruning, but usually improves the attractiveness of a plant. It allows you to get rid of totally unwanted growth and lets you keep favorite plants that would otherwise become too big to be grown in the home. A drastic cutting back often improves growth by ridding the plant of old, weak sections and encouraging new, strong shoots with short gaps between the leaves. Citrus and azalea plants (*Rhododendron simsii*) benefit from this type of pruning.

Cutting back straggly growth
Fast-growing plants which climb, or are trained round hoops and canes, can lose their shape after one, two or three seasons' growth. Jasmine (*Jasminum* sp.) is a climber which needs particularly drastic cutting back. Do not be afraid to cut out all but the newest growth; if the plant is cut back in early spring, it will be covered with new growth by the summer.

1 If growth round the hoop becomes very straggly, cutting back will provide attractive, bushier new growth.

Cutting back to create close growth
Plants with long stems, such as ivies (*Hedera* sp.) or philodendrons, may develop large gaps between the leaves in winter. This may be due to insufficient light or overcrowding. To correct the condition, the stems affected must be cut back to allow new, close growth (the tips can be used as cuttings). The initial cause of the problem must then be identified and improved.

1 Stems with large gaps between leaves, particularly those of trailing plants, will look better if cut back.

Cutting back a tall plant
Cutting back usually encourages new growth, so merely snipping away the top 4-6in of a large plant will only prove a temporary solution. When a rubber plant (*Ficus elastica*) or rainbow plant (*Dracaena marginata*) almost reaches the ceiling, it needs shortening by about 3ft if you want to keep it indoors for a few more years. The plant may look odd for several weeks but once the new leaves appear the cutting back will have been worthwhile.

1 A favorite plant which has grown too tall can be cut back drastically and kept in the house for a few more years.

Flowers on long stalks
Deadhead plants such as African violets (*Saintpaulia* hybrids), whose flower stalks arise from the base of the plant, by pulling and twisting out the whole stalk.

Flowers on short stalks
Deadhead flowers in clusters, or on short stalks arising from a main stem, by pinching them off between your thumb and index finger.

Pinching out

Growing tips should be pinched out frequently on plants that would naturally grow long unbranched stems, but which look better when growth is more compact. Pinching out also prevents climbers and trailers becoming too straggly.

How to pinch out *right*
Nip out the growing tip or point with your index finger and thumb.

2 Unwind the stems from the hoop and cut them off, using sharp scissors, until only two of the youngest stems remain.

3 Wind the remaining stems round the wire hoop and secure with wire plant ties.

2 Using sharp scissors, cut the stem back to the point (node) where tight growth exists, taking out the elongated, leggy growth.

3 If the plant is then given the correct growing conditions, the new growth will have short gaps between the leaves.

2 Use pruners to remove the head of a woody-stemmed plant. Cut down by as much as half its original height.

3 Staunch any flow of latex with a dusting of powdered charcoal. Give the plant the kind of growing conditions it needs to grow at its best and new leaves will be produced in four to six weeks.

Training plants

Many house plants can be trained to grow in a variety of shapes, by appropriate pruning or pinching out to obtain a bushy plant or a tall plant with a bare stem, known as a standard, or by training the plant to grow round a support. Most plants attain a rewarding shape within a few years.

Growing a standard

1 Remove all the side shoots that form on the main stem, but leave the foliage.

2 At the desired height, pinch out the growing tip. Remove foliage from the stem.

Growing a bushy plant

1 Pinch out the growing tips to encourage the development of side shoots.

2 Maintain the bushy shape by pinching out the growing points of new side shoots.

Training plants around a support

Support can be provided by fastening the stem of the plant to thin canes, bamboo, wire hoops or trellises pushed into the potting mixture. Ties made of twine, raffia, soft wire rings or wire-and-paper twists can be used. Fasten them so that they secure the stems, but not so tight that they will bite into the stems as they thicken.

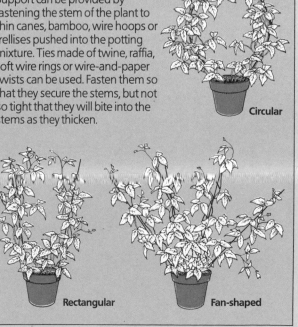

Circular

Rectangular

Fan-shaped

Propagation 1

All plants eventually reach the stage when they cease to be as attractive as they once were and need replacing with younger, more vigorous specimens. Propagating your own plants is a cheap and satisfying way of rejuvenating your house plant stock.

There are two main ways in which new plants can be produced—they may either be grown from seed (see p.269) or propagated vegetatively.

Vegetative propagation

This method of propagation involves taking a specific part of a plant and encouraging it to make roots of its own, so that it can establish itself and become a plant in its own right. Generally, but not always, plants propagated vegetatively look just like the original plant the section was taken from. Virtually any part of a plant can be used: plantlets that develop on leaf surfaces or on trailing stolons, offsets and stem or leaf cuttings. Alternatively, clumps may be divided (see p.267), or stems layered or air-layered (see p.268). You can propagate some plants by more than one of the methods mentioned, others can only be propagated in one particular way. Quick rooting and establishment is, in all cases, vital. The faster the section can make roots of its own and become established as a separate plant the safer it is; unrooted sections are at risk from wilting, rot and a number of other hazards. Special rooting mixtures are available for the propagation of cuttings—these hold plenty of air and water, but have few nutrients, which would scorch the new roots.

With practically all types of vegetative propagation, the best season to choose is the spring, just as new growth is starting.

Equipment for propagating plants

Jam jar propagator

Paintbrush

Plastic bag propagator

Plant labels

Hormone rooting powder

Labelling pencil

Peat tray

Peat pots

Peat pellets

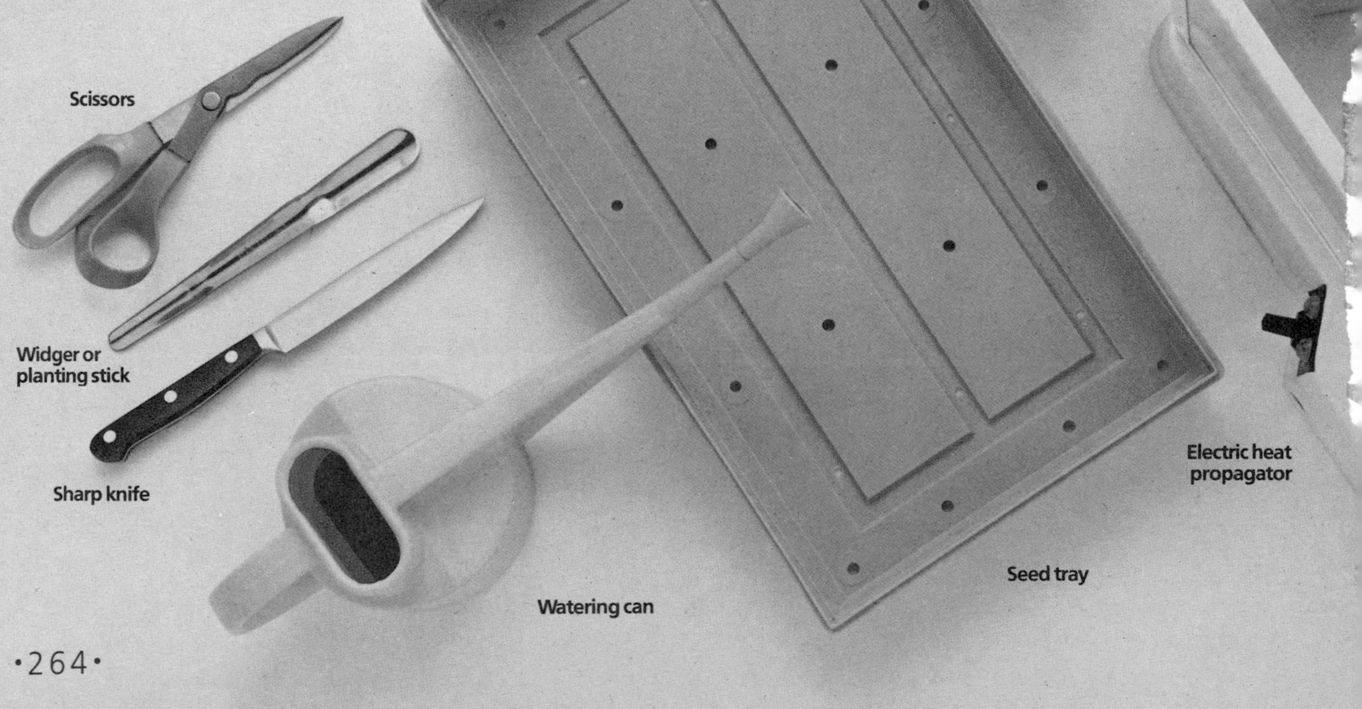

Scissors

Widger or planting stick

Sharp knife

Electric heat propagator

Watering can

Seed tray

Cold propagator

Propagating from stem cuttings

Most house plants can be propagated from stem cuttings of one kind or another. Cuts should be made with a really sharp knife or razor blade, as bruised or split stems are liable to rot. If possible, water the plant about two hours before taking the cutting, as this ensures that the stems and leaves are fully charged with moisture. If you have to use a flowering stem, gently pinch off the flowers first. Coating the cut end of the stem with hormone rooting powder will hasten the rooting process.

Rooting a soft-stemmed cutting in water

1 Make a clean cut just above a leaf axil or node; the parent plant can then make new shoots from the top or upper leaf axils.

2 Make another cut immediately below the lowest node or leaf axil of the cutting and gently remove the lower leaves.

3 After approximately four weeks, 1-1½in of new root will have formed, and the cutting can then be transferred to its potting mixture.

Rooting a soft-stemmed cutting in potting mixture

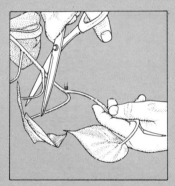

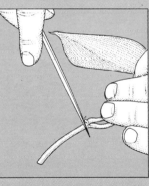

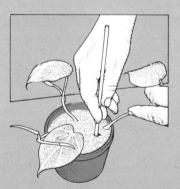

1 Select a healthy stem, with about three nodes spaced fairly close together, and make a clean cut, giving a 4-6in "tip" cutting.

2 Trim the cutting just below the lowest leaf node and remove the lower leaves to prevent them rotting in the rooting mixture.

3 Make some holes with a stick and plant several cuttings in the same pot, gently firming the mixture with your fingers.

Taking a woody-stemmed cutting

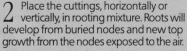

1 To propagate a woody-stemmed plant, remove any lower leaves that remain and cut the stem into short pieces, each of which should include at least one node. The rooting process may take several weeks longer than with a soft-stemmed plant.

2 Place the cuttings, horizontally or vertically, in rooting mixture. Roots will develop from buried nodes and new top growth from the nodes exposed to the air.

Propagation 2

Propagating from leaf cuttings

Some plants can be propagated from leaf cuttings. A complete leaf, with its leaf stalk attached, is pulled or cut from the parent plant and then grown in barely moist rooting mixture, or, in certain cases, water. The leaves should be inserted into the mixture at a 45 degree angle, and may be rested against the pot edge to give them maximum support; the cut end should not be buried too deeply. The new roots and shoots will develop from the cut end of the leaf stalk, or along the leaf edges (veins). Leaf cuttings may be planted singly in small pots, or a number may be planted together in larger pots or shallow trays. Enclosing the container in a plastic bag creates a humid atmosphere and usually eliminates the need for further watering. African violets (*Saintpaulia* hybrids) and rhizomatous begonias are examples of popular house plants which can be repro-duced in this way. The leaves chosen should be neither too old nor too young, so—in the case of an African violet, for example—the extreme inner and outer leaves of the rosette should not be used. Large-leaved begonias should not have their leaves cut into sections, as they are then liable to rot, but the leaves can be used whole if their outer edges are trimmed off to reduce leaf area and loss of water by transpiration.

Rooting leaf cuttings in potting mixture

1 Remove one complete leaf with a sharp knife or razor blade, and trim the stalk to a length of 1½-2in.

2 Plant the leaf in barely moist rooting mixture and cover the pot with a plastic bag to increase humidity.

3 When new plantlets appear at the base of each leaf, cut away the parent leaf.

Rooting leaf cuttings in water

1 Remove a healthy leaf with a leaf stalk attached, and trim the stalk to a length of 1½-2in.

2 Cover a water-filled jar with plastic and insert leaves through holes punched in the plastic.

3 Roots and small plantlets will form underwater. These can then be separated and planted in potting mixture.

Rooting leaf sections in potting mixture

The leaves of certain plants, including the mother-in-law's tongue (*Sansevieria* sp.), Cape primrose (*Streptocarpus* hybrids) and emerald ripple peperomia (*Peperomia caperata*), can be cut into pieces, which are rooted separately to produce many new plants. A cluster of plantlets will push up through the mixture from a section of Cape primrose leaf and, most probably, just a single plantlet from the cut base of each piece of mother-in-law's tongue leaf. The segments of leaf must be inserted base down-wards in the rooting mixture—otherwise no roots will develop.

Mother-in-law's tongue and Cape primrose leaves should be cut crosswise at 2-3in intervals and then planted almost vertically in a sandy rooting mixture, with between a quarter and a half of the section buried. Emerald ripple peperomia leaves should be cut into four sections (one cut down the leaf, one cut across it) and planted with a cut edge just in contact with a barely moist rooting mixture. If leaves from a variegated mother-in-law's tongue plant are used (as shown here), the new foliage which is produced will revert to plain green.

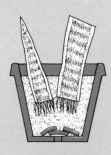

1 Remove the parent plant from its pot and select a healthy, mature leaf which is unblemished. Cut or break off the leaf at the base.

2 Cut the leaf crosswise, with a sharp knife, at 2-3in intervals. Each large leaf will provide several segments from which new plants can be propagated.

3 Plant the leaf cuttings together at a slight angle in the rooting mixture. They may be supported by plant labels or rested against the pot side, if required.

4 New roots will develop from the buried cut edge of each leaf section. When the plantlets are well-developed, pot them up and treat them as mature plants.

Propagating from plantlets

A number of house plants make "plantlets" —small replicas of themselves—on their leaves or at the ends of stolons or arching stems. Pickaback plants (*Tolmeia menziesii*) produce plantlets on their leaves, while strawberry geraniums (*Saxifraga stolonifera*) produce plantlets on stolons. If plantlets are left on the parent plant until they are well developed, they can usually be detached and potted up to develop roots of their own in a rooting mixture. Alternatively, strawberry geraniums and spider plants (*Chlorophytum comosum*) can be layered (see p.268), although plantlets may be less inclined to make roots of their own while they continue to be sustained by the parent through the linking stem.

1 Cut off a leaf or stolon (shown above) which bears a well-developed plantlet. Leave about 1in of the leaf stalk or stolon attached to the plantlet. Bury this stalk in a pot of rooting mixture with the plantlet resting on the surface.

2 Cover with a plastic bag to provide extra humidity. Roots should develop in three weeks.

Propagating from offsets

These are small plants which appear around the base of mature plants. Most grow directly from the stem but some may be produced on long stalks or stolons. Bromeliads and succulents often produce offsets at the base, and many of the spherical cacti make clusters of them. If offsets are to survive on their own, they should not be detached until they are well established and have developed the normal shape and characteristics of the parent. Well-developed offsets often have some roots of their own already formed, and this inevitably makes subsequent establishment easier and quicker.

1 Choose an offset, ideally one which already has some roots attached, and gently break it off the main stem. This may be done at the same time as you repot the parent plant.

2 Plant the offsets in barely moist rooting mixture in separate pots. Place the pot in a plastic bag until active growth indicates that the offset is well rooted.

Propagating by division

Plants such as African violets (*Saintpaulia* hybrids), most ferns and some cacti can usually be divided by taking them out of their pots and firmly but gently pulling apart obviously separate sections, each comprising a single or small cluster of plants and a healthy root system. It may be necessary to tease or wash away some of the potting mixture so that you can see the separate sections. Sometimes these are joined together with tough thickened roots, and you may need a sharp knife to make the division. In addition, ferns often have densely packed fine roots that make pulling the sections apart difficult.

1 You may need to use a knife to start a division so that you can get your thumbs into the cut area and successfully lever the sections apart, dividing the root ball equally.

2 Pot up the divisions at the same level as previously, in a pot slightly larger than the root spread. Water sparingly until sections get established and new growth appears.

Propagation times

Soft-stemmed cutting in water: four to six weeks for adequate roots to form; then transfer to potting mixture.

Soft-stemmed cutting in potting mixture: three to four weeks for adequate roots to form.

Woody-stemmed cutting in potting mixture: eight to ten weeks for adequate roots to form.

Whole leaf in potting mixture: three to four weeks for adequate roots to form; then a further two to five weeks before new topgrowth appears.

Whole leaf in water: three to four weeks for adequate roots to form; then transfer to potting mixture.

Leaf section in potting mixture: four to six weeks for adequate roots to form; then a further four to eight weeks before new topgrowth appears.

Plantlet in potting mixture: three to four weeks for adequate roots to form; then a further two to five weeks before an attractive-looking new plant develops.

Offset in potting mixture: three to four weeks for adequate roots to form; then a further two to three weeks for a plant of a useful size to develop.

Division in potting mixture: two to three weeks for a plant of a useful size to develop.

Propagation 3

Layering

This is the process by which roots are encouraged to form on a trailing stem while it is still in contact with the rest of the plant. Layering is practiced in the garden when semi-woody stemmed shrubs have their stems bent down and held in contact with the soil to encourage them to make roots. It is not often practiced indoors except with heartleaf philodendrons (*Philodendron scandens*) and ivies (*Hedera* sp.)—both of which make aerial roots at the nodes or leaf joints. As with the propagation of plantlets (see p.267), the stems are brought into contact with a suitable rooting mixture in a nearby pot. Many creeping plants are constantly sending roots down into the potting mixture over which they grow. The new growths can be cut from the parent plants and potted up separately at virtually any time.

1 Bring the stem into contact with a pot containing suitable rooting mixture, securing it firmly in place with a hairpin or a piece of bent wire. Heap a little rooting mixture over the point of contact to further encourage rooting.

2 New roots form within three to four weeks at the node, and a young plant will begin to grow. When this happens, cut the new plant free, taking care not to spoil the shape of the parent. Several plants can be propagated in this way simultaneously.

Air layering

Air layering is a way of propagating a prized plant that has grown too big for convenience or one that has lost some of its lower leaves and is starting to look untidy. It is often used for woody-stemmed plants that do not root quickly from cuttings and are so stiff that their stems cannot be bent down for layering.

The woody stem is "injured" to encourage it to put forth roots at the point of injury; the top section is then cut off and potted up. One method involves making a single upward-slanting cut in the stem, but this puts it in danger of being broken off. A somewhat safer way of air layering is described here.

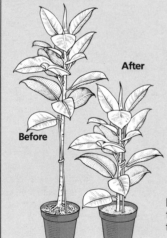

Before / After

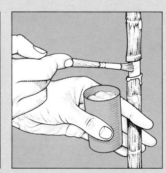

1 Score out two rings, ½-¾in apart, just below the lowest healthy leaf on the stem. Peel off the bark between them, leaving the stem tissue undisturbed.

2 Brush the stripped area of stem with a thin layer of hormone rooting powder to encourage the rapid production of new roots.

3 Using insulating tape or strong thread, secure the end of an oblong piece of plastic around the stem, just below the point at which the stem is cut.

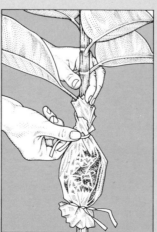

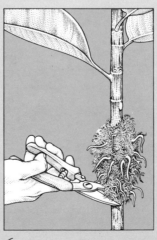

4 Pack the cuplike plastic sheath with moistened sphagnum moss. This is the most effective rooting medium for air-layering.

5 Lash the top of the plastic around the stem to ensure that the moisture cannot escape. The cut section of stem should now be completely covered.

6 After several weeks, roots will appear through the moss. Remove the plastic cover and cut the stem cleanly, just below where the roots are growing.

7 Plant the new root ball in a pot large enough to allow a 2in space around it. Fill with a suitable potting mixture, and water sparingly until well established.

Growing from seeds

Very reliable strains of seeds are available for such popular house plants as wax begonias (*Begonia semperflorens-cultorum*), black-eyed Susan vines (*Thunbergia alata*), silk oaks (*Grevillea robusta*), German violets (*Exacum affine*) and impatiens (*Impatiens wallerana* hybrids), and the best hybrid forms can often be raised in this way.

Seeds are best sown in a suitable peat-based rooting mixture (see p.264). Use half-pots, pans or seed trays depending on the quantity of seed being sown. Very small seed, such as that of begonias (*Begonia* sp.) and African violets (*Saintpaulia* hybrids), resembles dust, and is best sprinkled over the surface of the rooting mixture. Slightly larger seeds can have a shallow layer of finely sieved mixture placed over them, and sizeable seeds should be buried at one and a half times their own depth. Once water has penetrated the outer coating of the seed, growth begins and, from that point onwards, a constant supply of moisture

is needed. Any drying out is fatal, but too much water will result in rotting, so a balance must be struck.

Temperatures above 60°F are needed for swift germination and some of the sub-tropical and tropical plants need much higher levels. Some seed germinates best in the dark, other types need light to grow—so always follow the instructions on the packet. It is very important to give small seedlings the quantity of bright light they need from the very earliest stages of growth. If a seedling starts to make elongated growth, due to insufficient light, it will never develop into a really satisfactory plant. Containers should be placed near to a source of bright light as soon as the first seedlings start to appear. However, it is important to avoid hot direct sunlight that could cause scorch and certainly dry up the surface of the mixture. It is a good idea to check trays, pots and pans every day to ensure the various needs of the seedlings are being met.

Sowing seeds

1 Spread a thin layer of gravel in the bottom of a tray—this provides good drainage and prevents waterlogging. Cover the gravel with a layer of suitable rooting mixture.

2 Mark out shallow furrows as a guide for sowing. Scattering seed indiscriminately over the whole surface will often result in overcrowding of seedlings.

3 Take small pinches of fine seed from a hand-held container and sprinkle them along the furrows. Larger seeds can be individually spaced at regular intervals in the furrows.

4 Cover the seeds, if appropriate, and thoroughly moisten the mixture with a fine mist-sprayer. Then place a sheet of glass or clear plastic on top and put the tray in a warm place.

Thinning out

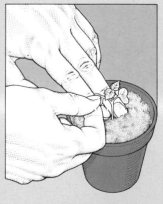

1 At an early stage, carefully thin out seedlings growing very close together. This gives those that remain a better chance of thriving.

2 The spaces between remaining seedlings should be roughly equal to their height. Use your fingertips to carefully firm the mixture around each one.

3 When a seedling has developed at least two true leaves, gently remove it from the mixture using a plant marker, or something similar, to ease out the young roots.

4 Transfer each seedling to a pot containing mixture suitable for the adult plant. Ensure that the lower leaves are not buried and avoid handling the stem.

Problems, pests and diseases 1

Healthy, well-maintained house plants grow sturdily, look good and are less likely to develop problems or be attacked by pests or disease. Unhealthy plants are usually the result of poor environment, neglect or wrong treatment—actual pests or diseases are, in fact, rarely to blame.

The first step to ensuring that your plants remain in peak condition is to choose them carefully, bearing in mind the amount of time and effort you can devote to them and the conditions you have to offer. Buy a specimen which looks healthy and protect it on the journey home. A plant will also need a period of acclimatization to its new surroundings; try to ensure it is placed in a suitable position and not moved for a few days. It is unwise to introduce a new plant into an existing collection until it has been carefully examined; ideally, it should be isolated from your other house plants until it can be given a clean bill of health.

Preventive action

The successful way to care for any plant is to give it neither too much nor too little of the essential growth factors: water, food, light, warmth and humidity. Apart from meeting your plants' specific growing needs, though, it is well worth devoting a few minutes, every week or two, to cleaning them and generally looking them over. Turn over the leaves and examine the undersides carefully—this will help you to spot any problems at an early stage. Should signs of ill health or pest infestation be apparent, immediate action must be taken if the plant is to be saved. Also pay close attention to the growing points; these, being soft and succulent, are more liable to attack by aphids than older, leathery leaves. In several flowering plants, such as the Cape primrose (*Streptocarpus* hybrids), the leaves are rarely attacked—it is the flower stalks and flower buds that are the susceptible parts. Some pests are a little choosy about their host plants, appearing only on certain species. Others are less discriminating and will attack any plant.

Routine maintenance

The action of cleaning a plant often dislodges the odd pest and may even prevent a real infestation. Household dust spoils the look of leaves and, to some extent, clogs the pores through which they breathe—it also reduces the amount of light which can be used for photosynthesis. See that plants are not crowded together so closely that air cannot circulate freely between them, or that some fail to get enough light because others are shading them. Remove any yellowing or damaged leaves and take off all flowers as they fade. Flower stalks should be taken off right to the base when all the individual blooms on the stalk are finished. Leaving sections of stalk behind can cause rotting in the plant's center.

Keeping plants clean

Plants which are kept indoors are bound to get dusty, so a regular cleaning program is essential. Clean leaves look more attractive and they allow a plant to function more efficiently. Various methods of cleaning are given below, depending on the size and texture of the plant's leaves. By far the most effective method of cleaning a plant of any shape or size is to stand it outside in a gentle shower, in a sheltered position, during the milder months. Rain water leaves no nasty white deposit behind and the leaves are thoroughly freshened by the experience.

Wiping with a damp cloth
Plants with large, smooth leaves can be cleaned with a damp sponge or soft cloth. Use a weak solution of soapy water and give a clear rinse afterwards. A shower will also benefit these plants, but ensure that the water pressure is not high enough to damage the leaves.

Removing faded leaves and flowers
Remove any faded flowers or yellowing leaves that are due to old age, taking them right off to the base. Snip off brown leaf tips with sharp scissors. As these are usually due to dry air, increase the level of humidity provided.

Routine checklist for ensuring healthy plants

In the majority of cases, ailments that affect house plants are not due to actual disease or infestation by pests. It may just be that one or more of the plant's growing needs are not being met. The following checklist will help you to determine the likely reason behind any symptoms of ill health displayed by your plants. If more than one of the plant's growing needs are not being met, it will be necessary to correct them all, to ensure healthy plant growth. If any symptoms persist, examine for any likely pests or diseases.

- Are you overwatering?

- Are you underwatering?

- Is the plant getting the sort of light it prefers?

- Is the temperature too high or too low for proper growth?

- Is the level of humidity conducive to the plant's needs?

- Have you remembered to cater for any winter rest the plant may need?

- Does the plant stand in a draft?

- Is the pot size correct?

- Are the roots of the plant completely filling the pot?

- Is the plant growing in the right sort of potting mixture?

- Would the plant benefit from being grouped with others?

- Is the plant dusty and in need of a clean?

Cleaning a plant with hairy leaves
Hairy-leaved plants will be damaged if
you attempt to clean them with a damp
cloth, as the hairs trap the water, causing
rotting. You can, however, "sweep" away
any dust which may have accumulated
by using a soft, dry ½in paintbrush.

Immersing a small plant
On warm days it is possible to wash
leaves clean of dust by inverting a small
plant and submerging it in a bowl of
lukewarm water to which a little soap
has been added. Swirl the plant around
gently for a few seconds, remove it from
the water and allow it to drain.

Examining for pests
It is a good idea to inspect your plants
carefully at regular intervals. Pay particular
attention to tender growing tips and the
undersides of the leaves; scale insects
and aphids are especially likely to
congregate there. Watch out for the
sticky honeydew that these pests exude,
as this may encourage sooty mold.

Physiological problems

The most common problems met
with in house plants are caused by
overwatering, underwatering, fluctuating temperatures, drafts, strong
sunlight causing leaves to scorch, cold
water causing spotting on the foliage,
and low levels of humidity.

Too much or too little water
Overwatering is a very common problem and can be a killer. The dangers
of underwatering are less, but the
signs of both faults are very similar:
in each case the plant droops or wilts
because it is not absorbing enough
water. Consistent overwatering, when
water is frequently given to an already
moist potting mixture, means that air
cannot reach the roots, so they stop
growing and start to break down and
die. With little or no roots, a plant
cannot take up enough water to
sustain it. To prevent overwatering,
only water when the potting mixture
starts to dry out, and wait until this
happens again before giving more
water. If a plant prefers a moist potting
mixture, keep it moist all the time, but
never sodden wet (see p.251).
   If a plant is underwatered, it will be
obvious that there is little or no water
left in the mixture; there may also be a
considerable gap between the root
ball and the inside of the pot where the
potting mixture has shrunk and, in the
case of a soil-based potting mixture,
the surface may become caked hard
or even cracked.

Fluctuating temperatures
When temperatures fluctuate by more
than 15°-18°F, leaf drop may occur. Aim
at keeping the temperature fairly even,
with only a slight fall at night. Avoid the
opposite—cool days when the heating
is turned off and warm evenings when
the heating is turned on. It is better to
keep all but the most warmth-loving
plants at a lower temperature all the
time, moving them to a room that is
not directly heated at night.
   When temperatures soar, African
violets (*Saintpaulia* hybrids) and many
other gesneriads will drop most or all
of their flower buds; during a heatwave
try to keep temperatures down and
increase the level of humidity.

Drafts
Plants abhor drafts: the thin and
more delicate fern fronds will be black-
ened by them, the leaves of angel
wings (*Caladium hortulanum* hybrids)
and painted-leaf begonias (*Begonia
rex-cultorum*) will droop, and crotons
(*Codiaeum variegatum pictum*) will
drop their leaves. Avoid sites next to
drafty or open windows and, at
night, do not leave plants behind
drawn curtains.

Sun scorch
The leaves of plants that prefer to
grow in some shade can easily develop
brown dehydrated patches if exposed
to really strong sunlight. Those plants
that can tolerate direct sun, but which
are not used to it, can be scalded by
sudden exposure. Always acclimatize
plants gradually to brighter light.

Insufficient light
If a plant is not receiving enough light,
its growth will be generally sluggish.
Flowering plants will not bloom as they
should, and flower buds may drop off.
The new leaves of plants with variegated foliage will revert to a uniform
green. To ensure that all parts of the
plant receive sufficient light, turn plants
regularly, or place them where a reflective surface can throw light on to the
side facing away from the light source.

Cold water spots
African violets (*Saintpaulia* hybrids),
gloxinias (*Sinningia speciosa*) and a
number of other gesneriads can have
their leaves marked with lighter
colored patches if they are watered
with cold water, or if water is allowed
to collect on the leaves at the time of
watering. Use tepid water and avoid
wetting the foliage.

Incorrect humidity
Low levels of humidity can cause
browning of leaf tips and leaf edges;
this is particularly obvious on plants
with thin leaves, such as peacock
plants (*Calathea makoyana*), spider
plants (*Chlorophytum comosum*) and
many ferns. Increase humidity by
regular mist-spraying and by standing
plants on trays filled with moist pebbles.

Problems, pests and diseases 2

Pests

House plants are sometimes attacked by insects and other pests which eat their leaves, stems and roots or suck their sap. A minor infestation is hardly noticeable and often does little damage but, if left unchecked, numbers quickly build up and then serious harm can be done. The ways in which pests arrive on plants vary, but new plants should always be thoroughly checked and infested plants should be moved away from healthy ones. Some pests prefer to feed on particular plants and will leave others alone, while others are less discriminating. A few types, such as aphids and whiteflies, are very common—they thrive throughout the world, adapting to very different conditions, and are extremely difficult to get rid of—others need special conditions to do well and are therefore easily discouraged.

Aphids

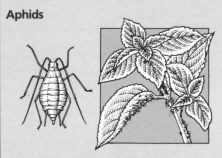

Aphids, commonly called "greenflies" or "plant lice", which may be black, brown, gray or light yellow as well as green, suck sap and multiply at an alarming rate. They molt their skins, and the white cases are found on infested plants.

What they do Apart from sucking sap, which debilitates the plant and causes distortion, aphids carry incurable viral diseases and exude a sticky honeydew on which a black fungus called sooty mold can grow.

Susceptible plants All plants which have soft stems and soft leaves; these include cyclamens (*Cyclamen persicum* hybrids), impatiens (*Impatiens* sp.) and German violets (*Exacum affine*).

Treatment Individual pests can be removed by hand, but a suitable insecticide is needed in most cases.

Caterpillars and leaf rollers

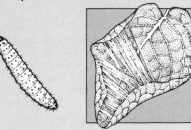

Caterpillars, such as those found in the garden, rarely attack house plants but an infestation may occasionally be caused by moths or butterflies which fly in and lay their eggs on stems or leaves—usually the leaf undersides. Sometimes a problem on plants summered outdoors is the thin caterpillar of the tortrix moth.

What they do They roll themselves up in a young leaf, inside a protective web, and eat young stems and growing points, ruining the symmetry of a plant.

Susceptible plants All soft-leaved plants, such as Swedish ivies (*Plectranthus australis*), nerve plants (*Fittonia verschaffeltii*) and geraniums (*Pelargonium* sp.).

Treatment Individual caterpillars can be picked off by hand and destroyed, but a more serious attack will need treating with a suitable insecticide.

Fungus gnats or sciarid flies

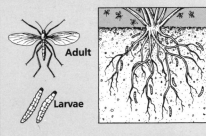

Adult

Larvae

Also known as "mushroom flies", these are tiny, rather sluggish creatures that hover above the surface of the potting mixture and do no real harm.

What they do The flies lay their eggs in the mixture and the hatched larvae feed on dead matter, including decaying roots. The larvae are unlikely to damage live roots on mature plants, but will sometimes attack those on very young seedlings.

Susceptible plants Fungus gnats exist in practically all peat and peat-based products. This means that plants such as creeping figs (*Ficus pumila*), African violets (*Saintpaulia* hybrids) and most types of fern are especially likely to suffer from them.

Treatment The condition can be treated by drenching the mixture with an insecticide when it is relatively dry, but the flies are really more of a nuisance than a pest.

Mealy bugs and root mealy bugs

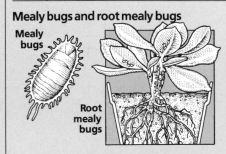

Mealy bugs

Root mealy bugs

Mealy bugs resemble white woodlice; they are oval in shape and around ¼in long. They can wrap themselves in a sticky white "wool" which repels water (and insecticide).

What they do Mealy bugs are sap suckers and excrete honeydew. A severe attack can result in leaf fall. Root mealy bugs congregate on the roots and create little patches of white wool.

Susceptible plants Mealy bugs tend to attack citrus, cacti or succulents, but may appear on virtually any plant. Cacti, geraniums (*Pelargonium* sp.) and African violets (*Saintpaulia* hybrids) are particularly liable to attack from root mealy bugs.

Treatment Systemic insecticides can be effective against mealy bugs, if used repeatedly. For root mealy bugs, drench the potting mixture with an insecticide at least three times at two-weekly intervals.

Red spider mites

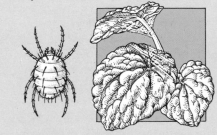

These minute reddish pests thrive in hot, dry air. The mites are barely visible to the naked eye, but their webs are the tell-tale indication of their presence.

What they do Red spider mites suck sap and spin very fine, silky webs on the undersides of leaves. Infestation results in leaves becoming mottled and rusty, new growth being stunted and, in severe cases, leaf fall occurring.

Susceptible plants English ivy (*Hedera helix* hybrids) and spider plants (*Chlorophytum comosum*) are two popular house plants which may be prone to attack.

Treatment As the mites dislike moisture, regular spraying with water will discourage a serious attack, but insecticides must be used in severe cases. Apply weekly, directing the spray on to both upper and lower leaf surfaces.

Scale insects

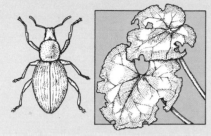

Most scale insects are brown or yellowish in color; they appear mainly on the undersides of leaves and are particularly partial to crevices. The young insects are very active and move about over the plant, but mature pests remain stationary, enclosed in their waxy cover, and appear as circular or oval raised discs.

What they do Both suck sap and excrete sticky honeydew—often the first sign that they are present is when this sticky residue is noticed on leaves or furniture. Honeydew may lead to infection by sooty mold.

Susceptible plants All plants are vulnerable to attack, but some types of scale insects prefer particular plants. The citrus family and ferns—especially bird's nest ferns (*Asplenium nidus*)—are most susceptible.

Treatment Spraying is not very effective, due to the hard protective coating of the adult insects, so systemic pesticides should be used.

Vine weevils

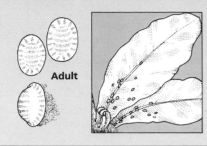

These pests are more common outdoors and in greenhouses. Adult weevils are large and almost black in color; their grubs are cream-colored.

What they do Adult pests bite pieces out of the foliage, leaving a permanent scar. The grubs eat roots, tubers and corms. Often, the first sign of their presence is when a plant droops and an inspection may reveal that it has no roots left at all!

Susceptible plants The most commonly affected plants include orchids, cyclamen (*Cyclamen persicum* hybrids), African violet (*Saintpaulia* hybrids) and all types of rosette-shaped succulents.

Treatment Adult pests can be removed by hand and destroyed, and the potting mixture should be drenched with a suitable insecticide. A plant without a root system cannot usually be saved.

Whiteflies

These tiny, white, mothlike creatures are sometimes found in the home, but are more common in greenhouses or conservatories. When whiteflies appear indoors, they have usually been brought in with temporary flowering pot plants.

What they do They settle mainly on the undersides of the leaves, sucking sap and depositing sticky honeydew. Their almost translucent larvae are often present in large numbers on the undersides of leaves.

Susceptible plants Whiteflies tend to attack certain flowering plants, such as fuchsias and geraniums (*Pelargonium* sp), grown during the summer in the garden.

Treatment These are persistent pests which may prove difficult to eradicate. Repeated applications of a spray insecticide for the larvae and a systemic kind for the adults will eliminate them in time.

Leaf miners

Leaf miners are the slim, sap-sucking maggots of a small fly. They can sometimes be seen if the leaves are examined closely.

What they do The grubs tunnel between the surfaces of the leaves of certain plants, causing a mosaic of irregular white lines. The progress of leaf miners is usually rapid and the appearance of a plant will quickly be spoiled if no action is taken.

Susceptible plants Chrysanthemums (*Chrysanthemum* sp.) and cinerarias (*Senecio cruentus* hybrids) are the most popular house plants likely to be attacked by these pests. Plants that are purchased are unlikely to be affected, but cinerarias grown by the amateur from seed can be at risk.

Treatment Damaged leaves should be picked off and a spray insecticide used on the leaves. Alternatively, a systemic insecticide can be applied to the potting mixture.

Earthworms

Although they are to be encouraged in the garden, where their feeding enriches the soil and their movements serve to aerate it, earthworms that get into the potting mixture of house plants can be a nuisance.

What they do Constant burrowing among the roots causes disturbance and loosens the potting mixture. Their presence is usually noticed when heaps of their casts appear on the surface of the mixture and plants seem loose in their pots.

Susceptible plants Worms may infest any plant which is left in the garden during the summer. They enter the mixture through the drainage holes in the pot.

Treatment Water affected plants with permanganate of potash solution and pick off any worms that surface. Tapping the pot will cause them to surface.

Slugs and snails

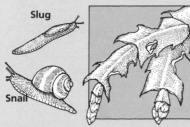

Slugs and snails will not survive in the home for long, as their presence is soon noticed and they can be easily picked off by hand and destroyed. They can, however, be troublesome in greenhouses and conservatories.

What they do Both are very fond of juicy stems, and can eat away large sections of them rapidly. They are most active at night and during prolonged wet spells outdoors.

Susceptible plants Plants that are left outside in summer and autumn can be seriously damaged by these pests. Christmas and Easter cacti (*Schlumbergera* and *Rhipsalidopsis* sp.) are especially at risk because of their succulent stems.

Treatment Protect all indoor plants while they are outdoors by sprinkling slug pellets around them. Renew pellets frequently as rain washes out the chemicals.

Problems, pests and diseases 3

Diseases

House plants are not prone to many air-borne diseases and, of those that are found, most gain a foothold because the plant has been overwatered, or because water has lodged in leaf axils causing conditions in which fungi and bacteria can thrive. Damaged leaves and bruised stems may spark off one of several bacterial diseases, and overcrowding, resulting in a lack of adequate air circulation, can also spell trouble. Many pests transmit diseases, and an infestation will, in any case, weaken a plant and make it more susceptible to disease. Always remove diseased sections as soon as you see them, and isolate an affected plant from the rest of your collection whilst treatment is being given.

Blackleg

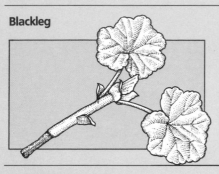

This disease, also known as "black rot" and "black stem rot", strikes plants just where the stem meets the potting mixture, but spreads both upwards and downwards to the roots. An attack rarely occurs unless the potting mixture is kept too wet for too long, but stem cuttings are liable to be affected during propagation.
Susceptible plants This disease is most common on geraniums (*Pelargonium* sp.).

Treatment Always use free-draining potting mixtures and be particularly sparing with water during the period that geranium cuttings are rooting. Avoid damaging stems and always remove faded leaves. There is no cure for this disease but cuttings taken from the tops of stems that are unaffected can be rooted—dip the cut ends into hormone rooting powder containing fungicide.

Gray mold

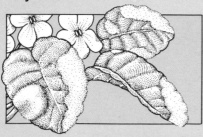

This fungus, which is also called "botrytis", usually starts growing on fallen leaves and flowers, but can also start when water lodges in the axils of the leaves. It strikes quickly when temperatures are low and the air is moist, and rarely in warmer weather and in dry air. Whole leaves or stems can be affected, assuming an unpleasant, fluffy-gray, moldy appearance.
Susceptible plants Gray mold affects plants with soft stems and leaves, such as African violets (*Saintpaulia* hybrids), cinerarias (*Senecio cruentus* hybrids), angel wings (*Caladium hortulanum* hybrids) and purple velvet plants (*Gynura aurantiaca*).
Treatment Fading leaves should be removed, and plants should be watered and mist-sprayed less frequently. A suitable fungicide may have to be used in severe cases, and to prevent further attacks.

Sooty mold

Sooty mold grows on the sticky honeydew secreted by pests such as aphids and scale insects. As such, it is a sure sign that a plant is infested with some sort of sap-sucker. The mold itself looks just like a thick layer of soot and feels sticky. Although sooty mold does not directly attack the leaves, its presence spoils the appearance of the plant, clogs the breathing pores of the leaves, and reduces photosynthesis by obscuring light.
Susceptible plants Citrus plants are particularly liable to be affected.
Treatment Regular washing of the leaves with soapy water avoids the possibility of an attack, and is the only way of washing off the objectionable mold once it appears. The best means of treatment is to attack the sap-sucking pests which deposit the sticky honeydew.

Mildew

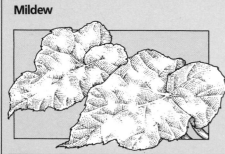

Mildew appears as powdery white patches on leaves, stems and, occasionally, flowers. These patches can be distinguished from gray mold by the absence of fluffy growths. Stricken leaves become distorted and fall from the plant. Low temperatures combined with high humidity, poor air circulation and overwatering provide ideal conditions for mildew.
Susceptible plants Soft-leaved and succulent-stemmed plants, including some begonias, are particularly susceptible; other kinds of begonia, even when growing alongside affected plants, are not attacked.
Treatment To treat plants affected by mildew, pick off all affected leaves and spray the rest of the plant with a fungicide.

Stem and crown rot

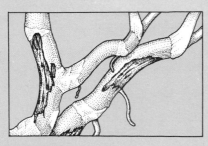

If the stem of a plant starts to go soft and slimy, the reason may be stem rot. Low temperatures and soggy potting mixture may cause plants to become infected. An attack of crown rot will cause the leaves to be eaten away from the center outwards.
Susceptible plants Plants with soft stems, such as impatiens (*Impatiens* sp.) and German violets (*Exacum affine*), are prone to stem rot. Other susceptible plants are cacti; when soft, dark-brown or black patches appear near to potting mixture level, it is likely to be stem rot. Rosette-shaped plants, such as echeverias (*Echeveria* sp.) and African violets (*Saintpaulia* hybrids), are liable to attack from crown rot.
Treatment An attack is usually fatal but unaffected sections may be dusted with sulphur and re-rooted if their shape justifies their being retained.

Diagnosis chart

The diagnosis chart below should enable you to determine what is wrong with your plant. Most problems occur because of incorrect growing conditions but, if the symptoms continue, check the plant for any likely pests and diseases, and treat accordingly.

Signs of pests

● Distorted stems and leaves ● Damaged flowers ● General air of lack-luster ● Sticky "honeydew" substance on leaves and stems *Occurs throughout the year*	Aphids (plant lice or greenfly)
● Mottled or finely pitted leaves ● Curled up leaf edges ● Fine silky webbing on leaf undersides and leaf axils *Occurs throughout the year*	Red spider mites
● Sticky substance on leaves which may turn black ● Waxy brown or yellow encrustations on leaf undersides *Occurs throughout the year*	Scale insects
● Yellowing leaves ● General air of debility ● Tufts of waxy, white wool in leaf axils and around areoles of cacti ● "Honeydew" on leaves or on cactus stems *Occurs throughout the year*	Mealy bugs
● Poor growth and yellowing leaves ● Clumps of white, waxy bugs on roots *Occurs throughout the year*	Root mealy bugs
● Crescent-shaped sections eaten out of leaf edges of plants with thick, succulent leaves *Occurs in spring and summer*	Vine weevils (adults)
● Wilting of the whole plant when potting mixture is still moist ● Roots or tubers eaten away *Occurs in spring, summer and autumn*	Vine weevils (larvae)
● Sticky "honeydew" on leaves ● Pure white insects resembling moths on leaf undersides *Occurs in summer and autumn*	Whitefly
● Minute, sluggish, brown flies circling above potting mixture ● Pilot of "soil" made by tiny larvae appear under the pot *Occurs throughout the year*	Fungus gnats
● Nibbled leaves and stems ● Rolled up leaves with fine sticky webbing holding them together ● Distorted growth caused by leaves or shoots being "stuck" to their neighbor *Occurs throughout the year*	Leaf rolling caterpillars

Signs of disease

● Fluffy gray mold on half-rotted leaves *Occurs from autumn to spring*	Gray mold (botrytis)
● Soft, slimy stems ● Black or brown decayed areas *Occurs in autumn and winter*	Crown or stem rot
● Thin, black, sootlike deposit on leaves and stems growing on the "honeydew" secreted by sap-sucking insects *Occurs in summer and autumn*	Sooty mold
● Powdery white patches on leaves and stems ● Twisted leaves ● Leaf fall and possible total defoliation *Occurs in spring and autumn*	Powdery mildew
● Black shrivelled sections of stem just above the potting mixture *Occurs in late autumn and winter*	Blackleg

Other danger signs

● Pale elongated growth with large gaps between the leaves ● Small new leaves, small or few flowers ● Variegated leaves lose color contrast ● New shoots that should be variegated appear plain green	Lack of sufficient light
● Large, irregularly shaped, light-brown patches on leaves ● Drooping leaves and stems ● Stunted flowers and unduly short or misshapen flower stalks	Too much sun or unaccustomed sun. Light too bright for those that prefer some shade
● Brown leaf tips and leaf edges ● Some leaf curl	Air too dry and/or potting mixture allowed to dry out too much between each watering
● Blackening or shrivelling of small leaf sections ● Serious leaf drop of large-leaved plants	Drafts or too cold a position
● Green slime on clay pots ● Algae, moss and other plant growth on the surface of the potting mixture ● Yellowing leaves and leaf drop ● Wilting of plant	Overwatering

Problems, pests and diseases 4
Pesticides

All types of pesticide are labelled as to their contents and the pests or diseases they should be used against. Always follow strictly any specific instructions, such as the dilution ratio and the method of application.

Contact insecticides

Insecticides are most commonly applied in liquid form as a fine spray, so that they hit the pest directly and, with luck, kill it quickly before it has time to multiply. These "knock-out" sprays work on contact, affecting the insect's respiratory system or otherwise destroying it.

Most sprays have an unpleasant smell and should not be inhaled. Take plants to be treated out into the garden or on to a balcony, as good ventilation while spraying is essential.

Some insecticides are poisonous to animals, birds and fish, and need careful handling. Others may not be suitable for particular plants, or broad families of plants, since their chemical content could burn the leaves and possibly do more harm than the pests. The label should warn you of this.

Systemic insecticides

Systemic insecticides work in another way. They are taken up by the sap—either from the potting mixture or through the leaves—and the sap-sucking or leaf-chewing insect is poisoned. Some stay as a thin film on the surface of the leaves, killing the insects that eat them; these are often called "stomach insecticides". Systemics can be applied in a number of ways: they can be watered on to the mix, sprinkled over it in the form of granules or pushed into it as a "pin" or "spike". They can also be sprayed on to the foliage of plants; the active ingredients work their way into the sap and circulatory system of the plant and poison pests taking them in. All systemics are relatively long-lasting and they can kill "newcomers" (pests that arrive on the plants some time after the application of the chemicals), whereas contact sprays only affect insects that they make direct contact with.

Some insecticides combine both the knock-out effect and the long-term systemic coverage. New products are regularly appearing, which is just as well since some pests eventually develop a resistance to one chemical. Vary your insecticide from time to time to avoid the possibility of resistance build-up.

Fungicides and bactericides

The best way to prevent disease is to ensure that your plants are grown in the conditions they prefer. Because disease is less frequently met with than attack by pests, it can be controlled by a much smaller range of chemicals. These are known as fungicides, which combat fungal diseases, and bactericides, which combat bacterial diseases. Most of these act systemically and are therefore capable of combating disease which occurs in any part of a plant. They are also unlikely to harm healthy plants, as can unsuitable insecticides, and are not usually harmful to people.

Fungicides and bactericides are most effective when applied in advance of attack, and it does no harm to use them purely as a precautionary device.

Application methods

Insecticides, fungicides and bactericides are packaged in various forms and can be applied in a number of ways. In addition to the normal sprays, aerosols, dusts, granules and spikes, diluted chemicals can be used as a bath into which small plants can be dipped. When it is necessary to treat sub-soil pests by soaking the potting mixture, a watering can may be used to apply the insecticide. In all instances, great care should be taken to follow the manufacturer's instructions and to ensure adequate ventilation is provided when applying the chemicals.

Spraying
Coat all parts of the plant evenly, paying particular attention to the under-sides of leaves. If possible, use sprays and aerosols outside so that the spray is not breathed in.

Soaking
Chemical solutions can be applied to the potting mixture using an ordinary watering can—but avoid splashing the leaves. Always use at the recommended strength.

Dusting
Dusting powders are especially useful on cut or bruised leaves. Give upper and lower surfaces a thorough coating. The potting mixture can also be dusted.

Sprinkling
Sprinkle granules evenly on to the potting mixture. The chemical is gradually released with each successive watering.

Inserting a spike
Push the spike into the potting mixture using a pencil or your finger. This method is quick and convenient.

How to apply pesticides

Key

- Soaking (solid drop)
- Spraying (open drop)
- Dusting (■)
- Granules (▲)
- Pellets (●)

	Benomyl	Carbaryl	Diazinon	Dicofol	Dimethoate	Dinocap	Disulfoton	Malathion	Metaldehyde	Nicotine sulfate	Permanganate of potash	Pyrethrum with Resmethrin	Rotenone	Safer's Soap	Comments
Aphids			Soaking, Spraying		Spraying		Spraying, Granules	Soaking, Spraying		Spraying		Spraying	Spraying, Dusting	Spraying	
Blackleg															No known cure
Caterpillars		Spraying	Spraying		Soaking, Spraying								Soaking, Spraying		
Earthworms											Soaking				
Fungus gnats								Soaking, Spraying		Soaking		Spraying		Spraying	
Gray mold (botrytis)	Spraying														
Leaf miners					Spraying		Spraying, Granules	Spraying							
Leaf rollers		Spraying	Spraying		Spraying										
Mealy bugs and root mealy bugs			Spraying		Soaking, Spraying		Spraying, Granules	Soaking, Spraying		Spraying		Soaking, Spraying		Soaking, Spraying	
Powdery mildew	Spraying					Spraying									
Red spider and other mites				Spraying	Soaking, Spraying		Spraying, Granules	Soaking, Spraying				Spraying		Spraying	
Scale insects					Soaking, Spraying		Spraying, Granules	Soaking, Spraying						Spraying	
Slugs and snails									Pellets						
Sooty mold															Remove with a damp sponge
Stem and crown rot															No known cure
Vine weevils					Soaking, Spraying										
White flies			Spraying		Soaking, Spraying		Spraying, Granules	Soaking, Spraying				Soaking, Spraying	Soaking, Spraying	Spraying	

Glossary 1

Adventitious roots Roots appearing in an unusual place, such as on stems or leaves, e.g., on the stems of cuttings placed in water or on the leaves of some succulent plants.

Aerial roots Roots that appear at nodes. They are mainly used for climbing but are also capable of absorbing moisture from the air. Many only develop properly if they can grasp a suitable rooting medium such as sphagnum moss, e.g., the philodendrons and their relatives the Swiss cheese plant, pothos vine, devil's ivy and arrowhead plant.

Annual A plant grown from seed that completes its life cycle in one season. Annuals must be thrown away once this cycle is complete. A number of perennial plants are treated as annuals (a recommendation is made in *The Plant Finder's Guide*), because of the difficulty of overwintering them or because they seldom look attractive in subsequent years, e.g., German violet. See also *biennial, perennial*.

Anther The male part of the flower which produces pollen.

Areole An organ unique to the cacti, consisting of a cushion or hump from which the spines and flowers arise.

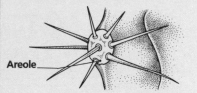

Areole

Axil The angle between the leaf or leaf stalk and stem from which new leaf or side-shoot growth and flower buds arise. Buds found here are known as axillary buds. Side-shoot growth is prevented if they are pinched out.

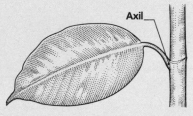

Axil

Berry A succulent fruit in which the usually small but hard seeds are embedded in the fleshy pulp. This pulp is usually brightly colored to attract animals and birds.

Biennial A plant grown from seed that takes two growing seasons to complete its life cycle. A rosette of leaves is produced in the first year, the flowers in the second. Biennials should be thrown away once this cycle is complete as it is difficult to make them flower again, e.g., foxglove. See also *annual, perennial*.

Bleeding When sap flows freely from a damaged stem. This is particularly obvious in such plants as the crown-of-thorns and rubber plant which bleed a milky-white latex. The flow can be staunched by applying powdered sulphur or charcoal. See also *latex*.

Bract A modified leaf, often colorful, which backs relatively insignificant flowers and acts as a method of attracting pollinating insects and birds, e.g., the petal-like red bracts of the poinsettia and the bell-shaped bracts of the paper flower.

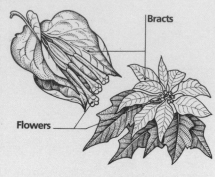

Bracts

Flowers

Bud An embryo shoot, leaf or an immature flower. A terminal growth bud is situated at the tip of a stem or side shoot, an axillary bud is one found in the axil of a leaf stalk. Growth buds are normally protected from damage and cold by closely overlapping scales or sheaths. See also *sheath, axil*.

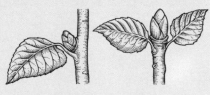

Axillary bud   Terminal bud

Bulb An underground storage organ containing a young plant. The organ stores food during the rest period and usually a complete embryo flower, e.g., tulip, daffodil. See also *corm, tuber*.

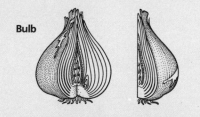

Bulb

Bulbil A small immature bulb attached to a parent bulb, it can also appear on the stems or leaves of the parent plant, e.g., some lilies.

Calyx The collective name for the ring of green sepals which surrounds the petals in most flowers. The calyx protects the developing flower buds. See also *sepal*.

Capillary action Also known as capillary attraction, this is the drawing up of water by a thread or hair. The term is also used to describe the way potting mixture draws up water when the pot and mixture are placed in direct contact with a dish or bowl of water.

Cereal Plants of the grass family cultivated for their seed as food, e.g., wheat, barley. See also *grass*.

Chlorophyll The green pigment found in the stems and leaves of plants.

Compound leaf A leaf divided into two or more segments, e.g., umbrella plant. See also *pinnate, palmate*.

Corm An underground storage organ made up of a thickened stem covered with a thin papery skin. At the top of the corm a bud produces both roots and shoots, e.g., crocus, sword lily. See also *bulb, tuber*.

Corm

Corolla The collective name for the ring of petals. The corolla may be made up of separate petals or the petals may be fused into one unit. See also *flower, petal*.

Crown The growing point of a plant, particularly of a rosette-shaped plant, e.g., African violet. The crown can also be the basal part of a herbaceous plant where the root and shoots meet. See also *root crown*.

Cultivar A type of plant or flower that has been developed in cultivation and named by the plant breeder. Cultivar names are enclosed by quotation marks to distinguish them from the scientific names. See also *variety*.

Cutting A term usually applied to a stem cutting. This is a section of stem, 3-4in long, (usually the growing tip), which is used in propagation to root and develop into a new plant.

Deciduous A plant that loses its leaves at the end of the growing season. These plants do not make good house plants as they are not decorative and usually need a cold resting period. New leaves appear in the spring. See also *evergreen*.

Dieback The death of a section of stem. This is often caused by faulty pruning.

Double flower Flowers having at least two layers of petals. Often the stamens and pistils at the center of the flower are replaced by more petals. Double-flowered forms are usually cultivars, e.g., modern roses. See also *single flower, semi-double flower*.

Double flower

Epiphyte A plant that grows on another plant but is not a parasite. Epiphytes use the host plant purely as an anchor and take no direct nourishment from it. Many bromeliads and ferns are epiphytes, producing strong, wiry roots which cling to tree trunks and branches, and other plants.

Etiolation The technical name for pale, sickly growth. The gaps between the leaves become greater and the flowers fewer. Insufficient light and overcrowding cause the condition.

Evergreen A plant which retains its leaves throughout the year. See also *deciduous*.

Exotic A plant introduced from abroad. The term is often applied to plants that have their origins in tropical and sub-tropical regions. Most house plants, therefore, are exotic.

Eye The center of a flower, which is often a different color to the rest of the bloom, e.g., black-eyed Susan vine, primrose.

Family A term used to describe a large association of plants in which certain characteristics are constant. Many genera make up one family, e.g., *Compositae* is the family name for all the plants with daisylike flowers. See also *genus, species*.

Filament The stalk supporting the anther. These two parts make up the stamen. Normally, many filaments are clustered together in the middle of the flower, e.g., passion flower. See also *stamen, anther*.

Floret A small flower among many others making up a flower head, e.g., most daisy flowers are made up of many florets.

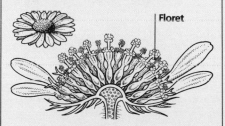

Floret

Flower Usually the most striking feature of a plant, this is an organ of very specialized parts concerned with sexual reproduction. Some plants produce flowers that carry only male parts (stamens), or female parts (pistils). These parts are usually surrounded by a ring of colored petals and green sepals, although there are many variations of this pattern. Some plants have both male and female flower heads on the same plant but, in most plants, both male and female parts are enclosed in the same flower head. Begonias are an example of a flower which is either male, when it is a collection of bright petals with pollen-filled stamens, or female, when it has a large winged seed sac backing the petals.

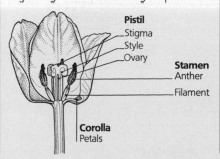

Pistil
Stigma
Style
Ovary

Stamen
Anther
Filament

Corolla
Petals

Forcing The technique of bringing a flower into growth ahead of its natural season. Usually a term applied to spring bulbs when they are encouraged to flower early. Azaleas and cyclamens are also "forced".

Frond Botanically, a term used to describe the deeply dissected "leaves" of ferns which bear spores and arise from a rhizome. It is also loosely applied to palm leaves.

Fruit A widely used term that describes any mature ovary bearing ripe seeds. The outer covering may be soft and fleshy, such as the berries of the Christmas cherry, or a dry pod with hard seeds inside, such as the seed pod of the Cape primrose. See also *nut, berry*.

Genus (pl. genera) A group of allied species. Usually a group of plants (though sometimes only one) which are similar in structure and which most probably evolved from a common ancestor. The genus name always begins with an upper case letter, e.g., English ivies belong to the genus *Hedera*. See also *species, family*.

Germination The first stage of a seed's development into a plant. The first visible stage is the sprouting of the new seedling. Germination can be swift (four to six days), or take many weeks or even months. It is a dangerous period as the seed is no longer protected by the hard outer casing, and strong roots and leaves have not yet developed.

Gourd The large, fleshy fruit of climbing and trailing annual plants native to tropical America. The dried fruits can be used in decoration.

Grass Annual or perennial plants of the family *Gramineae*. In the home, their decorative seed heads and threadlike stalks can be used in flower arrangements or dried for winter decoration. See also *cereal*.

Growing tip Also known as growing point, this is the tip of a shoot from which vigorous new growth emerges.

Hardy A plant capable of surviving outside throughout the year, especially in areas where there is the possibility of a sustained frost. English ivy and camellia are examples of hardy house plants.

Herbaceous A word usually associated with perennial plants whose growth dies down in the late autumn and is replaced with fresh growth the following spring. Plant material is stored as a bulb, corm, rhizome or tuber, e.g., begonia, daffodil. Herbaceous plants never have woody stems. See also *woody*.

Hip A fleshy type of fruit, especially common in the rose family.

Hybrid A plant derived from two genetically different parents. Cross fertilization is common between plants of different species within the same genus. Plants arising from such crossings are known as primary hybrids; they usually have some of the characteristics of both parents, but may favor one more than the other. Cross fertilization is possible, but rare, between plants of different genera, e.g., *Fatshedera* is a hybrid of *Fatsia* and *Hedera*. These crossings are known as bigeneric or intergeneric hybrids. Many naturally occurring hybrids are sterile.

Inflorescence A group of two or more flowers on one stem. An inflorescence may vary considerably in shape from the narrow and spikelike lavenders and sword lilies to the broad round heads of hydrangeas and Egyptian star clusters. See also *raceme, panicle, spike, umbel*.

Juvenile Usually applied to the leaves of a young plant that are different in shape from those of a more mature plant, e.g., eucalyptus foliage, which is round when taken from young plants and thin and pointed when taken from older trees. The leaves of young philodendrons may also be a different shape to those of older plants.

Latex A free-flowing, milky-white fluid which exudes from plants such as crown-of-thorns and rubber plants if stems are cut or damaged. See also *bleeding*.

Leaf The energy-producing organ of the plant. Light striking the green part of the leaf starts the process of photosynthesis. Sepals, petals, tendrils and bracts are thought to be modified leaves. In most cacti, the stems take over the function of leaves.

Leaflet A part of a compound, pinnate leaf, properly known as a pinna. See also *compound leaf, pinna, pinnate*.

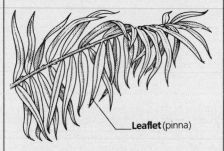

Leaflet (pinna)

Leaf mold Partially decayed leaves used in potting mixtures to provide nutrients, bacterial activity and an open, free-draining consistency. More correctly known as humus, it may be difficult to buy but can be found under deciduous trees (leaf litter) or made by composting fallen leaves.

Margin The border of a leaf or flower petal. This may be lobed or toothed, or of a different color to the main body of the leaf.

Node A stem joint at which the leaves are borne. The node may be notched or swollen and is a point from which the new roots of such plants as ivies and philodendrons are commonly made.

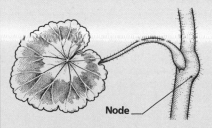

Node

Nut A type of fruit consisting of a hard or leathery shell enclosing a seed that is often edible. See also *fruit*.

Glossary 2

Offset Also known as an offshoot, this is a new plant produced by the parent at its base, or on short stolons, and is normally detachable from the parent. See also *stolon*.

Ovary The basal part of the flower in which the seeds are formed. The ovary wall becomes the fruit wall. See also *flower*, *fruit*.

Palmate A term applied to compound leaves with several leaflets arranged fanwise from a common point, shaped like a hand, e.g., false aralia. See also *compound leaf*.

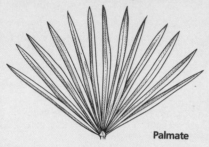

Palmate

Panicle A type of inflorescence consisting of a large branched cluster of flowers, each with a number of stalked flowers, e.g., lilac, most grasses. See also *inflorescence*.

Perennial A plant that lives for an indefinite period, e.g., African lily. Perennials can be herbaceous or woody. See also *annual*, *biennial*.

Petal Usually the showy part of the flower. Petals protect the center of the flower and, when colored, are intended to attract pollinating insects to the stamens and pistils. Sepals are often confused with petals. Petals may be few (three in many tradescantias) or many (as in a double-flowered rose). They are collectively known as the corolla. See also *sepal*, *stamen*, *pistil*, *flower*, *corolla*.

Photosynthesis The process by which carbon dioxide is converted into carbohydrates within the leaf. It is sparked off by light striking the green pigment in leaves and stems. See also *chlorophyll*, *leaf*.

Pinching out Also known as stopping. A form of pruning practiced by gently pulling off, with forefinger and thumb, the soft growing tips of shoots to induce bushiness.

Pinna An individual section of a much divided leaf or frond, commonly known as a leaflet. Used when describing fern fronds. See also *frond*, *leaflet*.

Pinnate A term used to describe a compound leaf that is divided into several or many pairs of oppositely arranged pinnae (leaflets), e.g., parlor palm. See also *compound leaf*, *leaflet*, *pinna*.

Pistil The female part of a flower, comprising stigma, style and ovary. See also *stigma*, *style*, *ovary*, *flower*.

Plantlet A young plant. The stage beyond that of a seedling, but also used to describe "offspring" that are produced on leaves or stolons, e.g., pickaback plant. See also *seedling*.

Raceme A type of inflorescence. An elongated, unbranched flower head, each flower having a short stalk. The flowers normally develop and open from the bottom of the raceme, higher ones opening as the lower ones fade, e.g., hyacinth. See also *inflorescence*.

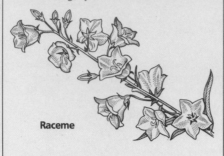

Raceme

Rest period A period within the 12-month season in which the plant should be allowed to become inactive, producing little or no leaf or root growth.

Rhizome A creeping stem, usually horizontal and often underground, from which leaves, side shoots and roots appear. It often acts as a storage organ to enable plants to survive through a short period of drought, e.g., painted-leaf begonia.

Rib A main or prominent vein of a leaf.

Root The lower part of a plant, normally in the potting mixture, which serves to hold it firm and pass nourishment and water to it from the potting mixture. There are two types of root: fine, fibrous roots and the larger, single tap roots. Most plants have one type of root or the other; few have both.

Root ball The mass of potting mixture interspersed with roots seen when a plant is taken from its pot. Examination of the root ball is a way of establishing whether a plant needs repotting or potting on.

Root crown The basal part of a plant, where the stem meets the roots.

Root hair The fine feeding hairs covering the surface of the roots. These are microscopic and cannot be seen with the naked eye.

Rosette An arrangement of leaves radiating from a distinct center, e.g., African violet.

Runner A creeping stem, running along the surface of the potting mixture, which takes root at its nodes and produces a new plant at that point. See also *stolon*.

Scurf Fine, scalelike particles on leaves or stems giving them a gray or silvered appearance, e.g., silver crown.

Seed The fertilized and ripened part of a flowering plant (ovule), capable of germinating and producing a new plant. Seeds range in size from very tiny to around 8in in diameter. Most seeds are pea-sized.

Seedling A young plant, raised from seed, which still possesses a single unbranched stem.

Semi-double flower A flower with more than one layer of petals but with fewer than a

fully double bloom, e.g., some African violets. See also *single flower*, *double flower*.

Semi-double flower

Sepal The outer part of a flower, often green, which protects the middle of the flower and the more delicate petals. Flowers such as the anemone are actually made up of sepals rather than petals. See also *calyx*, *petal*.

Sheath A protective wrapping for a growing point, e.g., rubber plant.

Shrub A woody-stemmed bushy plant, smaller than a tree and usually with many stems which branch near the ground. It is often difficult to define the difference between a large shrub and a small tree. Most house plants are shrubs rather than trees. See also *tree*, *woody*.

Single flower A flower with the normal number of petals, e.g., Marguerite daisy. See also *double flower*, *semi-double flower*.

Single flower

Spadix A small spike with minute flowers embedded in it, usually surrounded by a spathe, e.g., the center part of a flamingo flower. See also *spathe*.

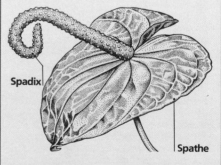

Spadix

Spathe

Spathe A prominent modified leaf or bract surrounding the spadix. Usually fleshy and white, sometimes colored, e.g., flamingo flower. See also *spadix*.

Species The members of a genus are called species. From its seed each persistently breeds true to type in its main characteristics. A plant's name is made up of at least two parts: the name of the genus and the name of the species, e.g., *Coleus* (genus) *blumei* (species). See also *genus*, *family*.

Spike A type of inflorescence, in the form of a long unbranched flower head. Very similar in appearance to a raceme except that the individual flowers of a spike have no stalks, e.g., sword lily.

Spike

Spore Minute reproductive bodies produced by ferns and mosses—the equivalent of seeds in a flowering plant. Spores are held in spore cases on the underside of some fronds (some fronds are sterile and do not bear spore cases) and may be arranged in a number of patterns—herringbone, marginal or scattered.

Stalk The organ supporting the flower (flower stalk), the leaf (leaf stalk) or the anther (filament). See also *filament*.

Stamen The pollen-bearing male organ of a flower, comprising a filament and two anther lobes containing pollen. See also *filament, anther, flower*.

Stigma The tip of the female reproductive organ (pistil) on which the pollen settles. See also *flower, pistil*.

Stolon A creeping stem that produces a new plantlet at its tip or wherever it touches the potting mixture. See also *runner*.

Stomata The pores through which gases enter and leave the plant. They are usually situated on the underside of the leaves.

Style The style supports the stigma, holding it in an effective place for pollination. See also *stigma, pistil, flower*.

Succulent A plant which has fleshy leaves or stems capable of storing water. Usually plants from arid areas, e.g., Chinese jade.

Sucker A shoot arising from below the surface of the potting mixture, usually from the roots of a plant.

Tendril A wiry projection from the stem that twines around a support and enables a plant to climb. The tendrils may be spiralled, e.g., passion flower, or forked.

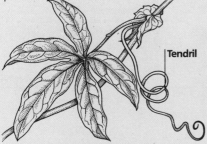

Tendril

Topdressing The process of replacing the top few inches of potting mixture with fresh mixture as an alternative to repotting. Topdressing is most useful for plants that have grown too large for moving into bigger pots. It involves carefully scraping away some of the old potting mixture in spring, doing as little damage as possible to the roots, and firming in fresh mixture.

Transpiration The continual, natural water loss from leaves. This may be heavy or hardly noticeable, depending on the time of day or time of year—factors which affect the relative humidity. Heavy transpiration in warm weather causes wilting, which is damaging to the plant.

Tree A woody-stemmed plant with an obvious trunk topped with branches. See also *woody, shrub*.

Tuber A thick, fleshy stem or root which acts as a storage organ. Some tuberous-rooted plants lose their leaves and stem in the autumn and the tuber stores food for renewed growth the following spring, e.g., begonia. Occasionally tubers are produced on stems, e.g., rosary vine. See also *corm, bulb*.

Tuber

Turgid A term applied to plants that are "crisp" and healthy as their cells are full of water. Also applied to cuttings that have obviously produced roots of their own and are taking up sufficient water for their needs.

Umbel A type of inflorescence. A flower head in which the individual flower stalks arise from a common point. Commonly known as a cluster, e.g., regal geranium, hydrangea. See also *inflorescence*.

Umbel

Undulate A leaf margin or petal that has a wavy edge. Undulate does not refer to toothed or serrated edges.

Variegated A term applied to leaves streaked or spotted with another color (usually cream or yellow). Variegation is usually the result of a mutation and is sometimes due to a virus infection; rarely is it natural or built-in. Variegated-leaved plants are popularly cultivated and need good light to maintain variegation. In some cases, cuttings from certain variegated-leaved plants produce plants with plain green leaves.

Variety A word used to refer to variations of the plant that have occured in the wild, but sometimes incorrectly used to describe a form developed in horticulture. Cultivar is a more accurate term for the latter. Varietal names are printed in italics. See also *cultivar*.

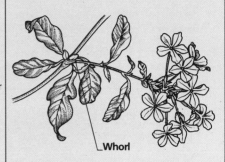

Whorl

Whorl A circle of three or more leaves or flowers produced at the nodes on a stem or stalk, e.g., Cape leadwort.

Wintering A term used to describe the simulation of winter conditions indoors to encourage winter- and spring-flowering bulbs to make good roots before top growth starts.

Woody Refers to plants which have hard stems which persist above ground all year, e.g., paper flower. See also *herbaceous*.

Index

Page numbers in *italic* refer to
illustrations and captions

·A·

Abutilon hybridum, color guide, *203,
205*; description and culture, 218,
218
A. hybridum "Canary Bird", descrip-
tion and culture, 162, *162*
A. pictum "Thompsonii", 162
Acacia longifolia, 22; description and
preparation, 222, *222*
Acanthus spinosissimus, description
and preparation, 220, *220*
Acer, 37
A. japonicum "Aureum", foliage,
225, *225*
A. palmatum "Dissectum", *74*
A. platanoides "Goldsworth Purple",
foliage, 228, *228*
Achillea, 88
A. filipendulina, description and
preparation, 216, *216*; dried, *105,
108, 231*
A.f. "Coronation Gold", *88, 216*
Achimenes grandiflora, 63; descrip-
tion and culture, 181, *181*
Adiantum hispidulum, 66, 183
*A. raddianum, 21, 39, 56, 58, 66,
247*; description and culture, 183,
183
A.r. microphyllum, 183
Aechmea fasciata, 46; color guide,
207; description and culture, 172,
172
Aeschynanthus lobbianus, *43*
Aesculus hippocastanum, 108
African daisy, dried, *108*
African hemp, *119, 133*; description
and culture, 164, *164*
African lily, *88, 144*; description and
preparation, 217, *217*
African violet, *25*, 244, 258, *259*,
266, 267, 269, 271, 272, 273; color
guide, *203, 207*; description and
culture, 175, *175*
Agapanthus africanus, description
and preparation, 217, *217*
A. campanulatus, 144
A. "Headbourne Hybrids", *88*
Agave victoriae-reginae, 70; description and culture, 200, *200*
Aglaonema crispum "Silver Queen",
19; description and culture, 164,
164
Agrostis, dried, *237*
A. curtisii, dried, *236*
air-drying flowers, 96-7, *96-7*
air-layering, 268, *268*
airplants, 147, *147*
Alchemilla vulgaris, 157; description
and preparation, 214, *214*; dried,
100, 230
Algerian ivy, *13, 138*; description and
culture, 184, *184*; foliage, 227, *227*
Allamanda cathartica, description
and culture, 186, *186*
Allium, description and preparation,
216; dried, *100, 103, 233*
A. giganteum, 156
A. schoenoprasum, 157
Aloe aristata, description and
culture, 199, *199*
Alstroemeria, 84
A. pelegrina, 25; description and
preparation, *213, 213*

aluminium plant, description and
culture, 162, *162*
Amaranthus albus, dried, *230*
A. caudatus, dried, *108*
amaryllis, *59*, 60, *118*, 257; descrip-
tion and culture, 194, *194*
amethyst violet, description and
culture, 176, *176*
Ammobium alatum, dried, *104*
Ananas bracteatus striatus, 174
A. comosus "Variegatus", descrip-
tion and culture, 174, *174*
A. nanus, 174
Anaphalis margaritacea, dried, *231*
Anemone coronaria, 23; description
and preparation, 222, *222*
angel wings, *18, 19, 29, 271*; descrip-
tion and culture, 182, *182*
Anthemis cupaniana, 88
A. tinctoria, dried, *231*
A.t "E.C. Buxton", *88*
Anthurium, 33
A. andraeanum, 24, 44; color
guide, *206*
A. scherzeranum, description and
culture, 182, *182*
Aphelandra squarrosa "Louisae", *47*;
description and culture, 182, *182*
aphids, 272, *272*
Aporocactus flagelliformis, description and culture, 201, *201*
A. mallisonii, 201
Arabis alpina "Rosea", dried, *233*
Aralia chinensis, foliage, 224, *224*
Araucaria heterophylla, 20; descrip-
tion and culture, 166, *166*
arching plants, guide to, 168-71,
168-71
Armeria maritima, dried, *235*
arrangement, flowers and foliage,
77-93, *77-93*; plants, asymmetrical,
32; contrast, 34, *34-5*; groups, 32,
32-3; principles of, 32-5, *32-5*;
symmetrical, *32*
Artemisia "Douglasiana", foliage,
227, *227*
A. "Powis Castle", foliage, 227, *227*
artificial flowers, *142*
artificial light, 258-9, *258-9*
Arum italicum "Pictum", *92*
Arundinaria, 118
Asparagus asparagoides, 183
A. densiflorus, 51
A.d. "Sprengeri", *56, 58*; description and culture, 191, *191*
A. falcatus, 183
A. setaceus, 16, 56, 58; description
and culture, 183, *183*
Aspidistra elatior, 20, 148; description and culture, 165, *165*
Asplenium nidus, 20, 56, 58, 146, 245,
273; description and culture, 173,
173
Aster novi-belgii, 41, 81; description
and preparation, 219, *219*
Astilbe japonica, dried, *234*
Astrophytum myriostigma, 70; description and culture, 198, *198*
Aucuba japonica "Variegata",
description and culture, 182, *182*
Australian maidenhair fern, *66*
autumn cut flowers, guide to, 218-21,
218-21
autumn flower arrangement, 90-1,
90-1
Avena, dried, *100, 108, 237*
avocado pear, *130*

azalea, 244; description and culture,
179, *179*

·B·

baby's breath, *24, 40, 83, 84, 131*;
description and preparation, 213,
213; dried, *96, 100, 104, 231*
baby's tears, *29, 30, 37, 124,
131*; description and culture, 192,
192
bactericides, 276-7
Ballota pseudodictamnus, foliage,
227, *227*
bamboo, *118*
bamboo palm, description and culture,
170, *170*
banana plant, *152*
Banksia menziesii, dried, *238*
barberry, *90*
barley, dried, *100, 237*
basket plant, *43*
baskets, arrangements in, 48-9, *48-9*;
dried-flower arrangements, 100-2,
100-2; hanging, 54-8, *54-8*;
humidity, *247*; pot-pourri, 106-7,
106-7; wicker, 56-8, *56-8*; wire,
54-5, *54-5*
bathrooms, decoration with plants,
144-7, *144-7*
bead plant, color guide, *204*, description and culture, 192, *192*
bear's breeches, description and
preparation, 220, *220*
Beaucarnea recurvata, 13, 28, 122;
description and culture, 171, *171*
bedding geranium, *240*, color guide,
205
bedrooms, decoration with plants,
140-3, *140-3*
beech, *108*; dried, *237, 239*
Begonia, 269
B. "Elatior", *35*; color guide, *202,
203, 204, 205, 206*; description
and culture, 176, *176*
B. fuchsioides, description and culture, 168, *168*
B. masoniana, 183
B. rex-cultorum, 20, 30, 46, 272;
description and culture, 183, *183*
B. semperflorens-cultorum, 62, 269;
color guide, *202*; description and
culture, 176, *176*
B. "Tiger Paws", *49, 68*; description
and culture, 193, *193*
B. tuberhybrida, 25, 176; color
guide, *203*
Belgian evergreen, *245*; description
and culture, 163, *163*
bells-of-Ireland, *24*; dried, *104*
bent grass, dried, *237*
Berberis thunbergii "Atropurpurea",
foliage, 228, *228*
B.t. "Rose Glow", *90*
Bergenia, foliage, 224, *224*
Billbergia nutans, description and
culture, 173, *173*
bird-of-paradise, *24*; description and
culture, 164, *164*
bird's nest bromeliad, *13*; description
and culture, 175, *175*
bird's nest fern, *20, 56, 58, 146,
245*, 273; description and culture,
173, *173*
bishop's cap, *70*; description and
culture, 198, *198*
black calla, *92*

black-eyed Susan vine, 269; color
guide, *203*; description and
culture, 185, *185*
blackleg, 274, *274*
black locust tree, foliage, 225,
225
blazing star dried, *234*
bleeding stems, sealing, 81, *81*
blue-flowered torch, description and
culture, 173, *173*
blushing bromeliad, *18*; description
and culture, 174, *174*
boat lily, description and culture,
166, *166*
bonsai, 74-5, *74-5*
Boston fern, *17, 28, 56, 138*; description and culture, 170, *170*
botrytis, 274, *274*
bottle brush, dried, *233*
bottle gardens, 66-7, *66-7*
Bougainvillea buttiana, description
and culture, 187, *187*
bracken, dried, *237*
Brassica oleracea acephala, 48
bristle bent, dried, *236*
Briza media, dried, *236*
brome grass, dried, *237*
Bromus, dried, *237*
Browallia speciosa, description and
culture, 176, *176*
B. viscosa, 176
Buddleia davidii "White Cloud", *88*
bulbs, fiber, 255, *255*; growing
indoors, 59-61, *59-61*; guide to,
194-5, *194-5*
bulrush, *59*
Burgundy philodendron, description
and culture, 187, *187*
bushy plants, guide to, 176-83,
176-83
butterfly bush, *88*
button fern, *28*; description and
culture, 168, *168*

·C·

cacti, 70-1, *70-1, 126*, guide to,
196-201, *196-201*; humidity, *247*;
removing from pots, 257
*Caladium hortulanum, 18, 19,
29, 271*; description and culture,
182, *182*
calamondin orange, description and
culture, 162, *162*
Calathea makoyana, 19, 271; description and culture, 165, *165*
California privet, foliage, 225, *225*
calla lily, *120*; description and
preparation, 213
Callistemon citrinus, dried, *233*
Campanula isophylla, 55; color guide,
202, 207; description and culture,
191, *191*
Cape ivy, description and culture, 184,
184
Cape leadwort, *29*; color guide, *206*;
description and culture, 186, *186*
Cape lily, *81*; description and preparation, 218, *218*
Cape primrose, *36*, 266, 269; description and culture, 175, *175*
capillary mats, 250, *250*
Capsicum annuum, color guide, *203,
204*; description and culture, 180,
180; dried, *239*
carbon dioxide, 242, *242*
care of plants, 241-77, *241-77*;

artificial light, 258-9, *258-9*; diseases, 274-7, *274*; feeding, 252-3, *253*; humidity, 247, *247*; hydroculture, 260-1, *260-1*; light, 244-5, *244-5*; pests, 272-3, *272-3*; pots, 254, *254*; potting mixtures, 255, *255*; potting on, 256-7, *257*; problems, 270-7; propagation, 264-9, *264-9*; pruning, 262-3, *262-3*; repotting, 256-7, *257*; signs of ill-health, 243; temperature, 246, *246*; topdressing, 256-7, *257*; training, 262-3, *262-3*; vacations, 250, *250*; watering, 248-51, *249-51*
carnation, *25*; description and preparation, 214, *214*
Carthamus tinctorius, dried, *232*
Caryota mitis, 117
cast-iron plant, *20, 44*, 148; description and culture, 165, *165*
Catalpa bignonioides, foliage, 225, *225*
caterpillars, 272, *272*
Catharanthus roseus, color guide, *202*
celosia, dried, *232*
Celosia argentea "Cristata", dried, *232*
Centaurea cyanus, 23
Cephalocereus senilis, description and culture, 197, *197*
cereals, dried, 236-7, *236-7*
Cereus peruvianus, 44
  C.p. "Monstrosus", description and culture, 197, *197*
Ceropegia woodii, *15, 45*; description and culture, 201, *201*
Chamaedorea elegans "Bella", *68, 120*; description and culture, 171, *171*
  C. erumpens, 171
Chamaerops humilis, 117; description and culture, 167, *167*
chestnut vine, 155
chilli pepper, *42*; dried, *239*
chincherinchee, *83*; description and preparation, 222
Chinese hibiscus, color guide, *204*; description and culture, 178, *178*
Chinese jade, description and culture, 197, *197*
Chinese lantern *142*; dried, *232*
Chionanthus virginicus, dried, *108*
chives, 157
Chlorophytum, 121, 152, *152*, 267
  C. comosum, 247, 271, 272
  C.c. "Vittatum", *54*; description and culture, 190, *190*
Christmas cactus, 244, 273
Christmas cherry, *65*; description and culture, 180, *180*
Christmas decorations, *105*
Christmas pepper, color guide, *203, 204*; description and culture, 180, *180*
Chrysalidocarpus lutescens, 120
Chrysanthemum, 23, 63, 64, 244, 273; description and preparation, 223, *223*; dried, *230*
  C. frutescens, *7, 42, 62*
  C. morifolium, 62, 64, 156; color guide, *203, 204*; description and culture, 181, *181*
  C. parthenium, 157
cineraria, *142*, 273, 274; description and culture, 179, *179*
Cissus antarctica, description and culture, 186, *186*
  C. rhombifolia, *16, 51, 54*, 150, *152*; description and culture, 184, *184*

Citrofortunella mitis, description and culture, 162, *162*
Citrus limon, 162
claw cactus, description and culture, 200, *200*
clay pots, *254*
climates, in the home, 114-5, *114-5*
climbing plants, guide to, 184-7, *184-7*; training, 50-3, *50-3*
Clivia miniata, 156
clove pinks, description and preparation, 214, *214*
coconut palm, *12*, description and culture, 169, *169*
Cocos nucifera, *12*, description and culture, 169, *169*
Codiaeum variegatum pictum, *18, 30, 132*, 271; description and culture, 164, *164*
cold water spots, 271
Coleus blumei, *18, 62, 124*, 247; description and culture, 177, *177*
color, color wheel, 78-9, *78-9*; flower arranging, 78-9; guide to flowering house plants, 202-7, *202-7*; leaves, 18, *18-19*; plant arrangements, *34*
columnea, *21*; description and culture, 189, *189*
Columnea banksii, *21*; description and culture, 189, *189*
coneflower, *90*; description and preparation, 218, *218*
conservatories, decoration with plants, 154-7, *154-7*
containers, 254, *254*; grouping in, 46-9, *46-9*; groups, 30, *30*; hydroculture, 260, *260*; matching plants to, 28-31, *28-31*; unusual, 31, *31*
Convallaria majalis, description and preparation, 210, *210*
cool conditions, in the home, 115
copper beech, foliage, 228, *228*
Cordyline terminalis, *8, 19*, 245; description and culture, 163, *163*
cornflower, 23
Cornus alba "Elegantissima", foliage, 226, *226*
Cortaderia, 152
  C. selloana, dried, *236*
Corylus maxima "Atropurpurea", foliage, 228, *228*
Cotinus coggygria, foliage, 228, *228*
Cotoneaster, *90*, 151
  C. "Cornubius", description and preparation, 223, *223*
  C. horizontalis, foliage, 224, *224*
cotton, dried, *238*
Cotyledon orbiculata, 196
  C. undulata, description and culture, 196, *196*
country style, 40-1, *40-1*
crab apple, *90*, 151; description and preparation, 210, *210*
Crambe maritima, foliage, 227, *227*
Crassula arborescens, description and culture, 197, *197*
  C. ovata, 197
creeping fig, *12, 32, 53*, 272; description and culture, 193, *193*
creeping plants, guide to, 192-3, *192-3*
Cretan brake fern, *56, 58*; description and culture, 183, *183*
Crinum, 81
  C. powellii, description and preparation, 218, *218*

Crocus, 59; description and culture, 195, *195*
croton, *18, 30, 132*, 271; description and culture, 164, *164*
crown rot, 274, *274*
crown-of-thorns, description and culture, 196, *196*
Cryptanthus bivittatus, description and culture, 174, *174*
Cucurbita pepo ovifera, dried, *238*
Cupid's bower, *63*; description and culture, 181, *181*
Cupressus glabra, 92
cut flowers, arranging, 77-93, *77-93*; autumn arrangement, 90-1, *90-1*; autumn flowers, 218-21, *218-21*; cutting, 80-1, *80-1*; foliage, 224-8, *224-8*; guide to, 209-28, *210-28*; preparing, 80-1, *80-1*; principles of arrangement, 83-5, *83-5*; spring arrangement, 86-7, *86-7*; spring flowers, 210-3, *210-3*; summer arrangement, 88-9, *88-9*; summer flowers, 214-7, *214-7*; supports, 82, *82*; winter arrangement, 92-3, *92-3*; winter flowers, 222-3, *222-3*
cut-leaf elder, foliage, 225, *225*
cut-leaved finger plant, *132*
cuttings, hydroculture, 262; leaf, 266, *266*; stem, 265, *265*
Cyclamen persicum, 121, *136*, 156, 272; description and culture, 180, *180*
Cymbidium, 6, 117
Cynara scolymus, description and preparation, 219, *219*
Cyperus, 44, 73
  C. alternifolius, 122, 144
  C.a. "Gracilis", description and culture, 166, *166*
cypress, 92

·D·E·

daffodil, as bulbs, 59, 60-61, description and culture, 194, *194*; as cut flowers, *7, 86, 87*, 151, description and preparation, 210, *210*; sealing cut stems, 81, *81*
Dahlia, 81, *90*; description and preparation, 220, *220*
  D. "Authority", *220*
  D. "Glorie van Heernstede", *220*
  D. "Little Conn", *220*
  D. "Rokesley", *220*
daisy bush, 7
day length, 244
day lily, *150*
daylight, 244-5
deadheading, 262
decorative qualities, 11-25, *11-25*
Delphinium, 81, *96*; description and preparation, 216, *216*
  D. consolida, 88, dried, 100, 104, 106, 122, 223, 234
  D. elatum, 22; dried, *234*
delta maidenhair fern, *21, 34, 39, 56, 58, 66*, 247; description and culture, 183, *183*
Dendrobium, *25*; description and preparation 223, *223*
desiccants, drying in, 97, *97*
devil's ivy, description and culture, 188, *188*
Dianthus "Allwood's Cream", *215*
  D. "Arthur Sim", *215*
  D. barbatus, description and

preparation, 215, *215*
  D. caryophyllus, *25*; description and preparation, 214, *214*
  D. "Comoco Sim", *215*
  D. "Crowley Sim", *214*
  D. "Fragrant Ann", *215*
  D. "Inchmery", *215*
  D. "Joker", *215*
  D. "Portrait", *215*
  D. "Purple Frosted", *214*
  D. "Zebra", *215*
Dieffenbachia, 155
  D. amoena, 163
  D. exotica, *17*, 163
  D. maculata, description and culture, 163, *163*
Digitalis, 98; description and preparation, 216, *216*
  D. grandiflora "Ambigua", *216*
  D. purpurea, 216
  D.p. "Alba", *216*
dining rooms, decoration with plants, 130-5, *130-5*
Dipsacus fullonum, dried, *239*
diseases, 274-5, *274*
division, 267, *267*
Dizygotheca elegantissima, *17, 29*, 245; description and culture, 165, *165*
dock, dried, *235*
dogwood, *84*
donkey's tail, description and culture, 201, *201*
Dracaena marginata, *8*, 116, 150
  D.m. "Tricolor", description and culture, 167, *167*
  D. sanderana, 245; description and culture, 163, *163*
drafts, 271
dragon tree, *8*, 150
dried flowers, air-drying, 96-7, *96-7*; arranging, 95-111, *95-111*; arranging in baskets, 100-2, *100-2*; chains of, *111*; corn stars, *110*; decorations, 110-1, *110-1*; dried-flower trees, 104-5, *104-5*; drying, 96-9, *96-9*; floral balls, *110*; in glycerine, 98, *98*; guide to, 229-39, *229-39*; in desiccants, 97, *97*; pot-pourri, 99, *99*; pressing, 98, *98*; wreaths, 108-9, *108-9*
dumb cane, *17*, 155
dwarf coconut palm, *14*; description and culture, 170, *170*
earth star plant, description and culture, 174, *174*
earthworms, 273, *273*
Easter cactus, *42*, 273
Easter lily, 60
Echeveria, 274
  E. agavoides, description and culture, 200, *200*
  E. derenbergii, description and culture, 200, *200*
Echinocereus grusonii, description and culture, 199, *199*
Echinops ritro, 88; dried, *235*
Egyptian star cluster, description and culture, 177, *177*
elatior begonia, *35*; color guide, *202, 203, 204, 205, 206*; description and culture, 176, *176*
elder, *90*
elephant's ear, foliage, 224, *224*
elephant's ear philodendron, *15*
emerald fern, *51, 56, 58*; description and culture, 191, *191*
emerald ripple peperomia, *20, 34*, 266;

description and culture, 180, *180*
English holly, *83*; description and preparation, 222, *222*; foliage, 226, *226*
English ivy, *19, 28, 40, 64, 121, 122, 134, 156, 261*; description and culture, 190, *190*; foliage, 226, *226*
entrances, decoration with plants, 148-51, *148-51*
Epipremnum aureum, description and culture, 188, *188*
Eranthis hyemalis, description and preparation, 223
Eremurus, 124; description and preparation, 214
Erica, dried, *100*
Eryngium giganteum, 88
   E. maritimum, dried, *99, 100, 104, 108, 235*
Eucalyptus, dried, *236*
   E. gunnii, 88; foliage, 227, *227*
Euonymus japonica "Ovata-aurea", foliage, 225, *225*
   E. sachalinensis, description and preparation, 219, *219*
Eupatorium purpureum, dried, *233*
Euphorbia, description and preparation, 212, *212*; sealing cut stems, 81
   E. characias, 212
   E. griffithii "Fireglow", *212*
   E. milii, description and culture, 196, *196*
   E. polychroma, 212
   E. pseudocactus, 140
   E. pulcherrima, 6, 23, 155, 244; description and culture, 179, *179*
   E. robbiae, 212
   E. tirucalli, 113
   E. wulfenii, 212
European cranberry bush, *90*; description and preparation, 221, *221*
European elder, foliage, 226, *226*
European fan palm, *117*; description and culture, 167, *167*
everlasting, dried, *100, 104, 108, 110, 230, 231, 233*
Exacum affine, 25, 62, 272, 274; color guide, *207*; description and culture, 178, *178*
eyelash begonia, *49, 68*; description and culture, 193, *193*

·F·

Fagus, dried, *108*
   F. sylvatica, dried, *237, 239*
   F.s. "Purpurea", foliage, 228, *228*
false aralia, *17, 29, 245*; description and culture, 165, *165*
false safflower, dried, *232*
Fatshedera lizei, description and culture, 165, *165*
Fatsia japonica, 12, 29, 36, 121, 269; description and culture, 181, *181*
feeding, 252-3, *253*; hydroculture, 260
fennel, *150, 157*
fern leaf yarrow, description and preparation, 216, *216*
fern potting mixture, 255, *255*
Ferocactus latispinus, description and culture, 198, *198*
fertilizer, 252-3, *253*
feverfew, *157*
Ficus benjamina, 9, 17, 134, 131; description and culture, 171, *171*

F. elastica, 154, 269; description and culture, 163, *163*
F. lyrata, 122, 163
F. pumila, 12, 53, 272; description and culture, 193, *193*
F. retusa, 74
fiddle-leaf fig, *122*
fiddle-leaf philodendron, *16*
filtered sun, in the home, 114-5, 245, *245*
finger plant, description and culture, 169, *169*
fish-hook cactus, description and culture, 198, *198*
fishtail palm, *117*
Fittonia verschaffeltii, 18, 272; description and culture, 193, *193*
   F.v. argyroneura "Nana", *66, 193*
flaming sword, *245*; description and culture, 172, *172*
flamingo flower, *33, 44*; color guide, *206*; description and culture, 182, *182*
floral foam, 82
florist's chrysanthemum, *62, 64*; description and culture, 181, *181*
florist's cyclamen, description and culture, 180, *180*
flower arranging, 77-93, *77-93*; *see also* cut flowers; dried flowers; foliage
flowering maple, color guide, *203, 205*; as cut flowers, description and preparation, 218, *218*; as house plants, description and culture, 162, *162*
flowering onion, description and preparation, 216; dried, *103, 156, 233*
flowering tobacco, description and preparation, 221
flowers, shape, *24, 24-5*; size, *22, 22-3*; *see also* cut flowers; dried flowers
fluorescent light, 258, *258*
Foeniculum, 150
   F. vulgare, 157
foliage, guide to, 224-9, *224-9*; dried 236-7
foliar sprays, *253*
foxglove, *98*; description and preparation, 216, *216*
foxtail lily, *124*; description and preparation, 214
Fragaria vesca "Alpine", *53*
Freesia, 151; description and preparation, 212, *212*
Fritillaria, description and preparation, 210
fritillary, description and preparation, 210
fruits, dried, *238-9*
Fuchsia, 142
fuchsia begonia, description and culture, 168, *168*
fungicides, 276-7
fungus gnats, 272, *272*

·G·

Gardenia, 144
Garrya elliptica, 92
gentian, *25*
Gentiana, 25
geranium, *40, 41, 62, 272, 273, 274*; color guide, *205*; description and culture, 177, *177*

Gerbera, 97
   G. jamesonii, 24, 128; description and preparation, 217, *217*
German violet, *25, 62, 272, 274*; color guide, *207*; description and culture, 178, *178*
Gladiolus, 25, 85; description and preparation, 215, *215*
   G. "Albert Schweitzer", *215*
   G. "Madam Butterfly", *215*
   G. "White Angel", *215*
globe amaranth, dried, *235*
globe artichoke, description and preparation, 219, *219*
globe thistle, *88*; dried, *235*
gloxinia, *6, 271*; color guide, *205, 207*; description and culture, 175, *175*
glycerine, preserving in, 98, *98*
golden barrel cactus, description and culture, 199, *199*
golden-feather palm, *120*
golden marguerite, *41, 88*; dried, *231*
golden pincushion, description and culture, 198, *198*
golden privet, foliage, 227, *227*
golden trumpet, description and culture, 186, *186*
golden yarrow, dried, *105, 108*
Gomphrena globosa, dried, *235*
Gossypium, dried, *238*
gourds, *148*; dried, *238*
grape hyacinth, dried, *99*; description and culture, 195, *195*
grape ivy, *16, 51, 54, 150, 152*; description and culture, 184, *184*
grasses, dried, *236-7, 236-7*
gray mold, 274, *274*
greater periwinkle, foliage, 226, *226*
greenfly, 272, *272*
Grevillea robusta, 17, 269; description and culture, 166, *166*
   G. triternata, dried, *236*
groundsel, foliage, 227, *227*
grouping plants, 32-5, *32-5*, 46-9, *46-9*
Guzmania lingulata, 28, 56, 58, 245; color guide, *205*; description and culture, 174, *174*
Gynura aurantiaca, 21, 274; description and culture, 191, *191*
Gypsophila paniculata, 24, 83, 84, 96, 131; description and preparation, 213, *213*; dried, *100, 104, 231*

·H·

halls, decoration with plants, 148-51, *148-51*
Hamamelis mollis, 92
hanging baskets, 54-8, *54-8*
hare's foot fern, description and culture, 169, *169*
harestail grass, dried, *236*
heartleaf philodendron, *13, 15, 50, 136*; description and culture, 188, *188*
heat, conditions in the home, 114-5
heath, dried, *100*
Hedera canariensis, 13, 138; description and culture, 184, *184*
   H.c. "Variegata", foliage, 227, *227*
   H. colchica "Paddy's Pride", *92*
   H. helix, 19, 28, 40, 64, 121, 122, 134, 156, 261; description and culture, 190, *190*
   H.h. "Argento-variegata", foliage, 226, *226*

Helianthus annuus, description and preparation, 220, *220*
Helichrysum bracteatum, description and preparation, 219, *219*; dried, *96, 100, 104, 108, 110, 111, 231, 232, 233*
Helicotrichon sempervirens, foliage, 227, *227*
Helipterum humboldtianum, dried, *231*
   H. roseum, dried, *100, 104, 108, 110, 230, 233*
hellebore, *92*
Helleborus corsicus lividus, 92
Hemerocallis, 150
herbs, 136-7, *157*
Hibiscus rosa-sinensis, color guide, *204*; description and culture, 178, *178*
Hippeastrum, 59, 60, 118, 257; description and culture, 194, *194*
history of indoor plants, 8-9
honeysuckle, foliage, 225, *225*
hop-clover, dried *99*
Hordeum vulgare, dried, *100, 237*
horse chestnuts, dried, *108*
Hosta, foliage, 227, *227*
   H. plantaginea, foliage, 224, *224*
Howea belmoreana, 6, 8, 14, 119, 122; description and culture, 170, *170*
   H. forsterana, 170
Hoya bella, description and culture, 189, *189*
humidity, 247, *247*; conditions in the home, 114-5; incorrect, 271
hyacinth, *61*; description and culture, 195, *195*
Hyacinthus orientalis, 61; description and culture, 195, *195*
hybrid tea rose, description and preparation, 216, *216*
Hydrangea, 96, 120
   H. macrophylla, dried, *103, 234*
hydroculture, 72-3, *72-3*, 260-1, *260-1*
Hypericum androsaemum "Tutsan", *88*
   H. inordorum, description and preparation, 218, *218*
Hypoestes phyllostachya, 19, 30, 65, 68; description and culture, 179, *179*

·I·J·

Ilex aquifolium, 83; description and preparation, 222, *222*
   I.a. "Golden Queen", foliage, 226, *226*
immortelle, dried, *108, 235*
Impatiens, 54, 156, 272, 274
   I. wallerana, 62, 269; color guide, *205, 206, 207*; description and culture, 177, *177*
Indian bean tree, foliage, 225, *225*
insecticides, 276-7, *276*
Ipomoea batatas, 73
Iris, 85; description and preparation, 212
   I. foetidissima, 92
   I. pallida, 43
   I. reticulata, description and culture, 194, *194*
Italian bellflower, *55*; color guide, *202, 207*; description and culture, 191, *191*
Japanese anemone, *40*
Japanese angelica, foliage, 224, *224*
Japanese barberry, foliage, 228, *228*

Japanese fatsia, *12, 29, 36, 121, 151,*
269; description and culture, 181,
181
Japanese maple, *74;* foliage, 225, *225*
Japanese spindle tree, foliage, 225,
225
Jasminum polyanthum, description
and culture, 186, *186*
Joe pyeweed, dried, *233*
juniper berries, dried, *99*
Justicia brandegeana, color guide,
206

·K·L·

Kafir lily, *156*
Kalanchoe blossfeldiana, 24; color
guide, *204;* description and culture,
197, *197*
kangaroo vine, description and
culture, 186, *186*
Kentia palm, *6, 8, 14, 119, 122;*
description and culture, 170, *170*
kitchens, decoration with plants,
136-9, *136-9*
Kniphofia uvaria, description and
preparation, 221, *221*
lace aloe, description and culture,
199, *199*
ladder fern, *152*
lady's mantle, *157;* description and
preparation, 214, *214;* dried, *100,*
230
Lagurus ovatus, dried, *236*
landings, decoration with plants, 152,
152-3
larch, dried, *108*
Larix, dried, *108*
larkspur, *122;* dried, *96, 99, 100, 104,*
106, 233, 234
Lathyrus odoratus, description and
preparation, 217, *217*
Laurus nobilis, dried, *99*
laurustinus, *92*
Lavandula, dried, *99*
L. *angustifolia,* dried, *235*
lavender, dried, *99, 235*
layering, 268, *268*
leaf cuttings, 266, *266*
leaf miners, 273, *273*
leaf rollers, 272, *272*
leaves, color, 18, *18-19;* plant
adaptations, *243;* preserving in
glycerine 98, *98;* pressing, 98, *98;*
shape, 16, *16-17;* signs of ill-
health, *243;* size, 14, *14-15;*
texture, 20, *20-1; see also* foliage
Leea coccinea, description and
culture, 171, *171*
lemon-scented geranium, dried, *99*
leopard plant, *128*
Leucospermum nutans, 25; description and preparation, 221
Liatris spicata, dried, *234*
light, 244-5, *244-5*
lighting plants, 36-9, *36-9,* 114-5;
artificial, 258-9, *258-9;* backlighting,
37, 38; downlighting, *37;* frontlighting, *37, 38;* natural light, *36;*
sidelighting, *39;* uplighting, *37;*
on windowsills, *36*
Ligularia, 128
L. *dentatum* "Desdemona", *90*
L. *ovalifolium* "Albo-marginatum",
foliage, 227, *227*
L.o. "Aureum", foliage, 225, *225*
Ligustrum vulgare "Aureo-varie-

gatum", foliage, 226, *226*
lilac, *83, 84, 142;* description and
preparation, 210, *210*
Lilium, 128, 156; description and
preparation, 211, *211*
L. *auratum, 128*
L. *longiflorum,* 60
L. *regale, 45, 134*
lily, *128, 156;* description and
preparation, 211, *211*
lily-of-the-valley, description and
preparation, 210, *210*
Limonium latifolium, dried, *100, 103,*
104, 108
L. *sinuatum,* dried, *100, 104, 230,*
233, 234
L. *suworowii,* dried, *232*
liquid fertilizers, 253
little club moss, *68;* description
and culture, 192, *192*
little nerve plant, 66
living rooms, decoration with plants,
116-29, *116-29*
lobelia, 62
Lobelia erinus pendula, 62
Lonas inordora, dried, *108*
Lonicera brownii, 134
L. *nitida* "Baggesen's Gold", foliage,
225, *225*
love-in-a-mist, *41;* dried, *100, 103,*
108, 239
love-lies-bleeding, dried, *108*

·M·

Madagascar periwinkle, color guide,
202
magnolia, foliage, 224, *224*
Magnolia grandiflora, foliage, 224,
224
Mahonia, 92
M. *aquifolium,* dried, *100*
maize, dried, *239*
Malus, description and preparation,
213, 213, 218, 218
M. *eleyi, 213*
M. "Golden Hornet", *90*
M. "John Downie", *218*
Mammillaria, 70, 156
M. *bocasana, 70*
M. *hahniana,* description and
culture, 199, *199*
M. *rhodantha,* description and
culture, 198, *198*
M. *zeilmanniana,* description and
culture, 199, *199*
mantelpieces, 126, *126,* 127, *127,*
131
maples, *37*
Maranta leuconeura erythroneura, 21;
description and culture, 178, *178*
marguerite daisy, *42, 62, 88*
marsh rosemary, dried, *232*
Matthiola incana, 81; description and
preparation, 212, *212*
M.i. "Parma Violet", *212*
M.i. "Princess Alice", *212*
M.i. "Yellow of Nice", *212*
mealy bugs, 272, *272*
Michaelmas daisies, *41;* description
and preparation, 219, *219*
Microcoelum weddellianum, 14;
description and culture, 170, *170*
Mikania ternata, description and
culture, 185, *185*
mildew, 274, *274*
milkbush, *113*

mimosa, *22;* description and
preparation, 212
miniature iris, description and culture,
194, *194*
miniature wax plant, description and
culture, 189, *189*
mini-climates, 114-5, *114-5*
mirrors, 145, 148, *150*
mist-spraying, 247, *247*
mock orange, foliage, 225, *225*
molded wax plant, description and
culture, 200, *200*
Moluccella laevis, 24; dried, *104*
Monstera deliciosa, 16, 124, 144, 269;
description and culture, 187, *187*
moss-poles, making, 50-1, *50-1*
mother-in-law's tongue, 148, 244,
266; description and culture,
167, *167*
mullein, foliage, 227, *227*
Musa, 152
Muscari, dried, *99;* description and
culture, 195, *195*
Myrtus communis, 33

·N·O·

Narcissus, as bulbs, *59, 60-1, 83,* 86;
description and culture, 194, *194;*
as cut flowers, 7, *86-7;* description
and preparation, 210, *210;* sealing
cut stems, 80, *81*
N. "Armada", *86*
N. "Barrii", *86*
N. "Cheerfulness", *210*
N. "Cragford", *60*
N. "Fermoy", *86*
N. "Golden Ducat", *210*
N. "Golden Harvest", *86*
N. "Ice Follies", *86*
N. "Inglescombe", *210*
N. "Mary Copeland", *210*
N. *medioluteus, 86*
N. "Mrs Backhouse", *210*
N. "Pheasant's eye", *210*
N. "Soleil d'Or", *86*
Neoregelia carolinae "Tricolor", *18;*
description and culture, 174, *174*
Nephrolepis, 152
N. *cordifolia, 152,* 170
N. *exaltata* "Bostoniensis", *17, 28,*
56, 138; description and culture,
170, *170*
Nertera granadensis, color guide,
204; description and culture, 192,
192
nerve plant, *18, 66, 272,* description
and culture, 193, *193*
New Zealand flax, foliage, 228, *228*
Nicotiana affinis, description and
preparation, 221
Nidularium fulgens, 175
N. *innocentii, 13;* description and
culture, 175, *175*
Nigella damascena, dried, *100, 103,*
108, 239
nodding pincushion, *25;* description
and preparation, 221
Norfolk Island pine, *20, 32;* description
and culture, 165, *165*
nursery beds, hydroculture, *261*
oats, dried, *100, 108, 237*
offsets, 267, *267*
old lady cactus, *34;* description and
culture, 199, *199*
old man cactus, description and
culture, 197, *197*

old-man's-beard, dried, *108*
Opuntia microdasys, 29; description
and culture, 197, *197*
oranges, pomanders, *107*
orchid, *25, 77, 84, 117;* description
and preparation, 223, *223*
Oregon grape, dried, *100*
ornamental kale, *48*
ornamental oats, foliage, 227, *227*
Ornithogalum thyrsoides, 83; description and preparation, 222
overfeeding, 252
overwatering, 251

·P·

Paeonia, description and preparation,
214, 214
P. *lactiflora, 214*
P. *officinalis, 214*
P.o. "Rubra-plena", *214*
painted lady, description and culture,
200, *200*
painted-leaf begonia, *20, 30, 40, 272,*
description and culture, 183, *183*
painted nettle, *18, 62, 124, 247,*
description and culture, 177, *177*
painter's palette, *24*
pampas grass, dried, *152, 236*
Pandanus veitchii, description and
culture, 173, *173*
pansy, *24;* description and preparation,
213, *213*
Papaver, 81; description and
preparation, 215; dried, *100, 103,*
104, 238
paper flower, description and culture,
187, *187*
parlor palm, *68, 120;* description and
culture, 171, *171*
parsley, *157*
Passiflora caerulea, 16, 52; color
guide, *207;* description and culture,
185, *185*
passion flower, *16, 52;* color guide,
207; description and culture, 185, *185*
peacock plant, *19, 271;* description
and culture, 165, *165*
pearl everlasting, dried, *231*
Pelargonium, 272, 273, 274
P. *crispum,* dried, *99*
P.c. "Variegatum", description and
culture, 176, *176*
P. *domesticum,* description and
culture, 178, *178*
P. *hortorum, 24,* 178; color guide,
205
Pellaea rotundifolia, 28; description
and culture, 168, *168*
Pentas lanceolata, description and
culture, 177, *177*
peony, description and preparation
214, *214*
Peperomia caperata, 20, 266;
description and culture, 180, *180*
peppermint-leaved geranium, *40*
Persea americana, 130
Persian ivy, *92, 151*
Peruvian apple cactus, *44;* description
and culture, 197, *197*
Peruvian lily, *25, 84;* description and
preparation, 213, *213*
pesticides, 276-7
pests, 272-3, *272-3*
Petroselinum crispum, 157
Philadelphus coronarius "Aureus",
foliage, 225, *225*

Philodendron bipinnatifidum, 16, 132;
   description and culture, 169, *169*
P. "Burgundy", description and
   culture, 187, *187*
P. hastatum, 15, 187
P. scandens, 13, 15, 50, 136;
   description and culture, 188, *188*
Phormium tenax "Purpureum", foliage,
   228, *228*
photosynthesis, 242, *242*, 244
Physalis alkekengi, dried, *232*
P. a. "Gigantea", *142*
pickaback plant, 267; description and
   culture, 190, *190*
pictures, 128, *128-9*
Pilea cadierei, description and culture,
   162, *162*
P. spruceana, 162
pine cones, dried, *108, 111*
pinks, *37*
Pinus, dried, *108, 111*
Pittosporum tenuifolium "Garnettii",
   foliage, 227, *227*
P. tobira, foliage, 224, *224*
plantain lily, foliage, 224, *224*,
   227, *227*
plant care, 241-77, *241-77*; artificial
   light, 258-9, *258-9*; diseases, 274-5,
   274-5; feeding, 252-3, *253*;
   humidity, 247, *247*; hydroculture,
   260-1, *260-1*; light, 244-5, *244-5*;
   pests, 272-3, *272-3*; pots, 254,
   254; potting mixtures, 255, *255*;
   potting on, 256-7, *257*; problems,
   270-7; propagation, 264-9, *264-9*;
   pruning, 262-3, *262-3*; repotting,
   256-7, *257*; signs of ill-health,
   243; temperature 246, *246*;
   topdressing, 256-7, *257*; training,
   262-3, *262-3*; vacations 250, *250*;
   watering, 248-51, *249-51*
plant form, 12, *12-13*
Platycerium bifurcatum, 21, 54, 148;
   description and culture, 191, *191*
Platylobium angulare, dried, *236*
Plectranthus australis, 152, 272;
   description and culture, 193, *193*
P. oertendahlii, 193
Plumbago auriculata, 29; color
   guide, *206*; description and culture,
   186, *186*
plush vine, description and culture,
   185, *185*
poinsettia, 23, 155, 244; description
   and culture, 179, *179*
poison primrose, 25, 49, 62; color
   guide, 202; description and culture,
   181, *181*
polka-dot plant, 19, 30, 65, 68;
   description and culture, 179, *179*
polyanthus, description and
   preparation, 213
Polypodium aureum "Mandaianum",
   description and culture, 169, *169*
Polystichum setiferum, foliage, 224,
   224
pomander, *107*
ponytail, *13, 28, 45, 122*; description
   and culture, 171, *171*
poppy, description and preparation,
   215; dried, *100, 103, 104, 238*;
   sealing cut stems, 81
Portea petropolitana extensa, *37*
pot-pourri, in baskets, 106-7, *106-7*;
   making, 99, *99*
potbound plants, *257*
pothos vine, 16, 28, 30, 72; description and culture, 188, *188*

pots, 254, *254*; hydroculture, 260, *260*;
   removing plants from, *256*
potting, 256, *256-7*
potting mixtures, 255, *255*
potting on, 256-7, *257*; in hydroculture, 261
powder-puff cactus, *70*
prayer plant, *21*; description and
   culture, 178, *178*
pressing leaves, 98, *98*
Primula malacoides, 181
   P. obconica, 25, 49, 62; color
      guide, *202*; description and culture,
      181, *181*
privet, foliage, 226, *226*
problems, 270-7
propagation, 264-9, *264-9*; air
   layering, 268, *268*; division, 267,
   267; offsets, 267, *267*; plantlets,
   267, *267*; layering, 268, *268*; leaf
   cuttings, 266, *266*; seed, 269, *269*;
   stem cuttings, 265, *265*; vegetative,
   264-8, *264-8*
Protea, dried, *238*
pruning, 262-3, *262-3*
Prunus, description and preparation,
   213, *213*
   P. serrulata "Kwanzan", *213*
   P. s. "Shirotae", *213*
   P. s. "Ukon", *213*
   P. subhirtella "Autumnalis", *92*
Pteridium aquilinum, dried, *237*
Pteris cretica, 56, 58; description
   and culture, 183, *183*
Pteris tremula, 183
purple velvet plant, *21*, 274; descrip-
   tion and culture, 191, *191*
purple-leaved filbert, foliage, 228, *228*
Pyrus calleryana "Chanticleer", *213*

·Q·R·

quaking grass, dried, *236*
queen agave, *34, 35, 70*; description
   and culture, 200, *200*
queen's tears, description and culture,
   173, *173*
rabbit's ears cactus, *29*; description
   and culture, 197, *197*
ragwort, *90*
rainbow plant, *116*; description and
   culture, 167, *167*
rat's tail cactus, description and
   culture, 201, *201*
Rebutia minuscula, description and
   culture, 198, *198*
red crown, description and culture,
   198, *198*
red-hot poker, description and
   preparation, 221, *221*
red spider mites, 272, *272*
reed mace, *236*
regal geranium, description and
   culture, 178, *178*
regal lily, *45, 134*
removing plants from pots, *256*
repotting, 256-7, *257*
Rhapis excelsa, description and
   culture, 170, *170*
Rhipsalidopsis, 273
   R. gaertneri, *42*
Rhododendron, description and
   preparation, 211, *211*
   R. simsii, 244; description and
      culture, 179, *179*
Rhoeo spathacea "Variegata",
   description and culture, 166, *166*

Robinia pseudoacacia, foliage, 225,
   225
rock cress, dried, *233*
room decoration, 113-57, *113-57*;
   bathrooms, 144-7, *144-7*; bedrooms, 140-3, *140-3*; conservatories,
   154-7, *154-7*; dining rooms, 130-5,
   130-5; entrances, 148-51, *148-51*;
   halls, 148-51, *148-51*; kitchens,
   136-9, *136-9*; living rooms, 116-29,
   116-29; mini-climates, 114-5,
   114-5; stairs, 152-3, *152-3*;
   sunrooms, 154-7, *154-7*
root mealy bugs, 272, *272*
Rosa, description and preparation,
   216, *216*, 221; dried, *232*
   R. "Goldgleam", *216*
   R. "Margaret Merrill", *216*
   R. "Message", *216*
   R. moyesii, *221*
   R. "Pascali", *216*
   R. rugosa, 221
rosary vine, *15, 45*; description and
   culture, 201, *201*
rose, description and preparation,
   216, *216*; dried, *232*; hips, description and preparation, 221, *221*
rose pincushion, description and
   culture, 199, *199*
rosette-shaped plants, guide to,
   172-5, *172-5*
rubber plant, *154*, 269; description
   and culture, 163, *163*
Rudbeckia, description and
   preparation, 218
   R. fulgida deamii, *90*
Rumex acetosa, dried, *235*

·S·

saffron spike, *47*; description and
   culture, 182, *182*
sagebrush, foliage, 227, *227*
St John's wort, description and
   preparation, 218, *218*
Saintpaulia, 25, 244, 258, 259, 266,
   267, 269, 271, 272, 273; color
   guide, *203*, *207*; description and
   culture, 175, *175*
Salix alba, foliage, 227, *227*
Sambucus nigra "Albo-variegata",
   foliage, 226, *226*
   S. n. "Aurea", *90*
   S. racemosa "Plumosa Aurea",
      foliage, 225, *225*
Sansevieria, 244, 266
   S. trifasciata, 148
   S. t. "Laurentii", description and
      culture, 167, *167*
Saxifraga stolonifera, 267; description and culture, 190, *190*
   S. s. "Tricolor", *19*
Scabiosa caucasica, dried, *239*
scabious, dried, *239*
scale, plant arrangements, *35*
scale insects, 273, *273*
scarlet star, *28, 56, 58*, 245; color
   guide, *205*; description and culture,
   174, *174*
Schlumbergera, 155, 244, 273
   S. "Bridgesii", 200
   S. truncata, description and culture,
      200, *200*
sciarid flies, 272, *272*
Scindapsus pictus "Argyraeus", 16, 28,
   30, 72; description and culture,
   188, *188*

Scirpus cernuus, 59
sea holly, *88, 99*; dried, *100, 104,
   108, 235*
sea kale, foliage, 227, *227*
sea lavender, dried, *100, 103, 104,
   108*
seasonal guide, flowering house
   plants, 208
Sedum maximum "Atropurpureum",
   foliage, 228, *228*
   S. morganianum, description and
      culture, 201, *201*
   S. spectabile "Atropurpureum", *90*
seed, propagation, 269, *269*
seed heads, dried, *238-9*
Selaginella apoda, 192
   S. kraussiana, *68*
   S. martensii, *68*; description and
      culture, 192, *192*
   S. pallescens, 192
self-watering devices, 250, *250*
Senecio cruentus, *142*, 273, 274;
   description and culture, 179, *179*
   S. macroglossus, description and
      culture, 184, *184*
   S. maritima, foliage, 227, *227*
   S. "Sunshine", foliage, 227, *227*
shady positions, in the home, 115,
   245, *245*
shrimp plant, color guide, *206*
silk oak, *17*, 269; description and
   culture, 166, *166*
silk tassel bush, *92*
silver crown, description and culture,
   196, *196*
silvered spear, *19*; description and
   culture, 164, *164*
Sinningia, 6
   S. pusilla, 175
   S. speciosa, 271; color guide, *205*,
      207; description and culture, 175,
      175
skylights, 152, *152*
slow-release fertilizers, *253*
slugs, 273, *273*
smoke tree, foliage, 228, *228*
snails, 273, *273*
soft shield fern, foliage, 224, *224*
Solanum capsicastrum, 65, *139*;
   description and culture, 180, *180*
Soleirolia soleirolii, 29, 30, 37, 124,
   131; description and culture, 192,
   192
sooty mold, 274, *274*
sowing seed, 269, *269*
Sparmannia africana, 119, *133*;
   description and culture, 164, *164*
Spathiphyllum "Clevelandii", 122, 156;
   color guide, *202*; description and
   culture, 169, *169*
sphagnum moss, 255
spider chrysanthemum, *43, 151*
spider plant, *54, 121*, 152, *152*, 247,
   267, 271, 272; description and
   culture, 190, *190*
spindle tree, description and
   preparation, 219, *219*
spotted dumb cane, description and
   culture, 163, *163*
spotted laurel, description and
   culture, 182, *182*
spraying, water, 247, *247*
sprays, foliar, 253
spring cut flowers, guide to, 210-3,
   210-3
spring flower arrangement, 86-7, *86-7*
spurge, description and preparation,
   212, *212*

staghorn fern, *21, 44, 54, 148*; description and culture, 191, *191*
stairs, decoration with plants, 152-3, *152-3*
statice, dried, *96, 100, 104, 230, 233, 234*
stem rot, 274, *274*
stems, cutting and preparing, 80, *80*; sealing bleeding, 81, *81*
Stephanotis floribunda, description and culture, 185, *185*
stick yucca, *13, 17, 35, 145, 148, 245*; description and culture, 167, *167*
stinking iris, *92*
stock, *40*, 81; description and preparation, 212, *212*
stonecrop, 90, foliage, 228, *228*
straw flower, description and preparation, 219, *219*; dried, *96, 100, 104, 108, 110, 111, 231, 232, 233*
strawberry geranium, *19*, 267; description and culture, 190, *190*
Strelitzia reginae, 24; description and culture, 164, *164*
Streptocarpus, 36, 266, 269; description and culture, 175, *175*
styling with plants, art deco, 45, *45*; country style, 40, *40-1*; ethnic style, 42, *42*; high tech, 44, *44*; oriental style, 43, *43*
succulents, 70-1, *70-1*, guide to, 196-201, *196-201*; humidity, 247
summer cut flowers, guide to, 214-7, *214-7*
summer flower arrangement, 88-9, *88-9*
sun scorch, 271
sunflower, description and preparation, 220, *220*
sunlight, in the home, 114-5, 244-5, *245*
sunrooms, decoration with plants, 154-7, *154-7*
Swedish ivy, 152, 272; description and culture, 193, *193*
sweet pea, description and preparation, 217, *217*
sweet potato, *73*
sweet William, description and preparation, 215, *215*
Swiss cheese plant, *16, 124, 144, 269*; description and culture, 187, *187*
sword lily, *25*; description and preparation, 215, *215*
symmetrical arrangements, *32*
Syngonium podophyllum "Imperial White", description and culture, 187, *187*
Syringa, 83, 84, 142; description and preparation, 210, *210*

·T·

Tanacetum vulgare, 41, dried, *96, 230*
tansy, *41*; dried, *96, 230*
tartarian dogwood, foliage, 226, *226*
teasel, dried, *239*
temperature, 246, *246*; fluctuating, 271
terraria, 68-9, *68-9*
Tetrastigma voinieranum, 155
texture, leaves, 20, *20-1*; plant arrangement, *34*
thrift, dried, *235*
Thunbergia alata, description and culture, 185, *185*

thyme, *40*
Thymus vulgaris, 40
ti plant, *8, 19,* 245; description and culture, 163, *163*
Tillandsia argentea, 147
  T. bulbosa, 147
  T. butzii, 147
  T. cyanea, description and culture, 173, *173*
  T. ionantha, 147
  T. juncea, 147
tip yucca, *29, 34, 35*
Tolmiea menziesii, 267; description and culture, 190, *190*
topdressing, 256-7, *257*
Tradescantia, 117, 152, 261
  T. albiflora "Albovittata", *72*; description and culture, 189, *189*
  T. fluminensis "Variegata", *63*, 189
  T. sillamontana, 189
trailing plants, guide to, 188-91, *188-91*
Transvaal daisy, *24, 128*; description and preparation, 217, *217*; dried, *97*
tree ivy, description and culture, 165, *165*
trees, bonsai, 74-5, *74-5*
Trifolium agrarium, dried, *99*
Triticum vulgare, dried, *100, 108, 110*
trumpet honeysuckle, *134*
tuberous begonia, *25*; color guide, *203*
tulip, as bulbs, description and culture, 195, *195*; as cut flowers, *81, 124, 131, 136, 140, 146*, description and preparation, 211, *211*
Tulipa, as bulbs, description and culture, 195, *195*; as cut flowers, *81, 124, 131, 136, 140, 146*, description and preparation, 211, *211*
  T. "Aster Neilson", *211*
  T. "Black Parrot", *211*
  T. "Blue Parrot", *211*
  T. "Captain Fryatt", *211*
  T. "China Pink", *211*
  T. "Dyanito", *211*
  T. "Flying Dutchman", *211*
  T. "Greenland", *211*
  T. "May Blossom", *211*
  T. "West Point", *211*
  T. "White Triumphator", *211*
tumbleweed, dried, *230*
Tutsan St. John's wort, *88*
Typha latifolia, dried, *236*

·U·

umbrella plant, *43, 44, 73, 122, 144*; description and culture, 166, *166*
underfeeding, 252
underwatering, 251
upright plants, guide to, 162-7, *162-7*
urn plant, *46*; color guide, *207*; description and culture, 172, *172*

·V·

vacations, care of plants, 250, *250*
variegated pineapple, description and culture, 174, *174*
vegetative propagation, 264-8, *264-8*
Veitch screw pine, description and culture, 173, *173*
Verbascum, foliage, 227, *227*
Viburnum opulus "Fructo-luteo", *90*
V.o. "Xanthocarpum", description and preparation, 221, *221*

V. rhytidophyllum, foliage, 224, *224*
V. tinus, 92
Vinca major "Variegata", foliage, 226, *226*
vine weevils, 273, *273*
Viola wittrockiana, 24; description and preparation, 213, *213*
Vitis vinifera "Purpurea", foliage, 228, *228*
Vriesea fenestralis, 172
  V. psittacina, 172
  V. saundersii, 172
  V. splendens, 245; description and culture, 172, *172*

·W·

wandering Jew, *18, 261*; description and culture, 189, *189*
warm conditions, in the home, 114-5
water, cold water spots, 272; hydroculture, 260, *260-1*; plant requirements, 242, *242*
water gardens, 72-3, *72-3*
watering, 248-51, *249-51*; overwatering, 251; reviving plants, 251; *251*; self-watering devices, 250, *250*; underwatering, 251; winter, 251
wattle, description and preparation, 222, *222*
wax begonia, *62, 269*; color guide, *202, 206*; description and culture, 176, *176*
wax flower, description and culture, 185, *185*
weeping fig, *9, 17, 134, 141,* description and culture, 171, *171*
West Indian holly, description and culture, 171, *171*
wheat, dried, *100, 108, 110*
white button flower, dried, *230*
whiteflies, 273, *273*
white sails, *122, 156*; color guide, *202*; description and culture, 169, *169*
white-scented jasmine, description and culture, 186, *186*
white willow, foliage, 227, *227*
white yarrow *88*
wicker baskets, hanging, 56-8, *56-8*
wild flowers, *126*
wilting, 243
window-boxes, *62-6, 62-6*
winged everlasting, dried, *104*
winter aconite, description and preparation, 223
winter cut flowers, guide to, 222-3, *222-3*
winter-flower arrangement, 92-3, *92-3*; hallways, 151, *151*
winter-flowering cherry, *92*
winter-flowering jasmine, *151*; description and preparation, 223, *223*
wintering plants, 246; watering, 251
wire netting, cut-flower supports, 82, *82*
witch hazel, *92*
woodland strawberries, *53*
wormwood, foliage, 227, *227*
wreaths, dried flowers, 108-9, *108-9*; for mantelpieces, 127, *127*

·X·Y·Z·

Xeranthemum annuum, dried, *108, 235*
yarrow *88*; dried, *41, 231*
yellow yarrow, *88*
Yucca elephantipes, 13, 17, 29, 145, 148, 245; description and culture, 167, *167*
Zantedeschia aethiopica, 120; description and preparation, 213
Zea mays, dried, *239*
Zebrina pendula, 18, 261; description and culture, 189, *189*
Zonal geranium, *24*

Acknowledgments

Author's acknowledgments

I should like to thank the following for their help:
Elizabeth Eyres who has edited the book and Jane Owen who has laid it out so delightfully.
Priscilla Ritchie who has given invaluable help in creating studio
shots in my absence, together with the photographer, Dave King.
Richard Gilbert who has performed monumental work on the horticultural
wants of plants—not my forté.
And lastly, Hilary Bryan-Brown, my secretary, who has coped amazingly
with both a new set of plant names and my handwriting!

Dorling Kindersley's acknowledgments

Richard Gilbert for all his tireless work and efficiency; Chris Thody for finding
plants; Helen Claire Young and Tina Vaughan for design assistance; Caroline
Ollard and Sophie Galleymore-Bird for editorial assistance;
Vickie Walters for picture research; Sue Brown and Sarah Hayes Fisher for styling;
Judy Sandeman for production; Richard Bird for the index;
Adrian Ensor for black and white prints; Sebastian von Mybourg at
The Flowersmith; Anmore Exotics; The Vernon Geranium Nursery; The Royal
Horticultural Society; Holly Gate Cactus Nursery; Syon Park Garden Centre; Clifton
Nurseries Ltd; Coolings Nursery; Bourne Bridge Nurseries; Inca (Peruvian Art and
Craft Ltd), 15 Elizabeth St, London SW1; The General Trading Company, 144
Sloane St, London SW1; Zeitgeist, 17 The Pavement, London SW4; Ceramic Tile
Design, 56 Dawes Rd, London SW6; Chris Frankham of Glass House Studios; Neal
Street East, London; and Habitat.

Illustrators

David Ashby Will Giles Tony Graham Nicholas Hall Coral Mula Sandra Pond James Robins Lorna Turpin

Photographic credits

EWA Elizabeth Whiting and Associates CP Camera Press SG Susan Griggs Agency DK Dorling Kindersley **T** = top, **B** = bottom, **L** = left, **R** = right, **C** = centre

1, 2, 3, 4, 5 Philip Dowell/DK; **6L** Ken Kirkwood/English Style (courtesy of Margot Johnson); **6C** Michael Boys; **6R, 7L & R;** Michael Dunne/EWA; **7C** Lucinda Lambton/Arcaid; **8L** Andreas Einsiedel/EWA; **8C** Richard Bryant/Arcaid; **8R** Michael Boys; **9L** Richard Bryant/Arcaid; **9C** John Hollingshead; **9R** Michael Dunne; **10, 11** Linda Burgess; **12, 13, 14, 15, 16, 17, 18, 19, 20, 21, 22, 23, 24, 25** Philip Dowell/DK; **26, 27** Linda Burgess; **28, 29** Dave King/DK; **30CL** Fuer Sie/CP; **30T, CR & B** Dave King/DK; **31T** Mon Jardin et Ma Maison/CP; **31BL** Schöner Wohnen/CP; **31BR** Michael Boys/SG; **32TL & TR** Dave King/DK; **32B** Michael Nicholson/EWA; **33** Jean Durand/The World of Interiors; **34T** Tom Dobbie/DK; **34B** Dave King/DK; **35T** Tom Dobbie/DK; **35B** Dave King/DK; **36T** Michael Boys/SG; **36B** John Vere Brown/The World of Interiors; **37L** Dave King/DK; **37TR** Michael Nicholson/EWA; **37BL & BR, 38T & B** Tom Dobbie/DK; **39T** Dave King/DK; **39B** IMS/CP; **40T** Fuer Sie/CP; **40B** Dave King/DK; **41TL & TR** Linda Burgess; **41B** Dave King/DK; **42TL** Michael Boys/SG; **42TR** Linda Burgess; **42B** Dave King/DK; **43L** Tom Dobbie/DK; **43R** Michael Boys/SG; **43B** Dave King/DK; **44TR** Linda Burgess; **44TL** Richard Bryant/Arcaid; **44B** Dave King/DK; **45TL** IMS/CP; **45TR** Schöner Wohnen/CP; **45B, 46, 47T & C** Dave King/DK; **47B** Geoff Dann/DK; **48, 49, 50** Dave King/DK; **51L** Michael Dunne/EWA; **51TR** Jessica Strang; **51B, 52, 53T & BR** Dave King/DK; **53BL** Hus Modern/CP; **54** Spike Powell/EWA; **55** Dave King/DK; **56, 57, 58** Trevor Melton/DK; **59T** Linda Burgess; **59B** Schöner Wohnen/CP; **60** Dave King/DK; **61BL** Pamla Toler/Impact Photos; **61BR** K-D Buhler/EWA; **62TL** John Moss/Colorific; **62TR & B** Pamla Toler/Impact Photos; **63, 64** Dave King/DK; **65T & B** Linda Burgess; **66, 67, 68T** Dave King/DK; **68BL** Michael Boys/DK; **68BR** Geoff Dann/DK; **69, 70, 71TL & R** Dave King/DK; **71BL & R** Tom Dobbie/DK; **72, 73T & BL** Dave King/DK; **73BR** Michael Boys; **74T & BR** Dave King/DK; **74BL** Schöner Wohnen/CP; **75** Dave King/DK; **76, 77**

Linda Burgess; 78, 79 Philip Dowell/DK; **80, 81, 82, 83, 84, 85, 86, 87, 88, 89, 90, 91, 92, 93** Dave King/DK; **94, 95** Linda Burgess; **96, 97, 98, 99T** Dave King/DK; **99B** Linda Burgess; **100, 101, 102** Trevor Melton/DK; **103TL** Jessica Strang; **103TR & B** Linda Burgess; **104, 105T & BL** Dave King/DK; **105 BR** Tom Dobbie/DK; **106, 107, 108T** Dave King/DK; **108B** Zuhause/CP; **109, 110, 111** Dave King/DK; **112, 113** Schöner Wohnen/CP; **114TL** Michael Dunne; **114TR** Bill McLaughlin; **114BL** Ron Sutherland; **114BR** Schöner Wohnen/CP; **115TL** Jessica Strang; **115BL** John Vaughan/The World of Interiors; **115C** Jacques Dirand/The World of Interiors; **115TR** Dave King/DK; **115BR** Femina/CP; **116** John Hollingshead; **117T** Schöner Wohnen/CP; **117B** Tim Street-Porter/The World of Interiors; **118T** Ken Kirkwood/English Style (courtesy of Tricia Foley); **118B** John Vaughan/The World of Interiors; **119TL** Michael Boys; **119TR** Schöner Wohnen/CP; **119B** Michael Boys; **120L** Schöner Wohnen/CP; **120R** Clive Helm/EWA; **120B** IMS/CP; **121** Dave King/DK; **122T** IMS/CP; **122C** Michael Boys; **122BL** Michael Dunne; **122BR** Ken Kirkwood/English Style (courtesy of Michael Baumgarten); **123** John Vaughan/The World of Interiors; **124TL** Ken Kirkwood/English Style (courtesy of Lesley Astaire); **124TR** Michael Boys; **124CL** Ken Kirkwood/English Style (courtesy of Lesley Astaire); **124CR & B** Michael Boys; **125** John Vaughan/The World of Interiors; **126TL** Ken Kirkwood/ English Style (courtesy of Stephen Long); **126TR** Schöner Wohnen/CP; **126B** Peter Woloszynski/The World of Interiors; **127** Dave King/DK; **128TL & TR** Michael Boys; **128TR** Michael Boys/SG; **128B** Jessica Strang; **129** Schöner Wohnen/CP; **130** Peter Woloszynski/The World of Interiors; **131TL** Michael Boys; **131TR** Ken Kirkwood/English Style; **131B** Schöner Wohnen/CP; **132T** M Deneux/Agence Top; **132B** Neil Lorimer/EWA; **133T** Hussenot/Agence Top; **133B** Schöner Wohnen/CP; **134T** Michael Boys; **134B** Kent Billequist/CP; **135** Tim Street-Porter/The World of Interiors; **136T** Richard Bryant/Arcaid; **136CL** Michael Dunne; **136CR** Jessica Strang; **136B** Ken Kirkwood/English Style (courtesy of Lesley Astaire); **137T** Schöner Wohnen/CP; **137B** Bill McLaughlin; **138TL** Suomen/CP **138R** Schöner Wohnen/CP; **138BL** Michael Dunne; **139** Dave King/DK; **140T** Spike Powell/EWA; **140B** Femina/CP

141T Lucinda Lambton/Arcaid (courtesy of Virginia Antiques, London W11); **141R** Schöner Wohnen/CP; **142TL** Lucinda Lambton/Arcaid; **142TR** Mon Jardin et Ma Maison/CP; **142C** Linda Burgess; **142B** Lucinda Lambton/Arcaid; **143** James Wedge/The World of Interiors; **144T** Jessica Strang; **144BL & BR** Schöner Wohnen/CP; **145TL** Lucinda Lambton/Arcaid (courtesy of Tessa Kennedy); **145TR** Bill McLaughlin; **145B** Clive Frost/The World of Interiors; **146TL** Lucinda Lambton/Arcaid (courtesy of Lyn le Grice Stencil Design, Bread St, Penzance, Cornwall); **146TR** Michael Boys/SG; **146BL & BR** Lucinda Lambton/Arcaid; **147** Dave King/DK; **148T & B** Michael Boys; **149** John Vaughan/The World of Interiors; **150TL** Bill McLaughlin; **150TR** Ken Kirkwood/English Style (courtesy of Philip Hooper); **150B** Jessica Strang; **151** Dave King/DK; **152T** Ken Kirkwood/English Style (courtesy of The Victorian Society); **152BL** Richard Bryant/Arcaid; **152BC** Michael Dunne; **152BR** Spike Powell/EWA; **153** Jacques Dirand/The World of Interiors; **154** Ron Sutherland; **155TL** Tim Soar/Arcaid; **155TR** Bill McLaughlin; **155B, 156TL** Linda Burgess; **156TR** Jessica Strang; **156B** Ken Kirkwood/English Style (courtesy of Matyelok Gibbs); **157TL** Linda Burgess; **157TR** Michael Boys; **157B** IMS/CP; **158, 159** Andreas Einsiedel/DK; **162, 163, 164, 165, 166, 167, 168, 169, 170, 171, 172, 173** Tom Dobbie/DK; **173TL** Dave King/DK; **174, 175, 176, 177** Tom Dobbie/DK; **177TL** Dave King/DK; **178, 179, 180, 181, 182, 183, 184, 185, 186, 187, 188, 198, 190, 191, 192, 193** Tom Dobbie/DK; **194, 195** Dave King/DK; **196, 197, 198, 199, 200, 201L** Tom Dobbie/DK; **201R** Dave King/DK; **202, 203, 204, 205, 206, 207** Ian O'Leary/DK; **209** Dave King/DK; **210, 211, 212, 213, 214, 215, 216, 217, 218, 219, 220, 221, 222, 223, 224, 225, 226, 227, 228** Trevor Melton/DK; **229** Dave King/DK; **230, 231, 232, 233, 234, 235, 236, 237, 238, 239** Philip Dowell/DK; **240, 241** The Design Group; **242, 246, 254, 255** Dave King/DK; **258L** IMS/CP; **258R, 259L** Dave King/DK; **259R & B** Femina/CP; **264** Dave King/DK.

Front cover photograph Dave King
Photograph of John Brookes Tom Dobbie